Advanced Selling For Dummies®

Cheat Sheet

Seven-Step Sales Presentation

Although every sale is somewhat unique, the process generally takes seven steps. Knowing these steps in advance can improve your chances of making the sale:

1. **Greet your customer.** Making a great first impression is key.

2. **Ask questions.** You don't know what to sell a client until you know what the customer wants.

3. **Identify your client's need.** Based on the answers to the questions you asked, you can lead your client through the process of identifying her need. Even though you're taking the lead, you want your customer to feel as though she identified the need herself.

4. **Highlight possible solutions.** Guide the client through the process of identifying possible solutions, one of which should be the product or service you're selling.

5. **Weigh the costs and benefits.** The client should be well aware of cost-to-benefits ratio. Are the benefits going to justify the costs?

6. **Address client questions and concerns.** A client who has questions and concerns is typically ready to buy. Be responsive at this critical stage in the selling process.

7. **Closing the transaction.** When the customer is ready to buy, stop selling and take the order. All too often, salespeople continue to sell at this stage, giving the client an opportunity to back out.

Acting Like an Entrepreneur

Throughout *Advanced Selling For Dummies*, I encourage you to consider yourself a business — You, Inc. When you're selling as a small business, you should be doing the following:

- Take responsibility for your own success.
- Set sales goals.
- Draw up a business plan.
- Invest in your success by obtaining the equipment and resources you need.
- Develop productive partnerships.
- Develop systems and procedures, so you can easily delegate work.
- Hire assistants to take on some of the workload both at home and at the office.
- Market yourself online and off to give yourself a brand presence.

For Dummies: Bestselling Book Series for Beginners

Advanced Selling For Dummies®

Taking the STREBOR Approach to Sales Success

Awhile back, I realized that "Roberts" spelled backwards is "streboR," and I worked out a system for effectively implementing any plan for success. When you're ready to put your plan into action, follow the STREBOR System:

S Sticktoitism is the dogged determination required to ensure that you follow through on your plan.

T Training provides you with the know-how and skills to properly execute your plan.

R Results are what you build on as you attain higher and higher levels of success.

E Enthusiasm provides you with the ambition and energy required to follow through.

B Benefits and rewards give you the motivation to succeed.

O Optimism is the confidence that enables you to overcome obstacles.

R Reach is your commitment to taking risks and seizing opportunities that make you grow both professionally and personally.

Maximizing Your Upside

To maximize success in your sales career, you have to avoid anything that could limit your upside. Following are some suggestions on how to maximize your upside:

- **Pick the right product or service to sell.** You should be selling something you know a lot about and can be passionate about. If what you're selling doesn't make you want to get up in the morning and sell it, find something else to sell.

- **Focus on your best customers.** Identify your top 5, 10, 25, and 100 customers and focus your efforts on them. Replace your worst customers — they will suck the energy and resources right out of you.

- **Choose a great company to work for.** Ideally, your company and manager should support and believe in you.

- **Hire well-qualified assistants.** If you don't have an assistant, you are one. You will always be strapped for time unless you start hiring assistants to take over some of the work.

- **Expand time.** You can expand time by becoming more productive. Adopt technologies that improve your productivity, team up with others to build creative synergies, and hire assistants to take on some of the workload.

For Dummies: Bestselling Book Series for Beginners

Advanced Selling

FOR

DUMMIES®

by Ralph R. Roberts with Joe Kraynak

BICENTENNIAL
1807
WILEY
2007
BICENTENNIAL

Wiley Publishing, Inc.

Advanced Selling For Dummies®

Published by
Wiley Publishing, Inc.
111 River St.
Hoboken, NJ 07030-5774
www.wiley.com

For general information on our other products and services, please contact our Customer Care Department within the U.S. at 800-762-2974, outside the U.S. at 317-572-3993, or fax 317-572-4002.

For technical support, please visit www.wiley.com/techsupport.

Wiley also publishes its books in a variety of electronic formats. Some content that appears in print may not be available in electronic books.

Library of Congress Control Number: 2007933276

ISBN: 978-0-470-17467-8

Manufactured in the United States of America

10 9 8 7 6 5 4 3 2 1

About the Authors

Ralph R. Roberts' sales success is legendary. He has been profiled by the Associated Press, CNN, and *Time* magazine, and was once dubbed by *Time* magazine "the best selling Realtor® in America." In addition to being one of the most successful salespeople in America, Ralph is also an experienced mentor, coach, consultant, and author. He has penned several successful books, including *Flipping Houses For Dummies* and *Foreclosure Investing For Dummies* (John Wiley & Sons), *Sell It Yourself: Sell Your Home Faster and for More Money Without Using a Broker* (Adams Media Corporation), *Walk Like a Giant, Sell Like a Madman: America's #1 Salesman Shows You How To Sell Anything* (Collins), *52 Weeks of Sales Success: America's #1 Salesman Shows You How To Close Every Deal!* (Collins), *REAL WEALTH by Investing in REAL ESTATE* (Prentice Hall), and *Protect Yourself from Real Estate and Mortgage Fraud* (Kaplan).

Although Ralph has many varied skills and interests, his true passion is selling . . . and showing other salespeople how to boost their sales and profits. In *Advanced Selling For Dummies*, Ralph reveals the practical sales tips and tricks he's gathered over the course of his more than 30-year career and challenges you to put them to work for you.

Ralph also serves as Official Spokesman for Guthy-Renker Home, a company dedicated to equipping home buyers, sellers, and real estate professionals with the tools, information, and community setting they need to achieve mutual success. Visit www.HurryHome.com and www.RealtyTracker.com to experience the exciting innovations that that Guthy-Renker Home offers now and is planning for the future.

To find out more about Ralph Roberts, visit www.AboutRalph.com.

Joe Kraynak is a freelance author who has written and co-authored dozens of books on topics ranging from slam poetry to computer basics. Joe teamed up with Dr. Candida Fink to write his first book in the *For Dummies* series, *Bipolar Disorder For Dummies,* where he showcased his talent for translating the complexities of a topic into plain-spoken practical advice. He then teamed up with Ralph to write the ultimate guide to flipping houses — *Flipping Houses For Dummies* and delivered an encore performance in *Foreclosure Investing For Dummies*. In *Advanced Selling For Dummies,* Joe and Ralph join forces once again to deliver the full-court-press approach to sales success.

Dedication

From Ralph: To the many salespeople, companies, and organizations I have mentored and coached who have actually had the sticktoitism to put into practice the lessons they have learned . . . and succeeded because of it.

From Joe: To my brother Greg, the salesman of the family, whose talents and skills I appreciate infinitely more after working on this book.

Authors' Acknowledgements

Although we wrote the book, several other talented individuals contributed to its conception, development, and perfection. We give special thanks to the following contributors, who collaborated with us on the development of chapters in their areas of expertise:

Terry Wisner created the Personal Partnering Process™ to help people become more successful both personally and professionally. He shares his insights from over 30 years of sales and human performance improvement in Chapter 7.

Kandra Hamric (www.KandraHamric.com), a top virtual assistant, speaks on the topic of maximizing productivity with virtual assistants, and she shows you in Chapter 13 just how to use assistants to take your business to the next level.

Terry Brock (www.terrybrock.com) is a professional speaker and a columnist for *Business Journals* around the United States. In Chapter 14, Terry reveals the secret of R-Commerce — a powerful networking concept that calls for refocusing your attention and energy on relationships—the unquantifiable factor in sales success.

Richard Nacht is the founder and CEO of Blogging Systems Group (www.bloggingsystems.com), a partner in the social media consulting firm of Nacht and Chaney, and a Fellow with the Society for New Communications Research. In Chapter 17, Richard offers practical advice on how to use social media in your marketing campaigns.

Michael Soon Lee (www.EthnoConnect.com), MBA, is a diversity expert who speaks around the world on selling to multicultural customers. In Chapter 19, Michael tests your Multicultural Sales Aptitude and then brings you up to speed in a hurry on how to improve sales to people from other cultures.

Ed Primeau (www.PrimeauProductions.com), is the founder of Primeau Productions Inc., a full-service multimedia production company to help professional speakers and entertainers promote their talents using the power of multimedia formats. In Chapter 16, Ed reveals the tricks of the multimedia marketing trade he has picked up and perfected over the years.

Dave Boufford (www.MrPositive.com), Mr. Positive, contributed the section "Revving up your mind with affirmations" in Chapter 2. In March of 1997, Dave made the leap to pursue his own dream of guiding others in developing and maintaining a positive attitude through his inspirational e-zines *Positive Thoughts* and *Positive News*.

Paul Doroh, cash buy agent and foreclosure expert, is an NCAA All-American soccer player and captain of two National Championship runner-up teams, as well as a licensed coach for several nationally ranked teams. In Chapter 20, Paul reveals ways to out-compete your competitors by treating them with respect and courtesy.

April Callis (www.springboard-consult.com) is a workplace issues and change management expert who has been featured in *Time* magazine and the *New York Times*. In Chapter 11, April contributed the section "Dressing for Success."

Pam Lontos (www.prpr.net), President of PR/PR, is a public relations specialist and consultant whose clients include Brian Tracy, Diane Ladd, and Ross Shafer. Pam was instrumental in guiding the content for Chapter 9.

Special thanks also go to acquisitions editor Lindsay Lefevere, who chose us to author this book and guided us through the tough part of getting started. Jennifer Connolly, our project editor, deserves a loud cheer for acting as a very patient collaborator and gifted editor — shuffling chapters back and forth, shepherding the text and photos through production, making sure any technical issues were properly resolved, and serving as unofficial quality control manager. We also tip our hats to the production crew for doing such an outstanding job of transforming a loose collection of text and illustrations into such an attractive bound book.

Throughout the writing of this book, we relied heavily on a knowledgeable and dedicated support staff, who provided expert advice, tips, and research, so we could deliver the most comprehensive and useful information. Lois Maljak proved invaluable not only as a resource person but also as the communications hub for the flurry of files and e-mail messages flying back and forth on a daily basis.

We owe special thanks to our technical editor, Jeff Lee, for ferreting out technical errors in the manuscript, helping guide its content, and offering his own tips and tricks and insights from the world of corporate sales.

Publisher's Acknowledgments

We're proud of this book; please send us your comments through our Dummies online registration form located at www.dummies.com/register/.

Some of the people who helped bring this book to market include the following:

Acquisitions, Editorial, and Media Development

Project Editor: Jennifer Connolly

Acquisitions Editor: Lindsay Lefevere

Copy Editor: Jennifer Connolly

Technical Editor: Jeff Lee

Editorial Manager: Michelle Hacker

Editorial Supervisor: Carmen Krikorian

Editorial Assistants: Erin Calligan Mooney, Joe Niesen, Leeann Harney

Cartoons: Rich Tennant (www.the5thwave.com)

Composition Services

Project Coordinator: Heather Kolter

Layout and Graphics: Jonelle Burns, Carl Byers, Joyce Haughey, Alicia B. South, Julie Trippetti

Anniversary Logo Design: Richard Pacifico

Proofreaders: David Faust, Tricia Liebig

Indexer: Aptara

Publishing and Editorial for Consumer Dummies

Diane Graves Steele, Vice President and Publisher, Consumer Dummies

Joyce Pepple, Acquisitions Director, Consumer Dummies

Kristin A. Cocks, Product Development Director, Consumer Dummies

Michael Spring, Vice President and Publisher, Travel

Kelly Regan, Editorial Director, Travel

Publishing for Technology Dummies

Andy Cummings, Vice President and Publisher, Dummies Technology/General User

Composition Services

Gerry Fahey, Vice President of Production Services

Debbie Stailey, Director of Composition Services

Contents at a Glance

Introduction 1

Part I: Mastering the Sales Success Mindset 9

Chapter 1: Boosting Sales with Advanced Selling 11

Chapter 2: Visualizing Yourself as a Power Seller 25

Chapter 3: Charting Your Roadmap to Sales Success 43

Chapter 4: Making Selling Your Hobby and Your Habit 57

Chapter 5: Setting the Stage for an Unlimited Upside 73

Part II: Pumping Up Your Sales Muscle 87

Chapter 6: Getting in Step with Your Customer 89

Chapter 7: Teaming Up for Success with Personal Partnering 105

Chapter 8: Embracing Change as a Growth Strategy 117

Chapter 9: Branding Yourself through Shameless Self-Promotion 131

Chapter 10: Stepping Out of Your Comfort Zone: Taking Risks 149

Part III: Equipping Yourself with Advanced Selling Tools and Resources 163

Chapter 11: Investing and Re-Investing in Your Success 165

Chapter 12: Putting the Latest Technologies to Work for You 179

Chapter 13: Picking the Right People to Fill the Gaps 197

Part IV: Prospecting for Sales Opportunities 213

Chapter 14: Harnessing People Power with R-Commerce 215

Chapter 15: Prospecting for Untapped and Under-Tapped Markets 231

Chapter 16: Tapping the Power of the Multimedia Marketplace 245

Chapter 17: Exploring Opportunities in the Virtual World: Social Media ...265

Part V: Teaming Up with Your Customers . . . and Competitors 283

Chapter 18: Focusing on Your Client's Success 285

Chapter 19: Selling to Multicultural Customers 299

Chapter 20: Playing Nice with the Competition 315

Part VI: The Part of Tens 329

Chapter 21: Ten Power-Selling Tactics and Techniques 331

Chapter 22: Ten Ways to Break Your Sales Slump . . . or Avoid It Entirely.............337

Index 343

Table of Contents

Introduction 1

About This Book...1
Conventions Used in This Book 2
What You're Not to Read 2
Foolish Assumptions 3
How This Book Is Organized...3
    Part I: Mastering the Sales Success Mindset......................4
    Part II: Pumping Up Your Sales Muscle.............................4
    Part III: Equipping Yourself with Advanced Selling Tools
       and Resources..4
    Part IV: Prospecting for Sales Opportunities 5
    Part V: Teaming Up with Your Customers . . . and Competitors 5
    Part VI: Part of Tens 5
Icons Used in This Book..6
Where to Go from Here...6

Part 1: Mastering the Sales Success Mindset......................9

Chapter 1: Boosting Sales with Advanced Selling 11

Defining and Achieving Your Own Destiny 12
    Establishing a positive mindset....................................12
    Setting stimulating goals 13
    Plotting your course 13
    Implementing your plan 14
Weaving Advanced Selling into Your Life................................14
    Envisioning your success 15
    Walking the walk 15
Recruiting People Power to Fuel Your Success..........................17
Selling Yourself: Self-Promotion 19
    Identifying your unique selling point.............................19
    Branding yourself 20
Prospecting for Ideas and Leads 21
Unlocking the Secret of Mutual Success 21
    Making your customers successful.................................22
    Making your customers' customers successful 23
    Focusing your efforts on underserved clientele 23
    Declaring peace with your competitors 23
    Tapping the power of professional associations.................24

Chapter 2: Visualizing Yourself as a Power Seller 25

  Sidling Up to Top Sellers 25
    Identifying your sales heroes...26
    Shadowing top sellers...29
    Revving up your mind with affirmations...30
    Reminiscing on past successes 35
    Surrounding yourself with positive people.....................................36
    Waking up with a positive plan..37
  Defining "Success" in Your Own Terms 37
  Envisioning Your Future Success 38
    Envisioning the ideal...39
    Imagining how you're going to act 39
    Acting out your reality...40
    Applying visualization to sales 40

Chapter 3: Charting Your Roadmap to Sales Success 43

  Drawing Up Your Sales Plan...43
    Determining where you are..44
    Setting a goal..45
    Setting a timeframe 46
    Identifying your objectives 46
    Figuring out a strategy...47
    Identifying tasks 48
    Identifying resources 49
  Prioritizing Your Tasks 50
  Putting Your Plan into Action with the Strebor System 51
  Tracking Your Progress 52
  Holding Yourself Accountable 52
  Celebrating Your Success...53
    Rewarding yourself for a job well done..53
    Rewarding yourself for a job about to be well done.......................54
  Revising Your Roadmap 54
    Assessing your progress . . . or lack thereof...................................55
    Correcting for wrong turns 55
    Building on success 56

Chapter 4: Making Selling Your Hobby and Your Habit 57

  Making Selling Your Hobby...58
  Thinking Like an Entrepreneur...59
  Greeting the Day with the Power Selling Attitude 61
  Engaging People Throughout Your Day 62
    Projecting a professional image 63
    Making a great first impression 63
  Discovering New Sales Techniques 64
    Reading up on new selling strategies 65
    Tuning into sales tapes and CDs 65
    Attending sales seminars and workshops 66
    Swapping secrets with colleagues..67

Buying to learn...67
Test-driving new techniques...67
Keeping Pace with Your Industry...68
Practicing Your Sales Skills in Real-World Scenarios...............69
Negotiating in the office 70
Sharpening your sales skills at home 70
Connecting with the restaurant staff 70
Negotiating upgrades at the airport 71
Engaging the taxi driver...72

Chapter 5: Setting the Stage for an Unlimited Upside **73**
Grasping the Concept of Upside 74
Spotting the Five Limitations to Upside......................................74
Wrong product or service 75
Wrong customer or client...75
Wrong company or manager...77
An I-can-do-it-all mentality 78
Time constraints..78
Finding the Right Product or Service 78
Listing products and services packed with potential 79
Assessing multimedia marketing opportunities..................80
Spotting franchise opportunities 80
Pursuing High-Quality Customers..81
Identifying the qualities of good customers 81
Discovering more best customers 82
Acquiring Support and Resources..83
Delegating Time-Consuming Tasks 84
Expanding Time..85

Part II: Pumping Up Your Sales Muscle **87**

Chapter 6: Getting in Step with Your Customer **89**
Knowing Why Buyers Buy...90
Identifying the seven buyer motivations..............................90
Identifying motivations for buying your product or service.........92
Collaborating on the Purchase Decision.....................................93
Calling attention to the problem or need..............................93
Identifying possible solutions..94
Weighing costs and benefits 95
Second guessing the decision...95
Brushing Up on a Few Power-Selling Techniques 96
Dealing with the decision maker 96
Mastering the meet and greet...98
Energizing the conversation 99
Asking questions to draw out the information you need 99
Mirroring your customer..101
Looking for win-win opportunities.......................................101

Changing "no" to "know" 102
Knowing when to stop 102
Practicing Your Sales Presentation 102
Role playing...103
Watching and listening to yourself work........................103
Teaming up with a trainer 104

Chapter 7: Teaming Up for Success with Personal Partnering 105

Flagging Areas for Improvement 106
Performing a self assessment 106
Taking a sales skills assessment test 107
Gathering insight from colleagues 107
Collecting customer feedback 108
Listening to the boss...108
Targeting Key Skills...108
Teaming Up with Your Personal Partner...................................110
Finding a good match 111
Sharing your priorities and plan 112
Setting the ground rules 113
Keeping each other on track...113
Reviewing, celebrating, and recycling 115

Chapter 8: Embracing Change as a Growth Strategy 117

Working On Your Business...118
Keeping an Eye on How Customers Buy 118
Getting a handle on the basics 118
Asking the right questions 119
Staying on top of changes 121
Changing the Way Customers Buy 121
Looking for cross-selling opportunities..........................121
Identifying new selling methods 123
Identifying revenue-generating opportunities 123
Prepping your customers for the coming changes 124
Serving the savvy consumer...124
Tweaking Your Current Marketing and Sales Strategy 125
Keeping score: What works? What doesn't? 126
Finding the "Why" behind Your Customer's "No" 127
Leaving a proven product alone 128
Capitalizing on Changes in the Industry 128

Chapter 9: Branding Yourself through Shameless Self-Promotion . . .131

Discovering the You in Unique 132
Changing Your Name?...136
Crafting a Unique Selling Proposition (USP)............................136
Moving from features to benefits to solutions...............137
Crafting your personal-professional USP 138
Implementing your USP in marketing and sales............139

Designing a Consistent Look and Feel 139
Establishing Brand Presence on the Internet 140
Boosting Your Street Cred 142
    Speaking to local groups 143
    Volunteering your time and expertise 145
    Becoming the resident expert 146
    Meeting and greeting the general public 147

Chapter 10: Stepping Out of Your Comfort Zone: Taking Risks 149
Marking the Boundaries of Your Comfort Zone 149
Envisioning Life Outside of Your Comfort Zone 152
    What's the worst that can happen? 152
    What's the best that can happen? 153
    What if you don't even try? 153
    Estimating your ROR (Return on Risk) 155
Reducing the Fear Factor 156
    Researching the viability of an idea or opportunity 157
    Following the trailblazers 157
    Assembling your own advisory board 158
    Setting achievable milestones 158
    Focusing on the present 159
Looking for Trouble . . . and Finding Opportunity 160
Regaining Your Footing When You Stumble 161

Part III: Equipping Yourself with Advanced Selling Tools and Resources 163

Chapter 11: Investing and Re-Investing in Your Success 165
Focusing on Productivity Instead of Cost 166
Prioritizing Your Investment Needs 167
    Dressing for success 167
    Pursuing education and training 169
    Gearing up with the equipment you need 170
    Investing in marketing materials 171
    Investing in support personnel 171
    Investing in yourself 172
Financing Your Investments 172
    Finding freebies 173
    Bartering for what you need 173
    Convincing management to invest in you 174
    Sharing resources 175
    Securing a small-business loan 175
Tabulating Your Time Budget 176
    Knowing how you spend your time 176
    Identifying time wasters 177
    Finding and making time 177

Chapter 12: Putting the Latest Technologies to Work for You 179

Overcoming Resistance to New Technology 179
    Assuming a playful attitude 180
    Overcoming objections to the cost..............................181
    Getting over the feeling that it's unproven 182
Pumping Up Your Productivity with Computers and Software..............182
    Becoming a road warrior 183
    Mastering a contact management program 184
    Knowing your way around a presentation program 185
Tapping into the Web...187
    Researching customers and competitors 187
    Gathering leads...188
    Marketing and advertising on the Web.............................190
    Networking with colleagues online...................................190
    Discovering new sales "secrets"..191
Tuning in with the Latest Communication Tools....................................191
    Optimizing the power of your phone system 192
    Improving e-mail efficiency 194
    Hopping on the BlackBerry bandwagon............................194
    Keeping in touch with instant messaging 195
    Teleconferencing over the Internet....................................195

Chapter 13: Picking the Right People to Fill the Gaps 197

Identifying Outsourcing Opportunities 198
    Taking inventory of everything that needs to get done 198
    Highlighting tasks that only you can perform 199
    Highlighting tasks you love doing 199
    Pinpointing what you hate doing 199
    Taking inventory of missing skills 201
    Tabulating time-wasting tasks 201
Designing an Efficient System...203
    Breaking tasks into steps...203
    Assigning tasks to assistants 204
    Targeting specific projects 204
Hiring and Firing...205
    Recruiting top-notch personnel 205
    Assigning meaningful job titles..208
    Empowering your personnel and letting go......................209
    Rewarding productive personnel 209
    Knowing when to fire an employee.....................................210
Scaling Your Work Force with Virtual Assistants....................................211

Part IV: Prospecting for Sales Opportunities 213

Chapter 14: Harnessing People Power with R-Commerce 215
Embracing the R-Commerce Philosophy 216
    Exploring R-Commerce applications.................................216
    Retooling your mind 218
Discovering the Four C's of R-Commerce.................................218
Getting Well Connected 219
    Identifying networking opportunities 220
    Soft-networking...221
    Scouting for force multipliers 221
    Gathering vital information 223
    Building a database...223
    Giving memorable tokens...225
    Joining and leading your trade association 225
    Getting noticed in the community 226
Becoming the Go-To Guy or Gal 228
Building R-Commerce with Your Clientele................................229

Chapter 15: Prospecting for Untapped and Under-Tapped Markets 231
Seeing Business Where It Isn't...231
Considering a Different Demographic 233
    Targeting a generation 234
    Selling to the disabled 238
    Overcoming racial and ethnic barriers 238
    Shifting your gender focus 240
Going Global: Exploring International Markets 241
Exploring Other Sales Channels 241
Looking for Bundling Opportunities..242
Partnering with Other Product or Service Providers...............243
Discovering Another Use for Your Product or Service 244

Chapter 16: Tapping the Power of the Multimedia Marketplace ...245
Marketing Yourself and Your Product in Print 246
    Advertising in print publications 246
    Moonlighting as a journalist 247
    Writing and distributing your own press releases.........249
Getting Some Free Publicity..251
Advertising on Television 252
    Producing your commercial..252
    Picking the right station and time slot 254
Getting on the Radio 255
Marketing on the Internet 256
    Setting up your own Web site 256
    Launching and maintaining a blog 258
    Driving traffic to your Web site and blog 259

Adding audio and video content 259
Connecting with customers via e-mail...260
Keeping customers posted with a newsletter 262
Staying in touch via instant messaging 264
Launching a Direct-Mail Campaign 264

Chapter 17: Exploring Opportunities in the Virtual World: Social Media 265

Grasping the Concept of Social Media 266
Applying social media to marketing and advertising 267
Putting the "social" in marketing media.......................................267
Assessing the pros and cons of social media and networking.....269
Drawing Attention to Yourself with Blogs 273
Updating your blog with fresh content 273
Populating your blog with relevant links 274
Getting your blog discovered on Technorati.................................275
Distributing your content with Really Simple Syndication (RSS) ...275
Converting blog traffic into sales 276
Establishing a Presence in Virtual Communities 277
Marketing on MySpace 277
Getting some air time on YouTube...279
Dig it, man, Digg it! 280
Living a "Second Life" 281

Part V: Teaming Up with Your Customers . . . and Competitors 283

Chapter 18: Focusing on Your Client's Success 285

Getting to Know Your Client's Business 286
Researching your client's business..287
Finding out about your client's client..288
Discovering What Your Client Needs to Succeed 289
Identifying specific needs..290
Adjusting your business model to meet client needs...................292
Integrating Sales with Product Development and Client Service 293
Communicating Your Commitment to Your Client 294
Reinforcing a positive relationship 295
Fielding complaints 296

Chapter 19: Selling to Multicultural Customers 299

Testing Your Multicultural Aptitude 300
Busting Common Myths 303
Mastering the Multicultural Meet and Greet 305
Following your customer's lead 306
Gauging your customer's personal space 306

Establishing eye contact . . . or not.................................307
Greeting the female companion 308
Asking customers to explain their culture...................308
Adjusting Your Sales Presentation for Cultural Differences 309
Changing your office décor...............................310
Choosing effective presentation media......................310
Speaking the language 310
Leading customers through the purchase process 311
Haggling with Multicultural Buyers 312
Surviving your first group negotiation 312
Negotiating before, during, and after the signing of the contract....313
Adjusting Customer Service for Different Cultures 313

Chapter 20: Playing Nice with the Competition **315**
Seeing the Upside of Letting Down Your Guard 315
Studying Your Competitors.................................317
Identifying your competitors 318
Scoping out the competition.............................319
Avoiding the Copy Cat Syndrome 320
Focusing on your business...............................321
Sparking creativity 321
Launching ideas into action.............................322
Gaining a gadget edge 323
Referring Customers to Your Competitors and Affiliates 323
Redirecting your worst customers to the competition................324
Sending business to your affiliates 324
Partnering with Your Competitors to Create Win-Win Opportunities....325
Harnessing the power of affiliates and competitors...............325
Bridge burning creates tiny towns.........................327

Part VI: The Part of Tens.................................329

Chapter 21: Ten Power-Selling Tactics and Techniques **331**
Focusing on Relationships, Not Sales.........................331
Generating Positive Publicity for You and Your Company 332
Implementing an Hour of Power 332
Working Your Way to the Decision Maker........................333
Being Yourself...333
Focusing on Ends . . . and Letting the Means Fall into Place.................334
Categorizing Your Customers................................334
Asking for Referrals 335
Staying Put . . . Rather Than Job Hopping 335
Just Do It!...336

**Chapter 22: Ten Ways to Break Your Sales Slump . . .
or Avoid It Entirely** 337
    Steering Clear of Sales Slumps 337
    Motivating Yourself with Added Incentives..............................338
    Steering Clear of Negative People and Situations.....................339
    Starting Right Now 339
    Re-Committing Yourself to Success 340
    Ramping Up Your Marketing Efforts 340
    Revisiting Your Relationships.....................................341
    Reviewing Your Records 341
    Consulting Your Supervisor, Mentor, Personal Partner, or Coach........342
    Getting Your Friends and Family Involved..............................342

Index *343*

Introduction

You can find all sorts of books and tapes revealing the "secrets" of sales success — books on solution selling, strategic selling, new strategic selling, spin selling, question-based selling, customer-centric selling, how to close a sale, and so on. Becoming a top salesperson, however, requires much more than asking a customer questions and then pitching your products and services.

Those who achieve the pinnacle of sales success act more like entrepreneurial small-business owners. They market and advertise, engage in unrelenting shameless self-promotion, constantly expand their address books with new contacts, develop synergistic partnerships, investigate new markets, take risks, implement the latest technologies to boost productivity, hire assistants to grow their business, and much more.

In *Advanced Selling For Dummies,* I reveal the not-so-secret secret to becoming your own best-seller — you have to develop a positive attitude, work hard and smart, and stick to it. You need to get up to speed with 21st century business management and discover the power of virtual assistants, blogs, email drip campaigns, Internet lead generation, social media, and other cutting edge and bleeding edge tools and resources.

I show you how to do everything I've done over the past 30 years and continue to do as a highly successful salesperson. Follow in my footsteps, and you're much more likely to attain the sales success you're committed to achieving.

I have to warn you, though — what I do is not easy. This is not a Ten-Minute Guide to Sales Success. You have to work at it. When I tell you to make 100 phone calls a day, you have to do it. When I tell you to hire an assistant, don't tell me you can't afford to. When I tell you that you need to set up your own Web site or blog, don't give me some excuse that you don't have the technological know-how. Just do it. You can start slow, but schedule it and get 'er done.

About This Book

Far too many salespeople relinquish themselves to what they consider is a painful reality — they can't sell, because nobody wants what they're selling. Mediocre salespeople are constantly telling me, "Bring me a customer, and I can sell." They rely far too much on the company they work for to market the products and services and they do little or nothing to market *themselves*.

Entrepreneurial salespeople, on the other hand, blame nobody. Instead, they drum up their own business. They make business happen. They become revenue-generating machines, no matter where they work or what they sell.

In this book, I offer you a vast collection of strategies, techniques, and tips on how to become a revenue-generating machine. I show you how to believe in and motivate yourself, develop a winning game plan, hone your sales skills, market yourself online and off, take yourself to the next level with personal partnering, embrace change, take risks, become more productive with the right technologies and assistants, tap the power of R-Commerce through networking and personal partnering, and much more.

Advanced Selling For Dummies is designed to present this loose collection of sales tips and tricks in an easily digestible format that enables you to skip around. You can certainly read the book from cover to cover, but if you prefer to focus first on a specific area, such as blogging, you can simply skip to that chapter and dive right in.

Conventions Used in This Book

Compared to other selling programs and books, *Advanced Selling For Dummies* is anything but conventional, but I do use some conventions to call your attention to certain items. For example:

- ✓ *Italics* highlight new, somewhat technical terms, such as *R-Commerce,* and emphasize words when I'm driving home a point.
- ✓ **Boldface** text indicates key words in bulleted and numbered lists.
- ✓ `Monofont` highlights Web site, blog, and email addresses.

In addition, even though you see two author names on the cover of this book — Ralph and Joe — and I consulted with half a dozen experts who specialize in various areas of selling, you see "I" throughout the book when I, Ralph, am describing my personal experiences with selling and offering my expert advice. Joe's the wordsmith — the guy responsible for keeping you engaged and entertained and making sure I've explained everything as clearly and thoroughly as possible. Joe is admittedly not much of a salesperson, although he did manage to sell me on the idea of working with him . . . or did I sell him on the idea of working with me?

What You're Not to Read

Although I encourage you to read this book from cover to cover to maximize the return on your investment, *Advanced Selling For Dummies* facilitates a skip-and-dip approach. It presents the information in bite-sized bits, so you can skip to the chapter or section that grabs your attention or meets your current needs, master it, and then skip to another section or simply set the book aside for later reference.

Feel free to skip any sections you feel as though you've already mastered. If, for example, you feel as though you are a highly motivated person who doesn't need to set goals, you can safely skip Chapter 2, "Visualizing Yourself as a Power Seller." If you already have several assistants to support your efforts, skip Chapter 13, "Picking the Right People to Fill the Gaps."

You can also safely skip anything you see in a gray shaded box. I stuck it in a box for the same reason that most people stick stuff in boxes — to get it out of the way, so you wouldn't trip over it. However, you may find the stories and brief asides uproariously funny and perhaps even mildly informative (or vice versa).

Foolish Assumptions

The biggest foolish assumption I make in this book is that you've already had some basic training on the fine art of selling. Specifically, I assume you've already read the first book in this "mini-series," *Selling For Dummies* (Wiley) by Tom Hopkins, one of my earliest role models. Hopkins gets you up to speed in a hurry on the art of selling, the need to know your products and your customers, and how to sell effectively throughout the "seven-step selling cycle." If you haven't yet read *Selling For Dummies,* put down this book right now, buy that book, and read it. I'll be waiting for you when you're done.

The other foolish assumption I make is that you're committed to your own success. Becoming a top-producing salesperson is hard work and requires *sticktoitism* (pronounced stik-to-it-izm) — a word I've been using since the 1970s to describe the determination and dogged perseverance required to achieve success and build wealth. I could use "stick-to-itiveness," which happens to appear in the dictionary, but I like my word better.

I can't force you to put into action the strategies and systems I describe in this book. You have to be so committed to your success that you take the next step and practice what I preach. Although it's difficult, it is not impossible. I do it, and I know dozens of "average" salespeople who have managed to put my recommendations into practice. They've since become much more than average, and you can expect the same results.

How This Book Is Organized

I wrote this book so you could approach it in either of two ways. You can pick up the book and flip to any chapter for a quick, stand-alone mini-course on a specific advanced selling topic, or you can read the book from cover to cover. To help you navigate, I took the 22 chapters that make up the book and divvied them up into six parts. Here, I provide a quick overview of what I cover in each part.

Part I: Mastering the Sales Success Mindset

Attitude plays a major role in success. If you believe in yourself, your company, your customers, and your products and services, you have most of what you need to succeed. In this part, I show you how to visualize yourself as a top-producing salesperson, draw up your personalized plan for success, make selling more of a hobby and a habit instead of a boring job, and remove any obstacles that may be limiting your upside. When your mind is right and your vision clear, you are well-prepared to implement the sales strategies and systems that can significantly boost sales.

Part II: Pumping Up Your Sales Muscle

The chapters in this part lead you through your sales calisthenics and reveal various techniques to take your skills to the next level. In Chapter 6, I offer a more advanced perspective on selling basics, showing you how to approach a customer, ask questions, deliver your presentation, and eventually close the sale.

In the remaining chapters, I reveal techniques I practice to become a more effective salesperson, enhance my career, and get more out of life, both professionally and personally. Here you discover how to implement a self-improvement strategy called personal partnering, embrace change as a growth strategy, build a brand presence through shameless self-promotion, and take the risks necessary to achieve higher levels of sales success.

Part III: Equipping Yourself with Advanced Selling Tools and Resources

As an entrepreneurial salesperson, you are a small-business owner. As such, you need to invest time and money in building your business. The chapters in this part show you just how to accomplish this. In Chapter 11, I guide you in selecting the self-improvement tools and resources that promise the biggest return on your investment of both time and money. In subsequent chapters, I focus on getting you geared up with productivity-boosting technologies and personnel that enable you to achieve higher levels of success than would otherwise be possible.

Part IV: Prospecting for Sales Opportunities

Good salespeople target markets. Great sales people become targets. They create a high profile and put a human face on whatever they sell, so that prospective customers come calling. The chapters in this part show you how to take a long-term approach to sales by building a strong reputation as the go-to guy or gal for a particular product or service. You may not see immediate results, but over time, all of your efforts eventually pay off. You no longer have to sell — you simply facilitate the purchase.

Part V: Teaming Up with Your Customers . . . and Competitors

One of the best ways to become a top producer is to surround yourself with success. Make your customers, colleagues, and even your competitors successful, and you soon find that the culture of success you built around you lifts you higher and higher. The chapters in this part reveal various strategies for ensuring the success of your customers, multicultural clients, and your competition. Here you also discover the powerful paradox of giving to give instead of giving to get.

Part VI: Part of Tens

Every *For Dummies* title comes complete with a Part of Tens — two or more chapters that each contain ten strategies, tips, tricks, or other important items to keep in mind. In *Advanced Selling For Dummies*, the Part of Tens offers ten power selling tactics and techniques and ten ways to break out of a sales slump. Not only do you receive the tools required to succeed, but you also get the motivation to use those tools.

Icons Used in This Book

Throughout this book, I've sprinkled icons in the margins to cue you in on different types of information that call out for your attention. Here are the icons you'll see and a brief description of each.

I want you to remember everything you read in this book, but if you can't quite do that, then remember the important points I flag with this icon.

Tips provide insider insight from behind the scenes. When you're looking for a better, faster, cheaper way to do something, check out these turbo tips.

"Whoa!" This icon appears when you need to be extra vigilant or seek professional assistance before moving forward.

Where to Go from Here

Advanced Selling For Dummies offers you a collection of sales tools you can add to you repertoire in any order you wish. The more you add, and the faster you add them, and the more use you make of them, the higher you climb and the faster you get there.

If you're looking for a quick course on advanced selling, check out Chapter 1, which provides a sampler plate with a small taste of everything contained in the book. I strongly recommend that you read Chapter 2, as well, where Mr. Positive (Dave Boufford) and I motivate you and assist you in setting your course. If you don't have a positive attitude and a clear vision of where you're going, you have very little chance of getting there. Chapter 9 on shameless self-promotion is also a must-read.

You also don't want to miss the chapters I collaborated on with other sales specialists, including

- Chapter 7, "Raising the Bar with Personal Partnering"
- Chapter 13, "Picking the Right People to Fill the Gaps"
- Chapter 14, "Harnessing People Power with R-Commerce"
- Chapter 17, "Exploring Opportunities in the Virtual World: Social Media"
- Chapter 19, "Appealing to Multicultural Clientele"

My wish is that you achieve whatever level of sales success you dream of *and* work hard enough and smart enough to attain. Keep in mind that this wish can be a curse. If you don't put into practice what I recommend in this book, you are most likely to remain an average or below-average salesperson. For average people, that may be good enough, but this book isn't for average salespeople. You're better than that, and you deserve more than that. Your spouse and family deserve more than that, too. If you're going to be away from your family for 8 to 12 hours a day, you'd better make sure that they're benefiting from your efforts while you're at work. After all, why take time away from your family only to pursue mediocrity?

Part I

Mastering the Sales Success Mindset

The 5th Wave   By Rich Tennant

So—what the heck are you selling?

In this part . . .

In any field of endeavor, especially selling, success requires the right mindset, the proper attitude. You have to visualize yourself as the success you want to be, set challenging goals, develop a rock-solid game plan for achieving those goals, and then make selling an activity that's as natural as breathing.

In this part, I show you how to get in character and sell *yourself* on the idea of success. As long as you believe you can be a top seller and then start acting like you are, you can't help but become the sales success you're destined to be.

Chapter 1

Boosting Sales with Advanced Selling

In This Chapter

▶ Defining success on your own terms

▶ Fueling success with people power

▶ Believing in and then selling yourself

▶ Generating ideas, leads, and opportunities

▶ Building a culture of success

Advanced selling is the full-court press approach to achieving success. It requires clear vision, careful planning, shameless self-promotion, a discerning vigilance, the ability and willingness to take calculated risks, and a dogged determination that I like to refer to as *sticktoitism*.

Advanced selling is about more than boosting sales and profits, although that's certainly a part of it and is probably the biggest reason you're reading this book. The strategies and tips you master as an advanced seller can also be applied to other aspects of your life to achieve both your professional and personal goals.

In this chapter, I reveal what goes into making a top-producing salesperson and assist you in discovering what you need to accomplish to achieve your goals, whatever they may be.

Defining and Achieving Your Own Destiny

Selling is like life itself — you're free to define "success" in your own terms and then plot your own course to get there. For one salesperson, success may be measured in status, and being the top salesperson in the company would be the ultimate achievement. For someone else, success may mean lots of money to afford a certain lifestyle. Others may want more time to spend with friends and family or an early retirement. You may have some other goal in mind.

Your destiny is yours to define and achieve. Don't let anyone else define what "happiness" should mean for you. Even if you were to achieve your goals, your happiness and satisfaction would always elude you, because you would be achieving someone else's dream.

In the following sections, I guide you through the process of establishing a positive mindset, setting goals, and plotting your course. For additional details, check out Chapters 2 and 3.

As motivational speaker Art Fettig told me, "It's hard to be healthy, wealthy, and happy at the same time." However, striving to achieve a balanced life that leads to health, wealth, and happiness is certainly a noble pursuit.

Establishing a positive mindset

Success stands at the end of many different journeys, but it always begins with the right attitude — a positive mindset. If you've been around negative people all your life, your mindset may be holding you back.

Just as buggy software can bog down a computer and cause it to crash, negative thoughts can slow you down and derail your efforts to succeed. You may have to reboot your mind and fill it with positive affirmations and a strong belief that you are perfectly capable of achieving your dreams. Here are some suggestions on how to give yourself a positive attitude adjustment:

- ✔ Find a sales hero — a role model to inspire you.
- ✔ Shadow a successful salesperson to find out how they achieve success.
- ✔ Read inspirational books or listen to motivational tapes.
- ✔ Fill your mind with positive affirmations.
- ✔ Hang out with positive people and avoid naysayers.

Surround yourself with positive thoughts, people, and experiences, so negativity has no space to take root and grow. If negative thoughts begin to creep in, visit my friend Mr. Positive, Dave Boufford, at www.MrPositive.com. He can get you pumped up in a hurry.

You would be surprised at the number of top salespeople or speakers who would welcome the opportunity to meet with you, share a cultural event, or join you for dinner when they're passing through your town. If you know that one of your sales heroes is going to be in town, try to contact the person and arrange a meeting. This can be the perfect opportunity to meet your hero in person and begin a relationship that may develop into a mentoring situation.

Setting stimulating goals

Most sales coaches stress that goals should be realistic, which is somewhat true, but realistic goals that don't make you stretch are of little use. I prefer to encourage the salespeople I coach to set stimulating goals. A goal should always make you reach outside your comfort zone. It should always include some level of risk. A good goal should include the following:

- ✔ Statement of the goal
- ✔ Starting date
- ✔ Completion date
- ✔ Statement of how success is going to be measured

Sales quotas can do more harm than good, particularly if they are pinned to a deadline. A sales quota can often make you so motivated to close a sale that you're powerless to negotiate with the buyer. Buyers are often well aware of sales quotas and can use them to negotiate a more attractive price and terms. Try to think of different goals, such as acquiring a certain number of new customers or increasing the number of cold calls you make by a certain percentage.

Plotting your course

The best laid plans of mice and men may often fail, but trying to achieve a goal without having a solid plan in place is pure folly. Plot your course from point A to point B, so you know where you are, where you're going, and how you're going to get there before you even take that first step:

1. **Determine where you are first.** By logging your point of departure you can more effectively measure your progress later.

2. **Set your goal or destination, as described in the previous section.**

3. **Include a timeframe to keep yourself on track.**

4. **Identify your objectives.** Objectives are like milestone markers, rewarding you when you complete each leg of the journey.

5. **Plan an overall strategy for achieving success.** What sort of tactical plan can ensure success with the least amount of effort?

6. **Identify tasks.** Break the process down into individual tasks to make the plan feel less overwhelming and more manageable.

7. **Identify the resources you have on hand, including personnel and equipment.**

Don't get hung up thinking that you have to do everything yourself. Identify the tasks you are well-qualified to perform and then delegate the remaining tasks to more capable people who have more time. A good rule of thumb for hiring people is this: If you earn more than enough per hour to cover the cost of hiring someone else to do the work, hire someone. Also, if you can do more and sell more with an assistant than you can without one, hire the assistant. At least try it. See Chapter 13 for more about hiring the right people to fill the gaps.

Implementing your plan

Sales and business consultants often discover that clients are more than willing to pay them $300 or more per hour for advice and then rarely put that advice into practice. They know what they have to do to achieve success, but they're unwilling to take that essential next step — implementing the plan.

After setting your goal and drawing up a solid plan, put your plan into action. If it doesn't quite work, make the necessary adjustments and try again. Successful businesspeople rarely succeed on their first attempt. They fail, learn, make adjustments, and persist. Unsuccessful people fail and give up or never even get started. I've known salespeople who have stuck with a prospect for 14 months and then given up only to discover that the customer decided to buy in the 15th month. If it were easy, everyone would do it.

Weaving Advanced Selling into Your Life

Watch the top performers in any profession and you observe a quality that they all share — almost every single one of them loves what they do. Even if they weren't getting paid to do what they do, they'd probably still be doing it.

My co-author, Joe, spent some time with the folks at Incredible Technologies, creators of the most popular coin-op video game on the planet — Golden Tee Golf. He interviewed the game testers — the quality control people who tested the video games 8–12 hours a day. One of the questions he asked was, "What do you guys do when you get home at night?" Their answer, "We play video games."

To become a top salesperson, you have to love selling, and then you have to live it, as I explain in the following sections.

Don't let success drive you to failure. If you're a top salesperson, you will eventually be asked to be the sales manager. I highly recommend that you pass on this "promotion." Managing salespeople is no job for a top sales-person. It's downright toxic. Not only would you find it frustrating, but you would probably end up driving the other salespeople right out the door. If you own your own business, avoid promoting your top salesperson to man-ager for the same reasons.

Envisioning your success

What does sales success look like to you? Are you sitting in an office all day making cold calls? Driving around from one disinterested client to another trying to drum up business? Or do you have people calling *you* to place orders? Do you have to hire an assistant to handle the extra business? Do you have more opportunities than you can possibly pursue?

Your first step in achieving success is to envision it. Most people can't get past this first step, because they don't even know what they would love to do. Dream, and then jot down a detailed description of that dream, so you can close your eyes and see it playing out in your mind.

Prior to May 6, 1954, the date on which Roger Bannister ran a mile in under 4 minutes, people thought that running a 4-minute mile was physically impossi-ble. As soon as Bannister did it, other runners were miraculously able to run 4-minute miles. Why could they do it now when they couldn't before? Because now they could see themselves doing it.

Walking the walk

You can talk the talk. You know what you should be doing to achieve the suc-cess you desire. The next step is to walk the walk. For salespeople, walking the walk consists of doing the following:

  ✓ **Practicing your craft.** Practice selling at work, at home, at the airport, in the taxi, at the grocery store, and wherever else you happen to be in contact with other people. The key to selling is being able to establish personal relationships with your clients. Practice by making meaningful connections with everyone you meet.

✔ **Taking risks to stretch your limits.** The people who make the most money take the biggest risks, and that applies to sales as much as it applies to anything in the world of business. You have to be willing to invest money and take some chances. Otherwise, you're little more than an hourly employee hired to take orders.

✔ **Embracing change as a growth strategy.** The Internet, new technologies, and the global economy have combined forces to accelerate change to a dizzying pace. The only way to survive and thrive in this environment is to embrace rather than resist change.

✔ **Investing in your own success.** As an entrepreneurial salesperson, you have to act like a business, and that means investing in your own growth and development, the latest gadgets to boost sales and productivity, and support personnel, so you have more time to spend on what you do best and what earns your company the biggest profits. Besides, walking around with the latest gadgets is cool. Sometimes, I forget to pack one of my gadgets just so I have an excuse to buy the latest version.

✔ **Playing with new technologies.** Tech savvy customers are relying more on the Internet for their information and are using a variety of communications technologies to keep in touch, including cell phones, e-mail, text messaging, VoIP (Voice Over Internet Protocol or Internet phones), and blogs. To stay in touch with the latest generation of shoppers, you'd better be tech savvy, too.

✔ **Hiring an assistant.** Hire or be hired is what I say. Hire people to take on tasks that they can perform better, faster, and cheaper than you can, and then treat them well. The more work you can outsource to others, the more time and energy you can spend on dollar-intensive activities. See the following section, "Recruiting People Power to Fuel Your Success," for details.

✔ **Achieving a balanced lifestyle.** Being a successful human being means much more than achieving career success. It means remaining healthy, building rewarding relationships, supporting your community, and perhaps even raising children. Failing in one area of your life can lead to failures in other areas.

✔ **Giving without expectations.** Sales coaches often recommend that you "give to get." I'm telling you to "give to give." If you're expecting something in return, you're not really giving — you're bartering. Give for the sheer pleasure of giving.

Work on being successful in all areas of your life. Without the strong relationship I have with my wife and children, I would not have achieved the same level of success in my career. Success feeds on success, and, unfortunately, failure feeds on failure. Encourage everyone around you to set goals and pursue their dreams.

Stay the course

During my recent stay at the Hilton Hotel in Glendale, I met a young man, a bartender who seemed a little down in the dumps. I had to ask—the best salespeople always ask questions, the right questions. I asked what was going on in his life, and he started talking right away—the best bartenders always do.

He had been engaged, and his fiancé had recently called off the engagement. He wanted to be a full-time fireman, and she wasn't so sure she wanted to be included in the pursuit of that dream. Now he was deep in debt, having borrowed to pay for a fancy engagement ring.

I advised him to continue to work, live at home, pay off his jewelry debt, and do everything possible to keep moving forward toward his goal of joining the fire department. People in these situations often give up and settle for something short of their dreams, and I hate to see young people snuff out their dreams in the prime of their lives.

Fortunately, he loves peanut butter and jelly sandwiches, which will certainly help him meet his budget, conserving funds to pay off debt and stay focused on providing a great service to his community. I wish him well.

If the path to your dreams seems a little rocky, don't give up and settle for less. Stay the course.

Recruiting People Power to Fuel Your Success

Overachievers are often self-reliant types who refuse to ask for any assistance. They like to achieve everything on their own, so they can take full credit. When you're in sales, that approach is nonsense. The fact is that you can do more and do it better by harnessing the power of people.

If you need proof, just look around at the major corporations. Do you think they could be major corporations without hiring people? Think of yourself as a mini-corporation, You, Inc. When you want to grow your business, you'd better hang out the Help Wanted sign and start interviewing some qualified candidates. Here are some tips for harnessing people power to fuel your success:

- ✔ **Identify the missing links to your success.** What do you want to do that you can't do because you are lacking the time or expertise? As soon as you know what you need and don't have in terms of talent, skill, and time, you have a pretty good idea of the people you need to hire or partner with — people who have what you need.

✔ **Outsource time-consuming chores.** Figure out how much you earn per hour. If you earn $50 an hour selling and you're cleaning your house over the weekend when you can hire someone for $10 an hour to do it, that's borderline insane . . . unless, of course, cleaning your house is therapeutic or something you enjoy doing. Hire someone so you have more time to implement the strategies I present throughout this book.

✔ **Get yourself an intern.** Colleges and even some high schools have internships or coop programs in which students are willing to work for free or for a pittance in exchange for job experience. Look into these programs for some cheap and often highly qualified workers.

✔ **Hire the talent you're missing.** Salespeople rarely hesitate to invest in a gadget or service they think they need, but when I recommend that they hire an assistant, they immediately find all sorts of excuses. The fact is that hiring an assistant has never been easier. You can even hire a virtual assistant, as explained in Chapter 13, so you don't have to deal with messy payroll issues and benefits. A virtual assistant works as a freelancer for however long you need the assistant's skills.

✔ **Cash in on R-Commerce (Relationship-Commerce).** On its surface, the economy is driven by the exchange of goods and services, but beneath this surface economy is the real economy, driven by relationships. By focusing on your relationships with customers, colleagues, and even your competitors, you can grow your sales infinitely more than by focusing simply on the exchange of goods and services. See Chapter 14 for details.

✔ **Team up with a personal partner.** It's far too easy to skip out on your responsibilities when you're accountable only to yourself. By teaming up with a personal partner to set goals and keep one another on track, you can achieve much higher levels of success than by acting alone. In Chapter 7, I show you how to choose a personal partner and work together to ensure mutual success.

✔ **Pick the brain of a mentor or coach.** Success leaves big footprints, so follow those footprints by taking on a mentor or hiring a sales coach to advise you. A mentor or coach can often point out shortcuts you may have missed, expose you to incredible opportunities, and make sure you're doing everything you need to do to stay on plan.

✔ **Become a mentor.** You may think that mentoring a student or a salesperson who's less qualified, less experienced, or less successful than you would be a huge expenditure of time, and perhaps it is, but what you get in return usually makes up for it. A younger student can often teach you a thing or two about using the latest technologies or expose you to new marketing and sales techniques. In addition, if you establish a solid relationship, your student promises to become a major networking asset later in his career.

Selling Yourself: Self-Promotion

Sure, you're selling products and services, but when your customers choose to buy from you rather than from one of your competitors, they're buying into you. Although you may market and sell a host of products, remember that your major marketing campaign should center mainly on you. You are your own company, and by promoting yourself properly and persistently, you ensure a long and successful future in sales.

People generally buy from people they know and trust. That's why even though shoppers may be able to go on the Internet and buy something for considerably less than the street price, they often choose to shop at the local store — a brick-and-mortar establishment. Your reputation should be so solid that you essentially become a brick-and-mortar establishment unto yourself.

By shamelessly promoting yourself, you create the image — the impression — you want people to have of you. Cold calls become warm calls, because people already feel as though they know you. Do it right, and you won't even have to call . . . people who want what you're selling are going to call you.

To engage in effective shameless self promotion, you first have to find something in yourself to promote, and then promote it, as explained in the following sections.

Identifying your unique selling point

In the good old days, you knew who you were doing business with. Maybe it was Ted the TV guy, Melvin the milkman, Beatrice the beautician, Clare the cleaning lady, Fran the financial planner, or Ralph the Realtor (always thinking of Me, Incorporated). In a small town there was usually one person known as the go-to guy or gal for each product or service. Nowadays, particularly in big cities, you may find dozens or even thousands of suppliers from which to choose. To stick out (in a good way, of course), you want to pick something about you that's unique or create some memorable persona, so when prospective customers think of the product or service you're selling, they immediately think of you.

Several years ago, I decided to make an 11-foot-tall, 500-pound nail my unique thing. You can skip to Chapter 9 to find out more about it or visit www.BigNail.com. I purchased the Big Nail on eBay, stuck it on a trailer, and pulled it around town to various fundraising events for special causes. I also placed the Big Nail logo on all my marketing materials. Needless to say, it created a lot of positive buzz.

Discover your Big Nail and make it the center of your self-promotional campaign. A clear, central focus on something that can really get you pumped up can generate a lot of energy and, more importantly, draw a lot of attention.

Branding yourself

Think of Martha Stewart, The Donald, Oprah, Britney Spears, Paris Hilton. As soon as you see or hear the name, that person's face probably pops into your mind. And you probably can describe what each person does. That's because these people have brand presence. Through their own self promotion and a lot of help from the media, these folks have achieved celebrity status.

While you may not crave celebrity status or want the paparazzi photographing you while you're on vacation, you can achieve a certain level of brand presence on your own by creating your own buzz-marketing blitz:

- ✔ **Market yourself on paper.** Start slow with your own business cards and brochures. Hand them out to everyone you know and everyone you meet.

- ✔ **Market yourself in the media.** Are you an expert on what you sell? You should be. Leverage your expertise in your marketing efforts. Offer to write articles for local newspapers and magazines. Call the local TV and radio stations and offer your services as a local expert for news stories related to your area of expertise. Offer to speak to local groups for free. I gave more than 1,000 free speeches before I ever was able to charge a fee.

- ✔ **Market yourself on the Internet.** Every salesperson should have at least one Web site or blog. I have over 200, including AboutRalph.com (professional services site), BigNail.com (about branding), GetFlipping.com (to promote *Flipping Houses For Dummies*), FlippingFrenzy.com (about real estate and mortgage fraud), RalphRoberts.com (a real estate site), and KolleenRoberts.com (a tribute to my older daughter). The Internet is an entirely separate world, a virtual world, where more and more people are spending more and more of their time. You have to be there to meet and greet these tech savvy customers.

- ✔ **Advertise everywhere.** Wherever people who buy the products and services you sell happen to hang out or obtain their information, you should be there. If your customers watch TV, you should be on TV. If they tune into the radio, they should be able to hear your voice occasionally. If they read the papers, you should have an ad in the paper.

I put my phone number and e-mail address on *everything*. That makes some salespeople a little nervous, because they don't want everyone calling them at all hours of the day and night. I have assistants who handle much of the added work, and I strongly recommend that you do the same. Yes, having to field calls, answer questions, talk with reporters, write articles, and do all that other self-promotional stuff requires more time, energy, and effort, but if you want to be the top salesperson in your industry, that's what it takes.

Prospecting for Ideas and Leads

The paradox of giving is that the more you give, the more you receive, especially when you're not trying to receive. It just snowballs. One opportunity leads to another. I post an article on one of my blogs, and a reporter calls to interview me. That interview gets posted, a publisher notices it and calls me to write a book. The book is published, and I get more reporters calling.

Sometimes, I attend a conference for the sole purpose of attending a few workshops and honing my sales skills. The workshops can all be terrible, but I always manage to bump into someone, start conversing, and we come up with an idea for a new business venture or product.

These opportunities arise through no real conscious effort to pursue a particular opportunity. However, they wouldn't happen if I wasn't proactive in marketing myself and maintaining productive relationships. To open yourself to more leads and opportunities, I recommend you do the following:

- ✔ Hand out your business card to everyone you know and meet.
- ✔ Post an article at least once a week on your Web site or blog.
- ✔ Contribute to online discussions on message boards and blogs that pertain to your products and services — get involved in these online communities.
- ✔ Remain positive and upbeat. Nobody likes a wet blanket. You should also consider steering clear of discussions about politics, religion, sex, and schools.
- ✔ Become a member, preferably a leader, in your trade association.
- ✔ Attend conferences regularly, and offer to speak or deliver workshops on your areas of expertise.
- ✔ Keep in touch with everyone in your address book, preferably by way of personal phone calls.
- ✔ Talk to reporters — they can get the word out for you.
- ✔ Volunteer for an organization you trust, but avoid committees. Most salespeople are very civic minded, but a committee can really sap your enthusiasm.

Unlocking the Secret of Mutual Success

Selling is all about establishing mutually beneficial relationships, and when you think about it, that's the type of relationship we strive for in every aspect of our lives. The most productive relationships are those in which each person involved thrives independently and can bring something of value to the relationship.

In business, particularly in sales, making everyone around you successful delivers several things of value:

- ✔ **Return business:** Satisfied customers are more likely to come back to you the next time they're in the market for your product or service . . . assuming they think of you, which is why it is so important to keep in touch with customers.

- ✔ **Increased sales volume:** A successful business customer is more profitable and has the money to purchase more products and services from you.

- ✔ **Positive referrals:** When customers are happy, particularly if you had something to do with it, they're more likely to refer you to other people they know.

- ✔ **Positive testimonials:** Testimonials are great to include in sales letters, brochures, and other marketing materials. If future prospects know that you've helped others, they have more trust that you can help them.

- ✔ **Increased opportunities:** Focusing on your customer's success often opens your mind to new ideas for additional products and services and perhaps even new divisions or businesses you can start.

In the following sections, I offer some suggestions on how to ensure your own success by making everyone around you more successful.

Making your customers successful

Your customer's success is your success, so it is in your best interest to make your customer as successful as possible. That doesn't mean giving away your products and services. It does mean enabling your customer to tap the full potential of what you're selling and to assist your customer even when that assistance doesn't directly boost sales.

You may be called on to offer your customer some free advice, refer them to other companies for products and services you don't sell, or even do a little head-hunting for them to steer them in the direction of the most qualified personnel in your area.

Become your own customer, as much as possible. Try to buy the same product or one that's similar to what you sell from another salesperson to discover insights from your customer's point of view. (You don't actually have to buy it.) See Chapter 18 for additional strategies and tips for establishing mutually beneficial relationships with your customers.

Making your customers' customers successful

As an entrepreneurial salesperson, always think one step ahead — that means considering your customer's customer. The single most important contribution you can make to your customer's success is contributing to the success of your customer's customer.

In many cases, this is primarily the responsibility of your company's CEO or product development division, but because you probably have more direct contact with customers, you may need to carry the message back to your company. If you're selling to a business that sells your product to consumers, keep that consumer, the end user, in mind.

Focusing your efforts on underserved clientele

Your market is likely populated with a portion of un-served or underserved clientele, particularly minority customers that you and your competitors have ignored. Ensuring customer success often calls for paying some attention to this market sector.

Chapter 19 offers specific suggestions for appealing to minority, multicultural clientele. Salespeople who are able to implement some of the strategies discussed in this chapter often reap incredible rewards because they find that they have no competition for these customers. By making a few adjustments, you can corner the market and expand your world view at the same time.

Declaring peace with your competitors

Establish relationships with your competitors like the relationships you have when you compete against friends in a friendly game of tennis. Try your best to pummel the competition, but don't take it personally. You never know when you may need to ask one of your sworn enemies for a favor or when an opportunity to work together may present itself.

In Chapter 20, I point out several potential benefits of playing nice with the competition and show you how to collaborate effectively when given the opportunity. I also show you ways in which you can cut in on your competitor's profits . . . nicely, of course.

Why share your secrets?

Whenever I speak, coach, or publish a book revealing my "secrets" of success, people often wonder why I would share these secrets. Why not just keep all of this to myself? Why risk revealing anything of value to the competition?

Someone asked Ira Hayes, the top salesperson at NCR (National Cash Register) many years ago, these same questions. At the time, Hayes was touring the country, telling everyone his secrets to achieving phenomenal sales. When someone asked why he would come and speak to the sales people at a company that was one of NCR's major competitors, Hayes said something like, "Well, nobody at my company is following my advice, so I don't expect that any of you will follow it either."

I carefully screen candidates before I agree to coach or mentor them for this very reason — I can't teach someone who won't put my advice into practice.

Declaring peace with your competitors doesn't mean waving the white flag. It's about playing fair, and I don't mean county-fair nice. You're still a gladiator fighting for your life in the great arena of life, so don't go soft. Just keep in mind that your competitors can come in handy at times.

Tapping the power of professional associations

As you're making the rounds to boost the performance and productivity of everyone around you, don't overlook your colleagues. Join and lead your trade association, and give back to the industry that toasts and butters your bread.

Honor your duty to give back to your industry. Once a year, you should offer to speak at an industry event or at least act as a member of a discussion panel. Find a way to give back and pass along the wisdom you've acquired.

In Chapter 14, I point out the many benefits of being a member of your trade association and the bigger benefits of taking on a leadership position. By making your colleagues more successful, you do your part to create a healthy, thriving industry that's good for everyone — suppliers, salespeople, clients, consumers, and yourself. In addition, you gain professional contacts, many of whom are leaders in the industry.

Chapter 2

Visualizing Yourself as a Power Seller

In This Chapter

▶ Selecting top-notch role models

▶ Crowding out negative thoughts with positive statements

▶ Getting comfortable with yourself

▶ Defining what you mean by "success"

▶ Visualizing your future success

*P*ower selling is about faith, and faith is a funny thing. While most people believe it when they see it, people with faith see it because they believe it. The "power" in power selling comes from believing — believing in the product or service you're selling, in your customers or clients, in your personnel, and especially in yourself.

The first step to becoming a power seller, is to believe in yourself. Visualize yourself as a success, and you're a big step closer to becoming a success. In this chapter, I show you how to establish a power-selling mindset by identifying your sales role models, packing your brain with positive thoughts, and envisioning your future success. By following the advice I offer in this chapter, you can gain the belief that empowers you to achieve your dreams.

Sidling Up to Top Sellers

To be good at anything, hang out with the people who are the best. To be a good father, be around good fathers. To be a good friend, hang out with the people who are good friends and work toward being a good friend to them. To be a good salesperson, rub elbows with the top salespeople. By surrounding yourself with the best, you benefit in at least two ways:

Those people motivate you to strive for excellence.

They model the skills you need to achieve your desired level of excellence.

As Charlie "Tremendous" Jones use to say, "You're only as good as the books you read, the people you meet, and the tapes you listen to." And in the sections that follow, I give you the tools you need to both find and follow the best people who can inspire you to success.

Identifying your sales heroes

To figure out how to envision yourself as anything, watch a kid. Kids have heroes — maybe their favorite baseball or soccer player, an astronaut or movie character, a teacher or parent, or perhaps even a superhero like Wonder Woman or Spiderman. Kids who really get into it pretend to be the hero. They talk the talk, walk the walk, and for some fleeting moment during the day, they *become* that hero, at least in their own minds.

Of course, the heroes you need aren't likely to be wielding their powers on the silver screen or hitting homeruns — you need heroes that can help you envision yourself as a sales success. Throughout these sections I show you how to figure out just what makes a good sales hero as well as how to start your own growing list of heroes.

My sales heroes

I've gathered a my own list of sales heroes to share with you. These are people who, through their words and examples, have inspired and guided me to my current success:

- Julia Rowland, my grandmother and owner of Fashion Treasure Jewelry — an accomplished saleswoman who embodied the joy of selling — inspired me to go for the gold when it came to selling on my own.

- Tony & Noel Fox of Fox Brothers Real Estate — the first real estate brokers, who hired me right out of high school and taught me the nuts and bolts of introducing myself to *everyone* and letting them know who I was and what I did. When I first started, they dropped me off at the local grocery store and told me to introduce myself to everyone and give them my card. For Tony and Noel, the weather was no excuse not to work. When it rained, I was in the grocery store; when it was nice I was on the door-to-door campaign. As a salesperson there is always something you can do!

- Ira Hayes, the original Ambassador of Enthusiasm, who taught me the power of the word "Great!" Hayes was a top salesman for NCR (National Cash Register) who led not only with words but also by example. I attended every one of his speaking events I could and wore out his tapes listening to them.

- Tom Hopkins, author of *Selling For Dummies* and the guy who wrote the first book of tips for real estate agents. Every top salesperson I know follows the Tom Hopkins approach to selling . . even if they don't know it's his approach. On Jan 23, 1986, I took his course on Closing the Sale for the '80s. He taught me the value of goals and the characteristics of a great salesman.

✔ Zig Ziglar, the sales superhero, who taught me that if you help enough people get what they want, you will get what you want.

✔ Charlie "Tremendous" Jones, who revealed to me the life-changing power of people and books.

✔ Art Fettig, who taught me the difference between a great salesperson and an order taker.

✔ Joe Girard, the top car salesman of all times, who happened to sell cars four miles from where I grew up. Over the years we would meet and have lunch. I soaked up everything I could to learn how to be the best salesman possible. Joe taught me that you could have a team and be more successful together.

✔ Floyd Wickman, a real estate agent in my area, who taught me to stay on track and be competent, confident, and natural. The same houses that Wickman sold for $17,000–$20,000 30 years ago, I now sell for $175,000–300,000! The National Association of Realtors commissioned Floyd, Danielle Kennedy, and me to go out to real estate offices across the country to critique offices and teams.

✔ Dick Runstatler, my favorite sales manager of all time, who let Ralph be Ralph and taught me how to handle stressful situations.

✔ Tom Desmond, a real estate agent I worked with at Earl Kiem real estate, who was constantly striving to improve himself. At the time, I thought his obsession with professional titles was silly. Only later did I realize that he was truly dedicated to being the best he could be.

✔ Earl Keim, a guy who could sell you the house next door, even if you didn't want it. He coined the phrase "Keim Sold Mine,"

expanded his brokerage to include hundreds of offices, and later became a speaker who passed along his words of wisdom known as "Earl's pearls." He taught me the value of branding.

✔ Lee Iacocca, who sold the government on bailing out the Chrysler Corporation with $1.2 billion. What I admire most about Iacocca is how he reacted during the Chrysler crisis — pulling an idea way out of the box to bail out the automotive company. No one would have expected that his crazy idea would be seriously considered, but he didn't let that stop him and he got it done — it was a good thing and the right thing to do.

✔ Norman Vincent Peale, best-selling author of *The Power of Positive Thinking*, who recognized the extraordinary in ordinary people and sincerely cared about other people. He saw opportunity and seized it.

✔ Mark Victor Hansen, the "Master of Mindset" and co-creator of *Chicken Soup for the Soul*, who taught me to reflect rejection and continue to pursue my passion. Mark was instrumental in helping me launch my writing career.

✔ Og Mandino (www.ogmandino.com), a humble, yet remarkable man who spent so much of his life striving to overcome his own personal challenges and sharing what he discovered through his writing and teaching. His legacy is a gift to us all.

✔ Tom Antion, the speaker's speaker, who taught me that if you can't talk to people, you can't sell.

✔ Les Brown, who taught me the power of living with a purpose.

Honing in on hero qualities

To simplify the process of envisioning yourself as a successful salesperson, identify your sales heroes — people whom you deem the ultimate salespeople. You're unique, of course, so you won't sell exactly the same way they do or even have the same personal or professional goals, but picking the right role models means you get:

- ✔ **Valuable resources for continuing education:** Your role model has probably read all the books, listened to the tapes, attended a host of seminars, consulted with hundreds of other salespeople in your field, and field-tested a variety of sales techniques. This person is uniquely qualified to provide you with shortcuts to success by showing you what works and what doesn't and pointing the way to other useful resources.

- ✔ **Inspiration to strive for higher levels of success:** When you hook up with a sales hero, you make a commitment to that person (often unspoken) to do your best. Just by having an accomplished salesperson guiding you, you work a little harder, knowing that your hero is watching and rooting for you.

- ✔ **Shortcuts to success:** Your sales heroes probably achieved success through a good deal of trial and error. They know what works and what doesn't. By listening to them, you can avoid much of the trial and error and pour more energy into acquiring techniques that really work.

Success leaves behind huge footprints. Follow those footprints to the person who left them and try to connect with that person. The most successful people are typically the most generous with their time and expertise. They're willing to share if you demonstrate an eagerness to learn. (See Chapter 14 for details about teaming up with others to build mutually beneficial relationships.)

Pinpointing the best people

Start a list of your own personal and professional heroes. They can be authors, speakers, colleagues, family members, friends, or neighbors. Anyone you admire is a perfect candidate to be a hero.

Role models can be from the past or present, near or far, in sales or out of sales, but they must be successful at what they do. If you haven't yet identified one or more role models, start looking:

- ✔ Identify the top sales person where you work and consider using that person as your role model.

- ✔ Check out other books by salespeople with proven track records including *Selling For Dummies*, by Tom Hopkins.

- ✔ Attend conferences where the top salespeople offer motivational presentations and sales seminars.

✔ Get involved in your trade association, as discussed in Chapter 16.

✔ Read biographies of historical figures you admire or are curious about.

✔ Ask people you admire who their role models are.

Shadowing top sellers

You can certainly start to form an idea of the salesperson you want to be by studying your sales heroes, attending their seminars, reading their books, listening to their tapes, and perhaps even meeting them in person. The best way to envision yourself selling the way they sell, however, is to observe them in action. Shadow superior salespeople and watch them ply their craft on the job.

I've had dozens of salespeople spend a day with me, simply observing what I do. I shadow other salespeople to pick up new strategies and tips from them. To remain on the cutting edge is a lifelong learning process, and shadowing is often the best training available.

Set a goal to shadow at least one other salesperson this month. If you work in an office with other salespeople, ask your manager to schedule a day when you can shadow the top salesperson in the company. In Chapter 8, I recommend *personal partnering* as another way to team up with colleagues to boost sales and improve your career.

The World's Greatest Salesman

I was fortunate enough to grow up in Metropolitan Detroit, where I had some incredible role models, including Joe Girard, the "World's Greatest Salesperson." Joe Girard has been listed in the Guinness Book of World Records as the Number 1 Retail Sales Person in the World for 12 years. In his 15 years as a new car salesman, Joe sold 13,001 cars (all retail sales, no fleet, wholesale, or used cars).

Joe believed that "sparks create fires," and he was constantly on the lookout for sparks he could use to motivate himself to make something happen. Joe started gathering sparks at an early age, growing up in one of Detroit's worst ghettos with a father who constantly berated him and told him that he would never amount to anything. Joe's first spark was his determination to prove that his father had been wrong. His second spark was to show his mother that her love for him and her faith in him had not been misplaced.

I was very fortunate to live in the same town as Joe Girard. Over the years, I would have lunch with him, and he served as my unofficial mentor. I listened to Joe, read stories about him, and visualized myself being a top salesperson, like Joe Girard. By modeling myself after a salesperson I admired, I was able to take a shortcut. I didn't have to discover strategies and tips, because Joe shared with me what he had already discovered.

If you're on a sales team in which each salesperson handles a different geographical area, making shadowing impractical, set aside a couple hours during a late Friday afternoon to share anecdotes, war stories, and situational analysis with the top or veteran sales people on your team. Do this regularly and you'll be amazed at the sharp reduction in the number of sales situations that catch you by surprise. In addition to benefiting from your own experience, you benefit from the experience of your fellow teammates. Harnessing the Power of Positive Thinking

I hate complainers; they always have excuses for why they're not successful.

They're not getting quality leads.

The sales quotas are too high.

The company doesn't provide enough support for the sales department.

The product or service is second rate.

The business is facing too much competition.

Blah, blah, blah.

Power sellers don't look for excuses. They have a can-do attitude that enables them to overcome any limitation. In the following sections, I show you how to develop this can-do attitude and crowd out counterproductive thoughts.

Death and incurable illness are the only two problems you can't solve. Every other problem in the world can be solved with time, money, human resources, or a combination of the three. Don't let problems get in the way of your success — solve them!

Revving up your mind with affirmations

Most of us grow up learning to put ourselves down for any real or imagined shortcoming. We grow up believing certain things about ourselves or comparing ourselves negatively to others. The use of positive affirmations is a technique to change that negative self-talk into something more positive. But even if you're one of the fortunate few not experience the negative self-talk, affirmations still can be a powerful ally in reaching your goals.

Affirmations are effective because they can fundamentally change a person's subconscious thought patterns. In the past few years the researchers have proven some very astounding facts that once were only theories, the most important of which (for our purposes) is that the subconscious mind is the true power center. It controls 97 percent of our actions, beliefs, behaviors, and attitudes.

In the following sections, my friend and colleague Dave Bouffard (a.k.a. Mr. Positive at www.MrPositive.com) and I bring you up to speed on the power of affirmations and show you how to use them to fuel a positive attitude that drives success from your subconscious mind throughout all aspects of your life.

An attitude of gratitude is absolutely essential in the practice of affirmations. Be thankful for everything you have.

Grasping affirmation basics

An affirmation is not simply a memo telling yourself what to think or how to behave. An affirmation must paint a picture or project an image in your mind and make an emotional connection. You must go beyond thinking the affirmation to feeling it. Otherwise, they simply have little or no effect on your long-term attitude and behaviors.

Below are a few basic affirmations that most people know and many have tried and may or may not have had success with:

"All I need is within me now."

"I love and accept myself exactly as I am."

"Money comes to me easily and effortlessly." (Replace "Money" with whatever you desire.)

"I am healthy in body, mind, and spirit."

"I am living my wonderful, ideal life."

"Every day in every way I am getting better and better!"

These basic affirmations are not bad, but they obviously don't evoke an emotional response and they're certainly not something we would consider sufficient for advanced selling.

Research has discovered that every negative thought requires 27 positive thoughts to cancel it out.

Composing your own advanced affirmations

Average affirmations are fine for average people, but when you're trying to take your sales career to the next level, average just isn't good enough. You want the deluxe models. So what separates an average affirmation from something more advanced? Advanced affirmations must meet the following four requirements:

✔ **Stated in the present tense:** Word the affirmation to express your ownership of it and convey the sense that you have already achieved what it states. All affirmation should begin with words like "I am . . ." or "I have . . .". For example, instead of saying, "I will have a rewarding job," say, "I have a rewarding job." Otherwise, you'll be waiting forever for that reward job to come your way.

✔ **Expresses a positive statement:** Affirm what you want, rather than what you don't want. For example, instead of saying, "I am no longer sick," you may say, "I am now perfectly healthy in body, mind and spirit." This reinforces your desired goal without confusing your subconscious mind with the mention of the undesirable condition.

✔ **Is short and specific:** Short affirmations are easy to say, and have a far greater impact at the subconscious level than those that are long and wordy. Keeping them short and specific to the point adds power as the idea is uncluttered by extraneous elements.

✔ **Is spoken with strong feeling:** The more emotion and feeling you put into your affirmations, the deeper the impression they leave on your subconscious. Your goal when stating your affirmations should be to fire up your passion so your can "see" your goal and create a strong emotional connection.

Checking out some advanced affirmation examples

If you're having trouble composing your own affirmations, you may find inspiration in affirmations that other salespeople have written. Here are some examples of advanced affirmations:

✔ I (state your name) easily attract everything I need for me to meet my sales goals. Leads, referrals and the right opportunities always come to me.

✔ I (state your name) am a selling professional who always goes the extra mile to serve my clients, exceeding their expectations and meeting their goals, and I always meet or exceed my professional goals.

✔ I (state your name) am dedicated to my personal and professional development. I read, listen to tapes, and attend training sessions to improve my skills. I am a lifelong learner who easily absorbs and applies what I learn to my life on a daily basis.

✔ I (state your name) take great care of my physical being. I exercise regularly, eat healthy, and get sufficient rest. My health is my true wealth. I am committed to my health and wealth!

✔ I (state your name) am confident, charismatic, and attractive to the people I meet in both my personal and professional life. I am a great listener and communicator.

Imprinting your affirmations into your subconscious

After you have composed the perfect affirmation for yourself, you can begin the process of imprinting your affirmation in your subconscious mind. To do an effective job of making your affirmation an integral part of your being, follow these tips:

✔ **Repeat your affirmation often:** The importance of repetition cannot be overemphasized. Your affirmation should become your mantra. Although you may not want to chant, you should play it over and over in your mind.

✔ **Express your affirmation emotionally:** Get involved, be passionate, move your body and feel it. Pretend that you already have what you are affirming. How would you feel and act. The feeling is vital and brings much more power to the process than just writing, typing, or speaking your affirmations.

✔ **Be persistent and consistent:** Continue to remind yourself of your commitment to your affirmation and strive to attain it. If you get distracted and wander off the path, recommit yourself to success.

✔ **Believe:** Ditch any doubts that may creep into your mind. You must willingly suspend any disbelief, just like when you read a book or watch a movie. Get into it. Don't overanalyze it or let the destructive voices of negative self-talk have a say in who you are. If you believe that the affirmation process will work for you, it will.

✔ **Personalize:** Personalize all of your affirmations, by stating your name. Your subconscious responds to your name (that's why in a crowd when someone speaks your name you hear it!). The more tools you use to reach your subconscious mind, the more powerful the process of using advanced affirmations is going to be for you, and the sooner you experience positive results.

Acquiring additional affirmation techniques

Many people who use affirmations to adjust their attitudes and drive their success simply repeat their affirmations in their minds, crowding out the negative self-talk and replacing it with positive self-talk. However, you can use a variety of techniques to imprint your affirmations on your mind.

Use the combo pack approach: Write out your affirmations, record them in your own voice, and use them when you exercise! Then read, listen, and say them daily.

Following are several techniques that we use to reinforce our affirmations:

✔ **Writing technique:** Consider writing down each affirmation 10 to 20 times a day for 30 days or journaling about your affirmations. Writing is a physical activity that can make the affirmation feel like a more integral part of your being.

✔ **Recorder technique:** Speak your affirmations into a tape or digital recorder and then listen to them first thing in the morning and just before you drift off to sleep at night. Your subconscious mind often pays better attention to your own voice.

Mix in your favorite music or natural sounds — anything that brings you into a positive emotional state and makes your mind more receptive to the message.

✔ **Exercise technique:** As you're working out, repeat your affirmations. You can say them out loud or in your head. This technique is especially effective if your affirmations have to do with health. You may say something like "Everyday in every way I'm getting better and better" or "I am strong, I feel great, I am healthy, I am healthy."

✔ **Mirror affirmation technique:** Stand in front of the mirror, look in your eyes, and speak your affirmations to yourself. The key is looking into your eyes and speaking out loud just as though you were closing a deal with a prospect. You are selling yourself your affirmation, so keep eye contact, stand tall, and put on your best smile, because this is the most important sales call you'll ever have!

Most people go through life looking others in the eyes to show they are being sincere and honest, but most people never truly look themselves in the eye! Try it. It's very, very powerful.

✔ **Anywhere technique:** Whenever you find yourself with a free moment, repeat your affirmations, in your car, in the elevator, at your desk. And if you have a negative thought or say something negative about yourself, immediately restate it in the positive.

✔ **Meditation technique:** If you enjoy meditation, simply add the repetition of your affirmations to your practice.

✔ **Trash can technique:** Whenever you find something in your life that isn't working or you don't like, write it down and throw it into the trash. By doing this, you are telling yourself, I want to be done with this problem, and then . . . be done with it.

✔ **The burning bowl technique:** The "burning bowl" ceremony is a simple process that works much like the trash can technique above. Write two lists — one is for all the thoughts and personal traits that you want to get rid of, and the other is for the positive thoughts and traits that fill the vacuum created by the departing thoughts. Light a fire in a bowl (outside on your BBQ or in your fireplace) and put the bad list in, and state that you release these thoughts/traits to the universe. Then as the flames continue to burn, read your new positive affirmations.

✔ **Candle technique:** Disconnect the phones and remove any other distractions. Sit in a quiet room, light a single candle, turn out the lights, and close the shades. As the flame burns, stare at it and softly repeat your positive affirmations out-loud. Continue repeating your affirmations for 10 to 20 minutes.

✔ **Integration technique:** Affirmations alone are insufficient in achieving your goals. They are the words and motivation required to trigger positive change and action, but real change and action are required to enable those affirmations to manifest themselves in your life. The integration technique calls on you to put those affirmations into practice. The rest is up to you, so get busy. Integrate congruent action with your affirmations and you will increase the speed of your results.

The best time to reaffirm your affirmations are in the morning, just before you get out of bed, while you are still in a semi-dreamy state, and at the end of the day just before you drift off to sleep. Of course, the more you repeat your affirmations throughout the day the better.

Reminiscing on past successes

Negative, self-defeatist thoughts often result from a perceived failure in the past — a perceived failure to achieve a goal that you set for yourself or that someone else set for you. Maybe the goal was "getting A's and B's," being happily married, having children, or being a successful doctor or lawyer. You didn't achieve whatever goal was set, so you may have some lingering doubts about your abilities.

For this very reason, a colleague of mine, Lois Maljak, keeps a journal. She calls it *journaling the journey.* Lois has written in her journals daily for over 25 years and has a complete chronicle of her life from the time she began writing and collecting photos and clippings. To Lois, her journey through life is more important than wherever she happens to end up. By looking back at her journal entries, Lois reminds herself of all of her wonderful accomplishments and experiences — traveling with her parents when her father was in the service, friendships she developed, family gatherings, raising her children, and so on.

When you notice that you're beating yourself up over some sale that fell through, a shortcoming you think you have, or an obstacle you think you can't overcome, jot down a list of what you've accomplished or at least think back to what you consider to be the major accomplishments in your life. Looking back reminds you that you managed to make it through overwhelmingly tough times in the past and gives you the perspective, strength, and encouragement to tackle today's apparently monumental problems.

Although celebrating past success can empower you to deal better with current challenges, don't get stuck in neutral reminiscing about past successes or trying to relive those moments. Your current reality is the present, and you eventually have to deal with it. Reach back to the past to gather the insight and strength you need to forge ahead and strive for even higher levels of future success.

Surrounding yourself with positive people

The world is full of optimists, pessimists, and people in between — those balanced souls who comprise the majority of the population. The world needs a little negativity. We need critics to set standards, sound the alarm when those standards aren't met, and point out problems. When you're in sales, however, critics can function as dream killers, especially if the criticism they offer is not constructive.

I'm not suggesting that you surround yourself with a bunch of yes men and women. I do suggest, however, that you gather around you people who believe in you and avoid those who don't. Surround yourself with people who will stand shoulder to shoulder with you even in the most dire circumstances. Check the roster and make sure you've packed it with positive teammates:

- ✓ **Your spouse or life partner:** My career really took off after I met my wife, Kathleen. Kathleen believes in me, assists me in running our businesses, shares goals, and opens my mind to new opportunities. A positive attitude begins with your family and closest friends and confidants, especially when you're in business for yourself.

- ✓ **Other family members:** Family members can be highly supportive cheerleaders or your most brutal critics. Because they know you so intimately, they can dredge up incidents from the past or point out shortcomings that nobody else is aware of. If a family member or certain family gatherings get you down, limit your time around them or avoid them altogether. When you're in business for yourself, you can use all the family support you can get, so try not to burn too many bridges.

- ✓ **Coworkers:** Positive coworkers naturally create a team-based atmosphere in which everyone joins forces to make each person achieve her maximum potential. Put a stop to any negativity you feel from a coworker, if possible. If it's not possible, avoid the person like the plague.

- ✓ **Supervisor:** A good supervisor acts less like an overbearing boss and more like a facilitator, communication hub, and mentor. If your supervisor makes you feel like a loser, consider confronting the person, avoiding her, or looking for another job.

Are you a positive support person? Do you demonstrate your belief in your family members, colleagues, friends, and neighbors, or are you overly critical? You can't expect to receive support unless you give it to others. Show others that you believe in them, and you can immediately boost the attitude and performance of everyone around you.

Waking up with a positive plan

The first 15 minutes of every morning, I spend planning my day. My co-author, Joe, plans for tomorrow at the end of the day. He also leaves something unfinished at the end of the day, so he has something to get him going the next day.

However you choose to do it, have a positive plan in place first thing in the morning. Draw up a to-do list, and then do it. A to-do list serves several purposes:

✔ Gives your day some structure, so you're not waiting around for something to happen

✔ Provides you with mini-goals to motivate you

✔ Rewards you with a sense of accomplishment and a feeling that you're making progress

Although your to-do list shouldn't be overwhelming, it should contain more tasks than you can possibly accomplish in a single day. Any downtime you have gives negative thoughts and too much opportunity to procrastinate and destroy your momentum. For more about planning your day, week, month, year, and life, check out Chapter 3.

How you manage your to-do list is less important than *that* you manage your to-do list. You can jot down a list of tasks on a Post-It note and stick it to your computer screen, carry the list around in your pocket, keep a day planner, record your tasks in a program like Microsoft Outlook, or type them into your PDA (personal digital assistant). Regardless of which method you choose to record your to-do list, make sure you remain accountable to it until you're ready to make the next day's list: Mark off tasks you've accomplished, make notes about tasks in progress, and note which tasks need to be revised or moved to another day.

Defining "Success" in Your Own Terms

Whenever I use the term *success* in this book, I'm usually talking about it in terms of meeting a sales quota or achieving your own goal of increased sales and revenue. *Success,* however, means whatever you decide it means for you. I've seen highly successful people who were terrible in business, and I've seen people who were highly successful in business but miserable failures in their personal lives. You are as successful as you feel you are.

Being healthy, wealthy, and wise, is very nearly impossible. When you become ill, health becomes your primary concern. When you need money or fulfilling work, your career becomes your focus. When you have problems in your personal life, those problems draw your attention.

To maintain some semblance of balance, I encourage you to develop a definition of success that fulfills all parts of your being:

- ✔ **Head:** Develop and challenge your mind by becoming a lifelong learner, and connect with people from varied backgrounds who are likely to challenge your current thinking.

- ✔ **Heart:** Meaningful relationships are key to developing understanding and empathy. Don't let your career get in the way of relationships with family, friends, neighbors, and even complete strangers.

- ✔ **Hands:** Hands represent action. Take action to improve the environment around you — your physical surroundings, family, community, and so on.

- ✔ **Soul:** Spirituality is key to gaining the perspective that you're a part of something much greater and developing a sense of interconnectedness.

Envisioning Your Future Success

I don't put much stock in palm readers, tarot cards, or crystal balls, but the futures they foretell do carry some validity. Alexander the Great was prophesied to become a great leader, and he certainly fulfilled that prophecy. The way I see it, however, is that the prophecy that was drilled into Alexander from the time he was a young boy motivated him to strive for what he truly believed was his destiny and spurred him on to achieving that destiny.

The most successful people in any field form a clear vision of their destiny, believe in it strongly, and work tirelessly to achieve it. Thus, their destiny ultimately becomes their reality. Those who seize their own destiny typically follow a three-step process:

1. **Envision the ideal.**

2. **Imagine how you're going to act when you've achieved that ideal.**

3. **Act the way you would act if you had already achieved that ideal.**

In the following sections, I describe each stage in the process in greater detail, so you can begin to achieve your destiny immediately.

Envisioning your success is the first step to building your own self-fulfilling prophecy.

Envisioning the ideal

Imagine yourself in the perfect position. Are you working for someone else or do you have your own business? Are you married or single? Do you have kids? If so, how many? Are you dressed in a suit and tie or do you dress casually for work? What kind of house do you live in? What kind of car do you drive?

A few people manage to stumble their way to becoming highly successful, but most highly successful people have a clear picture in their minds of what success is before they set out on their journey to get there. If your dream is to have your own business, imagine where it's located, what products and services it offers, how many people it employs, and how those people act.

With a clear vision in mind, you have a destination. You define your own destiny. Believe in that destiny, and you're already well on your way to making it your reality.

Imagining how you're going to act

Forget for awhile all the work required to achieve your destiny. Imagine that you've already achieved it and are living your dream. How do you dress? How do you carry yourself? How do you treat your customers, colleagues, and competitors?

The only difference between someone who's successful and someone who's not is that the successful person *acts* successful. Acting successful is being successful. By forming a clear image in your mind of how you believe you would act when you're living your dream, you know the type of behavior required to attain that dream. You can then begin to act out your reality, as explained in the following section.

Don't confuse acting successful with pretending to be successful and boasting about your success. Most people who spend a lot of time talking about how successful they are aren't successful. They're simply trying to convince themselves as much as they're trying to convince you. Boasting is a big turnoff that can destroy any future opportunities.

Your sales heroes and other role models can assist you in formulating what you consider to be successful behavior. Keep in mind, however, that you're a unique individual, and your view of success is whatever you determine it is. Never let others define you, and certainly never allow them to impose their limitations on you.

Acting out your reality

To avoid becoming simply a "legend in your own mind," translate the destiny you imagine for yourself (see the section, "Envisioning the ideal," earlier in this chapter) into behaviors. In other words, you've talked the talk, now start walking the walk. Start behaving as if you've already achieved your destiny.

Follow this bit of advice within reason, of course. If you imagine yourself as an independently wealthy philanthropist and start giving away all of your money and then some, you can get yourself into some deep trouble. Behaving as if you've already achieved your destiny means behaving in a business relationship according to your ideal vision. In other words, walk the walk.

Your family members and perhaps a few of your less ambitious colleagues may consider you delusional, but the only way you're going to improve your results as a salesperson is to improve the way you act. And if you're not acting in line with your ideal, you're not quite there and are highly unlikely of ever getting there.

This isn't a one-day or one-week free trial period or dress rehearsal. Behaving as if you've already achieved your destiny takes some practice, and you're likely to regress into your old behaviors once in awhile when you're first starting out. Stick with it. Eventually, any positive changes in your behavior will result in positive changes to the reality around you.

Applying visualization to sales

Envisioning your future success (see the section, "Envisioning the ideal," earlier in this chapter) and then behaving as though you've already achieved that success (see the section, "Acting out your reality," earlier in this chapter) are effective strategies for professionals, athletes, students, and anyone else with imagination and determination.

Power sellers often apply the strategies by imagining how they'll act on a sales call. Whenever I'm heading out to meet a client, I rehearse the entire meeting in my mind from the time I knock on the door until we sign the papers, reminding myself of exactly the way I need to behave to close the sale. Mentally rehearsing the flow of the conversation and potential objections can also ensure that you're prepared to be successful in the meeting and that you achieve all of your preconceived objectives.

As a salesperson, sell yourself on the fact that the sale is yours for the taking. Envision your meeting with the client. You can even write up a script and rehearse with your colleagues or with friends or family members to "get into character." You may even try practicing in front of a mirror. When the curtain rises, all the preparation you invested in rehearsals makes your sales presentation that much more natural and effective. Skip to Chapter 6, "Honing Your Craft," for additional advice on how to prepare for a sales call and improve your sales presentation.

Chapter 3

Charting Your Roadmap to Sales Success

··

In This Chapter

▶ Planning your strategy to increase sales

▶ Creating your to-do list

▶ Being accountable for your own success

▶ Enjoying the fruits of your labor

▶ Adjusting your game plan to maximize positive results

··

Success rarely happens by mistake. It requires planning, execution, and hard work. You set a goal, figure out how you're going to get there, pull together everything you need to execute your plan, and then work your plan the best you can in the hopes of boosting sales and profits.

In this chapter, you chart the course to your sales success, draw up a list of tools and resources required, and formulate a clear idea of how you're going to get from point A to point B. And if you happen to veer off course, this chapter shows you how to get back on track and perhaps even discover a couple detours to shorten the journey.

 Planning is always a necessity, whether you're just starting out, have achieved some level of success, or recently suffered a setback. Effective planning assists you in achieving success, avoiding failure, and recovering from disappointments. Always be planning.

Drawing Up Your Sales Plan

Stop thinking of yourself as a salesperson or an employee. I'm promoting you to entrepreneur. Whether or not you own your own business, you are a business — a revenue-generating entity . . . You, Inc. As such, one of your primary responsibilities is to draw up a business plan — in this case, a sales plan. You're going to plot point A (current sales) and point B (your sale goal) and then chart the course that leads you from point A to point B.

Drawing up a sales plan is a seven-step process:

1. **Determine where you are.**

2. **Set a goal.**

3. **Set a timeframe.**

4. **Identify your objectives.**

5. **Figure out a strategy.**

6. **Identify tasks.**

7. **Identify resources.**

The following sections describe these seven steps in greater detail.

Your sales plan may not work out quite the way you expect it to, but the process of planning forces you to think about your goals and more importantly *how* you are going to achieve those goals. Even if your plan is only 50 percent effective, that's 50 percent better than having no plan.

Determining where you are

I consult with both individual salespeople and small to large companies. You would be surprised at just how many of these individuals and companies are flying by the seat of their pants. Several don't even have a clear idea of where they are in terms of sales, revenue, and expenses or where they want to be one year or five years down the road.

First, you have to establish where you are in terms of sales and the effort you're investing in marketing to figure out where you're going in terms of sales, revenue, and growth. To get a clear idea of where you stand, jot down the following:

- Current gross sales annually.

- Amount of time you typically invest in your business annually.

- Sales-per-hour earnings: Divide your annual gross sales revenue by the number of hours you work per year.

- Annual sales expenses, including your personal outlay for marketing materials, equipment, supplies, and so on.

- Dollar investment per dollar of sales: Divide your annual sales expenses by your annual gross sales.

The most important numbers you jot down are your sales-per-hour earnings and dollar investment per dollar of sales. Think of these numbers as your *sales efficiency ratings.* They're sort of like golf scores — the lower the number, the fewer times you have to swing to score a sale. Track the numbers over time to measure your progress.

Setting a goal

By their very nature, sales goals are production-based — as a salesperson, your goal is to sell more stuff. Determination, effort, and your engaging personality are certainly important, but unless they generate more revenue, they don't really show up on the balance sheet at the end of the year. When setting a sales goal, focus on increasing revenue. Here are a few examples of sales goals:

- Increase gross sales by at least 20 percent.
- Increase the net profit on products and services by at least five percent.
- Line up 15 new customers.
- Increase existing customer orders by 10 percent.

Beware of sales quotas

Imposing a strict sales quota on yourself or having one imposed on you is often counter-productive. I prefer to steer clear of quotas, because they can lead to several negative consequences:

- **Derail the sales process:** Increased pressure to meet quotas can tempt you to push a prospective buyer right out of deciding to buy a product. You need to set your pace in relation to your customer, not in service to some arbitrary sales quota

- **Reduce the profit-per-sale:** Sales quotas are often attached to certain dates, such as end-of-month, end-of-quarter, and end-of-year. When buyers are aware of these quotas, they gain an upper hand in the negotiating process and can pressure you to accept a lower price simply to close the sale.

- **Crush a salesperson's confidence:** Failure can shake anyone's confidence. Conditions outside your control can cause you to miss the quota even if you did quite well given the conditions you were facing.

A sales quota, in and of itself is not necessarily a bad thing, but an obsession with meeting a quota can negatively impact sales and profits. Use a sales goal or quota only as a tool to motivate yourself and a milestone against which you measure your progress. Focus more on the objectives, strategies, and tasks you must accomplish in order to achieve your goal. In other words, focus on the process you're going to follow, and your productivity is almost guaranteed to rise as a result.

Note that these goals simply state the desired end result. They say nothing about how you're going to achieve that goal or the amount of time you have to reach your goal. You can work in these details later, as described in the following sections.

For more about goal setting, specifically for salespeople, check out *Selling For Dummies*, by Tom Hopkins. Hopkins devotes an entire chapter on how to set meaningful sales goals and hold yourself accountable.

Don't share goals with non-goal-setters, like your buddy who defines success as drinking a six-pack of beer every Friday night. People who don't set goals tend to put down those who do. They can kill your dreams.

Setting a timeframe

Setting open-ended goals is an invitation to procrastinate, so every goal should have a deadline. Now, I'm not saying that you should become obsessed with the deadline or let it influence sales negotiations or the way you treat your clients. A deadline simply enables you to measure your progress over time and make the necessary adjustments to your plan later.

After jotting down your sales goal, specify a timeframe for achieving that goal. If the goal seems unrealistic in terms of the timeframe, consider breaking down the goal into incremental goals. If you have a goal to sell 500 cars a year, for example, consider setting a goal to sell 40 cars per month. If that still seems overwhelming, think of it as selling two cars a day (based on a five-day workweek). And if the goal still seems unrealistic, consider trimming it back a bit. Goals should stretch you, not break you.

Have you ever noticed that the less time you have to complete a task, the more you accomplish? If you're constantly missing deadlines, you may be tempted to extend your deadlines. Instead of taking that approach, try tightening your deadlines to see what happens. Many people find that the tighter the deadline, the more energy they funnel into completing the task, and the faster they get it accomplished.

Identifying your objectives

Objectives answer the question "How I am going to achieve my goal?" without going into great detail. Following are some examples that pair up goals with objectives:

Goal: Increase gross sales by at least 20 percent.

Objective: Convert 20 percent more initial contacts into sales.

Goal: Increase the net profit on products and services by at least five percent.

Objective: Increase the markup on all products by five percent across the board.

Goal: Increase existing customer orders by 10 percent.

Objective: Improve relationships with existing customers.

While the goal is fairly concrete, the objective or the way you plan on achieving that goal can vary. If your goal is to increase sales by at least 20 percent, for example, you can achieve that goal with any number of different objectives, including the following:

✔ Convert 20 percent more initial contacts into sales.

✔ Ramp up prospecting efforts.

✔ Implement an Internet marketing program.

✔ Increase up-sell opportunities.

Figuring out a strategy

At this point, you should know what you're going to do and have a general idea of how you're going to do it, but now you need to answer the question "How am I going to fulfill my objective?" This is where strategy comes into play. Think of strategy as the bird's-eye-view of how you're going to fulfill your objective and hence achieve your goal. The following examples pair up objectives with strategies:

Objective: Convert 20 percent more initial contacts into sales.

Strategy: Focus efforts on high-quality leads.

Objective: Ramp up prospecting efforts.

Strategy: Devote one day per week to prospecting.

Objective: Implement an Internet marketing program.

Strategy: Launch a corporate Web site and blog.

Objective: Increase up-sell opportunities.

Strategy: Add a product line.

If you're having a tough time distinguishing between goals, objectives, and strategies, you're not alone. The differences are pretty subtle. Think of it this way: Say your goal is to learn a foreign language (Spanish, for example), here's how your goal, objective, and strategy may look:

Goal: Communicate with Spanish-speaking clients.

Objective: Study Spanish.

Strategy: Take Spanish classes at the city college.

Of course, I could achieve that same goal by fulfilling a different objective — for example, hiring a Spanish-speaking assistant. I could also meet my objective by employing any of several strategies for learning Spanish, including reading *Spanish For Dummies*, listening to Spanish lessons on tapes or CDs, or using computer-based Spanish learning software.

Don't spend too much time trying to distinguish the difference between objectives and strategies. As long as you have a goal and a clear vision of how you're going to achieve that goal, you're ready to identify the tasks you must accomplish to get there (speaking of which, see the next section, "Identifying tasks," to get started on that list).

Identifying tasks

If you think of your goal as your ultimate destination, the tasks are the steps you take to reach that destination (by executing your strategy and achieving your objective). Think of tasks as your to-do list. If you accomplish everything on your list, you can't help but achieve your goal . . . theoretically, at least.

Say you have a goal to increase sales by 20 percent. Your objective is to maximize up-sell opportunities, and your strategy is to add a new product line. Your tasks are then the steps you must take to add the product line. You may come up with something like this:

1. **Poll customers to determine market demand for various products.**

2. **Research products for salability and profitability.**

3. **Identify suppliers.**

4. **Compare prices, quality, and service.**

5. **Select products to include in new product line.**

6. **Market products to new and existing customers.**

When jotting down tasks you must accomplish, forget about the order of the tasks. Do a brain dump. Jot down all the tasks, and if they need to be accomplished in order, like steps, then you can go back and rearrange your list. What's most important is that the list covers everything.

Identifying resources

When you're drafting your roadmap to success, don't overlook the fact that you need to pack some supplies. In the case of planning to achieve a business-related goal, the supplies you need basically come down to time, money, equipment, and people (human resources). An effective plan identifies all the resources you need and ultimately functions as a grocery list, simplifying the process of procuring essential resources.

Getting buy-in: A tip for sales managers

If you're a sales manager, resist any urge you may have to impose your sales goals and plan on your sales staff. A much more effective approach is to involve your staff in setting their own goals. This approach offers several benefits, including the following:

✔ Sales reps are more likely to buy into the goals and take ownership of them.

✔ Sales reps may act more as entrepreneurs and have a stronger sense of empowerment and accountability.

✔ Diverse goals may encourage development of more creative and effective sales strategies.

✔ Setting goals as a team may foster cooperation among sales reps that could lead to increased productivity for the entire sales department.

As a sales manager, I would often set sales goals for my salespeople and share those goals with them. Unfortunately, this practice sent one of my best salespeople packing.

This particular real estate agent was one of the top salespeople I've ever trained. In one year,

he sold 157 homes, which is an incredible number. Unbeknownst to me, he had set sales goals and developed his own business plan. His goal was to sell 125 homes. My goal was for him to sell 175 homes. Both of our plans were designed to increase revenue. My plan called for selling 20 percent more houses while his called for selling fewer houses at a 20 percent higher profit. His plan would actually have resulted in a bigger boost in revenue than my plan had called for, with the added bonus of giving him more quality time with his family and friends.

Unaware that my top salesperson had his own plan in place, I shared with him the fact that I had expected him to sell 175 houses. Understandably, he felt as though I didn't appreciate his efforts. Before I could correct my mistake, my top salesperson was headed out the door to launch his own business. He's doing very well.

If you supervise a sales staff, I strongly encourage you to team up with your staff to set goals rather than imposing your goals on them.

To identify the resources required to accomplish your goal, answer the following questions:

- ✔ How many total hours are required to complete all tasks?
- ✔ How much time can I commit to the project?
- ✔ What expertise is needed that I don't currently have?
- ✔ How much money is this going to cost?
- ✔ Do I need any special equipment, such as a computer?
- ✔ Are some resources already available?

 When developing your resource list, don't limit yourself. Make it a wish list. Ideally, what would you need to accomplish all of the required tasks as quickly and easily as possible? Be creative. Once you have your wish list in place, you can edit it based on the amount of time, money, and existing resources you have at your disposal.

Prioritizing Your Tasks

When drawing up a sales plan, you may find yourself with dozens of tasks you must tend to. Your to-do list can become overwhelming, perhaps so overwhelming that it causes you to freeze up. Not knowing where to start, you can't get moving. If you find yourself in the deep freeze, take some time to prioritize your tasks.

Prioritizing tasks doesn't always mean that you tackle the most important tasks first. When arranging the items on your to-do list, you have several options:

- ✔ **Step-by-step:** If the tasks must be performed in a certain order, prioritizing is as easy as one, two, three. Arrange the tasks in the order you need to perform them, and then follow the steps.
- ✔ **Order of importance:** Complete the tasks that are key to the success of a project first.
- ✔ **Most profitable first:** If you have several tasks, and one particular task has the potential of making you some quick cash or increasing profits immediately, why wait? Do the money-making tasks first.
- ✔ **Hardest thing first:** If one task is significantly more difficult than the others, consider tackling it first. A difficult task can function as a huge mental block that prevents you from moving forward. Tackle the most difficult task first. When it's out of the way, the rest of the process is smooth sailing.

✔ **Easiest thing first:** If confronting the most difficult challenge first is just too overwhelming, deal with something easier. This can give you some momentum to move on to other, more difficult tasks.

✔ **Most obvious first:** A task may present itself as obviously something you must do immediately — perhaps you have all the resources you need, you have some free time, and you just realized that this is something you have to do.

Your first priority at the beginning of every day is to prioritize the items on your to-do-list. When I prioritize, I generally tackle the most difficult tasks first. I call the people I don't want to talk to, address any problems that cross my desk, and immediately tend to the task I'm most strongly inclined to avoid. I then focus on the most profitable activities, what I call *dollar-productive activities*, which I learned from the "Condo King," Allen Domb, while shadowing him. If I have any time left near the end of the day, I deal with the remaining items in their order of importance.

Putting Your Plan into Action with the Strebor System

Awhile back, I realized that "Roberts" spelled backwards is "Strebor," and I worked out a system for effectively implementing any plan for success. When you're ready to put your plan into action, follow the Strebor System:

S: Sticktoitism is the dogged determination required to ensure that you follow through on your plan.

T: Training provides you with the know-how and skills to properly execute your plan.

R: Results are what you build on as you attain higher and higher levels of success.

E: Enthusiasm provides you with the ambition and energy required to follow through.

B: Benefits give you the motivation to succeed.

O: Optimism is the confidence that enables you to overcome obstacles.

R: Reach is your commitment to taking risks and seizing opportunities that make you grow both professionally and personally.

Tracking Your Progress

Some people do a great job in the planning stage and may even succeed in executing their plans to perfection, but they drop the ball when it comes to tracking their progress. As a result, they don't know whether they're making any headway.

Put a system in place for tracking your progress. Following are some suggestions:

- ✔ **Checklists:** You can implement a system of annual, monthly, weekly, and daily checklists to keep yourself on track and measure your progress. Audit your lists at the end of each period to determine how well you've done and set more challenging goals moving forward. Start every day with a list of things to do in the order in which you need to do them and then — do them!

- ✔ **Success journal:** Make daily or weekly entries in your journal to keep track of what's working and what's not.

- ✔ **Idea of the week book:** Prompted by Ira Hayes, I've been keeping an idea of the week book for 25 years. In it, I jot down my idea of the week, and if the idea is worth pursuing, I give it a shot. Then I jot down the results.

- ✔ **Lifetime achievement book:** Think of this as the equivalent of a profit-and-loss statement. Instead of listing your financial profits and losses, you can describe your achievements and setbacks. Over time, the book comes to represent a measure of your success and can point you in the right direction.

Holding Yourself Accountable

Whether or not you have a boss, a manager, or a supervisor, as a power seller, you are ultimately your own boss and should be more demanding of yourself than any boss could ever be. The responsibility for achieving your goals sits squarely on your shoulders. It's up to you to hold yourself accountable.

As motivational speaker Bob Perks says, "Don't blame others for your failure to be fully accountable for your own life. If others are to blame then you have given them control."

If you're not qualified to hold yourself accountable, consider taking on a personal partner, as explained in Chapter 7, "Raising the Bar with Personal Partnering."

Celebrating Your Success

If you love to sell, chances are pretty good that you don't need much motivation to do it. For you, selling may be your essence, an intrinsic pleasure that you would continue to indulge in even if you were independently wealthy. Most salespeople, however, are better at selling when they have some external motivation — a reward for a job well done.

Although I love to sell, I dangle rewards in front of myself to rev up my sales engine. I encourage my sales staff and family members to reward themselves, as well, as a way of giving their goals a more emotional connection. After all, money is a meager measure of success. If that money represents a two-week vacation with your family, a car you've always dreamed of, or early retirement, then achieving your sales goals becomes much more meaningful.

In the following sections, I encourage you to pat yourself on the back for a job well done and reward yourself early as an added incentive to achieve your goals.

Rewarding yourself for a job well done

Sales goals can seem somewhat meaningless. Boosting sales by 20 percent or increasing your sales commissions by $50,000 a year are certainly noble goals for your company, but what do they mean for you as a person? To increase your motivation to achieve a goal, make your future success more meaningful by offering yourself a tangible reward. What do you want as a result of your efforts?

When you know what you want, create a mental image of it:

- **Write a detailed description of the reward.** Whether you want a fancy new car, early retirement, or the ability to help less fortunate family members and friends, describe your dream in detail, as if you were already living it.

- **Create a reward collage.** Cut out pictures that remind you of your reward and hang them on your refrigerator door or in your office or paste them on poster board to create a collage.

- **Sample the reward.** Get a small taste of the reward. If you're thinking of rewarding yourself with a fancy new sports car, for example, head down to the dealership and take it for a test drive. Craving a luxurious new home? Attend some open houses of homes that you think may fit the bill.

- **Share your vision.** Tell your family, friends, and colleagues about your dreams of success. In addition to creating a clearer mental image of the reward for you, this subtly makes you accountable to others and increases your motivation to achieve your goal.

Putting a face on your goals

I encourage the agents in my office to share their personal goals. One year, I took a large roll of paper, cut it into six-foot sheets, wrote an agent's name at the top of each sheet, and taped them up all over the building. I asked the agents to create a collage that would represent their goals. In addition to generating a deeper sense of camaraderie amongst the staff, I saw a near immediate boost in morale and productivity. The agents now had a clearer idea of what they were working for.

Goals can seem a little too nebulous at times. To bring them down to earth, put a face on them by connecting them with something you find rewarding. What's rewarding is different for everyone. Some people get excited about promotions and job titles, while others like money or time off. Find out what motivates you (and your staff, if you're a manager), and you will unlock the secret of happy production.

Rewarding yourself for a job about to be well done

When you get tired of rewarding yourself for all of your accomplishments, consider a different approach — reward yourself prior to achieving your goal. Occasionally, I use this method to motivate myself. I find the reward I want, charge it on my credit card, and then work to earn enough money to pay for the item before my credit card statement arrives in the mail and I actually have to pay for what I purchased.

Don't get into the habit of buying stuff that you don't have the money to pay for. That could get you into trouble. I'm merely suggesting that you try this approach for a change of pace.

Revising Your Roadmap

Drawing up the perfect sales plan and executing it to perfection doesn't necessarily guarantee success. In some cases, you may fall short of your goals. In more fortunate situations, your success exceeds your wildest imagination. Whatever the result, you usually have to revisit your sales plan regularly to see just where you've ended up and what adjustments are required to get back on track or change your direction to achieve even loftier goals.

In the following sections, I reveal the importance of revising your sales plan to accommodate unexpected shortcomings and take advantage of unanticipated success.

You're better off aiming too high and missing the mark than always achieving less ambitious goals. If you fall short of a goal, you can always extend the timeframe, but if you constantly meet unchallenging goals, you're never going to achieve your full potential.

Assessing your progress . . . or lack thereof

You set your goal and specified a timeframe for achieving it. When the time is up, revisit the goal to determine whether you've accomplished it. Assuming you set a measurable goal, you should come to one of three conclusions:

✔ You met your goal.

✔ You exceeded your goal.

✔ You didn't quite get there.

If you met your goal, kudos for you! Skip back to the section on rewarding yourself and collect your bonus. Then, return to the beginning of the chapter and set new goals. If you missed your goal or exceeded it, you have more work to do, as explained in the following sections.

Correcting for wrong turns

When you miss your goal, it can only mean only one of three things:

✔ **The goal and timeframe were unrealistic.** Perhaps you were a little too ambitious. That's perfectly understandable. As long as you're making progress, extending your deadline can put you back on track.

✔ **Your plan was flawed.** Plans don't always work. What's important is that you realize the plan was flawed before you pour any more time, money, or effort in it. You may have to dump the plan and start over or make some adjustments.

✔ **You failed to execute your plan properly.** If you dropped the ball during the execution of the plan, you can blame only yourself. Come clean about it and renew your commitment.

Although you may need to dump your plan entirely, avoid dumping something that works. A single triumph can be the seed that grows into a hugely successful new sales plan. Cut what doesn't work and build on whatever's working.

The journey to success is like sailing across the ocean. A minor change in course early in your journey can make a huge difference in where you ultimately end up. You don't always have to make sweeping changes.

Building on success

Sometimes, success can be more devastating than failure. You put a plan in place to increase sales. The plan is a resounding success. Product is flying off the shelves. Unfortunately, inventory is running low and you don't have another supplier lined up or you can't ship product fast enough to meet demand or you don't have the support staff in place to keep all of your new customers happy.

When you're checking your progress toward accomplishing a particular sales goal, be prepared for situations in which your success exceeds your expectations. An inability to change course to take advantage of unforeseen success can negatively impact your sales and is certain to leave you with a missed opportunity.

Chapter 4

Making Selling Your Hobby and Your Habit

In This Chapter

▶ Starting the day out right

▶ Tuning into the people around you

▶ Gathering new sales techniques

▶ Field-testing newly acquired techniques

*P*ower selling is a way of life. You gotta love it and live it and seize every opportunity to discover how to do it better. Every encounter is an opportunity for you to practice the art and science of selling, an opportunity to hone your skills.

I love selling, and I'm always selling something. Whether I'm eating out, boarding an airplane, riding in a taxi, or checking into a hotel room, I'm selling. I can usually talk my way into first-class seating on flights and first-class accommodations at hotels. Even when I fall short, I always meet someone, and every one of those someone's is a potential client and lead generator. Every encounter makes me a slightly better salesperson. As you begin to weave selling into every aspect of your life, you soon realize the infinite opportunities it draws into your life.

In this chapter, I encourage you and show you how to approach selling with the eagerness of an avid hobbyist. I show you how to start each day with the right mindset, tune in to the people around you, and become more sensitive to sales opportunities you may tend to overlook. I also show you how to practice your sales skills, so selling becomes more of a habit than a job.

Making Selling Your Hobby

A hobby can be a pretty intense activity that requires more energy and investment than a full-time job, but hobbies rarely make you tired, rundown, or stressed out. To the contrary. When you choose a hobby that's right for you, it recharges your batteries and makes you think more creatively. It makes you want to stay up late at night and gives you a reason to wake up in the morning. With a hobby, you learn without ever having to study, and you're naturally motivated to share information and insights with other enthusiasts.

I encourage you to approach selling as a hobby rather than a job. If you treat selling as a job, you're unlikely to have the determination and energy to be very good at it, and you're more likely to get burned out. Following are some tips that may be able to assist you in treating selling more like a hobby:

- ✔ **Stop thinking about it.** When you're immersed in a hobby, you rarely think about how enjoyable it is or how good you feel doing it. When you're getting paid to do something, however, you may be tempted to overanalyze it. Focus on your work, and you're going to have a lot more fun doing it.

- ✔ **Hang out with salespeople who love to sell.** Hobbies are often refreshing because they attract people who are enthusiastic about a common interest. The positive energy emanated by others can fuel your own enthusiasm.

- ✔ **Continue to challenge yourself.** Hobbyists often start with beginner kits and work their way up to more and more advanced projects. When you hit a plateau, raise the bar. You should always feel as though you're reaching for something higher.

- ✔ **Develop new skills.** Discovering new sales strategies and techniques keeps you moving forward and feeling as though you're making progress. See "Discovering New Sales Techniques," later in this chapter, for details.

- ✔ **Play.** Hobbies are simply an adult form of playtime. Be a little more playful in your job. Don't be afraid to be yourself and take some chances. Loosen up. Have fun.

The only difference between your hobby and your job should be that you *spend* money on your hobby and you *earn* money with your job. The money you earn is a measure of success, but satisfaction isn't always tied to a product or a paycheck. Selling is presenting an idea or sharing a moment with someone you may or may not meet again. Selling is about making that moment a positive influence on someone's day or life.

Mastering the Bob approach

I met Bob, the baggage handler, for the first time at Detroit Metro Airport when I was heading out on my first book tour for *Walk Like a Giant, Sell Like a Madman*. I was so excited about the book, I passed out copies to everyone I met, and when Bob greeted me at the curb, I immediately felt a blast of enthusiasm that earned him one of the first copies.

Bob may not consider himself a salesman, but he's one of the best I've ever met. Whenever I pull up to the curb during Bob's shift, he immediately greets me and tells everyone in line who I am and how excited he is to see me. He makes me feel like a rock star. In spite of all the Homeland Security policies, Bob remains positive and establishes a personal relationship with all of his clients, while processing passengers efficiently to get them to their gates as quickly as possible.

I don't know how much Bob earns, but with a few adjustments, a guy like Bob could probably earn ten times as much as the average baggage handler. Imagine if the baggage handlers all worked together, handed out business cards, and established relationships with their passengers. They could motivate one another to work harder, share tips on how to work smarter, market their services, and have much more fun. They could probably make as much as $15 an hour in salary and another $50 an hour in tips, earning a six-figure income.

Regardless of your occupation, you can boost your income and increase your job satisfaction simply by treating your job like a hobby and giving clients the service and attention they crave.

 Selling isn't for everyone. If you've done your best to make selling feel more like a hobby than a job, and selling still doesn't rev your engine, consider changing jobs. To perform at your peak in any field of endeavor, you gotta have passion — a bowl of sticktoitism with a big scoop of enthusiasm.

Thinking Like an Entrepreneur

Throughout the years, I've heard many salespeople, even good ones, utter phrases like, "You just get the customers in the door, and I'll do the rest." That's the sort of passive attitude that makes you an order taker, not a salesperson. According to the law of attrition, order takers are being eliminated, while the entrepreneurial power sellers achieve even greater success.

Order takers think and act much differently than entrepreneurs, which results in the entrepreneurs becoming power sellers. If you're an order taker, switch gears to a power seller by changing your mindset:

- **An order taker waits for success — a power seller pursues it.** At a restaurant, an order taker asks to take your order, whereas an entrepreneurial server says, "Let me tell you about our specials," and then proceeds to describe them in delicious detail and credits the chef. Instead of asking whether you're ready for your bill, the entrepreneurial server brings the dessert tray.

- **An order taker backs down in the face of a client's objections — a power seller comes up with answers to objections *before* the meeting even takes place.** Order takers pick only the low-hanging fruit, even if they can readily see better fruit a little higher up on the tree. When a great prospect raises an objection to the sale, which is often a sign that the client is interested, the order taker backs away, assuming she lost the sale. A power seller has already rehearsed how she's going to respond to the objection long before the prospect ever expresses it.

- **An order taker relies solely on the company for marketing — a power seller invests in his own shameless self promotion.** Long-term success demands that you become a brand name company unto yourself. Even if the company you work for does an outstanding job of building its own brand presence and generating business for you, you should be marketing yourself. See Chapter 9 for additional details.

- **An order taker complains when the company fails to supply him with the tools he needs to succeed — a power seller invests in his own success.** Although you should certainly try to convince the company to pick up the tab for the equipment and other resources you need, you shouldn't wait around for them to do it if they refuse. As a power seller, you are responsible for your own success. See Chapter 11 for additional details.

A true salesperson functions as an independent contractor. Think of yourself as a corporation — You, Inc. Your corporation can be as small or as large as you want it to be. You can invest as much or as little time as you want in making it a success. You can procure the supplies and human resources you need to take your corporation to the next level. Begin thinking as an entrepreneur, and your sales potential becomes unlimited.

If you don't already consider yourself an independent contractor, retool your thinking, and start behaving like an entrepreneur:

- If you're not already receiving commissions, negotiate commissions-based compensation with you supervisor or find a position with a company that pays its salespeople commissions.

- Develop your own sales plan, as discussed in Chapter 3.

✔ Don't blame or complain. As an entrepreneur, you are completely responsible for your own success.

✔ Set your own hours and schedule. You should be making a majority of the decisions that shape your day.

✔ Acquire the means to achieve your goals. If your company won't shell out the money for equipment, marketing materials, an assistant, or whatever else you need, pay for it out of your own pocket. For more ideas on how to invest in your own success, check out Chapter 11.

Twenty percent of all salespeople are making more money than the other 80 percent combined. Where do you fall in?

Greeting the Day with the Power Selling Attitude

Have you ever walked out of a store with something you purchased and suddenly realized that you really didn't need it or want it? I buy a lot of products, and this happens to me all the time. Even though I know all of the sales tactics and tricks, the salesperson was able to convince me to buy something I neither needed nor wanted. How was that possible?

When a salesperson is capable of selling me, it's usually because I like the person. Sure, she knows her product and asks questions to find out what I'm looking for, but my decision to buy is based on more than that. I end up liking the salesperson, and the main reason for that is because the person has confidence and an engaging personality. They've got *it*. Some don't have *it*. Some have *it* and just don't use *it*. The people who sell me have *it* and flaunt *it*.

Are you fair, good, very good, great, excellent, or *unbelievable?* Power selling is about being unbelievable. As a salesperson, you're selling more than a product or service. You're selling yourself. Sell yourself successfully, and prospective clients are much more likely to purchase whatever it is you're selling. Once you grasp advanced selling strategies and make them a part of who you are, you can hop to any company in any industry and sell anything.

If you're not meeting your sales goals, you may have to give yourself an attitude adjustment. Chapter 2 offers some suggestions on how to readjust your thinking to give yourself a more positive perspective, but indulge in anything that gets you revved up and in the proper mood:

✔ Listen to motivational tapes, CDs, or MP3s on your way to work.

✔ Pump yourself up with some uplifting music.

✔ Listen to something funny — a morning radio show or recordings of standup comedians.

✔ Exercise regularly so you feel physically fit.

✔ Eat foods that make you feel more energetic, and avoid foods that drain your energy. Check out *Nutrition For Dummies* for some suggestions.

✔ Change something in your work environment or redecorate your office.

✔ Try a new hairstyle or outfit.

When you don't feel good about yourself and what you're doing, prospective customers can sense your inner discomfort, and it can often make them feel uncomfortable around you. Do whatever it takes to feel good about yourself. This includes attending to any issues at home that may be dragging you down.

When I was 40, I was getting ready to go on a family trip to Florida. I had the bright idea to have my hair highlighted. My family was in shock. Mr.Guy Next Door, Mr. Most Successful in Real Estate had his hair highlighted! My family immediately sent me back to the hair salon. The moral to the story? If you're thinking of making a dramatic change in your appearance, consult your partner or someone else who has a vested interest in making sure you don't look like a fool.

Engaging People Throughout Your Day

Selling takes much more than pitching a product to a prospective customer. Selling is about building a mutually beneficial relationships. Work on improving your relationship skills. The more you practice, the more comfortable you become dealing with people, and dealing with people is what selling is all about. (It's not about the bottom line. That will take care of itself.)

To make selling more like a hobby and improve your ability to build relationships with people, engage people throughout your day. Whether you're out shopping, working out at the gym, standing in the elevator, or waiting in line at the movie theater, establish eye contact with someone and try to strike up a conversation. Every connection you make is an opportunity to practice your relationship-building skills.

In the following sections, I provide a couple tips on how to present yourself and make a positive first impression. Later in this chapter, in the section, "Discovering Opportunities to Ply Your Trade," I show you how to practice your sales skills in situations you may not associate with sales.

Projecting a professional image

A key factor in becoming a more engaging salesperson is to project a professional image — an image that conveys the fact that you know what you're doing and are genuinely interested in the people you meet.

Perception is reality. Your customer's perception of you is the only you she knows. By knowing what you're trying to present and becoming more sensitive to how people actually perceive you, you can close the gap between how people perceive you and how you want to be perceived.

Developing and projecting a professional image is a five-step process:

1. **Know what you're presenting by the way you dress, what you say, how you say it, how well you listen, and how you interact with people.**

2. **Become more aware of how people are perceiving you.** You may even consider asking a friend or colleague or even a client you feel comfortable with "how you come across to people."

3. **Draw up a list of image enhancements — adjustments you can make to improve your image.**

4. **Implement the positive changes from Step 3.**

5. **Jump back to Step 2 and repeat the process to make sure you're following your plan and that the changes you've made are having the desired effects.**

Attend to *all* of the characteristics that others perceive and use to form an opinion of you. If you're dressed well, present yourself with confidence, and then spew fourth foul language, those obscenities are likely to undermine all other efforts at projecting a positive image.

Making a great first impression

You don't get a second shot at making a great first impression, so do it properly right from the start:

1. **Smile.** A smile opens the doors to communication and invites the other person inside.

2. **Look 'em in the eye.** Actors often use a one-eye technique for close encounters, because if you try looking at both eyes, your eyes may move back and forth slightly, giving you that shifty-eyed look. Most people can't tell when someone's looking them in one eye instead of both, but they can tell if someone is looking at their eyebrows or forehead. Whatever you do, don't stare. If the other person glances away, you're probably staring.

3. **Shake hands.** Remember to maintain eye contact and a pleasant facial expression when you are shaking hands.

4. **Stand up straight but not stiff.** Imagine a string connected to the crown of your head that's pulling you upward and a string attached to your navel that's being pulled from behind you. Consider practicing good posture when you're standing in line, and practice enough to make it a habit.

5. **Watch what you say and how you say it.** Shoot for a G-rating on your vocabulary. Nobody's going to miss the four-letter words. Your nonverbal presentation is equally important. Speak clearly and loud enough for the person to hear without feeling as though you've cranked the speakers up too loud. Your tone of voice and facial expressions communicate more than you may realize.

6. **Move with conviction and confidence.** Practice giving yourself a reason to move. If you're heading over to the fax machine to pick up an incoming message, consider pretending that you're retrieving the president's schedule while he's waiting on the other line. This trains you to move with purpose.

Your standard meet-and-greet may not be appropriate for people from different cultures. To make sure you're accommodating clients and prospects from different cultures, check out Chapter 19, where diversity and sales expert Michael Soon Lee of EthnoConnect and I provide some additional guidance on dealing with multicultural clientele.

Discovering New Sales Techniques

Early in my career, I thought I knew everything about selling houses, and I was doing pretty well, but I wasn't what I would now consider a power seller. Shortly after Kathleen and I married, she suggested that we take a trip to San Francisco to attend the annual convention for the National Association of Realtors. I always assumed that conventions were a waste of time, but Kathleen loved San Francisco, and the convention gave us a convenient excuse to fly out there.

I signed up for a few seminars and workshops just to check them out, expecting them to simply rehash what I had already learned from the college of hard knocks. Boy, was I surprised! I was astounded at how little I really knew. I discovered much more effective ways of marketing and selling houses, boosting my profits, and making my business run more efficiently. I returned to Michigan packed with ideas and inspired by the top Realtors in the country, who all happened to be at the convention. Now I was kicking myself for not taking advantage of these opportunities earlier in my career.

To be a power seller, continually educate yourself and pick up new strategies and techniques from other sales people. In the following sections, I point out some of the best continuing education opportunities for salespeople.

You don't really know whether you're good at something until you know about that something and take it for a test drive. Sales books, CDs, seminars, workshops, and other educational resources expose you to different sales strategies and techniques you may not have been aware of and may be really good at. To remain at the top of your game, continue to seek out educational opportunities.

Reading up on new selling strategies

Throughout this book, I suggest various high-octane ways to boost sales and maximize your exposure to sales opportunities. I assume that you've already read a beginning-level book on sales, such as *Selling For Dummies*. I encourage you to sample some additional books, as well, and explore various sales strategies, including solution selling, SPIN selling, and question-based selling. In addition to strategies similar to these, in Chapters 6 and 21, I highlight several sales techniques that I like to use.

Every expert on the topic of selling has a slightly different approach. By reading widely instead of buying into a single strategy, you can form your own unique sales strategy that fits best with your personality and approach.

You don't have to start over to get your career on the right course. Make incremental adjustments one or two degrees at a time. A cruise liner doesn't turn 90 degrees at a time. It changes course by a few degrees at a time, which over the course of hundreds or thousands of miles makes a huge difference. Take the same long-term approach in your career. Otherwise, changes may seem too overwhelming, leading you to make no positive change at all. Visit www.simpletruths.com/aff/046/TTWD for an inspirational movie on the power of small changes called *212 Degrees*.

Tuning into sales tapes and CDs

Books are great for providing detailed information, but nothing can replace hearing the impassioned voice of a sales coach providing verbal instruction. Even though I read every book about selling that I can get my hands on, I still like to listen to authors on tapes and CDs. Now I even download podcasts and listen to them.

Tapes, CDs, and other recordings of books on tape have one added advantage — you can listen while you're on the road.

Several years ago, I was diagnosed as having ADHD (Attention Deficit Hyperactivity Disorder) and soon discovered that I could absorb more information by listening to audio clips played at twice the speed. For more information about ADD and ADHD, check out *ADD and ADHD For Dummies*, by Jeff Strong, Michael O. Flanagan, and Lito Tejada-Flores.

Attending sales seminars and workshops

Books and audio recordings are certainly informative, but mastering a new technique, particularly when it runs counter to something you've been taught in the past, requires practice and feedback. Seminars and workshops provide you with a more dynamic venue in which you can ask questions and perhaps even rehearse new techniques.

Of course, not all seminars and workshops are of equal value, so choose carefully and look for those that feature a combination of the following:

- ✔ **Panels of top producers:** You want to learn from the best, not those who may someday be best.

- ✔ **Big-name keynote speakers:** In addition to giving you the chance to rub elbows with success, this shows that the organization presenting the seminar has spent some money invested in it.

- ✔ **A wide variety of breakout sessions:** Selling is a multifaceted art form, so hone your skills in as many areas as possible.

- ✔ **Networking time:** Seminars expand what you know, but they also expand who you know. You often discover more in the hallways and at lunch than you do during the actual sessions. Meet the other attendees and as many of the presenters as possible. If possible, meet each presenter early on and obtain their materials, so you can determine which sessions to attend.

One-day motivational seminars are great if you're in bad need of a pep talk, but don't rely on them exclusively. Look for seminars that have more substance and provide you with educational opportunities to upgrade your skills.

Attending a seminar or workshop may require a significant investment of time and money, especially if you have to travel very far, but the return on your investment is usually worth it. In addition to obtaining practical sales training, you have the opportunity to meet other top salespeople, pick up additional techniques from them, and establish valuable professional connections.

When I go to a seminar with my assistant, I look for a central location to set up my office. It is usually near the bar or restaurant area, where I know people attending the seminar will congregate before and after each session. This gives us a great opportunity to meet and really get to know attendees.

Swapping secrets with colleagues

One of the bonuses of working in sales is that most salespeople love to talk . . . or maybe they just love to *hear* themselves talk. Whatever the case, they're usually willing to share what they've picked up in the course of their career. Get connected with as many salespeople as possible and pick their brains. Even if they sell in a completely different industry, they can offer tips and suggestions that can stimulate your own creativity.

Sharing works both ways. When a less experienced salesperson comes to you for assistance, don't hesitate to offer your advice. Teaching is often one of the best ways to master a technique, and I believe that if you learn something, you have an obligation to pass it along.

Buying to learn

Every time you go shopping for something — a computer, cell phone, TV set, car, house, whatever — you have an opportunity to watch another salesperson at work and pick up some new techniques.

After you buy something or decide not to buy something, do a brief analysis of why you decided to buy the product or service or decided against buying it. Whenever I go out to dinner, I observe the way the server tries to sell the dessert. Some servers simply ask, "Can I interest you in some dessert?" giving you the opportunity to say "No," in which case, the discussion is over. More savvy servers wave a dessert tray over the table, which usually sparks a lively discussion that convinces at least one person at the table to indulge. After one person orders dessert, the rest of the table usually follows suit.

Test-driving new techniques

Salespeople are notorious for not following advice. They read a book on a great new sales technique and a week later they're delivering the same sales pitch they've been using for the last five years. They hire a personal coach to train them, pay the guy $300 and hour or more, and then simply fail to put any of the training into practice.

I'm not saying you should immediately unleash your new, untested sales strategies on unsuspecting customers, but you should start to work new strategies into your repertoire as soon as possible.

A very effective way to begin implementing a new sales technique is to first rehearse the technique with a colleague — one of you plays the salesperson, and the other pretends to be the buyer. Consider switching roles, so you each have a chance to play salesperson and buyer. Some salespeople claim to learn more by playing the role of buyer. Keep in mind that mastering a new technique may require several role-playing sessions and considerable practice to work out the bugs.

Some sales techniques require you to master subtle tactics. Consider hiring someone who has mastered the technique to provide training, supervise role-playing sessions, and offer expert feedback.

Keeping Pace with Your Industry

A good salesperson can sell anything — cars, houses, insurance, video games, computers, shoes, you name it. A power seller loves what she sells. I sell houses, because I love the whole concept of homeownership — owning a piece of land, taking pride in my neighborhood, being able to renovate my home to suit my needs and tastes, and having an investment that gives me a tax break. I wouldn't buy a house from someone who didn't own one or a car from someone who didn't drive. I believe that you should love what you sell.

The Mickey Mouse maneuver

In May of 2006, I flew to Virginia with my daughter Kolleen and my two assistants, Lois and Kandra, to attend a Tom Antioch class on Internet marketing. On the flight home, all of us had seats in coach, and I decided to try to get us upgraded to first class.

When we arrived at the ticket counter, I struck up a conversation with the lady behind the counter . . . okay, so my wife calls it flirting, but that's beside point, right? I noticed she had nails that looked as though she were going to a ball or a New Year's eve party. I complimented her on her nails, and she smiled.

I then said, "Did your husband do that for you?"

She replied, "No, this is one of my luxuries. I have my nails done every month."

I said "Awesome!" I paused a few seconds and asked, "Are you a Mickey Mouse fan?"

She looked up at me and said, "How did you know?!"

I replied, "Because I'm a Mickey Mouse fan." (I didn't tell her that I saw she was wearing a Mickey Mouse watch.) My daughter had to turn around to hide her laughter — she had seen me work before.

The lady behind the counter then said, "Mr. Roberts, I have a critical problem. The plane is really full, and it would help me if I could put you and your daughter and assistants in first class. Would that be okay?"

And I said, "If that would help you and the airline, that would certainly be okay with us."

This opportunity came to me, because I embraced the person behind the counter as a real person. I engaged her in a conversation and established a connection — a meaningful relationship. Most people at airports are in such a hurry and so frustrated and angry that they overlook opportunities to connect with other people. As a salesperson, you should always connect.

Assuming you do love what you sell, my next bit of advice is something you will have no trouble putting into practice — keep pace with your industry. Subscribe to your industry's top magazines, journals, and newsletters; bookmark leading industry Web sites and visit them regularly; and share information with others in the industry.

A great way to keep up on late-breaking industry news is to sign up for Google News Alerts. Go to Google News at `news.google.com`, and then click News Alerts in the navigation bar on the left and follow the instructions to register and set up your alerts. You simply specify the news topics you want to be notified of, and when a story that matches your description is published, Google notifies you via e-mail.

By keeping up with the latest news and developments in your industry, you become a much more valuable resource person for your customers and can better understand their needs and the issues they face. In Chapter 18, I provide some additional suggestions on how to focus on your customers' success, which will drive your success to a higher level.

Keeping up on changes in the industry is much easier than having to catch up later. Be proactive in gathering information. In highly competitive markets, falling behind for even a short time can lead to disaster.

Practicing Your Sales Skills in Real-World Scenarios

You can apply sales skills to a host of different scenarios and situations, because selling primarily consists of engaging people in a discussion and then negotiating until you and the other party reach some agreement.

When you decide to make selling your hobby, start practicing your sales skills wherever and whenever you spy an opportunity. Sufficient practice makes selling more instinctive and natural and places your prospective customers at ease.

Effective selling requires an ability to adapt to different people and situations quickly and smoothly. This ability to adapt is sometimes referred to as *situational fluency.* When you know your product and what the customer needs and are comfortable with various sales techniques, you can customize your sales presentation on-the-fly to maximize its effectiveness in any given situation. With situational fluency, you're able to carry on a conversation with a prospective client without feeling as though you're pitching a product or service. Some salespeople seem to be naturals, but most of us have to practice.

In the following sections, I reveal several situations in which you can practice your sales skills without risking the loss of a sale.

Negotiating in the office

Unless you're acting as the salesperson for your own business, you have a boss or supervisor who's probably a pretty savvy salesperson. What better person could you possibly find to sell something to? If you can sell to your supervisor, you can probably sell to anyone. Following are some ways of practicing your sales skills at the office:

✔ Negotiate a raise or a higher commission.

✔ Convince your supervisor to buy you a tool that can make you more productive.

✔ Request additional sales training.

✔ Negotiate an additional perk for the sales staff.

Sharpening your sales skills at home

Most marriage and family counselors essentially provide sales training to their clients. They teach family members how to communicate more effectively. Just like family, clients are much more receptive to what you have to say if you first really listen to their needs and then address those needs.

Selling is all about guiding your clients to choose solutions that are best for their situation. What better way to practice selling than in your family, where you're genuinely committed to guiding family members in making the right choices?

Another benefit of practicing your sales skills on a family member is that your family is probably very sensitive to the feeling of being sold. If they feel that you're feeding them a sales pitch, they're likely to call you on it. Practicing with your family forces you to be more genuine.

Connecting with the restaurant staff

If you sell houses, cars, insurance, or something else that most people eventually need or want, I strongly recommend that you click into sales mode every time you eat out. According to my estimates, everyone knows at least 250 people, so if you can establish a positive connection with your server, you have an opportunity to sell to at least 250 more people.

The next time you go out to eat, commit yourself to selling to your server:

✔ Always greet the server with a smile and a compliment or some other positive remark. I often say something like "How did we manage to get the best server in the restaurant!" The server may have had a bad table just before you walked in, so always be positive.

✔ After dinner, leave your business card behind with a positive note on it, such as "Outstanding service and food!" If the service wasn't all that great, mention the food. If the food wasn't great, mention the service.

✔ Don't be chintzy on the tip. A 20 percent or better tip is the most memorable compliment you can leave behind.

Even if you're not selling something that everyone eventually needs or wants, you can still practice your sales skills at the restaurant by engaging your server in a conversation. Not only do get some additional practice under your belt, but you make the entire dining experience more enjoyable for everyone. Make it a habit.

Negotiating upgrades at the airport

I have so many frequent-flier miles racked up that I'm usually automatically upgraded to first class, but prior to this, on about 80 percent of my flights, I've been able to sell myself into a first-class seat. This is a great way to practice your sales skills.

When you arrive at the airport, you have three opportunities to negotiate a first-class seat:

✔ **At the curb:** If you fly frequently, establish long-term, positive relationships with the baggage handlers. Treat them with respect, get to know them personally, and tip them very well. Over time, you'll find that they provide you with preferential treatment. When I pull up at the curb in Detroit Metropolitan Airport, 100 people may be lined up to check their bags. In most cases, a baggage handler who knows me takes me right to the counter and tells the airline representative to "take care of my friend." If a first-class seat is available, I usually get it.

✔ **At the ticket counter:** Most travelers at the airport are pretty grumpy, so be the one person who cheerfully greets the person behind the counter. Offer a compliment. Strike up a conversation, and then look for an opening to request an upgrade.

✔ **At the gate:** If you couldn't get an upgrade at the curb or the ticket counter, you have two more chances at the gate. When you're checking in, engage the person behind the counter in a conversation. If that doesn't work, connect with a member of the crew or even the captain. People often don't realize that they can talk with the captain.

Selling taxi rides

I flew into Los Angeles and had booked a room at the Ritz Carlton, Laguna, Niguel, about an hour and fifteen minutes from the airport. On my way to the hotel, I struck up a conversation with the taxi driver. As usual, the driver asked me what I did for a living, and I explained that I was in sales — I sold houses. He asked me what he could do to increase sales. He wanted to sell more rides to the airport.

The first thing I told him to do was to have business cards printed up with his cell phone number on them, so people could call him directly instead of having to call a dispatcher. I jotted down his cell hone number, so I could call him whenever I needed a ride during my eight-day stay.

I called the driver the next day. When he picked me up, sure enough, he already had his business cards. He asked me if I had any other suggestions to boost his business. I noticed that he had bucket seats in the front of the cab. I said, "If I were you, I'd put a TV/VCR player between the seats and play movies. Your passengers could watch a movie on the drive from the airport to the hotel."

He wasn't too impressed with this suggestion. He replied, "But the ride is only an hour and fifteen minutes. They'd only be able to watch half the movie."

"Exactly," I said, "Then they'll have to call you for the ride back to the airport if they want to see the second half of the movie!"

Months later, I called the taxi driver to see how everything was working out for him. He was now running his own limousine service in Laguna.

This story doesn't really show you how to hone your sales skills over the duration of a taxi ride, but it does demonstrate an important point about sales — think creatively. By inventing ways to better serve your clients, you're one big step closer to meeting your sales goals.

Engaging the taxi driver

To me, everyone I meet is a mini-marketing machine for Ralph R. Roberts, Inc. Taxi drivers are no exception. They meet a lot of people in the course of the day, and if they can drop my name or pass my card along to a potential client, that's free advertising for yours truly.

Engaging a taxi driver in a conversation also provides you with another opportunity to ply your trade and generate ideas. After all, taxi drivers are entrepreneurial — in a way, they're salespeople. You may be able to pick up a sales strategy from them or pass one along.

Chapter 5

Setting the Stage for an Unlimited Upside

In This Chapter

▶ Identifying products packed with potential

▶ Replacing bad customers with good ones

▶ Getting your company to support your efforts

▶ Outsourcing tasks that others can handle

▶ Stuffing more production into less time

As an entrepreneurial salesperson, getting stuck in a dead-end job doesn't seem likely to happen. After all, when you're earning commissions, you can earn as much as you're willing to work, right? Well, maybe not. Salespeople can still get stuck in dead-end jobs by boxing themselves in — picking the wrong product or service, pursuing business from customers who demand too much attention, working for an uninspired company, or refusing to delegate tasks that others are perfectly capable of handling.

Limit your upside, and you can achieve only a limited level of success. It's like buying an eight-foot ladder when you own a two-story house. That ladder isn't going to get you on the roof.

Maximize your upside and you discover unlimited opportunities. You can continually expand and ramp up your efforts with additional resources and personnel. You never feel cramped, you always feel driven by a new challenge, and your dreams can become more and more expansive.

In this chapter, I introduce the four main limitations to a salesperson's upside and then reveal strategies for overcoming these limitations and maximizing your upside. Here you discover how to pick the right products or services to sell, liberate yourself from lousy customers, break through limitations set by your company, and hire assistants to improve your own productivity.

Grasping the Concept of Upside

If you're not quite sure what upside is all about, you're not alone. Few sales-people give it much thought, but it is something you should give careful consideration. Upside is simply your maximum potential. Think of it as an impermeable ceiling that won't budge. If you're selling something that only a half dozen people in the world would ever really need or want, your upside is pretty low. Sell something that everyone is in constant need of, like great tasting fresh water, and your upside is pretty much whatever you decide it's going to be.

In sales, you want to maximize your upside, so you're never at risk of hitting into that ceiling. The upside should be sufficient to accommodate your growth far into the future — ideally to the end of your career. You should never feel as though you've achieved all that you could possibly achieve.

Spotting the Five Limitations to Upside

A limitation to upside is any bottleneck in your sales system that slows you down and restricts your earnings potential. It can limit you from the supply side or the demand side, from the bottom up (not having the resources or personnel in place) or the top down (too narrow a market).

When you begin to feel as though something is holding you back, that some-thing is likely a limitation to your upside, and the first step in removing that limitation is to identify it. In the following sections, I describe the five types of limitations that may be holding you back.

Getting past the plateau

You reach plateaus in any challenging endeavor — physical training, a weight-loss plan, marriage, your job, you name it. When you're dieting, for example, you may lose a significant amount of weight and then, no matter what you do, you can't lose any more.

My friend, Pete Thomas, "The Biggest Loser" on NBC's competitive weight-loss show and my personal weight-loss trainer, told me that to get past the plateau, you have to "change it up." As he explains it, the body starts to lock calories in the storage pantry when it senses that it's being starved. Pete told me that I had to occasionally eat *more* so that my body would unlock the pantry.

The same is true in sales or any business venture. Once you've achieved a certain level of success, you often have to "change it up" — try something new, to start climbing to the next level. When your sales career feels as though it's a job rather than a challenging career, it's probably high time to "change it up."

Wrong product or service

You may be able to sell swimming pools in Alaska, but the effort is probably not worth it, and you're going to run out of customers pretty quickly. If possible, steer clear of products and services with a limited upside. Here are some red flags to watch out for:

- ✔ **Something you don't like:** Can you get excited about the product or service? If not, consider selling something else. If you're selling a product or service you don't believe in and can't get worked up about, then your upside is going to be limited by your lack of enthusiasm.

- ✔ **Fad item:** Don't jump on the bandwagon whenever any fad rolls into town. Sales are likely to go from boom to bust in a hurry, and eventually all the resources you invested in building a brand around that fad are going to be wasted. However, be aware of the difference between a fad (short term) and a trend (long term). Mistaking a trend for a fad could keep you from capitalizing on a lucrative opportunity.

Don't mistake a revolutionary change for a fad. Beanie Babies and pet rocks were clearly fads, for example, but blogging is a revolutionary change that's here to stay. Meeting Richard Nacht from Blogging Systems has provided opportunities that I couldn't have imagined before the days of blogging. For more about blogging, check out Chapter 17.

- ✔ **Poor quality:** A market always exists for second-rate products and services at low prices, but selling shoddy products and services ultimately harms your reputation, limiting your upside.

- ✔ **One-time purchases:** Avoid selling anything that a person buys only once during her life, such as cemetery plots. Houses, cars, candles, computer software, and IT servers that have a three-year lifecycle are examples of products that require renewal. You can afford to invest time and resources in establishing long-term relationships with clients, because you know that in the future, they'll be in the market for another house, car, candle, IT server, or whatever else they purchased from you.

- ✔ **Saturated market:** Some products are merely commodities, and competition in based solely on who can offer the lowest price. Competing on low price may work for some mega-giant retailers, but it usually means you're scraping the bottom of the barrel.

Wrong customer or client

If you operate in accordance with the credo that "the customer is always right," you're making a big mistake. Customers are often wrong, and when a customer is wrong, serving them can quickly become a costly full-time operation. Unless you can settle them down in a hurry and get their expectations in line, your best move may be to cut them loose.

Identify your worst customers and consider giving them *less* attention rather than *more* attention (which they demand). I know it's a little counterintuitive — the squeaky wheel is supposed to get the oil, but in sales, pulling back from a bad customer is a no-lose situation. The bad customer either goes elsewhere (to burden your competition) or decides to cooperate and become a more profitable and less burdensome source of revenue.

Use the following criteria to identify your worst customers:

- ✔ Doesn't pay or doesn't pay on time.
- ✔ Haggles over everything.
- ✔ Constantly complains.
- ✔ Badmouths you to other potential customers.
- ✔ Calls every 15 minutes.
- ✔ Distracts you from doing other dollar productive activities.
- ✔ Won't listen to reason.
- ✔ Consistently late or shows up without an appointment.

To identify your best and worst customers, determine how profitable each customer is. Gross sales is only one consideration. Also factor in the amount of repeat business the customer represents, the amount of time the customer requires, frequency and size of returns, payment issues, referrals you receive from that customer, how your relationship with that customer affects your status in the industry, and so on. Consider ranking customers and then work on finding replacements for the customers at the bottom of your list. See "Pursuing High-Quality Customers," later in this chapter for details on finding superior replacements.

Trust your instincts and act sooner rather than later. You can pretty much sense when a customer is going to require more work than the relationship is worth. No matter how hard you try, the results are going to be the same — frustration. Instead of wasting your time, energy, and resources on a customer, cut the cord. Let the customer cut his teeth on some other unfortunate salesperson.

Another way to handle bad customers or those you simply don't get along with is to refer the customer to another salesperson in your office who's likely to be a better match. If you have a sales team, discuss troublesome clients regularly and strategize on how to handle them. You may be able to keep their business in the family while shedding yourself of a burden.

Even when you're dealing with the worst customer in the world, remain respectful and polite, and let the customer down easy. Remain professional at all times. When I tell a customer, "I'd love to have ten more customers like you," it's a signal to my staff that this customer didn't make the cut. When I say, "I'd love to have ten thousand more customers like you," everyone gets on board.

Wrong company or manager

If you're not thriving in your current work environment, the reason may be that it's just not the right place for you. Perhaps you need a company that's more supportive or you simply need everyone to get out of your way, so you can sell. Assess your current company, being particularly sensitive to these warning signs:

- **Lack of support:** Ultimately, you're responsible for procuring the tools, materials, and assistance required to sell, but if you can't obtain what you need from the company and don't have the capital to obtain them on your own, you may be in a dead-end job.

- **Lack of training:** A sink-or-swim sales environment is perfect for salespeople who prefer a hands-off management style, but if you require a little more training, especially product training, and your company refuses to provide it, you may be in the wrong place.

- **Overbearing sales manager:** Top-producing salespeople who are promoted to sales managers make the worst managers about 99 percent of the time. If your sales manager is obsessed with sales quotas, disregards your opinions, berates you, or undermines your authority with customers or clients, you either have to convince your manager to step back or start looking for another job.

Don't quit your current position without careful deliberation. I coach many salespeople who are disenchanted with their jobs simply because the grass looks a little greener on the other side of the street. By implementing the strategies I suggest throughout this book, you're likely to discover that the job, your company, and your supervisor weren't the cause of your lackluster sales. If you're doing everything I recommend in this book, and your sales are still less than stellar, then the company you work for (or its products or services) may not be the right fit. If you decide to jump ship, check out "Finding a Supportive Company," later in this chapter, for criteria in selecting a company that treats its salespeople right.

An I-can-do-it-all mentality

Salespeople tend to be control freaks, and I still have a little control freak in me — okay, maybe a lot. Trying to do everything yourself, however, is a sure way to cap any hoped-for increase in productivity.

Do the math. You're only one person. You have 24 hours in a day and seven days in a week. You can boost your productivity with software and other tools, but time still limits how much you, yourself, can do. To dash those limitations, delegate less critical tasks to others.

Later in this chapter, in the section "Delegating Time-Consuming Tasks," I show you how to increase productivity by outsourcing some of your work-load. In Chapter 13, I provide additional guidance on how to assess your needs and hire the right people.

Time constraints

People often blame time for their limitations. After all, every day has only 24 hours, and every week has only seven days. When you see time simply as a single dimension, it can limit what you're able to accomplish. Those who see time as only one dimension in a multi-dimensional world, however, are able to transcend time and reduce its effect as a limiting factor.

Your reality consists of several dimensions, including time, money, technology, and human resources. By leveraging the power of technology, the talents of others, and resources from other dimensions, you can blow the cap off of your time limits. See "Expanding Time," near the end of this chapter.

Finding the Right Product or Service

The salability of some products boggles the mind. Who would ever think you could sell bottled water in a country in which every building has a faucet or drinking fountain? Yet, every year, Americans alone gulp down over 26 billion liters of bottled water. Unlimited upside? Sure, everyone needs water, but still it makes you wonder.

Bottled water aside, when you're looking for ways to boost sales, product selection has to factor in. If you're selling a product that has a narrow appeal, the market is saturated, or you're simply facing superior competition, you may be fighting a losing battle. Part of being a power seller is knowing how to pick a winner — a product or service with an unlimited upside. In the following sections, I reveal some guidelines for picking a more likely winner.

Listing products and services packed with potential

Before bringing a new product or service to market, successful companies typically perform market research to determine the viability of the product. They may research sales figures for other similar products, host focus groups, test the market on a smaller scale, and so on.

Chances are good that if you're selling for a fairly large company, they've already performed the necessary research and are aware of the product's market potential. If you're running your own business or trying to pick a company to work for that has products or services with the most potential, make sure those products and services have the following qualities:

- ✔ **Universal appeal:** The larger the market, the bigger the upside. Focusing on a niche market is fine, as long as that market has more consumers than you can possibly reach in the course of your career.

- ✔ **Opportunities for repeat sales:** Anything that people buy more than a couple times over the course of their lives is a candidate, including houses, cars, computers, phones, and, yes, bottled water. This allows you to establish relationships with customers that lead to repeat business, so you're not constantly searching for new customers.

- ✔ **Reliable consumer base:** A reliable consumer base is one that's not likely to disappear after a short period of time. In other words, don't chase fads. The more reliable the consumer base, the longer you can expect to be in the business of selling that product or service.

- ✔ **Something you won't tire of selling:** I love selling houses and can't imagine ever tiring of the process of finding the right homes for families. If you have to convince yourself that you like what you're selling, you're probably selling the wrong thing.

Pick a product you can build a career around — houses, cars, computers, productivity software, power tools, or something else that people are going to always need. Becoming a power seller requires that you build a brand identity. Even if you sell branded products, you still want your clients thinking about you as their go-to guy or gal who represents the company. Whenever a customer thinks of the product you sell, she should immediately think of you. I encourage you to pick a product with an unlimited and long-term upside, so you don't waste time building brand identity with a product that's destined to drop off the radar a few months or years down the road.

Assessing multimedia marketing opportunities

Some products have limited media potential — they may play well in TV ads but not in print or on the radio or they may play well in print but not transition to TV. You're not likely to see a huge boost in sale by advertising a specialty software program on TV, for example.

When looking for products and services with an unlimited upside, however, lean toward those that you can advertise and market effectively in as many media as possible — print, TV, radio, websites, blogs, direct mailings, email, and so forth. With more ways to reach prospective customers, you have more ways to expand your market.

Don't forget that you're a product, too. When I talk about looking for a product that has unlimited media potential, that includes You, Inc. Having the right face and presence for TV, a good voice for radio, and excellent multimedia presentation skills to establish a Web presence are all excellent assets for capitalizing on the multimedia marketplace. For techniques and tips on how to fully exploit the multimedia marketplace, check out Chapter 16.

Spotting franchise opportunities

In some industries, "unlimited upside" may include franchise opportunities. As an entrepreneurial salesperson, you may be able to create your own franchise by hiring other salespeople to work under you, paying them a slightly lower commission.

This approach, commonly referred to as *network marketing* or disparagingly compared to pyramid schemes, has been employed successfully by Amway and other companies for years. For about 20 years, I steered clear of network marketing myself, because I didn't want to look like one of those lowlifes who was running a pyramid scheme.

Now, I think of network marketing a little differently. I'm a top producer in the real estate industry, and I can provide valuable guidance to younger, less-experienced salespeople. They want to work for me, because they know they can be more successful with the training I provide. I want them to work for me, because they can assist me in selling more than I could sell on my own. I can set up a network in a minimal amount of time, and it requires very little effort on my part to manage.

When salespeople criticize network marketing as simply being a type of pyramid scheme, Tom Bagby asks them, "You mean like General Motors?" GM and all other corporations are set up so that the top people earn the most money from the labor of the employees. Network marketing isn't much different, as long as the company is on the level and is not simply out to rip people off.

Pursuing High-Quality Customers

Every salesperson has his share of high-maintenance customers. The expense and aggravation of keeping them satisfied isn't worth the revenue they generate. These are the customers who are dragging you down. Shedding yourself of the deadweights and removing these particular limitations to your upside is a "simple" three-step process:

1. **Fire your worst customers.**

2. **Retain your best customers.**

3. **Find more best customers.**

Identifying the qualities of good customers

Who qualifies as a best customer is up to you to decide. In the business world, "best customer" usually equates with "most profitable" customer, but profitability can be a little tough to pin down. When creating your list of credentials for a best customer, consider the following traits:

- **Places you first:** When the customer thinks of a product or service you offer, she thinks of you first.

- **Pays a fair price:** Customers who value the product and service you offer are willing to pay the going rate. Those who don't value what you have to offer are constantly low-balling you on price.

- **Challenges you:** When customers constantly raise the bar, requiring you to expand your knowledge, improve or add new skills, increase productivity, and so on, they're improving your business.

- **Allows you to do what you do well:** Customers should know your business sufficiently to ask you to perform in areas where you excel rather than pushing you into areas outside your realm of expertise.

- **Exposes you to new opportunities:** Your best customers are collaborators — people or companies with whom you develop mutually beneficial relationships. These customers steer business your way and may even offer some cross-marketing opportunities. I value this quality more than any of the others.

Discovering more best customers

When you have a favorite dish or dessert, you often want more of it. You want to know the ingredients and how the chef prepared it, so you can make it yourself and have it whenever you want. In sales, you want more customers like your best customer, so single out your best customer and then find out all the ingredients that make that customer your best:

✔ **Who your customer is:** Who are you really selling to? The user of the product or service or someone who sells to the user of the product or service? In some cases, this isn't as obvious as you may think, as shown in the following sidebar "Know your client and what you're selling." Once you've identified your customer, study the demographic — age, sex, race or ethnicity, household income, geographical location, and so on. Jot down anything else you can think of, particularly in respect to what that customer needs most to be successful.

✔ **What your customer does:** Get to know what your customer does for a living, where she hangs out after work, other products she buys, and so on. I'm not saying you should become a stalker, but gather as much information about the customer you can, through normal conversations and correspondence, to draw a detailed customer portrait.

Know your client and what you're selling

Recently, I was consulting with a top hair salon owner about seizing additional opportunities. I asked him who is best client was, and he singled out his regulars — those who had and held their appointments for many years. I disagreed. I told him to look at it a different way. His clients were actually the people on the floor who booked business. Instead of focusing on pleasing the people who walked through the doors for a manicure, massage, or wash and cut, he needed to focus on pleasing the hair stylists, manicurists, and massage therapists. They needed to be happy and growing in knowledge in order to properly service their customers' needs.

Several years ago, I consulted with a publicly traded submarine sandwich company that was in trouble. They thought they were selling sandwiches, which they were, in a sense, but what they were really selling were franchises. The franchises were in the business of selling sandwiches. After I was able to convince them that their real customer was the franchise owner, they began to cater to the needs of the franchise owners, who ultimately became more successful. The submarine sandwich company was able to transform itself from a publicly traded company that was in trouble into a successful company that ultimately went private.

Sometimes, simply knowing who your customers really are can revolutionize your sales approach and lead to incredible success.

Brainstorm a list of the seven top sources for more customers who are like your best customer. Perhaps targeting a certain geographical area would be best. If you met the person through an Internet promotion, that may be where you want to focus your efforts. Think in terms of what you need to do to get more customers like this.

 Getting more clients like your best clients often requires the assistance of your best clients. In Chapter 21, I reveal one of my favorite techniques for drumming up referrals from past clients — my Hour of Power. Don't underestimate the value of your best past clients.

Acquiring Support and Resources

Ideally, you're either self-employed or you work for a company that nurtures an entrepreneurial mindset amongst its salespeople. Your company and manager encourage you to set goals, establish your own sales plan and strategy, and provide you with the resources required to put your plan into action. If you find yourself in a less-than-ideal situation, you have several options:

- ✔ Equip yourself with the tools and resources you need.
- ✔ Leave and find a company that's a better match for you.
- ✔ Convince management to invest in your success.

Try the third (least drastic) option first. What do you have to lose? If you try to convince management to open the vault and they say "No," you haven't lost anything. The worst thing that can happen is that you get ugly about it and get fired, in which case you lose a job with a company that didn't support you.

Now, how do you go about convincing management to get you what you need? The best approach is to act as though you're starting your own business and trying to convince a bank executive to approve a small-business loan:

1. **Draw up your sales plan, as discussed in Chapter 3.**

2. **Meet with your sales manager to review your plan, highlighting the potential boost in sales and profits.**

3. **Provide your manager with an itemized list of tools, supplies, and other resources required to properly execute your plan, along with an estimated total cost and ideas for implementing your plan.** Include enough supporting documentation to convince the person to say "Yes." It's easier for them to agree if they can hear it, see it, and possibly test-drive it. Show and tell all the way to close.

In most well-run companies, new sales associates receive plenty of training and support. In situations in which the training and support are not provided, they are usually readily available upon request. Don't automatically assume that your company is unsupportive just because management doesn't take the initiative to offer resources to you. You may simply need to ask.

Lois, my trusted advisor, was passing through the building and bumped into a new sales agent who had been in the office periodically. He complained that he was unable to get any "Ralph time." She told him that she knew how to remedy the situation. As soon as he started showing up at sales meetings, showing up to training meetings, showing up to shadow Ralph, showing up and acknowledging that he was ready, willing, and able to learn, he would have Ralph time. Before you can expect to receive any additional support from management, establish yourself as a talented and hard-working sales-person. Nobody can support your efforts to improve sales if you're not doing your part.

If your supervisor shoots down your plan, do what you normally do when you're trying to sell something — head on up to the decision maker. The higher you climb up the ladder in the business world, the more likely you are to connect with someone who's entrepreneurial by nature and values people who have goals and plans.

Here's a tip for sales managers and supervisors — look for ways to make your salespeople more productive. I had a great salesperson who had an unreliable car and no sense of direction. She was constantly getting lost and spending half the day trying to find out where she was and where she was going. One day, she simply didn't show up to a sales acquisitions meeting. I found out that she was knocking on doors in a dangerous neighborhood. I purchased a company car with a GPS service, and it made her twice as productive. She still gets lost, but only when she tries to drive somewhere without the assistance of the GPS system.

Delegating Time-Consuming Tasks

When I set a goal to sell 300 houses in a single year, I immediately realized that I couldn't do it on my own. The volume of phone calls alone would have consumed the better part of each day. To achieve my stated goal, I had to outsource the most time-consuming chores and focus on what I was really good at — dealing directly with buyers and sellers. I decided to deal with clients and hire others to answer the phones, shuffle papers, and tie up the loose ends.

When considering limitations to their upside, many salespeople focus too much on product and market limitations and completely overlook their own limitations. They falsely assume that just because their job description includes a list of tasks, they're personally responsible for performing those tasks.

You're not responsible for doing everything. You're responsible for making sure everything gets done.

Your goal is to maximize your earnings potential. You do that by focusing on the tasks you do best and that bring in the money and delegating any tasks that meet one or more of the following conditions:

- ✔ Someone else can do it just as well for less money. If you earn $50 an hour, don't cut your grass if you can get it cut for $10 . . . unless, of course, mowing the lawn is therapeutic.
- ✔ Someone else can do it better.
- ✔ You don't like doing it — it drains your energy and motivation.

I like to tell everyone that I put up the Christmas lights at my house. I truly believe that I do it, but I don't get on the ladder or string the lights. I write the check. Okay, I don't even do that — my wife writes the check, but because I play a critical role in earning the money that results in having the lights hung, I feel as though I'm the person who hung the lights. By the way, I also clean the house.

Expanding Time

People often cite time as a upside limiter, but it's actually not. I'm no physicist, but time isn't as linear as most people think it is. Time is relative to how much you get accomplished in that amount of time. If I can get twice as much done in half the time it takes someone else, I've just expanded time by a factor of four.

I discovered the power of expanding time fairly early in my career. As you know by now, I sell the American dream of homeownership. At one point, I hit a sales plateau. I was selling more houses than anyone else I knew, but I wanted to sell even more, and there just wasn't enough time in the day. So, I expanded time and decided to make every minute worth more money.

I began double-booking appointments. Instead of showing a home to one set of buyers, I invited two sets of buyers to drive around with me and look at houses at the same time. I loaded them into my Suburban and showed them the same houses. I usually sold two houses on the same trip.

What if the two sets of buyers settled on the same house? It never happened. As soon as one couple identified the house they liked, the other couple reinforced the sale. They would go on and on about what a great house it really was and how the other couple had really discovered the perfect home. They actually helped me sell the house!

After this accidental success, I took this approach to the next level. I went out immediately and purchased a 16-passenger van. I figured if I could be so successful with so little planning, just think what I could accomplish by putting more effort and resources behind it.

We started marketing this new house-hunting approach, and people loved it. House hunting became more of a pleasure trip for my clients — an opportunity to socialize and gather input from other buyers. More and more couples signed up. I was driving three or four or five families around at a time to look at houses. As I traveled the area selling houses, I used the cellphone to call back to the office to get the paperwork ready. On my best day, I actually sold 14 houses from the van. This became so successful that we eventually had entire convoys out looking at homes.

Then, we took the next step — we started marketing to real estate investors. They would really get excited talking about the investment opportunities of certain properties, swapping stories, talking shop, trading secrets. The best day I ever had with an individual was nine houses, and this was to a guy who was just getting started. Since then, he has started his own real estate company and is using many of the same techniques he picked up from me.

Whenever you feel as though your head is hitting the ceiling, identify whatever is holding you down, and then remove it. Think creatively to discover ways to avoid limiting your upside. Don't let anything hold you down.

Part II
Pumping Up Your Sales Muscle

The 5th Wave   By Rich Tennant

"How about this-'It's not just CRAP, it's Mel's CRAP'? Shoot! I hate coming up with a sales pitch for this client!"

In this part . . .

Becoming a top salesperson doesn't just happen while you're catching some z's. You have to work at it. You have to train, practice, and hone your craft and then shamelessly self-promote until everyone knows who you are, what you do, and how they can contact you to buy whatever it is you're selling.

The chapters in this part provide you with a workout guide. Like most workout programs, you don't have to complete every exercise and implement everything I suggest, but the more you do, the more successful you can expect to become.

Chapter 6

Getting in Step with Your Customer

· ·

In This Chapter

▶ Brushing up on sales psychology

▶ Riding the waves of the buying cycle

▶ Exploring sales strategies and techniques

▶ Sharpening your skills

· ·

Selling is like ballroom dancing. To avoid stepping on your dance partner's toes, you learn the steps. You practice to get a feel for how your partner moves and make your movements more natural and fluid. Assuming you and your partner have mastered the steps and practiced sufficiently, you move effortlessly and gracefully across the dance floor, never missing a beat. Onlookers can't tell who's leading and who's following.

Selling requires a very similar finesse. With selling, the dance steps are the basic selling techniques you employ. Over time, you practice these techniques until they become effortless and fluid. To avoid stepping on your customer's toes, you get a feel for your customer — what your customer needs and how she goes about making a purchase decision. Done right, the process of buying and selling takes on the appearance of a graceful dance. You take the lead and guide your customer to making the right decision, but as you interact, neither of you seems to be leading the other.

While this is certainly an overly romanticized description of the sales process, it illustrates the three key factors for selling effectively:

✔ Knowing your customer

✔ Knowing how to sell

✔ Practicing, so selling becomes natural

In this chapter, I focus on the key factor of knowing your customer. I give you an inside look at how customers generally go about making purchase decisions, reveal several proven strategies that I've picked up over the course of my 30-plus years in sales, and show you how to practice your skills until you're the Fred Astaire or Ginger Rogers of sales.

Knowing Why Buyers Buy

Knowing why people generally buy stuff — especially your stuff — can assist you in making your customers more sensitive to their wants and needs. Until you know what your prospective clients want or need, you are in no position to sell them anything. All you can do is present the product and describe its features. When you know what the client is looking for, however, then you can *pitch* the product to their wants or needs and have a much more effective presentation.

In the following sections, I reveal the seven key buyer motivations and then show you how to identify these motivations as they play out in the marketplace.

Identifying the seven buyer motivations

So, why do people buy stuff? I can come up with at least seven motivations. In the following list, I describe these buyer motivations in greater detail:

- **Need/Problem:** Customers you contact may already be well aware that they have a need or a problem, but many others are totally clueless. Until your customer is aware of the problem and realizes that viable solutions are available, she sees no need for the product or service you're selling. Early in the process, either through advertising or your interview, raise your customer's awareness of the problem and pique her interest in seeking solutions. Only then are you prepared to lead your customer through the process of analyzing available solutions.

- **Greed:** Numerous products and services are designed to assist people in making more money. If you're in corporate sales, that's pretty much all you sell, because businesses are in the business of making money. If what you're selling can make people more productive, if it can boost revenue or cut expenses, then you have a product you can sell by playing to your customer's desire to make money.

For the health of your immortal soul, avoid becoming another late-night-TV guru peddling get-rich-quick schemes. These crafty salespeople sell the vision of future riches, more leisure time, and early retirement.

✔ **Fear:** Fear sells. Some claim that fear sells better than sex, and they may be right. Just think of all the advertising invested in marketing products that protect us from real or perceived threats: Satellite communications systems for cars, so drivers always have a lifeline, no matter where they may end up; Home alarm systems to provide early warning of break-ins or fire; Bottled water… because you never really know what's in that tap water; Duct tape and plastic sheeting in the event of a chemical weapons attack; insurance; and so on.

✔ **Pleasure:** If you're selling in a feel-good industry, such as vacation travel, spas, hobbies and handicrafts, or home décor, marketing to your customers' pleasures is paramount. But even in industries in which pleasure isn't the central focus, you can often sell luxury-class items by focusing on the pleasure they're likely to provide for the consumer. When a customer is in the market for an $80,000 car, for example, she's wanting something more than a comfortable ride to work. If you want to learn how to cater to pleasure, go to a boat show.

✔ **Vanity:** People not only want to feel good, they want to look good, and they generally want other people to think they look good, too. Whether you're selling cosmetics, clothing, jewelry, accessories, hair care products, plastic surgery, or a host of other personal care products and services your marketing and selling strategies need to target the customers' need to look good.

✔ **Impulse:** People often buy stuff because everyone else is buying it. Remember the poker chip craze around the turn of the century? You don't need to be a great salesperson to take advantage of a hot trend, because people know what they want and often purchase impulsively. Success depends more on distributing the product and placing it in high-profile locations to making the purchase more convenient.

✔ **Fatigue:** Pushy salespeople can be very successful simply by wearing the customer down, but I discourage you from taking this approach. It may work for a door-to-door salesperson who wanders from town to town, but when you're trying to build a reputation that secures you future business, bully tactics are counterproductive.

Sure, you're selling a product or service, but your customer buys to solve a problem or meet a need. Early on, focus more on your customer and on identifying problems or needs.

Picking up sales tricks from advertising

You can discover some great sales tricks by analyzing TV commercials and checking out ads in magazines. The next time you're watching TV or flipping through a magazine, pay close attention to the customer motivation the advertisement targets — need, greed, fear, pleasure, vanity, or impulse. A commercial for a new toothpaste, for example, may boast that the toothpaste reduces cavities, thus calling attention to a problem — cavities and dental bills. Another toothpaste commercial may focus on the product's ability to whiten teeth — playing on the customer's vanity.

You're likely to see commercials that call attention to common fears, as well — perhaps a commercial for a financial company that makes you wonder whether you're going to have enough money socked away for a comfortable retirement or a commercial for a home alarm system that automatically notifies the police department of any break-ins. You're sure to see plenty of commercials that cater to greed, too, especially those late-night infomercials.

You're probably already targeting these same buyer motivations when you make your sales presentations, but by becoming more consciously aware of them, you can become much more effective at it.

Identifying motivations for buying your product or service

Selling requires an ability to get inside the head of your customer and figure out why that person is likely to want or need the product you're selling. Of course, you don't really know what motivates your customer to buy until he tells you, but you can get a general idea by examining what your products and services have to offer:

1. **Jot down a list of products or services you're selling.**

2. **Next to each item, list all of the motivations that a customer may have to purchase the product or service.** You may find that the primary motive is to solve a problem or alleviate a fear, but secondary motivations may also come into play.

3. **Rank the motivations in order of strength.** Which motivation is most common and likely to convince your customer to make a purchase decision?

4. **Use the motivation rankings to assist your prospective customer in making the right purchase decision.** Read on for additional details on how to assess a prospect's needs and then pitch your products to those needs.

Collaborating on the Purchase Decision

Regardless of what you're selling and your customer's possible motivation for buying it, your customer follows a predictable pattern when making a purchase decision. The more aware you are of this pattern, the more effective you can be at teaming up with the customer to arrive at a mutually beneficial purchase decision. Regardless of what your customer's buying, she generally takes the following four steps in making a purchase decision:

1. **Identifies a problem or need, either on her own or with the assistance of someone in marketing or sales . . . not necessarily you**

2. **Searches for and compares products or services that meet her needs**

3. **Compares prices of comparable products and services**

4. **Measures the risk of purchasing or not purchasing the product or service**

Although customers often follow this step-by-step process in order, the decision process can take some rapid and unexpected turns, and the longer the customer takes to decide, the more jumbled the steps become. After assessing the risks of purchasing a product or service, for example, a customer may decide not to purchase and skip back to Step 2 or 3, so be prepared to make adjustments on the fly.

In the following sections, I describe each step in the purchase decision process and highlight what you should be doing at each stage to guide your customer in making the right decision.

Calling attention to the problem or need

As a salesperson, you essentially solve problems or serve people's needs. In most cases, however, your customer doesn't even realize that he has a problem or that the need exists. During this stage of the process, you're assisting the prospective client in identifying a need, and you can do it in either of two ways:

- ✔ **Advertising:** On its surface, advertising may appear to push a particular product or service, but the underlying message of almost all advertisements is that the customer has a need that's not being sufficiently met.

- ✔ **Interviewing:** If you sell by contacting customers directly, your early conversations are or should be centered on identifying your customer's needs or problems. In other words, you should be asking lots of questions directed at rooting out problems or needs that the prospect may or may not be aware of.

Ask questions before pitching what you're selling. You don't know what your customer needs or wants until that customer tells you, and once you know, you can more effectively pitch your product or service to your customer's needs. The more excited you are about your product, the more you need to avoid the temptation to start reciting a litany of product features. Early in the buying process, your goal is to gather information and understand the customer's needs. See "Asking questions to draw out the information you need," later in this chapter for details.

Identifying possible solutions

To be the best salesperson you can be, stop selling. Don't think of yourself as a salesperson. Think of yourself more as a friend or colleague who's helping his buddy solve a problem. If your friend came to you with a problem, you'd probably listen first to gather as much pertinent information as possible. You may even ask your friend whether she tried any solutions and, if she did, what the results were. You probably wouldn't simply dive in and start offering advice before you knew what was going on. (For more about the benefits of asking questions, see "Asking questions to draw out the information you need," later in this chapter.

After you and your customer identify a problem or need (for ideas on how to identify needs, see the section earlier in this chapter, "Spotting the problem or need"), the next step is to analyze possible solutions. To team up with your customer and identify the optimum solution, continue your interview — ask questions and listen carefully.

At this point, you should have identified the prospect's wants or needs. Now you can shift the interview to asking questions that identify possible solutions and determine whether what you're selling meets your customer's needs:

- ✔ **What do you do?** Instead of launching into a long-winded description of what your company does and what you have to offer, shift the focus to the customer's situation.

- ✔ **How are you currently doing it?** Your customer may already have a system or products in place. By understanding the customer's current solution, you're in a better position to demonstrate how your products and services can better meet those needs.

- ✔ **What are you trying to do?** Encourage your customer to present what she thinks would be the ideal solution or at least her vision of the results that would follow if the ideal solution were in place. The answer to the first question "What do you do?" tells you where the customer is right now, while the answer to this question tells you where the customer wants to be tomorrow.

✔ **What can I do for you?** After you know where the customer is and where the customer wants to be, this question flows naturally. You're essentially asking the customer, "How do you see me assisting you in getting from point A to point B?"

You may need to reword these questions so they're more applicable to what you're selling. I sell houses, for example, so instead of asking "What do you do?" and "What are you trying to do?" I may ask, "Where do you live?" and "Where do you want to live?" Someone selling computers may ask, "What do you use your computer for now?" and "What do you think you'd like to be able to do with your computer?"

Prospective customers often dismiss problems, convincing themselves that no satisfactory solution exists or that the solution is too costly or time consuming to pursue. When talking with the customer at this point, consider asking whether she has considered or even tried other solutions. By discussing these other solutions, you can get a better feel for what the customer *doesn't* want.

Weighing costs and benefits

Knowing that a solution is available, customers proceed to analyze the costs — more specifically, they analyze the costs versus the benefits. This is where the scales begin to teeter-totter, and where sticker shock begins to set in on big-ticket items or large-scale solutions.

At this stage in the decision-making process, you can be very successful by focusing the customer's attention on the consequences of not purchasing the product or service. If you're in corporate sales, for example, you may ask the customer how a decision not to move forward is going to affect production or plans for expansion. In real estate, you may ask a couple who's thinking of purchasing a more affordable house how much that's going to save them in the long run.

When customers are assessing the costs and benefits, remain in question mode. Don't simply point out the negative consequences. Ask questions that draw the customer's attention to the negative consequences of not moving forward.

Second guessing the decision

After people decide to purchase something, especially an expensive some-thing, they begin to have second thoughts. They start talking to colleagues, relatives, friends, neighbors, their hairdresser, you name it. Maybe they don't really need it. Maybe they can get it cheaper somewhere else. Maybe the evil salesperson is pulling a fast one over on them. Whatever the case, the cus-tomer gets a case of what's technically known as *buyer's remorse,* or more commonly as *cold feet*, and you'd better be ready with a pair of warm socks.

At this stage in the purchase decision process, you're essentially addressing customer concerns, fielding objections, and trying to keep the customer calm. For instance, in my industry (real estate), the buyer is excited about the home they just purchased. Then comes the home inspection. Many agents don't attend, which is a big mistake. The agent needs to be there to re-sell, confirm that the buyer is making a great decision, and overcome any obstacles with suggestions of how to resolve potentially deal-busting decisions.

In corporate sales, you also have to remain engaged with the prospect but for different reasons, especially if your company follows the hunter-farmer sales model — that is, the person who lands the deal (the hunter) is ultimately not the person who services the account (the farmer).). In this situation, the hunter needs to continue to remain engaged with the client to ensure quality service and continuity.

 Your ultimate goal is not to sell but to assist the prospective client in choosing the solution that's the best fit for them, even if this means not getting the sale. When you're not selling for commissions or bonuses but to satisfy your customers, you're doing it right, and the commissions and bonuses start flowing your way.

Brushing Up on a Few Power-Selling Techniques

Some people seem to be born to sell. They have personality plus. Anyone would buy anything they were selling. If you're one of these people, lucky you. You can safely skip this section and tend to other ways of increasing your sales and revenue.

For the rest of you who weren't quite born to be salespeople, there's still hope. By acquiring a few basic skills along with some turbocharged techniques described in the following sections, you can take your game to the next level and begin selling like a seasoned pro.

Dealing with the decision maker

You can waste a lot of time and energy selling to people who don't have the power to make the final decision. This is a bigger problem in corporate sales, where your initial contact is likely to be lower on the chain of command, but you may also encounter this problem if you're selling high-priced items to couples, such as houses, cars, or insurance.

Whenever you're selling, sell to the decision maker; otherwise, you're not selling — you're simply negotiating your way past the gatekeepers. In the following sections, I show you how to spot the decision maker and work your way up to the person you should be selling to.

Spotting the decision maker

Assuming you catch sight of the decision maker, identifying her is fairly easy. Look for the person who has the most power and control. When I'm dealing with a couple, I find that the decision maker of the two typically exhibits the following qualities:

- ✔ Sits in the front seat when we go to look at houses.

- ✔ Speaks on behalf of the couple. (When you ask a question, the non-decision maker looks at the decision maker.)

- ✔ Adjusts with the type of product they're purchasing.

Even though you may be consciously pitching the product to the decision maker, don't make the non-decision makers feel like second-class citizens. Treat everyone equally — not the same, but equally. Otherwise, you could lose the sale.

In corporate sales, spotting the decision maker can be much more challenging, because that person may be hiding behind a host of other managers, employees, voicemail, and e-mail. Once you find the person, however, the signs of power are similar to those you observe when selling to couples or families. The decision maker is the person that all other defer to.

Working your way to the decision maker

When you're selling to companies, the path to the decision maker is likely to be strewn with blockades and detours. In most cases, you first have to get past the automated gatekeepers — voice mail, caller ID, and e-mail. Then, if you're lucky enough to contact an actual human being, you're likely to find that the person isn't actually the decision maker. To take some shortcuts to the decision maker in a business setting, consider the following tips:

- ✔ Find out how purchasing decisions are typically made in the industry you're working in. Do companies typically have a purchasing department? Does the CEO or CFO make the purchasing decisions? Are decisions handled by individual department heads?

- ✔ Explore the company's Web site for any clues, looking for the names of department heads and other managerial personnel.

- ✔ Use the time-crunch technique. When meeting with prospective clients whom you suspect are not the decision makers, ask when they would like to have this solution implemented. If they say something like "two months," you can follow up by saying, "Two months? That's okay, but it's pretty aggressive. Who's involved in the decision-making, so I can assist you in meeting your timeline?"

- ✔ Network with current and former employees, customers, and suppliers of the company. See if any or your contacts can personally introduce you to the decision maker. See Chapter 14 for additional details on networking.

- ✔ Introduce yourself to the receptionist and ask who's in charge of (fill in the blank)? Filling in the blank with the department you want to deal with; for example, "Who's in charge of IT?" or "Who's in charge of printing?"

If you're not talking to the decision maker, you should be working your way up to that person. Don't waste time pitching your products and services to people who can't decide to buy them. If you have a contact at the company already, ask your contact to introduce you to Mr. and Ms. Decision Maker, so your contact can advocate for your solution.

Mastering the meet and greet

Your first meeting with a prospective client can set the entire tone of your relationship. Following are some guidelines to ensure that your relationship has a positive start:

- ✔ When meeting the client at her home, knock on the front door instead of ringing (just in case someone's sleeping), and take your shoes off at the front door.

- ✔ Shake hands and introduce yourself first. A firm, friendly handshake is best.

- ✔ Maintain eye contact without getting into a staring match.

- ✔ Pay attention to seating arrangements. When meeting a couple at their home or apartment, I try to move them to the kitchen table. The living room is for company; the kitchen is where friends and family typically feel most comfortable. If meeting in a public place, try to arrange it so that your back is facing a wall, so that you receive the full and undivided attention of your clients.

- ✔ If the client offers you a non-alcoholic drink, accept it or ask for water.

- ✔ Some small talk can break the ice and establish you in the eyes of your client as not only a salesperson but a human being, but don't force it, and always avoid discussing sex, politics, religion, or schools.

For additional tips on making a good first impression, check out Chapter 4.

Energizing the conversation

No matter how badly your day has gone, how tired you feel, or how much you'd rather be somewhere else, pump yourself up and pump some energy into the conversation.

I once had a reporter call for an interview on a very busy day when I had barely a moment to breathe. She asked whether she could tape the interview. I could have replied, "Sure, that's fine," but instead, I said, "Fire up your tape recorder and let's have some fun!" She laughed, and I could immediately feel the energy rise in both of us. The interview continued at the higher level of energy and resulted in a much more positive story.

By boosting the energy in the room, you put your client more at ease, jump-start their positive thoughts, and improve your chances of achieving your sales goal.

Asking questions to draw out the information you need

Earlier in this chapter, in the section "Identifying possible solutions," I encourage you to ask questions in order to assess your customer's needs. Asking questions is a critical part of selling effectively, because it enables your customer to feel more in control of making the purchase decision while providing you with the information you need to guide your customer in the right direction.

Realize, however, that all questions are not created equal. If you ask a yes/no question, and the answer is "No," the conversation is pretty much over. In the following sections, I offer some suggestions on how to phrase your questions in a way that keeps the conversation going and provides you with the information you need.

When phrasing your questions, consider asking customers how they *feel* about something rather than what they *think* about it. The purchase decision is often an emotional choice, so knowing how your customer feels can give you a better idea of what they really want.

Asking thought-provoking questions

The best questions are those that provoke thought and compel your customer to offer up details rather than simply yes/no answers. These questions may also demonstrate your understanding of the customer's situation or business and your genuine interest in discovering solutions that are best for them.

Following are some examples of improperly and properly phrased questions that can guide you in formulating your own questions:

> **Poor:** "Did you like the neighborhood where you're living?" (Requires a simple yes or no answer.)
>
> **Better:** "What are some of the best things about the neighborhood where you're living?" (Makes the person think and offer details about what she's looking for in a neighborhood.)
>
> **Poor:** "When do you think you'll be ready to make a decision?" (Can be answered with a simple response.)
>
> **Better:** "What needs to happen for you to be prepared to make a decision?" (Requires that the person consider factors that go into the decision process rather than simply a timeframe.)
>
> **Poor:** "Have you worked with any other service providers in the past?" (Calls for a simple yes or no answer.)
>
> **Better:** "What sorts of experiences have you had with other service providers?" (Requests additional information about other service suppliers that can assist you in determining what the client needs.)

Answering a question with a question

Customers can trap you with their own targeted questions. If you're not careful, you can actually un-sell your product by giving the wrong answer. When you're not completely sure from the way a customer asks a question what answer they're looking for, consider answering the question with a question of your own.

Buyers often ask me questions about houses, such as "How big is the yard?" Without knowing whether they want a big yard or a small yard or even what they consider big or small, I have only a 50/50 chance of giving the right answer, so I ask my own question, "How big of a yard are you looking for?" Once I have the answer, I can phrase my own answer more effectively. If they want a big yard, I may say, "This house has one of the largest yards in the neighborhood." If they want something smaller, I can say, "The lot is pretty average for this area." Same lot, but I'm framing the customer's perspective, and perspective is reality.

Some prospects can be downright hostile when asking questions, so be prepared to deflect as much of the hostility you can, remain calm, and turn around the situation with logical answers and perhaps a touch of humor. You can usually sense hostility when the prospect asks the same question over and over again. Knowing your product and your industry is the best defense, because it enables you to deliver logical answers. I like to add a little humor to defuse the situation.

Using yes/no questions tactically

You may be able to use yes/no questions, but I typically do this only sparingly. For example, I may ask a series of very easy questions that I'm almost certain my client is going to say "Yes" to, so I can get the client in the rhythm of saying "Yes." Then, I finish by asking for something I really want:

> "Is it okay to put a For Sale sign on your front lawn?"

> "Is it okay to schedule an open house."

> "Can we put a lockbox on your door, so other agents can show your home to more buyers?"

> "Can we add your house to multiple listing services to generate more interest?"

After about 10 to 15 of these easy questions, then I present the contract the homeowners can choose to sign to have me as their listing agent and say something like, "Great, let's get started. This is a listing contract . . ."

Ask little questions, listen carefully to the answers, ask more little questions, listen, and you're likely to get the order.

Mirroring your customer

Your customer is likely to feel more comfortable in your presence if he feels that you're on the same level with him. To evoke a sense of camaraderie in my clients, I often use a technique called *mirroring.* If my client talks loud, I raise my voice. If the client speaks softly I lower my voice. If my client prefers talking on the phone over meeting in person, I make more phone calls than visits. If my client seems a little timid, I tone down my presentation.

Think of yourself as the host at a dinner party trying to make your guests feel comfortable.

Looking for win-win opportunities

The more successful your customer is, the more successful you're likely to become, so throughout the decision-making process, your focus should be on doing what's best for the customer. What's best for your customer is what's best for both of you. Strive to make transactions mutually beneficial.

If your product isn't right for your customer or your customer can't really afford it, selling it to them anyway may book you one commission, but it's going to hurt you in the long run.

Changing "no" to "know"

Salespeople are no strangers to the word "no," but when a customer says "no" to me, I hear "know," as in the customer doesn't yet *know* enough to say "yes." If the customer really means "no," then you should certainly back off, thank the customer for her time, and move on. Customers often say "no," however, when they're simply having second thoughts and require a little additional information. Be patient and persistent.

Customers often turn most negative just prior to making a decision to make a purchase — just before signing on the dotted line. Furthermore, when they're considering buying from one of several salespeople, they often become most negative with the salesperson they're most likely to purchase from. This is a positive sign, so don't lose the deal by getting discouraged and giving up.

Knowing when to stop

Some salespeople become so excited when the customer finally decides to make the purchase, that they keep selling, going on and on about how happy the customer is going to be, what a good decision she made, blah, blah, blah. What they fail to realize is that this places them at an increased risk of losing the sale.

When the customer has decided to make the purchase, whether it took you 20 minutes or 20 days to make the sale, stop selling and seal the deal.

Practicing Your Sales Presentation

A sales presentation is only as good as it is natural, and to make it natural requires practice. Just think how stiff a group of actors would be staging a play after only a few rehearsals. The more you practice, the smoother your delivery and the better able you are to ad lib when your customer throws you a curveball.

Unfortunately, most of your practice in sales comes in the form of on-the-job training — you fail your way forward. If you're a quick learner, the pain is short-lived, and you eventually reap the rewards of your sacrifice. To relieve some of the pain and get you up to speed a little sooner, the following sections suggest various ways to get much more out of your practice sessions on or off the job.

In speaker circles, stage time is critical to honing your speaking skills. In sales, the most important place to practice is in front of the customer. It's no secret — the more you do it, the better you get at it. Real sales experiences, good or bad, make you a better salesperson.

Avoiding the urge to become a clone

My resistance to role playing comes from my own experience with it. Tom Hopkins, author of *Selling For Dummies,* was one of my early sales heroes. I did everything I could to look and act more like Tommy Hopkins, so I could achieve a similar level of success. After some time, I realized that being a Tommy Hopkins clone wasn't working for me, and I needed to bring my own personality into my presentations.

In Chapter 3, I encourage you to identify your sales heroes, so you can develop a clearer vision of the salesperson you want to be, but avoid the temptation to model yourself too closely after your hero. You have to own the way you sell. Your approach must be true to your personality and beliefs. Otherwise, customers are going to perceive you as a phony.

Role playing

Sales consultants often recommend role-playing with a colleague, which I suppose can be of some use, but I'm not a big fan of role playing. You're better off practicing new skills in an actual sales setting with a real customer. Having a more experienced colleague sit in on your presentation and provide feedback afterward is an excellent idea, as I discuss later in this chapter in the section, "Teaming up with a trainer."

Watching and listening to yourself work

Athletes often watch tapes of themselves in action, to see what they're doing right, what they're doing wrong, and what they can do better. In the midst of competition, they have only a vague feeling of whether they're doing everything right. The video recording enables the athlete to take a more critical view of her performance.

Try the same technique. Audiotape your presentation and listen to it later. If you hold sales presentations in your office, you may also consider videotaping a few presentations and watching them later. By hearing and perhaps listening to both yourself and your client, you can develop a clearer sense of what you're saying and the effect it has on a client. You can then "adjust your swing" accordingly.

After a presentation, most salespeople have an overly negative view of their performance. They may have done quite well, but walk away feeling as though they "blew it." Keep this in mind when you start to feel as though you blew a sale. You probably did much better than you think.

Teaming up with a trainer

If you're fortunate enough to work for a company that provides training for its salespeople, take full advantage of the trainer. If you do most of your sales over the phone, you may be able to record your sales calls (with the client's permission, of course), and then review those calls with your trainer to determine what you can do more effectively. If you meet clients in person, the trainer may be able to sit in on the meeting and provide feedback later.

Former salespeople often make lousy trainers. They often have big egos fueled by the belief that becoming manager was a huge promotion. They can't stop selling and insist on stepping in when they think you're about to lose a sale. These intrusive trainers can actually undermine your credibility with a client. A good trainer remains as invisible as possible and provides feedback to you later . . . in private.

If your company doesn't offer a trainer, consider asking a colleague you admire to provide some coaching or going outside the company and hiring a sales coach. A sales coach can often assist you in attaining both your professional and personal goals. One of the big things in my industry right now are real estate agent teams. Team members often swap tips and techniques and may even accompany one another on sales calls to pick up new strategies.

Chapter 7

Teaming Up for Success with Personal Partnering

In This Chapter

▶ Meeting personal partnering for the first time

▶ Assessing your current situation

▶ Developing a personal improvement plan

▶ Selecting a personal partner

▶ Celebrating your mutual success

*Y*ou probably have one or two nagging goals — maybe to run a marathon, learn a foreign language, or play a musical instrument. Perhaps you've even tried a couple times to achieve that goal, but became distracted by something that seemed more important at the time. Ten years later, you're kicking yourself for not following up.

What if you had shared your goal with someone close? What if you told someone that two years from today, you were going to run a marathon or strum a particular song on your guitar or spend a month in Costa Rica speaking only Spanish? What if you had shared your plan for achieving that goal, and told that person to hold you to it? What if both of you held each other accountable for actively pursing your individual dreams? Both of you would have significantly improved your chances of achieving your goals. This is what personal partnering is all about.

Perhaps you already practice personal partnering and aren't even aware of it, or maybe you call it something else, like the *buddy system*. If you're a member of a reading group, for example, you're already involved in a basic form of personal partnering. The group chooses a book to read and sets a date on which to discuss the book. You feel responsible for getting that book read by the specified date, so you can contribute something of value to the discussion. Without some peer pressure, you'd have a much easier time blowing it off, and you probably wouldn't read nearly as much.

In this chapter, I reveal the Personal Partnering Process — a personal change technique developed by my friend and colleague Terry Wisner, Founder of *Partnering To Success, LLC.* Terry has helped me modify the approach to better assist salespeople in using it to effect positive changes in their careers. Here you discover how to team up with your personal partner to prioritize your goals, support one another's efforts, and celebrate your achievements on your way to mutual success.

Flagging Areas for Improvement

Like any serious effort to make a positive change in your life, changing the way you sell begins with an honest assessment of your current skill set. Until you admit that you could be doing something better and then identify that something, you have no idea of what you need to work on.

Of course, assessing your sales skills sounds a lot easier than it really is. It requires that you admit your own shortcomings and take a step back to see yourself as others see you. In the following section, I show you how to gather the information required to identify areas for improvement, or what I like to refer to as *lesser strengths*.

Performing a self assessment

When trying to identify areas for improvement, start with yourself. What do you feel you could be doing or doing better to boost sales? You may, for example, feel as though you're not very good talking on the phone or maybe you think you need to develop computer skills. Look for your lesser strengths. The following list highlights some key areas to examine:

- Communicating over the telephone
- Communicating in person
- Obtaining high-quality leads
- Improving efficiency through technology
- Meeting clients for the first time
- Asking for referrals
- Developing an product expertise
- Researching the competition
- Networking and building productive relationships
- Finding out more about your customers

Throughout this book, I reveal strategies, skills, and techniques that can make you a more effective salesperson. As you discover new sales tools and methods you'd like to try, add them to your list.

Taking a sales skills assessment test

A sales skills assessment tool or test can assist you in evaluating your knowledge of the selling process and identifying your strengths and weaknesses. If your company doesn't offer a skills assessment tool of its own, use your favorite Internet search tool to look for "sales skills assessments." Most of the tools require that you complete a questionnaire online. The assessment service analyzes your answers and delivers a report highlighting your strengths and weaknesses.

I prefer assessment tools that offer what is called *360-degree feedback* — perspectives from your customers, your peers, your boss, and yourself. You recommend the raters you want to assess you, and the company gathers information from these people. By seeing yourself from different perspectives, you can build a skill set that enables you to improve relationships with all of those who have a vested interest in your success. The Booth Company at www.boothco.com offers several assessment programs.

Gathering insight from colleagues

If you work in proximity with other salespeople, they may witness your interactions with clients, either over the phone or in person, and they usually form an opinion of how you handle various situations. If they're polite, they may keep their comments to themselves, but keeping a secret doesn't assist you in identifying areas for improvement.

To break the ice, encourage your colleagues to open up by asking them to provide you with honest feedback. Tell them that you're trying to sharpen your sales skills and that you would appreciate any insights or recommendations they have to offer. Maybe you sound a little too abrasive on the phone. Perhaps you talk too much and listen too little. Whatever the case, these are things you should be aware of.

Don't kill the messenger. No matter how harsh the criticism, accept it without holding a grudge against the person who offered it. The person who cares for you is the one who tells you when you have something stuck in your teeth or quietly slips you a breath mint when you really need it, not the person who keeps it a secret.

Collecting customer feedback

Customers see you as nobody else sees you — from the perspective of someone who's going to purchase something from you. They can usually purchase whatever they want from three or four other people, but they chose you (or didn't choose you) for some reason, and you should know why. And when you want to know why, ask.

Whether someone chooses to buy from you or not, try to find out what went into the purchase decision and how your sales presentation affected their decision. Avoid yes/no questions, such as, "Are you satisfied with the purchase?" Instead, keep your questions open-ended to encourage customers to identify areas for improvement. Following are some questions you may consider asking:

"What factors did you consider in making your purchase decision?"

"What made you decide to choose the product you chose?"

"What could I have done better?"

"Why did you choose to purchase from <the other company>?"

Customers who are also in sales often provide the most insightful feedback. Getting feedback from salespeople who buy your products is like getting coaching from a professional golfer instead of some weekend duffer. Seek feedback from those who are most qualified to give it.

Listening to the boss

The quality of feedback from a manager or supervisor can range from totally clueless to remarkably perceptive, so I'm not about to tell you to blindly follow your manager's advice. You should, however, listen to what your manager has to say . . . he could be right, particularly if you've heard the same thing from someone else.

Your manager's compensation is probably tied directly to the success of his sales force, so everyone's best interest is served through collaboration. Consider discussing your proposed personal improvement plan with your boss before your annual review and requesting your manager's support in achieving your goals.

Targeting Key Skills

People who achieve excellence in a particular field are those who act with a singularity of purpose. They focus on a few things, or perhaps just one, and pour all of their energy and resources into achieving whatever they decide is most important. In short, they know how to prioritize.

You can work on identifying and prioritizing goals or areas of improvement alone or with your partner. I find that spending some time alone makes the time I spend with my personal partner that much more productive. If you're having trouble getting started, however, skip to the following section, "Teaming Up with Your Personal Partner," and find a partner first.

In Chapter 3, I lead you through the process of listing your goals, prioritizing, and then drawing up a plan to achieve those goals. You can use those same strategies to target the sales skills you want to work on first, but the personal partnering process prescribes a slightly more specific approach:

1. **List 100 (or so) sales skills you would like to sharpen.** List as many as you can think of.

2. **Underline the top seven skills you feel are most valuable and in need of development.** If you had only a month to significantly boost sales, which seven skills do you feel as though you would need the most work on?

3. **Highlight one big thing on the list.** You already know that if you try to do too much, nothing gets done right, so pick one skill you want to focus on: your product knowledge, computer knowledge, overall business knowledge, competitive knowledge, listening skills, whatever. Pick only one!

4. **Pick a couple of easy things.** These are skills you can acquire or improve with much less effort, such as buying a Blackberry device, sending thank-you notes or birthday cards to customers, or jotting down a to-do list first thing every morning. You get the idea . . . pick easy things you can do that will have a positive impact on your selling skills. Achieving small goals keeps you engaged in the change process.

5. **Write it down.** If you don't write it down, it doesn't get done, so develop a plan and write it down. Chapter 3 discusses planning in greater detail. Just make sure that your personal partnering plan is SMART:

   • **S**pecific: Provide enough detail to explain how the efforts will culminate in the desired change.

   • **M**easurable: Include intermittent goals, so you can track progress.

   • **A**ctionable: Specify tasks you're going to accomplish and the steps required to complete those tasks.

   • **R**ealistic: Set realistic objectives, to avoid frustration and disappointment.

   • **T**imed: Set deadlines for accomplishing each task and achieving the planned objective.

Balance is key to long-term success, so when you're prioritizing your goals, make sure they include your personal goals, as well. If you achieve your professional goals without achieving your personal goals, or vice versa, you're likely to be disappointed overall, which is a sign that you're not truly successful. I could never have achieved the success I've experienced without having a supportive family and a rewarding personal life. Balance enables you to achieve your full potential in all areas of your life.

Teaming Up with Your Personal Partner

Personal partnering takes more than simply connecting with someone you know, making a few promises, and then going your separate ways to pursue your dreams. It requires that you work closely together, support one another, and meet regularly to track progress and make any necessary adjustments. You need to find a compatible partner, share your priorities and your plan, set down the rules, and then team up to execute your plans.

The following sections show you how to locate a suitable partner and launch your partnership in the right direction.

Personal partnering with my brother

One of my earliest personal partners was my brother, David W. Roberts. We worked in real estate together in Detroit, and he later moved down to Florida. We made great partners, because we were both highly motivated and committed to one another's success, and we shared common interests and experiences, particularly in our professional lives — real estate. Having someone who understood the business and had experienced its ups and downs was a real plus.

Whenever we met, we discussed the books we were reading, the marketing ideas we were working on, strategies we tried that failed and those that worked, and the goals we had. We didn't share the exact, same goals, but we supported one another. Each meeting was an occasion for growth and development, and we have each managed to achieve much more as a result.

David is now the most successful real estate agent in all of Florida and possibly in the nation. His sales exceeded $200 million dollars last year. David has also achieved success as my personal partner, encouraging and supporting me to achieve higher and higher levels of success than I could ever have achieved without him.

Look for opportunities to develop productive partnerships in your own life. You may find the perfect partner in a colleague, friend, neighbor, sibling, or parent. The perfect partner could just be the next person you meet.

Finding a good match

Personal partnering is effective with just about any two or three people who are dedicated to one another's success, but it works much better when you share common interests and goals. Teaming up with someone in sales, who is probably more aware of what you're trying to accomplish and the challenges you're facing, is likely to be more productive than dealing with someone who just doesn't get it.

When you're in the market for a personal partner, look for someone who fits the following profile:

- ✔ A salesperson, ideally in the same or a related industry and with a skill set comparable or superior to yours

- ✔ A goal setter who shares the goal of improving her skills and who would like to see you become more successful

- ✔ A person you respect and who respects you

- ✔ A person you like and who likes you

- ✔ A person already with a plan or a willingness to develop such a plan

- ✔ An honest individual who won't pull punches

Some of the most productive partnerships arise when partners have complementary skill set or resources. Star Power CEO Howard Brinton partners with Top Producing Agents (top-selling real estate agents). He acquires their knowledge and shares it with the industry. The top producers get more recognition and more referrals, and they become members of a community. When you and your partner review one another's lists, look for opportunities to barter one another's skills and resources.

As you gain success, more people are going to seek you out to establish partnerships. Be selective. Partnerships can end up becoming very lopsided. Make sure you're partnering with someone who has something of value to bring to the table.

When choosing a personal partner, avoid the following:

- ✔ **Clients or customers:** Although you may have a productive client/server relationship, adding a personal partnership could strain the relationship, mixing personal matters with business.

- ✔ **Competing coworkers:** Internal competition in sales teams can often create an environment in which personal partnering is not conducive. If you find yourself in a situation such as this, consider looking for a partner who sells in another district or region or for different company altogether.

Although your partner should have a plan for improvement, you don't necessarily need to be working toward the same objective. What you're striving for can be totally different. What's important is that you and your partner support one another in your efforts to improve. And you can do this in either of two ways — through collaborative or cooperative partnering:

- ✔ **Collaborative partnering:** In a collaborative effort, partners share a common goal. This is the most common arrangement for coworkers who are striving to achieve a common goal, such as host an event, build a Web site, or attend a conference together.

 Working collaboratively does not necessarily mean that you and your partner are performing the same tasks. If you're attending a conference together, for example, you may split up to maximize your networking opportunities and attend different training sessions. If you're hosting a promotional event, one of you may be working on invitations, while another is lining up a caterer, and a third partner is developing marketing materials.

- ✔ **Cooperative partnering:** With cooperative partnering, partners don't share a common goal. Each partner is free to pursue her own goals but is still accountable to her partner, and partners must encourage and support one another in their individual pursuits.

Sharing your priorities and plan

Sharing your priorities and your plan with your partner is the unveiling of your vision for future success. Assuming you're both passionate about the journey you're embarking on and believe in the plan you're sharing with your personal partner, your first meeting is likely to be positive and brimming with energy.

As you review one another's plans, ask yourself and each other questions designed to flesh out the plan and make it more concrete, such as the following:

- ✔ Why is this so important to me?
- ✔ What will happen if I don't accomplish this?
- ✔ How will I know when I've met my goal?
- ✔ Who else, if anyone, needs to be involved?
- ✔ How are we going to celebrate after we both achieve our goals? As an incentive to support one another, you celebrate only after you've *both* achieved your goals. See "Celebrating your success," later in this chapter, for details.

The idea here is to support and hold each other accountable to make the planned improvements. Examine each other's plan in as much detail as necessary and ask additional questions to clarify key points. This feedback is essential in both finalizing the plan and communicating it to your partner.

Setting the ground rules

Although you can certainly formalize your personal partnering agreement by drawing up a contract and signing it, you can forgo the formalities and take a more casual approach, but you should always schedule a follow-up meeting and have a plan for tracking one another's progress. Specifically, you and your partner should come to an agreement that lays out the following ground rules:

- ✔ Frequency of follow-up contacts
- ✔ Method of following up: in person, via phone, email
- ✔ Guidelines for judging success
- ✔ Rewards for achieving stated goals
- ✔ Consequences for not achieving stated goals
- ✔ The support role that each person must fill

For details about keeping in touch and providing the necessary support, check out the next section, "Keeping each other on track."

Support and encourage one other's growth. Don't criticize or ridicule. You can't force your partner to implement her plan. Your role is part cheerleader, part taskmaster, and part facilitator. Your partner's desire to achieve her goals and to honor her commitment to you and to herself should be motivation enough to keep her on track.

Keeping each other on track

Personal partnering is effective only if you and your partner remain in contact, communicate clearly, provide the necessary encouragement and support, and hold one another accountable. In the following sections, I step you through the process of staying in touch and keeping one another on track.

What happens between you and your partner stays between you and your partner. Sharing goals requires a certain level of intimacy and trust and may reveal some vulnerabilities. Discuss this issue with your partner and commit to communicate in confidence. Don't fall into the common trap of being overly positive and constantly patting each other on the back. I tend to gravitate toward the source of compliments, so I've surrounded myself with people who don't hesitate to tell the truth — my wife, Kathleen; my handler, Lois; and my virtual assistant, Kandra.

Tracking progress

Staying on course is a lot easier than getting back on course after a long detour, and the best way to stay on course is to follow up with your partner frequently, particularly early on. You can follow up with actual face-to-face sessions, via telephone calls, through e-mails or instant messaging, or through whatever other communication channels you have available.

Follow-up schedules vary, depending on your and your partner's preferences, whether you're in the initial stages of executing your plans, and the specific tasks that your plans entail. If you plan on making one extra sales call per day, for example, your partner may check your progress daily for the first week, once a week for the next month, and then monthly for the rest of the year. If your objective were to average 30 lead-generating phone calls per month, you may consider scheduling feedback sessions on a weekly basis for the first month then monthly after that.

Time your feedback sessions to accommodate both your plan and your partner's plan. The goal is for both of you to succeed.

Providing BACKUP

Throughout the personal partnering process, both you and your partner need to support and encourage each other by offering BACKUP:

Be empathetic towards each other

Actively listen to one another

Constantly focus on the other's goals

Keenly watch for non-verbal signals

Understand . . . you may not know everything

Pursue the other's thoughts and feelings

Collaborative competition

When you're teaming up with a colleague to achieve a goal, collaborative competition can keep you both on track. Let's say for example, that you and your partner share the goal of making ten additional cold calls per month. You agree to keep each other posted of your weekly progress. After three weeks, you both observe the following pattern:

Week 1 Extra Cold Calls: You 3, Partner 1

Week 2 Extra Cold Calls: You 3, Partner 0

Week 3 Extra Cold Calls: You 2, Partner 2

By the end of the third week, you have eight new cold calls to your partner's 3. Your partner, who happens to be committed to your mutual success, can plainly see that she needs to get her booty in gear to meet her quota, and you realize that you need to offer some support. At this point, you may want to give your partner a call and offer some tips on how you go about generating cold calls.

Sharpening your listening skills

Listening to your partner isn't like listening to background music. Give your partner your full, undivided attention. Here are some tips for being a more active listener:

- ✔ **Create a positive environment.** Turn off cell phones and get away from external distractions as much as possible.

- ✔ **Ask first.** By asking your partner to go first, you show that you're genuinely interested in what they have to say, and it elicits the same courtesy from your partner.

- ✔ **Take brief notes.** Just jot down key points and any questions you have.

- ✔ **Listen attentively.** Sit with your body relaxed and facing your partner and establish eye contact.

- ✔ **Communicate nonverbally, too.** Use appropriate facial expressions to indicate that you're listening and hearing what your partner is saying. Be careful not to overdo it.

- ✔ **Ask probing questions.** Open-ended questions elicit more thought and deeper connection within the discussion. They also reveal that you're interested in hearing more.

The ability to ask intelligent questions and process what the other person has to say are critical sales skills. Use your feedback sessions with your partner to practice these skills. Chapter 6 offers additional tips on asking your customers questions.

Reviewing, celebrating, and recycling

Party time! When your relationship with your partner culminates in some level of mutual success, it's time to review your overall performance, celebrate, and draw up plans to build on that success. The following sections show you how to work on your endgame and enjoy the fruits of your labor.

Reviewing your overall performance

As you execute your plans, you have many opportunities to review your progress, and when you're about to wrap it all up, you have one final opportunity to review your overall performance. At this stage, you and your partner should sit down and run through the following questions:

- ✔ Did my objectives have enough stretch?

- ✔ Was I fully engaged in this change process?

- ✔ Did we meet our goals?

- ✔ What are some other self improvements I can make?

✔ Could I have been more helpful to my partner?

✔ How helpful was the personal partnering process?

Take a few moments together and discuss your responses with your partner. Try to quantify the results in numbers. Has this experience resulted in a boost in sales volume? Has it increased gross sales or decreased expenses? Has it improved your overall job satisfaction?

Building on past success

After you've wrapped up your review, jump back to the beginning of this chapter and launch a new improvement plan right away. The success of your previous plan and the positive energy that flows from that success is just the momentum required to make self-improvement a habit rather than a one-time event.

Share personal partnering with your friends and family. Parents can partner with their children to live healthier, more fulfilling lives. Couples can partner to achieve their financial goals. Friends can partner to diet and exercise or save up for a fun trip. Personal partnering is designed to make all aspects of your life more enjoyable and rewarding.

Celebrating your success

Okay, here's the fun part. During the planning phase, you and your partner must plan for at least one victory celebration to take place when you both achieve your goals. Following are some suggestions:

✔ Dinner at a fine restaurant

✔ Trip to the spa

✔ Weekend fishing trip

✔ Day at the races

✔ Shopping spree

Team up with your partner to plan a celebration suitable for the success you've both achieved, and don't worry too much about the expense — your future success will more than pay for it.

Chapter 8

Embracing Change as a Growth Strategy

In This Chapter

▶ Adjusting to changes in the way customers shop

▶ Tuning in to what's happening in your industry

▶ Taking the lead to improve products and service

▶ Shifting your strategy to seize fresh opportunities

The old saying, "The only constant is change," has never been more true. The rate of change is accelerating at a phenomenal rate of speed, fueled primarily by technology but also by the age of ideas and information. Each day delivers innovations in products and services, how they're marketed, where they're sold, how they're paid for, and how they're used. Changes in technology, society, politics, and other areas have revolutionized everything from what we eat and where we eat it to how we elect our political representatives. These same changes have probably already influenced the way you sell.

When change occurs, you essentially have three options: resist it, accept it, or seize it. Resisting a positive change typically results in falling victim to it. As soon as your competitors implement the change, you lose ground. Accepting the change keeps you in the running. Seizing the change and making it work to your advantage enables you to reap its full benefits and grow both personally and professionally.

In this chapter, I encourage you to embrace change as a growth strategy. I show you various ways to keep up on changes in your industry and changes outside your industry that affect the way customers shop for products and services. With the information in this chapter and the right attitude, you're well positioned to ride the next big wave of change to the shores of success.

Working On Your Business

Capitalizing on change often hinges on how well prepared you are when change and its twin sibling, opportunity, come your way, but many salespeople are so busy working *in* their business that they forget to work *on* their business. They're too busy trying to earn a living or make a sale and earn that next commission that they don't invest the time required to make their business more successful. You have to think, anticipate change, plan ahead.

Joseph Kennedy Senior purchased thousands of acres of land surrounding the oil fields of his days. Everyone knew that there was oil on the land, but they thought it was too deep for the oil rigs of the day. He bought it up for cents on the dollar because everyone else saw it as worthless. Joe Kennedy believed that American ingenuity would eventually produce an oil drill that could dig deep enough to tap into those fields. Obviously he was right.

You need to develop the same foresight and belief in the future that Joe Kennedy exhibited with his investments in those oil fields. Be willing to take a risk. Otherwise, you will spend your entire life scrambling for the next sale. Get involved with the industry leaders, so you know what's coming around the bend and can remain on the leading, bleeding edge.

Keeping an Eye on How Customers Buy

Top producing salespeople seem to have a knack for staying one step ahead of their customers. When retail shoppers started flocking to the Internet, the most successful retailers were already there. The next tier of successful retailers got there in a hurry. The few who resisted the change are still suffering the consequences, if they're not already out of business.

Of course, not every fad turns into a trend and eventually becomes tradition. Some fads simply fade. Remaining on top, however, requires that you tune yourself in to your customers' needs and how they research and ultimately purchase the products and services you sell. Use the following sections to get yourself geared up for changes in the ways that your customers find and buy your products and services.

Getting a handle on the basics

Effective marketing and selling requires a coordinated effort that communicates to the buyer throughout the entire purchase-decision cycle. As explained in Chapter 6, a buyer typically takes the following four steps when deciding to purchase a product or service:

1. **Identify a problem or need.**

2. **Search for products or services.**

3. **Compare prices.**

4. **Measure the risk of purchasing or not purchasing.**

These steps rarely occur in a single place over a set period of time. A consumer may view a television commercial for toothpaste, for example, research different brands of toothpaste on the Internet, and then compare prices and other products at the grocery or pharmacy before ultimately deciding to purchase a specific product.

Asking the right questions

To create an effective selling strategy, you need to identify the various ways that your customers arrive at a purchase decision and then develop a well-coordinated marketing and selling strategy that communicates your message to the customer at every step in the decision-making process. To get started, answer the following questions:

- ✔ **Where is my customer likely to first discover the problem or need?** Pharmaceutical companies market in doctors' offices and medical facilities where customers are likely to hear first about a problem. They also market on television and magazines to people who may have been diagnosed but are unaware of new treatment options. In some cases, you may be the person who first reveals the customer's problem or need.

- ✔ **Where is my customer likely to search for additional information?** The world is packed with resources for assisting people with their purchase decisions — magazine articles, Web sites, product comparison charts, store clerks, and so on. Identify the top sources that customers turn to when making a purchase decision, and make sure you have some input in what the sources say about your products and services.

- ✔ **Where can my customer go to check prices?** You should have a pretty clear idea of what your competition is charging and what they're offering at that price, but you should also know where your customers go to check prices. Do they compare prices online or at the store? Do they usually just ask you? Know where they're going to check prices and make sure your prices are included. If you're charging a little more, explain why. If you offer something extra, say so.

✔ **When customers have doubts about purchasing or not purchasing the product, where can they find assistance in resolving those doubts?** The final stages of the purchase decision are critical, and you want to be there when the customer is wringing her hands. Unfortunately, this is the time in major purchase decisions when friends and relatives commonly get involved and raise the prospective buyer's level of doubt. Keeping in touch with the customer during this time is key to closing the sale. Contacting the customer via phone or e-mail is often best, but if your customers commonly seek reassurance elsewhere, find out where and establish a presence there, if possible.

Following the Sears lead

The story of the Sears, Roebuck & Company provides a perfect example of how a company managed to make successful transitions to adapt to its customers' changing shopping habits.

Sears started out as a mail-order catalog company in the early 1890s, when Richard Sears decided to launch his own mail-order company, selling mostly watches and jewelry. At the time, most people in the United States (38 states at the time), were shopping at local general stores and paying steep prices for merchandise. Sears figured he could compete with these stores nationally without having to set up his own stores all across the nation.

In 1893, Sears met Alva Roebuck and they teamed up to establish Sears, Roebuck & Company. By 1894, they had a 322-page catalog and were selling a wide selection of merchandise, including bicycles, sewing machines, and sporting goods. By 1908, Sears was even selling mail-order homes — complete kits for building your own home. They actually sold over 100,000 homes by 1940, when they stopped selling the kits.

In 1925, Sears opened its first department store. Ironically, Sears started as a mail-order catalog store to compete with local stores and was now opening local stores of its own! Marketing itself to America as the working man's place to shop, Sears department stores became hugely successful.

After many years of expansion and diversification, Sears hit some hard times in the 1980s and '90s and nearly closed under bankruptcy. Everyone was migrating from shopping at department stores to shopping in specialty stores. This was the era of the gourmet of products.

In 1993, Sears started to turn it around. They realized that they were known primarily for their quality Craftsman tools and that people were beginning to forget about all of the other merchandise they carried, including kitchen appliances, jewelry, and apparel. To attract the customers they lost, Sears launched one of its most successful ad campaigns ever, inviting customers to "Come see the softer side of Sears."

In 2004, Ty Pennington joined forces with Sears, adding his flair for style and design. Pennington and Sears leveraged the power of the multimedia marketplace and tapped into the popularity of reality TV with the show *Extreme Home Makeover*. With more and more women becoming do-it-yourselfers and the engaging personality of Ty Pennington, Sears was again able to increase its market appeal, this time showing people shopping at Sears for products and using Craftsmen tools.

By remaining sensitive to the way its customers were shopping and even where they were being introduced to new products and brands, Sears was able to stage a comeback in a very competitive retail market.

Staying on top of changes

The way customers buy changes over time. Twenty years ago, nobody would ever have considered purchasing beer through the mail, but thousands of beer lovers are now beer-of-the-month subscribers who can go online to select the brands they want to try. Home buyers are spending more time researching homes on the Internet. People may even discover a new product by purchasing some totally unrelated other product. You can stay on top of these changes by working ahead of your customer — check out the following ideas to get started:

- ✓ **Use references and testimonials.** References or testimonials from other customers can often assist you when customers have doubts about purchasing or not purchasing products or whether to purchase from you or someone else. The more you can do to establish trust throughout the purchase decision-making process, the less likely your customer is going to bail out at the last minute.

- ✓ **Just ask!** Don't hesitate to ask customers how they found out about you and how they ultimately decided to purchase a product from you. When you notice a change in the way your customers shop, be prepared to change the way you sell. Every change you make is an opportunity for growth . . . a way to sell more effectively and gain a competitive edge.

Changing the Way Customers Buy

As new ways of shopping and gathering information become available, customers naturally adapt to the methods and tools that make the purchase experience faster, easier, and more enjoyable. As a salesperson, you have to adapt to remain in sync with your customers, but this is a more reactive approach to dealing with the ever-changing market.

You can also choose to become more proactive by introducing new ways of marketing and selling your products that make the purchase experience faster, easier, and more enjoyable. In the following sections, I show you how to become a more innovative sales person and create a unique buying experience for your customers that can perhaps lead to additional revenue-generating opportunities.

Looking for cross-selling opportunities

In the late 1970s along with buying and selling real estate and owning my sports bar, I decided to open an arcade. A building next door to my bar became available. I bought it and installed video games. I was amazed at the number of kids who streamed into and out of the building . . . and at the number of quarters that rolled my way. I had quarters galore.

Business was so good that when another nearby building became available, right behind the arcade, we bought it and opened up a hand car wash. Parents could eat lunch at the sports bar and kids could hang out at the arcade while the family's car was being cleaned. We took $20 customers and turned them into $75-to-$100 customers simply by increasing the number of services we were offering. Now it's called *cross-selling*. Back then I was just trying to stay ahead.

Cross-selling provides you with a great opportunity to stay ahead of your customers just by anticipating needs that can coincide with what you already provide. To begin thinking of ways to add products or services to your current lineup, start by asking yourself these questions:

- ✔ **What other products and services do these customers enjoy that compliment what I already provide?** For instance, if you own a coffee shop, it makes sense to sell some baked goods alongside a cuppa joe.

- ✔ **What other products and services do customers enjoy that fits their needs while they're shopping with me or taking advantage of my services?** Okay, two words here: vending machines. When you're at a hotel, waiting for an oil change, or at work, you often overpay for cans of sodas or bags of chips because they're conveniently located nearby. Discover your own rendition of a vending machine.

- ✔ **How can I make my customers' experience with me easier?** Several grocery stores have carts that you can pile a entire gaggle of youngsters into, but the smart ones charge money for use of grocery carts that look like cars, animals, and other shapes that play cartoons while you shop. A grocery cart isn't a product or service you normally purchase at a grocery store, but some creative thinking by grocery store chains made the connection that people would not only pay for use of the cart but would also likely shop for more because the kids would be occupied — double bonus!

- ✔ **What products or services can enhance the use of the product or service my customer just bought or uses regularly?** An obvious example of this would be a warranty. Warranties cost a little extra but give customers the peace of mind that they have recourse if something goes wrong, but it also shows them you're confident in the workmanship of your product or service.

- ✔ **What services or products do my customers often use immediately after using my products or services?** A business that creates marketing materials for businesses within its area can add a courier service to its line of services, making some extra money every time those materials have to be delivered to local businesses . . . don't forget rush charges!

Identifying new selling methods

In Chapter 5, I tell a story of how I invented a new way of selling homes. Facing what I believed to be a major obstacle standing in the way of my goal to sell more than 300 homes in a single year, I was struck by the idea to show homes to more than one set of buyers at a time. My invention was a resounding success with many, although certainly not all, of my clients.

Innovations are often born from problems — as the saying goes, "Necessity is the mother of invention." Use some standard problem-solving strategies to start generating ideas:

1. **Jot down a list of problems that you believe are preventing you from reaching you sales goals.**

2. **Jot down a list of customer complaints and suggestions.** As I explain in Chapter 18, your customers' problems are your problems. Any problem is fair game, whether you think it's getting in the way of increased sales or not. You never know where your inspiration is going to come from.

3. **Arrange your list of problems in order from most serious to least serious, and then pick the top five.**

4. **Brainstorm solutions to the selected problems.**

5. **Pick the top solutions for each problem and begin to implement them.**

Far too many salespeople trip on the last step. They come up with brilliant ideas on how to make the purchase process easier and more enjoyable for their clients, and that's the end of it. Put your ideas into action.

 When you're trying to invent new ways to sell, think less about the end result (increased sales) and more about the buying experience. Ask yourself what you could possibly do to make the experience more valuable and memorable for your customer.

Identifying revenue-generating opportunities

New ways to sell don't have to cost you more money. Some innovations can actually save you time and money or even lead to additional revenue-generating opportunities.

You may notice several businesses that are actually two or more businesses combined. Auto supply stores, for example, often have a service department. They know that many prospective customers aren't qualified to work on their own cars. By adding a service department, they can sell more parts and supplies, and the parts and supplies store can refer more customers to the service department.

A few years ago, a major computer and appliance store added onsite computer technical support as one of its services. Management realized that customers often had problems with the computer equipment they purchased and were reluctant to bring the equipment in for service. By adding onsite technical support, which customers were willing to pay for, the store solved a major headache for customers while adding a second revenue stream.

 Don't give away valuable services unless you absolutely have to. If your customers are willing to pay a little extra for education, training, superior customer support, or any other services you can offer, use your ideas to generate additional revenue streams.

Prepping your customers for the coming changes

Your customers may not appreciate some of the changes you try to implement, especially if they're stuck in their old ways of doing business, but if the change you're promoting is truly better for your customers, it's a change worth fighting for, and the best time to fight is before the fight even starts.

Before implementing some radical change in the way customers shop or buy, get some buy-in:

- ✔ Float the idea past a few customers to see what they think. You may be able to improve on the idea.

- ✔ Take it for a test-drive. Don't unleash your idea on all of your customers at once. Test it on a select group of customers and work out the bugs first.

- ✔ Keep your customers posted. If you're not sure how your customers are going to react, prepare them in advance to avoid the shock. If you're sure that your customers are going to love it, a little shock can be a good thing.

Serving the savvy consumer

Real estate agents have relied on the MLS (Multiple Listing Service) for years. The MLS contains descriptions of all the properties listed through real estate agents. Buyer's agents can read through the listings to find homes that may appeal to their clients. Early in my career, we used thick MLS books . . weekly publications. They were supposed to be confidential, but most of the top agents bought several copies and passed them around to clients.

Spotting golden opportunities

When I was younger and first starting out in my real estate career, I found that first-time home buyers were a good match for me. I genuinely enjoyed showing them houses, teaching them the basics, and assisting them in overcoming all the obstacles to buying their first home.

I advertised in print, and those advertisements were fairly productive, but I needed a way to establish direct contact with first-time buyers. After wracking my brain for several months, I realized that the one thing first-time home buyers needed more than anything else was education. They needed to understand the process of buying a home and financing their purchase (qualifying for a mortgage loan).

I decided to hold a seminar for first-time home buyers called "How to Buy a Home with Little or No Money Down." I hosted a few, small seminars at first, to gauge people's interest, and I realized that I could go much bigger with it.

I contacted a local mortgage company, title company, and home inspection company to sponsor the event, and they even assisted me in recruiting people to fill the seats. I hired Ticketmaster to sell tickets. All of these companies lent support and credibility. I did press releases and contacted the media. I sent flyers to apartment complexes to encourage tenants to think about their future. The tickets sold for $29 in advance and $39 at the door. Over 1,000 people showed up to that seminar. I didn't make a boatload of money, but many of those attendees turned into future clients.

Next came "Boris," an MLS that distributed listings over the phone lines. It was sort of like a fax or teletype machine. You could request the information you wanted. The Internet followed, allowing agents or members to access the information. Now, just about anyone can go on the Internet, find homes for sale, and compare prices. Check out HurryHome.com to see exactly what I mean.

Today's consumer is a new breed. The average consumer is tech savvy, well-informed, and pretty good at tracking down information. To serve today's consumer, you'd better know your stuff. Phony sales pitches and fluff no longer work. Provide the information and resources your customer needs to make a well-informed purchase decision and back it up with impeccable customer service after the sale.

Tweaking Your Current Marketing and Sales Strategy

You can always achieve a higher level of success, but not if you stick with the status quo. Top producing salespeople are constantly tweaking their packaging, marketing, advertising, and sales presentations to experiment with what they hope are more productive methods. Even a subtle change can dramatically boost sales.

In the following sections, you discover how to ruthlessly evaluate your sales strategies and techniques, toss everything that's not working, and experiment with other strategies and techniques that hold more promise.

Although you may have to drop everything you're doing and change direction 180 degrees, give it careful consideration before moving forward. Changing course a couple degrees at a time can revolutionize the way you sell over the course of your career.

Keeping score: What works? What doesn't?

Refrigerator magnets. I tried those. So did every real estate agent I ever met. Real estate agents are still giving those away in the hopes that they gain a coveted high-profile spot on every refrigerator in the neighborhood. Unfortunately, I didn't see much of a lift in sales after passing out all those magnets. I tried the personalized pens, too, with similar results. Sometimes, I found myself using another real estate agent's pen to sign the papers for a house I sold.

Sales extinction exhibit

With all of the products and sales methods that have fallen by the wayside, you could almost start your own sales museum, complete with a huge extinction exhibit. Following are some of the items I would consider including:

- The door-to-door salesman . . . made extinct by the Home Shopping Network and the Internet. Who would have ever thought that you could tune into your TV to watch product demonstrations and or order products online and have them shipped right to your house?

- The milkman . . . made extinct by convenience stores and groceries and the proliferation of multicar households.

- Telemarketers . . . not extinct yet, but the national do-not-call list has certainly put a dent in the population.

- TV antenna installers . . . replaced by the cable guy and satellite dish installers.

- Eight-track tapes . . . replaced by cassettes.

- Cassettes . . . replaced by CDs.

- CDs . . . replaced by digital recordings and players.

Don't get added to the list. By riding the waves of change, you don't have to face extinction. In fact, you can evolve to usher in the era of a new species of salespeople.

When you're looking for ways to freshen up your marketing program, make one change at a time and keep score as much as possible to see what works and what doesn't. If you run a television commercial, check to see how much new business it generated. Was it worth the cost? If you try a direct mailing campaign, compare your sales figures before running the campaign against sales figures from the month you ran the campaign and the month following the campaign. Make sure you're getting your money's worth, and if you're not, then try something else.

Don't completely dismiss a new idea just because it didn't work the first time. A television commercial may fail for any number of reasons. Perhaps it wasn't aired at the right time or it was a lousy commercial. Gather some feedback and criticism, try to figure out why it didn't work, and then make some adjustments to improve it. If it still doesn't work after you've made the necessary changes, then consider dropping it.

Finding the "Why" behind Your Customer's "No"

Customers usually have a pretty good reason for walking away without purchasing a product, and you need to know what that reason is, particularly if the reason is due to something you said or did or didn't say or do. If a sale falls through and you don't understand why, start asking questions and doing a little soul searching:

- ✔ Consider asking the customer directly, "So I can do a better job in the future, may I ask why you chose someone else?" or "What could I have done differently to have earned your business?"

- ✔ Ask yourself whether you did something to scare off the customer. I have learned that some people are turned away by my energy level. I have had to ratchet it down a notch by mirroring my customers. For more about the mirroring technique, check out Chapter 6.

- ✔ Ask yourself whether your pace was too fast or too slow. I tend to go too fast, making it impossible for some customers to keep up with me.

Don't always assume that the customer's decision to buy from someone else is your fault. In my business, many times another agent would build up the seller's expectations and end up winning the client. This is called "buying the listing." I tell prospective clients that I would rather let them down today and sell their house tomorrow than dazzle them today and disappoint them the next by not being able to sell their home.

Personalities don't always mesh. I'm an aggressive salesperson, which some sellers don't like. They prefer someone who's a little calmer. I've had sellers back away from working with me and then call me back when the agent they chose wasn't aggressive enough. Don't beat yourself up just because a few customers don't appreciate your style . . . they may come back to you, and if they don't, you have another group of buyers who are probably going to love your style.

Leaving a proven product alone

If you're selling products that require constant updating, such as computers, software, or video games, your company has no choice but to constantly seek to improve those products. In some cases, however, the product is perfectly fine. If it has a proven track record, leave the product alone and try changing everything else. Frequently, a subtle adjustment in packaging, marketing, or even your sales presentation can transform a mediocre-selling product into a smash hit.

In 1957 Tang was first introduced in the USA and received a lukewarm welcome. Sales didn't really take off until 1972, when Apollo flights were associated with the product. The manufacturer changed the packaging by including a map of the moon on the label and ramped up its marketing. The product became a huge seller without a single change to the product itself.

Sometimes you have to be brutally honest when analyzing what works and what doesn't. Now is the time to call up the harshest critics and creative thinkers. Toss everything that doesn't work and replace it with something that holds more promise.

Capitalizing on Changes in the Industry

Nowadays, an entire industry can undergo a transformation that seems to happen overnight. Remember the video arcades of the early 1980s? As soon as game systems became readily available for homes, video arcades disappeared from the landscape. Satellite radio has made the task of selling radio advertising that much more difficult. Rising oil prices influence car-buying decisions. Rising or falling interest rates affect the housing market.

Sales visionaries

Industry leaders are often visionaries who demonstrate how to capitalize on changes in the industry. Here some stories of some of the visionaries I find most inspiring:

- Dave Liniger, founder of ReMax, envisioned a national brand for real estate agents. He began a program for training agents and was the first to create real estate conventions. His first convention attracted only 16 participants. Now, the conventions draw over 10,000.

- Walt Disney saw that the car would become more affordable to more families and the day would come when families would want to drive to a single vacation spot that would offer something for kids of all ages.

- Guthy-Renker envisioned a multimedia marketplace in which a coordinated marketing through TV, radio, the Internet, and direct marketing could transform individuals into brands that could drive sales of various products. Guthy-Renker also applied its multimedia marketplace idea to the real estate industry through Guthy-Renker Home, using a community building concept to generate target leads for real estate agents.

- Ralph J. Roberts, Comcast founder (no relation to Ralph R. Roberts), popularized cable television. In 1963, Roberts purchased a 1,200-subscriber cable television system in Tupelo, Mississippi, that he eventually grew into the largest cable television company in the country, Comcast Corporation, employing 87,000 people and serving 24 million customers.

Consider adding your own name to this list of visionaries. You may think you're just in sales and that you're not a corporate mogul like these folks, but when you think about it, these people were selling, just like you. As they were selling and trying to make a living, they just happened to notice an opportunity. Instead of simply daydreaming about it, they seized the opportunity and made it happen. You can, too.

Although you're often powerless to stem the tide of changes in the industry, you need to remain well-informed and sensitive to changes that may affect what you sell and the way you sell it. Keep your finger on the pulse of the industry and any factors outside the industry that may trigger changes:

- **Read widely.** Changes in politics, the economy, or related businesses can affect your industry. In addition, reading widely can often open your mind to new ideas that can boost sales.

- **Read industry publications.** Subscribe to at least one trade publication, and then read it. All too often, I see people subscribe to journals or magazines and then just stack them in the waiting room.

- ✔ **Attend conferences.** When you want to hear the buzz, attend conferences and network with your peers. You can often spot upcoming trends long before they appear in the trade publications.

- ✔ **Research on the Internet.** Visit the Web sites of the industry leaders and look for clues as to what's coming around the bend. If they have a newsletter, subscribe to it.

- ✔ **Stay connected.** Talk with others inside and outside of the industry. In addition to gathering valuable information, you often find that chatting it up with other professionals sparks creativity and innovation.

Chapter 9

Branding Yourself through Shameless Self-Promotion

In This Chapter

▶ Discovering your marketable assets

▶ Proving you're special . . . on paper

▶ Giving your marketing materials a uniform look

▶ Making a name on the Internet

▶ Grooming yourself to become a recognized expert

*T*ypical sales people target markets, customers, and clients. Top-producing salespeople become the target — they market themselves. They build a strong brand presence, so that prospective customers and clients seek them out whenever they become aware that they need the product or service the salesperson represents.

Whenever I speak to salespeople, I like to ask, "Can you close your eyes and visualize the president of the United States?" Of course, everyone can do that. I then ask, "What does your spouse look like? What do your parents look like? What does your dog or cat look like? What does your car look like?" Everyone can visualize these persons, animals, or things, because they know them intimately and see them on a regular basis. The images are tattooed on their brain cells. That's what you're shooting for when you market yourself. You want everyone in your area to know who you are and what you do, so when they think of a product or service you sell, your face pops up first in their minds.

By investing some time, talent, and energy into building a brand presence or persona, you become a much more efficient and effective salesperson. Prospective customers and clients call you. Cold calls become warm calls. And because you've already established trust, you no longer need to convince prospective customers and clients that you're trustworthy.

In this chapter, I lead you through the process of finding something unique about you that you can market, and show you how to log all of your assets on paper to simplify the process of marketing those assets. I then reveal several different ways you can market yourself to build a brand identity that your customers, past, present, and future, won't be able to forget.

Don't read this chapter unless your ready, willing, and able to handle hundreds of phone calls and e-mail messages every week. If you're not geared up to handle the workload, hire an assistant, as explained in Chapter 13, to take on some or all of the burden. Be prepared for some added perks, as well. Shameless self-promotion often results in getting you the best table and service at local restaurants, complimentary products and services, and even opportunities for intriguing projects that may or may not be related to what you're currently doing. Prepare to be pleasantly surprised.

Discovering the You in Unique

What is it about you that people will remember? What would you like them to remember about you? Whatever that something is, that's what you want to promote.

A real estate colleague of mine in Montgomery, Alabama, Sandra Nickel, is known far and wide as "The Hat Lady." She wears a distinctive hat wherever she goes. Her hat logo appears on her business card, all of her correspondence, and even on her Web site Invest in Montgomery, Alabama (www.investinmontgomeryalabama.com). Sandra has a solid team of real estate professionals who handle the daily business. She functions as the rainmaker, ensuring that the phones keep ringing and the Internet remains abuzz with the voices of interested buyers and sellers. She tells the story of Midtown and volunteers tirelessly to improve the community. In the process, the Hat Lady attracts a lot of attention . . . and a lot of business.

Whatever you choose to be known for, make sure it's something you can be comfortable with for your entire career. As long as Sandra wants to remain the Hat Lady, she has to wear a hat.

Another of my colleagues Michael Scott Karpovich, who's a member of the NSA (National Speaker's Association, Michigan Chapter), wears two different colored tennis shoes. At every meeting, I find myself checking to see whether he has them on, and sure enough, he always does. When people point it out to him, he says, "Yeah, that's funny, I have another pair just like them at home."

I've tried several different slogans and other attention-grabbers to set myself apart:

"You win with Ralph Roberts!"

"It's a wonderful day in the neighborhood." (Mr. Rodgers inspired.)

"Call Ralphie." My dads' name was Ralph, so when I was growing up, everyone called me Ralphie, and sometimes people still call me that.

"Big Sh't." My Aunt Louise used to call me and my 50 cousins "little sh'ts." I returned the favor by calling her "Big Sh't." When I bought my first boat, I christened it "Little Sh't." When people ask me what it means, I say "Little Shot," but when Aunt Louise came to our lake house for the first time and saw the boat, she knew exactly what it really meant, and I could see the alligator tears welling up in her eyes.

Some of what I do may appear more than a little kooky to people who are more reserved, and I'm certainly not recommending that you do exactly what I do. Find a way to promote yourself that fits with your personality. If, however, you're extremely shy, that's something you're going to have to overcome.

In real estate, agents love to add their pictures to everything. Some even go so far as including their wives, children, and dogs in their marketing mug shots. I've never been particularly fond of using family portraits for promotion. I avoid using family for several reasons, one of which is that I can't stand sharing the stage with them when my marketing campaign is supposed to be all about *me*. The other, more important reason is safety. I suggest keeping your spouse and children out of your marketing efforts.

Even my closest advisor, Lois Maljak has jumped on the branding bandwagon. When she steps in front of an audience, she introduces herself as Lois . . .

" . . . most people spell it L-o-u-i-s, which is pronounced *Lew*-iss, but my name is spelled L-o-i-s. To help you remember my name, there are two famous Lois's: One is the Lois in the Bible, Timothy's grandmother who led Timothy to faith. The other famous Lois is . . ."

And the audience replies in unison, "Lois Lane!"

Lois replies, "Exactly! Lois Lane is right. And who does Lois Lane hang out with?

The audience yells, "Superman!"

And Lois says "Exactly! I would like to introduce you to Ralph Roberts!"

When Lois is finished, nobody in the audience could possibly forget her name. She's drilled it into their heads, complete with the proper spelling.

Pick something you want to be known for. This could be a hat, tie, fancy shoes, the car you drive, a childhood nickname, a physical trait, or anything else on which you can focus your personal marketing campaign on promoting. For me, it's the Big Nail, as explained in the following sidebar.

Shameless self-promotion stresses "self." Sure, you may put your company logo and name on your business card and correspondence, but You, Inc. is ultimately the company you're promoting. You, Inc. is the central focus of your marketing campaign.

Discovering my uniqueness in a really big nail

In 2003, I discovered my uniqueness on eBay, in the form of an 11-foot high, 500-pound nail. But this was no ordinary nail. This was the Big Nail, part of a very recognizable roadside attraction for anyone living in the Detroit metropolitan area, where I did business.

For nearly a half century, visitors and locals driving into Detroit, Michigan, from the Metro Airport have been welcomed by one of Motor City's most recognized symbols: the 80-foot-tall Uniroyal tire. First created as a Ferris wheel attraction for the 1964/1965 New York's World's Fair, the landmark's appearance had evolved to reflect over 40 years worth of changes in tire technology and style and stood as an important symbol of Uniroyal's long heritage in the metro-Detroit area

The Giant Tire has towered alongside Interstate 94 since 1965. In 1998, to demonstrate how their NailGard self-sealing passenger tire worked, Uniroyal placed an 11-foot high, 500-pound nail into the tread of the Giant Tire.

In the fall of 2003, as part of a $1,000,000 renovation to the 80-foot tire, Michelin, Uniroyal's parent company, removed the Big Nail from the tire and donated it to the city of Allen Park, Michigan. The City of Allen Park put the Big Nail up for auction on eBay, and a short time later, I placed the winning bid, and purchased the Big Nail for $3,000. The proceeds from the sale helped fund the Allen Park Historical Society's programs and facilities.

I bought the Big Nail simply because I wanted it, but it has turned out to be the perfect branding tool for me and my business. After all, nails build houses. My father was a builder. In the Oxford dictionary, "nail" means "to join together." I love joining together with my customers to join them with their dream homes. I love joining together with my community and with worthy charities to improve the world.

The Big Nail appears on my business card, letterhead, and Web site, and on the side of my Hummer, which is affectionately known as the Nail Mobile or "The Hammer." The Big Nail has taken on a life of its own as a retired cultural icon, making guest appearances at charity fundraisers, community parades, and other events, and has become so popular that she has her own assistant just to keep up with bookings and appearance coordination.

One of the Big Nail's most memorable retirement appearances was in a parade celebrating the Detroit Pistons' winning the 2004 NBA championship. Thomas "Hit Man" Hearns, another Detroit icon, rode with the Big Nail alongside of "the Nail Man" . . . that's me.

More serious salespeople may have scoffed at the idea of building a brand around something as silly as an oversized nail, but the Big Nail worked and continues to work for me (see my examples in the figure). Find your uniqueness, your Big Nail, and start marketing it.

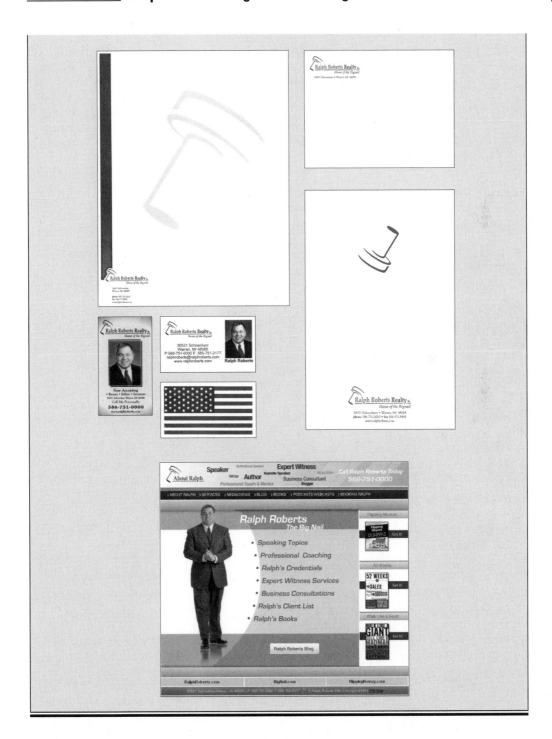

Changing Your Name?

Unique is good, but if your name is so unique that people can't pronounce it or so common that you sound just like any other Tom, Dick, or Harry, then you may want to consider changing it. To attain celebrity status in any field, you often have to think and act like a celebrity, and celebrities often change their names to make themselves more memorable. Here are some of the more famous people have opted for simpler, snappier names:

Donald James Yamcy became Don Adams

Tim Allen Dick changed his name to Tim Allen

Marion Michael Morrison chose to be known as John Wayne

Madonna Louise Veronica Ciccone shortened her name to Madonna

Donald Trump often goes by simply The Donald

 You certainly don't have to change your name to make your name into a brand, but some names are certainly easier than others. If your birth name poses too great of a challenge, you may want to consider using something that others are going to have an easier time remembering.

Crafting a Unique Selling Proposition (USP)

Why should your customers do business with you instead of one of your competitors? That's the question that your Unique Selling Proposition or Unique Selling Point (USP) needs to answer. Think of a USP as a sort of resume or curriculum vitae that's focused less on your knowledge, experience, and accomplishments and more on how your customers can benefit from your knowledge, experience, and accomplishments.

You may or may not decide to share your USP with prospective customers, but having a USP, in writing, serves three important purposes:

✔ Enables you to spot weak areas where you can improve

✔ Reminds you of the value you deliver to customers, so you can remind them of it

✔ Provides you with written content that you can use in other marketing materials you develop

---

U-S-... what?

Shortly after *Flipping Houses For Dummies* hit the shelves, someone at Guthy-Renker called to ask if I would be willing to develop some real estate content for a new Internet-based resource for real estate agents. Early in our discussions, my contact at Guthy-Renker Home said he could help get connected with some industry leaders, and he suggested that I put together a USP.

Prior to meeting with the people at Guthy-Renker Home, I had never even heard of a USP, but after my contact had mentioned it, "Create a USP" jumped to the top of my to-do list, and that was the first project I launched after returning home. As soon as I had my USP in hand, I quickly realized what a valuable marketing tool it really was. It has opened all sorts of doors for me since.

In the following sections, I show you how to get started on your USP, flesh it out with additional details, and then use it effectively in your marketing and sales campaigns.

 Check out my USP at www.AboutRalph.com. It may be a little on the long side, but it demonstrates how to structure and word a USP in a way that focuses more on benefits and solutions and less on features.

Moving from features to benefits to solutions

 Your USP is not about you, it's about what you can do for your customers that your competitors cannot or will not do. In your USP, you're selling yourself, but keep in mind that when you're selling anything, you're always selling to a customer. You need to prove to your customer that nobody can serve their needs better than you.

To focus your USP on addressing your customers' needs and providing solutions, begin connecting what you have to offer (features) to your customers' needs to develop a list of benefit statements, and then apply those benefit statements to the solutions that you offer. The following steps show you how:

1. **Divide a sheet of paper into two columns — what you have to offer on the left, and your customers' needs on the right.**

2. **In the left column, list your education, experience, skills, and anything else you have to offer.**

3. **In the column on the right, list your customers' needs.**

4. **Draw lines to connect each customer need with what you offer that best serves that need.**

5. **Write at least one benefit statement for each skill-need combination that expresses how you are uniquely qualified to serve the customer's need.** If, for example, you're a certified computer technician, you're selling computer equipment, and your customers often need technical support, one of your benefit statements may be, "Specialized training in computer service and repair make me uniquely qualified to answer any questions you may have regarding the setup and upgrading of your computer."

6. **Group related benefit statements into logical categories.** These categories should represent solutions to common problems that you solve for your customers.

After completing this exercise, you should have the content you need to actually put together your USP, as explained in the following section.

Crafting your personal-professional USP

Your USP is essentially *Your Name For Dummies*. Consider it a brochure that lays out exactly why your customer would want to buy from you rather than from any other salesperson on the planet. Your USP should include the following elements:

- ✔ **Your name:** You're marketing yourself, so your name is the title of your USP.

- ✔ **Your photo:** Obtain a professional photograph that has you looking professional. This is the image that you want to tattoo on your customers' brain cells.

- ✔ **A one-line summary of your USP:** This is a single phrase or sentence that describes your unique selling point.

- ✔ **Section headings:** Use plenty of headings to break down the material into easily digestible chunks.

- ✔ **Detailed information:** Go easy on the paragraphs, opting for lists, wherever possible, but provide plenty of detail under each heading, so you're reader is fully informed.

Include testimonials from other customers or clients, if you have testimonials. Including positive statements from other customers is a big plus, just be sure to obtain written permissions from your clients before quoting them.

Implementing your USP in marketing and sales

I created my USP when Guthy-Renker requested it. I sent the entire 22-page document in its full glory. I rarely use the whole USP in my marketing materials, but I constantly find myself copying and pasting paragraphs and lists when I'm creating proposals and presentations. I take the most pertinent information, paste it where needed, and then make a few modifications, if necessary, to blend it in with the other material.

You can also use your USP to remind yourself before sales calls and presentations exactly what you offer your customers that nobody else in your area can or will offer. Never forget your USP, and never let your customers forget it, either. That's why they buy from you.

Designing a Consistent Look and Feel

Some of the most creative salespeople I've met have the toughest time creating a brand presence. They get bored with having everything look the same. Their instinct tells them to use a completely different design for their business card, stationery, Web site, brochures, and so on. When creating a brand presence, however, consistency is exactly what you want. (For more about creating a brand presence, check out *Branding For Dummies* by Bill Chiaravalle and Barbara Findlay Schenck.)

Giving all of your marketing materials a unique look would be like dressing up in a different disguise every day of your life — your customers wouldn't be able to recognize you. To create a strong brand presence, use the same basic design, colors, fonts, and logo on all of your marketing materials, including the following:

- ✔ Business card
- ✔ Stationery
- ✔ Brochures
- ✔ Pamphlets
- ✔ Newsletters
- ✔ Press releases
- ✔ Websites
- ✔ Blogs

Tossing my business cards

A lot of salespeople I know treat their business cards like hundred dollar bills. They stick them in their wallets or purses and hand them out only to the people they regard as top candidates.

I treat my business cards more like rice at a wedding. I'll go to a sporting event, and when the crowd goes wild, I lean over the railing and toss a handful of business cards up in the air. Some people actually pick them up, stick them in their purses or wallets, and then call me when they're ready to buy or sell a house. I love when I ask someone, "So, how did you hear about me?" and they reply, "I caught your card flying through the air at the Pistons game."

Carry a stack of business cards with you wherever you go. Leave them on the counter at the local diner. Tack them up on the message board at your local grocery store. Hand them out to everyone you meet.

Unless you're a talented designer, don't trust your instincts. Hire a professional. Find some marketing materials you like and contact the company that sent them out to find out who did the design. Or, head down to your local full-service print shop and ask whether they know of any designers. After you settle on a design, color scheme, font, and logo, get some feedback from your better, honest customers before forging ahead. Once you pick a design, you should stick with it, so make sure you're going to be happy with it three or four years from now.

You're not a shameless self-promoter if you don't have a billboard. If you sell to the general public, get your photo pasted on a billboard along with a short, catchy slogan and your phone number, email address, and Web site address. Whenever I mention billboards, at least a few salespeople object on the grounds that they "don't want to scare customers away." Those who object usually have a low self-esteem. My response is this: "What do you want to do, scare them when they meet you for the first time? I believe you should give them fair warning." Thousands of people are likely to drive past the billboard daily, and most of them are likely to take notice. If you're in corporate sales, the billboard idea may not be right for you, but you should still be looking for other opportunities to get your face in front of prospective clients — perhaps by taking out an ad in an industry publication.

Establishing Brand Presence on the Internet

Your marketing materials may work great to establish a brand presence in the real world, but you also need to consider that other-world — the Internet. With more and more people shopping on the Web or at least seeking out additional product information on the Web, establishing a brand presence on the Internet is essential.

Establishing a presence on the Internet isn't quite as effective in building customer trust as having a brick-and-mortar business with a phone number and mailing address. The stronger your presence on the Internet, however, the more likely your customers are going to feel as though they're dealing with a legitimate business.

In Chapter 16, I show you how to take advantage of the multimedia marketplace and provide additional details on how to create a your own website and blog. Here's a checklist of what's required to build a brand presence on the Internet:

- ✔ **Register your own domain name.** (A domain name is a text-based address of a computer on the Internet. In `www.dummies.com`, `dummies.com` is the domain name. The domain name is also the part of an email address that comes after the @ sign.) The reason you want your own identifiable domain name is the same reason you want your own telephone number and address — it tells your customers exactly where to find you. If you start selling for another company, having a unique domain name enables your customers to follow.

- ✔ **Build your own Web site.** Well, you don't actually have to build it yourself. You can hire someone to do it, but you really should have your own website with a design that's consistent with the look and feel of your other marketing materials.

- ✔ **Build and maintain your own blog.** Whether or not you have a Web site, a blog enables you to join the blogging community. Establishing relationships in a community (online or off) is key to long-term sales success. If you're not blogging, start now. For more about blogging to sell, see Chapter 17. For a lot more about blogging in general, check out *Blogging For Dummies* by Brad Hill and *Buzz Marketing with Blogs For Dummies* by Susannah Gardner .

When posting material on you blog or on other online gathering places, such as MySpace and Active Rain, remain professional. I see young people posting material that they think is cool at the time, and they fail to realize that what they say is going to follow them for the rest of their lives. The same is true for adults, especially people who are in business. Before posting a message on your site, think about how that message reflects on you as a person and how it may affect the perception that future customers may have of you.

- ✔ **Contribute to other online communities.** Even if you have your own blog, you should establish a presence in other online communities, including MySpace. Contribute to other peoples' blogs and answer questions posted in message boards. Where appropriate, you can mention your own Web site and blog to drive traffic from these other communities to your landing pads on the Web.

✔ **Publish an eNewsletter.** An eNewsletter, which you can distribute via email or by posting it on your Web site, enables you to contact your customers regularly with valuable information and promotions without seeming to be just another pushy salesperson.

✔ **Add a signature to your e-mail messages.** Every e-mail program has an option to add a signature to all outgoing messages. Include in your signature your name, contact information, and a list of your accreditations, titles, and Web sites. Here's the signature I use:

Ralph R. Roberts GRI CRS

"Official Spokesperson of Guthy-Renker Home"

Author of *Flipping Houses For Dummies*

30521 Schoenherr

Warren, MI 48088

Office: 586-751-0000

Fax: 586-582-1694

Lois Maljak: 810-533-3448

ralphroberts@ralphroberts.com

www.realtytracker.com Guthy-Renker Home

www.aboutralph.com Speaking/Coaching

www.ralphroberts.com Real Estate Site

www.kolleenroberts.com Tribute

www.flippingfrenzy.com Mortgage Fraud Site

www.bignail.com Branding

www.macombcountyvoice.com Community

www.getflipping.com Flipping Houses Site

Establishing a presence on the Internet is not a one-time deal. Don't simply set up a Web site and then leave it to stagnate. Unless you keep fresh content coming, people are going to stop visiting. If necessary, draw up a schedule to freshen the content regularly, at least once a week.

Boosting Your Street Cred

When you find someone who knows what she's talking about, your natural inclination is to seek out that person whenever you need assistance with something in her area of expertise. If you find an excellent restaurant server who knows everything on the menu and how it's prepared and is attentive to your needs, you want to sit at that server's table every time you eat at that restaurant. If a certain financial advisor is known as the most successful and trustworthy in your area, that's the person you want handling your money.

In real estate, I specialize in several areas, including foreclosures and real estate fraud. When people have questions or concerns related to either of these topics, they often seek me out. They know that I'm a recognized expert. Maybe they read a quote from me in a news article, heard me on the radio, saw me on the news, or heard me speak to a local group. Whatever the case, they know my face, they're aware that I know what I'm talking about, and they trust me long before they meet me in person for the first time.

Become an expert in your industry. You don't have to be an expert on everything, but be an expert on something. Then, get out there and prove to the world that you're the expert you say you are. In the following sections, I show you where to go to start establishing yourself as the resident expert.

When you're first getting started, you may have to actively seek out speaking gigs and other opportunities to prove yourself the expert. Once you get the ball rolling, however, you can pretty much stop looking, because people are going to seek you out. All you have to do at this point is make yourself available.

Speaking to local groups

Local groups, including church groups; philanthropic organizations, such as Kiwanis, Rotary, and the Lions club; the chamber of commerce; and schools are always on the lookout for speakers with expertise on a wide variety of topics.

Many of these groups begin their regular meetings with a 15- to 20-minute speech, and the meetings are often packed with community and business leaders. This gives you the opportunity to get your face and message in front of many of the decision makers without having to make a heavy-handed sales pitch. If you do meet with these people later in a sales situation, they already feel as though they know you, making your job that much easier.

In the following sections, I provide some tips on how to get your start as a local public speaker.

You don't have to speak on a business-related topic. You can talk about whatever interests you — a hobby, marriage, the challenges of raising teenagers. As long as you're engaging, entertaining, and have something to say, your speech is likely to be memorable.

Honing your public speaking skills

Many salespeople who are comfortable speaking to individuals and small groups are terrified of delivering a speech to a large group of people. You can get therapy for that — behavioral therapy or cognitive behavioral therapy (CBT). This type of therapy is effective in assisting people with overcoming all sorts of phobias, including the fear of flying and the fear of public speaking.

Another (less expensive) approach is to join Toastmasters, an international club devoted to assisting its members in developing their public speaking and leadership skills. Toastmasters groups typically consist of 20 to 30 members who meet once a week for about an hour to acquire new skills and take turns practicing those skills and evaluating one another. To find out more about the organization and locate a group near you, visit www.toastmasters.org.

Work on your *elevator speech* — a prepared speech that you deliver whenever someone asks you what you do. I have several such speeches for different situations. If the person asking me "What do you do?" is likely to be buying or selling a house, I deliver the "I Sell the American Dream" speech. If I think they may be more interested in topics related to real estate and mortgage fraud, I deliver the "I Protect the American Dream" speech. Sometimes just for fun, I walk into the elevator, face the other passengers, and announce, "My name is Ralph Roberts, and I just lost my job at the Post Office." That usually loosens up the crowd.

Assessing the PR value of local groups

If you sell high-end stereo systems, you don't want to get stuck talking to the Women's Auxiliary. Of course, I don't know what you sell, so I can't exactly tell you which groups you want to speak to. I sell real estate, the books I write, and my services as a speaker and coach, so I speak to a wide variety of groups, including real estate investment clubs, homeowners associations, and neighborhood organizations that are interested in finding out what they can do to protect themselves against real estate and mortgage fraud.

Brainstorm a list of organizations and local groups in your area, and then prioritize the list. Highlight the groups that are most likely to put you in front of the movers and the shakers — these are the people who can open doors for you.

Getting your foot in the door

Selling yourself as a speaker is just like selling products, but first, you need a product to sell. Write a 15- to 20-minute speech, complete with a 1- to 2-page handout demonstrating that you have something to say. Shop it around to the leaders of the groups you want to speak to. Better yet, join the group, establish relationships with the group's leaders, and let them know that you're interested in addressing the group.

Don't just plan your marking campaign, work it. I recently drove past a business that was going out of business. Six people clad in sandwich boards were walking up and down the street to advertise the "Going Out of Business Sale." I thought to myself that if they had invested this much energy in promoting the business, the probably wouldn't be going out of business.

Delivering your speech

Whenever I speak to a group, I have three goals — to engage, entertain, and educate. I try to hook my audience from the very beginning, keep them laughing or crying, and pass along some valuable information or a bit of wisdom. When I succeed, everyone in the audience has an unforgettable experience. Hopefully, they undergo a bit of a transformation. And they always remember me.

Another way to encourage people to remember you is to offer them a gift — a handout with speaking points, a copy of an inspirational book, or some other token that they can look at later. Whatever you choose to give, make sure it reinforces your brand presence. It should include your name, contact information, Web site address, and so on.

After delivering your speech, hang around for the rest of the meeting and linger for awhile after the meeting. Attendees are most likely to seek you out following the meeting and introduce themselves. Be ready to hand them your business card or brochure.

For additional public speaking tips, tricks, and techniques, read *Public Speaking For Dummies,* 2nd Edition by Malcolm Kushner.

Volunteering your time and expertise

Branding is about more than giving yourself a high profile on the shelf. It's about earning a reputation as someone who is sincerely committed to building better communities, and that means volunteering your time and expertise.

As a salesperson, you have a unique gift to offer just about any nonprofit organization on the planet — your ability to sell and generate revenue. Every organization needs at least one salesperson to contribute to their fundraising efforts. If you want to take a break from selling, you can use your communication and organization skills in any number of ways.

Several sales gurus recommend that you "give to get." I prefer the "give to give" approach. Give for the sheer pleasure of giving. If you expect something in return, you're setting yourself up for disappointment. You may be so busy waiting for the expected return on your investment that you completely miss what you actually receive. In Chapter 14, I reveal the "give to give" lesson I learned from Art Fettig, something he calls *The Platinum Rule.*

When you're shopping for a nonprofit organization, try to find one that's a right fit for you and your business. I volunteer my time and expertise to Habitat for Humanity. I'm passionate about enabling every family around the world to realize the dream of homeownership, and Habitat for Humanity is the perfect fit for me. Try to find a way to give back to the community that supports your business. And don't just write a check — participate. Participating enables you to interact with community leaders.

Becoming the resident expert

Back in the days of local merchants, everyone knew who the town experts were. You could just stroll down Main Street and look for the sign. The same is true today, although the small town is now a global economy and Main Street is the Internet. To become the most successful merchant on Main Street, you need to become the resident expert — the person everyone thinks of when they think of buying whatever it is you sell.

The first step is often the hardest — actually becoming an expert. Posing as an expert when you're not truly an expert is a sure way to lose whatever credibility you have. Do your homework and become a true expert before you proclaim yourself one. In other words, don't say that you invented the Internet unless you really did.

After overcoming this initial challenge, you're ready to build credibility by doing any or (preferably all) of the following:

- Publishing articles magazines and journals.
- Writing a book. (If you can't find a publisher, self-publish. Books are like business cards on steroids.)
- Granting interviews to local reporters.
- Being interviewed on radio or hosting your own radio show.
- Appearing on television in both advertisements and news stories.
- Giving speeches to local groups or national organizations.
- Hosting a website or blog where you provide valuable information and guidance.

See Chapter 16 for additional details on tapping the full power of the multi-media marketplace and Chapter 14 for more information on the power of Relationship-Commerce.

Nobody likes a know-it-all, but everyone appreciates someone who really knows her stuff. By establishing yourself as the resident expert in a specific area, you become much more than a face and a logo — you become the go-to guy or gal, the person that other people seek out when they have a question or a problem.

Meeting and greeting the general public

If you sell to the general public, always be on the lookout for opportunities to connect with the man and woman on the street, particular those in your market. Everyone in your market should know who you are, what you do, and what you sell.

In the following sections, I describe two techniques I use to mix it up with prospective clients in my market. These techniques may not apply to all forms of selling, but they can help you stimulate your creativity to develop your own techniques.

Mastering the 10/10/20 technique

One of the not-so-secret secrets to sales success is to build on past success. That is what the 10/10/20 technique is all about, and here is how it works when applied to selling real estate:

When you list or sell a house, knock on the 10 doors to the left and right of the house you just sold and the 20 doors across the street and distribute your postcard with a handwritten note letting the neighbors know that you have listed or sold their neighbor's home.

That is it. That is all it takes to start generating new clients. It should take you less than an hour. Most of the neighbors are not going to want to talk with you at length. In less than an hour you have the potential of reaching 10,000 people.

Whoa! Where did that 10,000 number come from? According to my estimates, from attending weddings and anniversaries, every person knows at least 250 other people. By contacting 40 people in the area, you indirectly contact nearly 10,000 more, and everyone in sales, particularly in real estate, know that selling is all about meeting people and building relationships.

When is the best time to practice shameless self promotion? Right now, say you just sold a Chrysler 300 to a nice couple. Have another salesperson take a picture of you and your customers in front of the car and put it on a postcard. Ask permission to send the postcard out to their neighbors. You should also give them a stack of postcards, so when they get their new vehicle and drive it over to Aunt Sally's house they can give Aunt Sally a postcard.

If you're in corporate sales, tweak the technique. On your client's birthday, show up with a cake, introduce yourself around the office, let everyone know about the birthday, and present the birthday cake to your client. How many salespeople does your client know who would remember their birthday and do something to celebrate it? Your client will always remember you, and so will everyone else in the office. Take a photograph of your client and her coworkers, upload it to your blog with a brief message, and email your client sending a link to the page. You don't even have to wait for your client's birthday — simply show up to celebrate a "Just Because" day.

Sponsoring your own Flag Day

Every year in anticipation of the Fourth of July, my brother David, who's also a top-producing agent in Florida, and about 15 volunteers, including his own family members fan out across his farm area, planting 18-inch American flags on every lawn in the neighborhood — about 800 in all. The team meets at about 6:30 pm for pizza and soft drinks before setting out on its mission and wraps up a couple hours later. In the morning, they do one last drive around to make sure they haven't missed any homes. David also sends cards to all the people who receive the flags, saying, "Happy 4th of July, Enjoy your flag!"

The residents of David's small, tightly knit community love it, and every year, David receives about 50 handwritten letters from residents thanking him for their flags. The flags pull the residents of the community together and stand as a reminder of the fact that this community and the United States overall are great places to live. It also demonstrates David's commitment to the community.

Don't miss out on an opportunity to demonstrate your patriotism, give back to your community, and generate goodwill and positive PR. Purchase a few cases of attractive American flags, round up the troops, and fan out across your community to plant flags on the lawns and patriotism in the hearts of the residents of your community.

If you're in corporate sales, adjust the strategy to make it work for you. Perhaps you could put together a Fourth of July snack platter, complete with tiny American flags, a red-white-and-blue motif, and a stack of your business cards, and deliver it to your client's office the business day before the Fourth of July. Add a few firecrackers and ask the staff who in the office is the real firecracker. Include a few prizes just for fun. If you sell pharmaceuticals, stuff empty medicine bottles with small prizes and snacks, put a bowl of them in a central location where everyone meets to talk and laugh, and the office will never forget you!

Chapter 10

Stepping Out of Your Comfort Zone: Taking Risks

In This Chapter

▶ Defining your own comfort zone

▶ Imagining what life could be like

▶ Relieving your fear and trepidation

▶ Discovering opportunities in problems

▶ Failing toward success

Success isn't measured solely by achievement. It's also measured by failure. If you haven't failed, you haven't taken enough risk to test your limits, and you're probably not achieving the level of success you're capable of achieving.

You're likely to always feel some fear when facing the prospect of failure, but keep in mind that those who profit most take the biggest risks. This chapter shows you how to alleviate the fear of risk taking by carefully assessing the risks and the potential benefits, setting achievable goals, and preparing well in advance to minimize your risks.

Two types of failure exist — failure from poor planning and execution and failure from over-reaching. The type I discuss in this chapter is in the failure-from-over-reaching category, but in either case, as long as you learn from your mistakes and do your best not to repeat them, you're making progress.

Marking the Boundaries of Your Comfort Zone

Every time you say "I can't," you plot a point on the perimeter of your comfort zone. *You* define your limitations. And I stress the "You" for good reason — *you* have a choice to choose comfort and complacency over the potential uneasiness of stepping into the unknown. You have the choice of whether to gun for gold or settle for silver or bronze.

Recognizing the boundaries of your comfort zone, however, often signals the start of something better. Every time you find yourself saying "I can't" or "I won't," write down exactly what you can't or won't do. Then, try to identify the reason why. If you're having trouble getting started on this exercise, here are some common reasons why people claim they can't do something:

- **Insufficient funds:** You simply cannot afford to do what you really want to do.

- **Insufficient time:** 24 hours a day, 7 days a week just isn't sufficient.

- **Family limitations:** Your partner wouldn't go along with it or you have kids to support and simply can't afford to chase your dreams.

- **Lack of knowledge or skills:** You just don't know enough about it to actually do it or do it well enough to satisfy yourself.

- **Can't get a break:** A tight group has control over who's in and who's out, and you are definitely outside the circle.

- **Fear of failure:** You simply can't stomach the thought of what could happen if your best efforts fell short.

- **Fear of success:** This can be just as much of a hindrance as a fear of failure. Many people dread the thought of how their lives could change if they achieved their dreams. Would it be bring more work and responsibility than you could handle?

Taking calculated risks

I've risked and lost millions of dollars on various investments and business ventures, but I have also earned millions more by taking well-calculated risks and preparing a solid foundation first. I encourage you and others to try something different, but to do so in a way that minimizes your exposure to risk. Have a plan, human resources, financing, and your ability to sell in place, and you have a much better chance of turning risk into dollars.

Whenever I consult a company or coach sales agents, I test their temperament first to determine how much risk they're really willing and able to take on. My goal isn't to have them take on less risk but to take it on in such a way that limits their chance of failing.

Recently, a business owner retained me as his consultant during a period when he was planning to expand his business to an additional location. Everything looked great, but I advised him to pass on the expansion at this point and focus more on establishing the business. I wanted to see them become more of what they were, build their brand, strengthen their staff, and broaden their client base, before launching a new office. My reasoning was that I knew other opportunities would come but the stronger the foundation of the business, the more prepared they would be to take full advantage of the opportunities.

Take risk, but prepare well in advance to minimize the downside and maximize the upside.

I could go on and on. It's okay to admit these limitations. In fact, I want you to get them all down on paper or a white board or a chalkboard or wherever else you list things. Put all of your excuses . . . er . . . limitations out there, so you can see them, feel them, and get to know them.

After you have a complete and comprehensive list, go back over it and see how many of those limitations are really self-imposed. I would challenge you to find one limitation on your list that you couldn't overcome:

- ✔ **Insufficient funds:** You can always find someone to loan you the money if you have a great plan in place and the determination and resources to implement it. Head down to your local bank and start talking to people.

- ✔ **Insufficient time:** In Chapter 11, I show you how to make more time. In Chapter 5, I reveal the secret to expanding time by using technology and human resources to increase the amount you can accomplish in a set period of time.

- ✔ **Family limitations:** Healthy families support one another in their goals to achieve self-fulfillment. If your partner or other family members are not supporting one another, you may need some outside assistance. You should all be pursuing your dreams. That's what life is all about. Otherwise, you're simply taking up space and wasting resources.

If family members are not supporting you, consider the asking-for-forgiveness-instead-of-permission approach. Pursue your dreams, regardless of what they think. If they get upset and reprimand you for not consulting them, apologize. I know that the daytime talk-show hosts are going to criticize me for recommending this — you should always consult your partner. But I've been doing this for years, and sometimes it's the only way to get anything done.

- ✔ **Lack of knowledge or skills:** You can overcome this common limitation in one of three ways — learn it, hire it, or partner with it. I don't know one tenth of what I would need to know if I had to do everything by myself, but I know people who with the skills and knowledge I need. See Chapter 13 for additional details.

- ✔ **Can't get a break:** Make your own breaks.

- ✔ **Fear of failure:** Think of the worst thing that could happen. Is it really that bad?

- ✔ **Fear of success:** Think of the best thing that can happen. In most cases, the best that can happen is that you become incredibly busy. The additional business means more profit. More profit means you can hire more people to do the work for you. You now have more choices — work more or work less, focus on your business or focus on other, more gratifying pursuits.

Successful people view obstacles simply as speed bumps, not as impenetrable blockades. With a little ingenuity, you can overcome anything that initially appears to be a limitation.

Envisioning Life Outside of Your Comfort Zone

Dwight D. Eisenhower once said, "If you want total security, go to prison. There you're fed, clothed, given medical care and so on. The only thing lacking . . . is freedom."

Until you wander outside of your comfort zone, you really have no idea what it feels like there. It's sort of like deciding to live with your parents for the rest of your life or never leave the town you grew up in or refuse to leave your state or your country. By staying put, you never even have a taste of what's out there, good or bad. It's called being provincial — a fancy word for narrow-minded.

Some people are naturally compelled to set out on adventures. They're explorers who couldn't possibly sit in one place for any length of time. Others almost have to force themselves out of the comfort of their recliners. If you're one of these more sedentary folks, I offer a few words of advice, presented in the following sections, in the hope that they quell your concerns and kick you in your keister.

What's the worst that can happen?

I'm somewhat of a specialist in the foreclosure arena. My capable assistant, Lois Maljak may even be more accomplished in this field, especially when it comes to dealing with distressed homeowners who haven't quite lost their homes yet. In any event, I'm accustomed to working with people in the midst of what they consider to be the absolute worst thing that can happen to them — losing their home.

One of my main challenges in these cases is convincing the homeowners that they only stand to lose *this* home. They and their family are going to live somewhere. They are going to have another place to call home, another place to build memories. Losing this home is not going to destroy their family or their future . . . unless they let it.

I can't tell you the worst thing that can happen to *you.* I have experienced what I believe is the worst thing that could ever happen to me when my daughter Kolleen died at the age of 18, on Memorial Day 2006. Death is irreversible. Some illnesses are incurable. I suppose those are things that I would consider the worst things that can happen. Anything related to money is *not* something that is irreversible or incurable. I'm not saying that money is unimportant, but if going bankrupt is the worst thing that ever happens to you, you're pretty fortunate.

Think of worst things that you can imagine ever happening to you. If taking a risk in business exposes you to the chance that the worst things you can imagine really will happen to you, then you may want to step back. Otherwise, what do you really have to lose? My assistant's (Lois's) father would tell her that the definition of a problem is one that money can't solve. Everything else is just a nuisance.

What's the best that can happen?

You have this idea in your head of how you can be hugely successful. What if it really happened? Play it out in your mind. If you put your plan into place, and it worked to perfection, how would you feel? How would all the people around you feel? How much better would the world be? How would your family fare?

I spend a lot of time assisting salespeople with building a sales team, which is a huge risk. You reach a point in your career when you feel as though you've hit a plateau, and you can't sell more without a team of talented individuals supporting you. To take your sales career to the next level, you have to build a team, but that means leaving your comfort zone; giving up control; relying on others to do what you feel nobody can do better than you; training, motivating, and paying others; generating enough business to keep everyone busy and paid; and so on.

The risk discourages many salespeople from building teams, but that's mostly because they fail to see the upside — being able to focus on what they do best, outsourcing all of the tasks they find least rewarding, spending more quality time with family members; sharing their accomplishments with team members; learning new tips, tricks, and techniques from team members; boosting sales and revenue; and so on. Don't let the downside of risk cloud your vision to the point at which you are blind to the upside.

What if you don't even try?

What if you waited to do anything until you knew beyond the shadow of a doubt how it would turn out? You would never even be able to get out of bed. I would never have met my wife Kathleen. I wouldn't have had kids. And I certainly wouldn't have written this book. I would still be waiting until I knew what was going to happen. Where's the fun in that?

Insights from my trials and errors

When people meet me or anyone else who is currently successful, they tend to assume that the person could do no wrong — that every plan worked, every business was a phenomenal success, and money was never an object. This is rarely the case, and it certainly wasn't the case with me. I've seen more victory than defeat, but I've had my share of disappointments.

Here are some of my most memorable successful ventures:

✔ **Grass cutting:** My first business venture carried no overhead. I used my Dad's lawn mower, gas, oil, and repair services. This was one of the few totally risk-free businesses I've ever had. I cut it in high gear, mowing the neighborhood once, perhaps twice, a week. I made so much money that by the age of 16, I could afford to pass my lawn-mowing business to my younger brother Dave and try my hand at ice cream (see the section on failures) and then T-shirts.

✔ **T-shirts:** As a senior in high school, I took a silk screening class and learned how to make posters, T-shirts, and a host of other cool products. For most of my classmates, silk screening became a part-time hobby. For me, it became a business. I would purchase a gross of plain T-shirts, the class helped me make them, and then I would sell them. My top-selling shirt was "Steve Tyler, Aerosmith – Lord of the thighs." The business eventually folded. Upon graduation, I lost my market . . . and my free employees.

✔ **Real estate investment:** I was invited to speak to a group of investors about the foreclosure process in my area and actually became more involved in the investment group than I had anticipated. The organizer, Dick Mazur, had a unique way of pumping up the investors. He would canvass the room asking each person what he or she was willing to invest. When he arrived at the gentleman next to me, Dr. Lee, he said, "Dr. Lee, I have you down for a million dollars." Dr. Lee hesitated and said, "I promised my wife I would consult her before going forward with any new deals." I understood the potential in the deal, so I raised my hand, and Mazur called on me. I said, "I don't have to ask my wife. I would like to take the million dollar slot." Mazur said I was IN! I left the table, went to the restroom, called my wife, and begged her to let me do the deal. We spent $5 million and then we spent $30 million. Rip Hamilton of Detroit Pistons fame was the first purchaser in the subdivision that we developed on the property. It was a huge success.

Of course, I've had a good number of disappointments, which tend to be more entertaining for some reason. Here are a few of my all-too memorable failures:

✔ **Custom mirror installations:** In the late '70s I built a custom rack to put on my pickup truck. I didn't pound the spikes far enough into the steel body for them to hold, and they came loose and damaged the mirrors. I got pretty good at fixing the mirrors, so I decided to start my own business. After doing dozens of jobs and making a pretty good profit, customers started complaining. Apparently, the adhesive I used was eating the silver off the back of the mirrors. All my profits disappeared as I honored the warranties.

✔ **US Rental homes:** Along with a few friends who wanted to invest in real estate, I started a company called US Rental Homes. I saw a big demand for good, affordable rental properties. Our company published a daily listing of rental properties that people could subscribe to for $69. The trouble was that we had far more tenants than houses, so we had to refund everyone's money.

✔ **Ice cream:** Perhaps my most disappointing failure was my attempt to sell ice cream. At the age of 16, I purchased two ice cream trucks, figuring that I could drive one and hire someone to drive the other one. Only later did I discover that at the age of 16 I was not legally permitted to drive the truck. I ended up having to hire college students. I

hadn't counted on this expense or the cost of repairs or the loss of products when the generator broke down and all the ice cream melted. After a few years of frustration, I cut one truck from my fleet and sold the "business."

Throughout this book, I drive home the point that as a salesperson, you're an entrepreneur, and the more you think like one, the better you are going to perform. You have to try something new, take risks, and stick out your neck to achieve anything. You are likely to fail, but if you don't try, you've already failed.

If you don't travel to France, you have no idea what it's like there. If I haven't spent time with you, I really don't know who you are. If I haven't even tried to achieve my lifelong dream, I can't possibly achieve it. I would have as much chance at attaining my dream as I would have getting from Detroit to Los Angeles by sitting in my office and MapQuesting it.

Life is to be lived. The more fully you live it, the more of it you have. If you choose not to live life fully, you end up squandering opportunities and regretting it later. Attempting a great feat and failing at it is more noble than never making an effort.

Estimating your ROR (Return on Risk)

Businesspeople always talk about ROI (return on investment). I like to talk about ROR (return on risk). You approach ROR the same way you approach ROI — measure the potential upside against the potential risk to determine if attempting the venture would be "worth it." Following are some tips on how to approach ROR:

✔ Don't be concerned about what others think. It's your idea, your passion, and your life.

✔ Don't risk everything — separate your personal and professional risks When I first started, my wife was in on every deal. As my business grew, her name was off of every deal. If I lose everything, we can still live on what my family owns and vice versa.

- ✔ Ask for more then you want, to get what you need. Shoot for stars and land on the moon.

- ✔ Research carefully to take calculated risks, but don't use the need for more research as an excuse to avoid getting started.

- ✔ Develop a backup plan. If your plan doesn't quite work out or takes longer, what are you going to do?

- ✔ Start immediately, if not sooner.

Following are some signs that the risk may not be worth it:

- ✔ You could loose everything.

- ✔ The upside is negligible or non-existent.

- ✔ You haven't done any research.

- ✔ You have no backup plan.

Reducing the Fear Factor

Fear of failure is probably the second biggest cause of failure. The first is fear of the unknown — just watch any horror movie. The easiest way to overcome these fears is to take action. Don't succumb to the common affliction of paralysis by analysis. Simply forge ahead with your plans.

Making tactical use of your fears

I'm not sure I agree with Franklin Delano Roosevelt's quote that "We have nothing to fear but fear itself," at least in the context of sales. As I see it, my biggest fear has been my biggest asset.

Many people have a fear of flying, fear of public speaking, fear of death, and so on. The biggest fear I have is of being alone. I don't even have a key to my office building or my homes. I go places only when other people are there. When I first was married and had our daughter, Kolleen, I would pay someone to babysit while I was home, so that I would have someone to talk to. Or I would order a pizza and pay the delivery boy, Willie, to stay with me and keep me company.

When I described my fear to the people in my office, they didn't believe me. "How can you ride in the car alone?" they asked. I said, "I'm not really alone . . . I'm on the phone the entire time."

I think that if I weren't as afraid as I am of being alone, I would never have been as successful. I always was and always will be on the lookout for someone to do business with, whether it's a customer, a partner, an agent I'm training, or someone else. And as long as I'm looking for people, I am going to find them, connect with them, and produce something with them.

Identify your fears and try to transform them from liabilities into assets.

If you don't like that approach, I have some other suggestions. In the following sections, I reveal several techniques you can use to reduce and perhaps even eliminate the fear that's weighing you down.

Fear isn't necessarily bad. It can motivate you to achieve even higher levels of success, if you handle it properly. Let fear motivate you, not defeat you.

Researching the viability of an idea or opportunity

You may be able to ease into a risky venture through research and planning. I often encourage real estate agents to diversify by creating several departments in their real estate businesses — one for sellers, one for buyers, another for cash buys (investing in real estate), probate properties, public relations, foreclosures, and so on. In the foreclosure arena, I show them how to properly research foreclosure properties and have them sit in on three or more auctions before placing their first bid. After weeks of preparation, they feel much more confident and comfortable placing their first bid.

If you're afraid of implementing a new plan because of the risks you think are involved or the amount of time, effort, and money it may require, start researching. Read a book, search the Internet, and gather some facts. The mere act of taking the initiative to do some research can give you the momentum you need to actually launch your new idea.

To have any chance as a big game hunter, you eventually have to pull the trigger. I'm often accused of following the "ready . . . fire . . . aim" approach to business and sales. I don't always hit the mark, but at least I take plenty of shots. Don't get in the rut of thinking that research is an end in itself. You eventually have to make a decision and then take action. You won't hit anything if you don't pull the trigger.

Following the trailblazers

Chances are pretty good that someone has already attempted and perhaps even implemented, to some degree, whatever idea you have to boost sales or increase business. You just have to find out who.

Success leaves huge footprints that are pretty tough to miss. As you perform your initial research, keep an eye peeled for footprints and discuss your ideas with trustworthy colleagues and friends. Many times, simply talking about an idea generates enough buzz to drive the people you really need to talk to directly to your door.

After you have identified one or more individuals who've blazed the trails, contact them to discuss your ideas. The most highly successful people are usually the most generous with their time and expertise. After all, that's probably how they became highly successful. They may even be able to refer you to other specialists who can assist you in actually implementing you plan.

Assembling your own advisory board

Big companies and organizations often have advisory boards that guide the development of new ideas and departments. Consider taking the same approach as an individual.

I've leaned on dozens of experts in a wide variety of fields to guide me over the years, including Tom Hopkins, Zig Ziglar, Dennis Waitley, Mark Victor Hansen, Art Fettig, Howard Brinton, David Knox, Dave Beson, Stanley Mills, Steve Westmark, David W. Roberts, Cathy Russell, Danielle Kennedy, Floyd Wickman, Darlene Lyons, Karen Dice, Chip Neumann, Chip Cummings, Steve Stewart, Robert Kiyosaki, Norman Schwarzkopf, Ed Primeau, Terry Brock, Terry Wisner, Pete Thomas, Michael Soon Lee, Marge Fraser, Eric Pruitt, Richard Nacht, Stefan Swanepoel, Bob VanGoethem, Joe Sirianni, Tony Ferris, Jerry Toler, Dave Ebner, Steve Tarzy, Dan Brophy, Rachel Dollar, and Kathy Bott, to name a few of the thousands of those who have offered guidance, advice, time, and resources.

Jot down a list of the people you admire — successful people with the expertise to assist you. Pick the top 10 or 20 and place them on your personal advisory board. Enlist their insights and advice on your current projects and look to them in the future. In addition to providing you with guidance, these people will passively, and perhaps actively, hold you accountable for doing your best and achieving the goals you share with them.

Setting achievable milestones

Fear often takes hold when a project seems overwhelming. My plan to "change the world one million people at a time," sounds overwhelming at first, but I've managed to break it down — to divide and conquer. Using various technologies and media channels, I can actually communicate with audiences that are literally in the millions:

- **Blogging:** Blogging's online, all-the-time, on-demand venue enables me to post an article on the Web and make it available to billions of people around the world.
- **Books:** The numerous books I've written have sold hundreds of thousands of copies and provide me with the raw material I need to develop other products, articles, and commentaries.

- ✔ **Magazines and journals:** Magazines and journals, online and off, provide me with the opportunity to publish my ideas and even generate more traffic to my websites and blogs.

- ✔ **Press releases:** With a one-page press release, I can instantly connect with hundreds of thousands of people online and off to let them know what I'm up to.

- ✔ **Radio broadcasts:** Radio stations frequently call me for interviews and opportunities to present real estate investment seminars and talk on other topics.

- ✔ **Online podcasts and video:** These new media give me the power to broadcast audio and video recordings over the Internet to people across the nation and around the world.

- ✔ **E-mail:** Through e-mail blasts and drip campaigns, I connect with a million people each and every week. Every week, I have a unique and valuable message to offer my contacts, and e-mail gives me the means to distribute it quickly and economically.

To see just how my e-mail campaign works, send me an e-mail message at ralphroberts@ralphroberts.com, requesting to be added to my list or request my signature (the name I sign to my email messages), which I have been told gets passed around quite a bit. I often send out flash movies, inspirational poems, and other items that recipients highly value. In addition to receiving these free gifts, you get a glimpse of my marketing campaign in action.

Although I decided early on that I wanted to change the world one million people at a time, I didn't try to do everything at once. I started blogging at FlippingFrenzy.com. Reporters noticed my blog and contacted me for interviews. Online publications contacted me to write articles and commentaries. Book publishers contacted me to write books. All of a sudden, I had a great deal to say and hundreds of people providing me with the means of broadcasting my message to the audience of millions I had only been able to dream about.

When you have a vision that seems overwhelming and perhaps grandiose in the eyes of some, start breaking it down into more manageable units. Then, identify one task and get started. Getting started is often the hardest part. More likely than not, your momentum is going to carry you somewhere you've never imagined, so just get started and find out the rest later.

Focusing on the present

I'm not one of these people who preaches that you should throw caution to the wind, live for today, and let tomorrow take care of itself. I encourage people to plan well, save for the future, and remain fairly conservative with their family nest eggs.

Expanding business with a systems approach

I've achieved a great deal of success through what I like to refer to as a *systems approach*. I identify a business opportunity that's related to some business I'm already running. Then, I create a separate division or department for it, hire someone to run it, and add it to my collection of "small businesses." I created the following departments under the umbrella of Ralph R. Roberts Realty:

✔ **Buyer Department** services people who are buying a home. This enables me to service half of the real estate market. At the same time, buyers often generate more listings when they need to sell.

✔ **Listing Department** services people who are selling a home. Sellers are the cornerstone of any real estate business.

✔ **Closing Department** handles all of the paperwork, so my agents can focus more energy on the dollar-productive activities of buying and selling homes.

✔ **Cash Buy Department** enables me to move quickly on great investment properties. I figured that my agents and I are constantly

researching properties and talking with homeowners, so we may as well purchase some of the best buys.

✔ **Property Management** prepares the properties we purchase for sale or rent and manages the rental units. It also manages properties for other investors in the area who own rental units.

✔ **Foreclosure Department** is dedicated to assisting homeowners who are facing foreclosure. This department also purchases foreclosure properties at auction.

✔ **Public Relations & Marketing** ensures that me and my business are properly marketed to drive more business and opportunities our way.

This systems approach has diversified my business and enabled me and my employees to quickly adapt to changing market conditions. When the housing market is slow, we can capitalize on opportunities in the cash buy and foreclosure departments. When the housing market picks up, we can shift our energies to serving buyers and sellers.

When it comes to implementing a new strategy or technology that can boost business, however, don't let concerns about the future or about costs paralyze you. Jot down a list of tasks you must accomplish to achieve your goal, and then run through the list, tackling one task after another. Eventually, you discover that you've run out of tasks and have achieved your goal.

Looking for Trouble . . . and Finding Opportunity

Sales success often hinges on your ability not only to overcome adversity but to capitalize on it. Almost every invention came about as the result of someone recognizing a problem and coming up with a solution.

Spotting opportunities in foreclosures

Early in my career as a real estate investor, I made a mistake and lost one of my properties in foreclosure. It made me sensitive to the plight of homeowners who had experienced financial setbacks and were facing the loss of their home.

When I started my real estate business, I noticed that few real estate professionals devoted any time to or resources to assisting this segment of the market. Most of the investors working in the foreclosure arena were more interested in making a buck than in actually assisting the homeowners. Many of them added to the burden of the homeowners by presenting misleading or false information.

I saw an opening for investors who acted with integrity. I educated these distressed homeowners, let them know their options, and assisted them in selecting the most attractive option for their situation. As a real estate investor and agent, I could offer one option that most investors couldn't offer — to place the house on the market and sell it before the homeowner lost the home and all the equity they had in it. Sometimes homeowners would sell the house to me when they needed to make a quick decision, and other times, I would sell it for them so they could hold on to more of the equity.

I didn't always get the home or the listing, but I usually managed to benefit in some way. Over time, I established a reputation for acting with integrity. Many of the people I assisted became customers for life. Some referred to their friends and family to me when they were facing similar situations. Of course, a few people saw me as merely another opportunistic foreclosure investor, but you can't please everyone all the time.

The point of this story is that you can often turn problems, your own or someone else's, into a revenue-generating sales opportunity.

Now, you may wonder why I'm talking about inventors and inventions in a book about advanced selling, but as a salesperson, you have to be an innovator to be a top producer. Your job essentially consists of recognizing a customer's problem and then presenting an attractive, viable solution.

As an entrepreneurial salesperson, you can play an even greater role as innovator by recognizing problems that you or your customers face and turning them into revenue-generating opportunities. You may even be able to set up an entirely new division in your company to sell a related product or service or spin off a separate company.

Regaining Your Footing When You Stumble

When you're taking substantial risks, you're likely to lose your footing every so often and perhaps even fall flat on your face. I have suffered some hardships in my life, but with the help of family and friends and my policy of sticktoitism, I've managed to recover. You find out who your true friends and family members are during your darkest hours.

Remember that most often people fail their way to success. Success isn't for the faint of heart. Most people quit before they succeed. They just give up.

The steps to recovery function follow pretty much the same path, regardless of the cause of the failure:

1. **Cut your losses.**

2. **Identify what went wrong.**

3. **Fix the problems.**

4. **Regroup.**

5. **Try the same thing again with the required changes or try something else.**

One step I omitted because you already should have taken it is this — clean house. Purge your area of negative people, don't share your goals with people who are not goal-oriented, and surround yourself with positive goal-setters.

Michael Eisner, Chairman of the Board of the Walt Disney Company, once said, "Recovering from failure is often easier than building from success." Even when you succeed, you may feel as though the road ahead leads uphill. Continue to adjust your plan, gather resources, and recruit talented individuals to take full advantage of the success ahead.

And what happens if you go all in, risk everything, and lose? Then you have to start all over. That means evaluating what you do, how you do it, what you're selling, and your approach and trying something completely different. Starting from scratch is tough, but it can be done, and it always beats the alternative — giving up.

Part III

Equipping Yourself with Advanced Selling Tools and Resources

The 5th Wave   By Rich Tennant

"I was giving them a rousing motivational speech from my college football days, at the end of which everyone jumped up and butted heads."

In this part . . .

You may not have realized this, but you're not just a salesperson, you're a business — You, Inc. To flourish as a business, you have to invest in it. You have to be ready to spend some money, and in this part, I help you spend it . . . wisely, of course.

Here you discover what to spend your money on to get the biggest bang for your buck, how to better budget your time, and how to expand time while boosting revenue by equipping your business with the right technologies and hiring key personnel.

Chapter 11

Investing and Re-Investing in Your Success

In This Chapter

▶ Making productivity your priority

▶ Jotting down a list of must-haves

▶ Finding the cash to finance your success

▶ Finding and making more time

*T*he top 20 percent of professionals in any field invest 80 percent more time, money, and other resources on being the best. That's how they achieved their success, and that's how they continue to build on it. These top-20 percenters are constantly in the process of improving themselves, their customers, and everyone around them. They don't seek out ways to pass the time. They don't piddle away their resources on unproductive pursuits. And they certainly don't waste time and energy griping about how bad they have it. Instead, they seek knowledge and wisdom, more efficient systems, better technology, and solutions to problems. They invest in their own success.

This chapter shows you how to invest wisely in your own success. Here, I show you why investing in productivity almost always outweighs the cost of the initial investment. I then show you how to prioritize your investment needs, finance your investments, and make the best use of time.

By the end of this chapter, you should have a fairly good idea of where you need to begin your self-improvement program and how you're going to find the time and money to implement it.

 Invest in your own welfare — physical, emotional, spiritual, personal, and professional. As a healthy, happy, well-balanced individual, you are capable of accomplishing much more than if you focus on only one aspect of your well being.

Focusing on Productivity Instead of Cost

The old cliché "You have to spend money to make money" doesn't apply only to business owners or investors. It applies to salespeople, too. You can't compete in this world if you don't have a nice wardrobe; an attractive, comfortable car to drive clients around in when needed; a reliable computer; a cellphone; high-speed Internet; a Web site or blog; marketing materials; one or more assistants; and lifelong education and training. All of this stuff costs money.

You can't wait until you can afford it to lay out the cash for everything you need. As a real estate agent, you couldn't possibly get started in the business if you had to drive your clients around looking at houses in an old jalopy with no air conditioning or a broken heater. You couldn't compete without a computer and e-mail access or a cellphone number that your clients could call to get in touch with you immediately.

The cost of not having what you need to do your job better than any of your competitors is an expense you cannot afford. You may need to borrow from friends or family members, take out a loan at the bank, hit your boss up for an advance on your salary, barter, or figure out some other way to pay for it, but these tools and resources are necessities, not luxuries. See "Financing Your Investments," later in this chapter for details on how to make these necessities more affordable.

Don't quit your day job

If you're just getting started in sales, don't quit your day job until you have all the tools and resources required to make a smooth transition.

When I started selling real estate, I was working as a carpenter for my father's business. I worked from six in the morning until three o'clock in the afternoon as a carpenter and then sold real estate in the late afternoon and evenings, after most people returned from work.

I sold my first house to myself. I was going to use it as an investment property, so I stayed living with my parents. A few months later, my mother kicked me out of the family home. She said that if I was going to be a homeowner, I would have to live in the home.

I kept working with my father until I had all the tools I needed to become a full-time real estate agent, and then I made the leap. I've never gone back. Perhaps if I had tried to leap too soon, I would still have been a carpenter.

Keep your day job until you have what you need along with a little cash in your savings account to make it through any rough periods.

Prioritizing Your Investment Needs

As I repeat throughout this book, you are a business unto yourself, You, Inc. Every business starts with a solid business plan, which contains a complete list of all of the equipment and other resources required to get up and running. When you're drawing up your business plan for You, Inc., take this same approach. Create a list of everything you need, and then rearrange the items on the list to give the most critical items top priority.

In the following sections, I reveal the resources that most salespeople need to acquire. You may already have some of these resources in place, and your priorities are likely to differ depending on what you sell and the way you do business. If, for example, you interact with customers exclusively over the Internet, having an impeccable wardrobe and dressing for success may not be as important as having a top-of-the-line computer with reliable broadband Internet access.

Dressing for success

Dressing for success seems so cliché, so basic. So why am including it in a book on advanced selling? Because I regularly bump into very good salespeople who refuse to accept the fact that they may have to trade in their comfy pair of jeans for a suit or a pair of khakis and a polo shirt. Some are even trying to prove a point — that appearance *shouldn't* matter. While that may be a noble notion, the fact is that appearance *does* matter. Customers and clients, often unknowingly, judge your competence based on how you look.

For someone just starting out, dressing for success is key. If you're well established, your attire is less important. I have framed photographs and newspaper articles adorning the walls of my office of myself dressed in different ways. The most important thing when it comes to attire and fashion is that you dress for the occasion — for the customer or event. If you've never met the customer, play it safe and dress up rather than down.

If you need a few "better" reasons why dressing for success is important, here are a few:

- Fosters a sense of commonality
- Eliminates office distractions
- Creates a more favorable impression

Dress for the position you want

In Chapter 2, I encourage you to envision what success would look like to you and then start acting as though you're already the successful person you envision yourself to be. This includes dressing the part.

A hospital security guard I know had an effective way to create the perception of being qualified for the job he wanted. Each day, he came to work in a shirt, tie, and sport coat and would go to the employee locker room to change into his guard uniform. Before he left work each day, he changed back into his sports coat, shirt, and tie.

The other security guards and company personnel teased him a little at first, but management took notice, he was quickly promoted to the position he wanted, and the teasing soon ceased.

If you want to be successful, you have to look the part. Acting the part may not be enough.

In the late 1970s, John Malloy wrote a book called *Dress for Success* that prescribed a uniform of sorts for success in corporate America. In today's more casual corporate climate, you may be tempted to think that the days of dressing for success are over, but what has actually happened is that the wardrobe has simply changed clothes. Blue suits and red ties have been replaced with khakis and button-down shirts . . . with or without the ties.

Nowadays, dress for success means that you take your appearance out of the equation. You demonstrate that you're aware of your appearance, and you dress and groom yourself appropriately.

Consistency is key. If you wear a suit one day, jeans the next, and then a jacket and slacks, you're diluting your image . . . your brand presence. Consistency in grooming and attire triggers a very subtle, long-term shift in how others perceive you and perhaps even how you perceive yourself. Consistently present yourself as a professional. Make sure the image you project matches the person you want others to perceive that you are. Your image can make you the go-to guy or gal.

If you can't dress consistently, at least pack a change of clothes. I often dress in jeans to show investment properties, but any time during the day, a reporter may call to do a quick interview. When a reporter calls, I head back to the office and change into my more "professional" outfit to do the interview. Whenever I represent my company and employees, I want to project an appearance of professionalism.

Pursuing education and training

Early in my career, I scoffed at the need for education. I was young, hungry, and willing to work as hard as necessary to become the successful salesperson I wanted to be. And, boy, did I work hard. All of those people I made fun of — the people who were taking classes at night, learning new technologies, taking seminars and workshops, reading books, and attending conferences — they worked hard too, and they made a little less money than I did . . . at first. But then I discovered that they got where they were going a lot faster than I did.

Although on-the-job training is crucial for sales success, off-the-job training can provide you with shortcuts later in your career. This off-the-job training is equally valuable. Focus on the following areas in your continuing education as a salesperson:

- ✔ **Your sales craft:** By reading this book and putting my suggestions into action, you're already investing in this area. After mastering everything in this book, don't stop seeking even more ways to improve your craft.

- ✔ **Product research:** Be an expert on the products and services you sell. I know of several companies in which the sales staff is in constant communication with the people in product development, training, and customer service, in order to get up to speed on new products and services. If your company doesn't foster this kind of inter-department communication, recommend it to your corporate managers or implement an informal system on your own.

- ✔ **Customer research:** As a salesperson, you're in contact with current and prospective customers on a daily basis, but how much do you really know about them? Become more involved with your customers. Some companies require their salespeople to work in different departments, such as customer service and training, for a few days a year, so they have contact with customers in need and can develop a better sense of what customers are looking for. You may also consider getting more involved with customers in online discussion forums, blogs, and chat groups where customers in your industry are likely to hang out and look for information and guidance.

- ✔ **Competition research:** As an industry leader, don't fall into the trap of researching the competition in order to mimic them, but do keep an eye on what they're doing. Researching the competition enables you to identify areas where you need to improve and can often spark your own creative ideas for what you can do that your competition is not doing. See Chapter 20 for more suggestions on checking out the competition.

Harnessing the power of my ADHD

I have officially been diagnosed as having ADHD. Some would say that I'm suffering from ADHD, but I don't see it that way. To me, it's a blessing. It drives me to constantly seek out stimulating learning activities and even optimize learning opportunities.

In addition to reading, I often listen to CDs, MP3s, and Podcasts to explore a wide variety of topics. Recently, I discovered that if I accelerate the playback speed to twice the speed at which the narrator presents the material, I can pay better attention and retain more of the information.

I shared this observation with my doctor, who told me that I may have stumbled onto something. He suggested that he could possibly use this same approach to help his other patients with ADHD. My assistant has also speeded up her reading to me as I work on another computer, place phone calls, and read e-mails on my Blackberry.

If you have a "disability," look for ways to transform your liability into an asset. You never know what untapped energies you can harness with a little creative thinking.

Education can take many forms from the most formal (taking classes) to the least formal (searching the Internet for information). I encourage you to seek out a wide variety of educational opportunities, including workshops, seminars, distance learning, reading books and magazines, hiring a coach, and so on. No form is better than any other, but you quickly discover that some forms of education and training open your mind in ways that other forms do not.

Gearing up with the equipment you need

Whether you work out of your home or are a road warrior, you need equipment to do your job. The not-so-good-old-days of simply showing up in a suit and delivering your sales pitch are over. The modern salesperson requires a fully-equipped, Twenty-First Century office, complete with the following:

- ✔ Computer
- ✔ All-in-one printer, fax machine, copier, scanner
- ✔ Broadband Internet access
- ✔ Cellphone
- ✔ Blackberry device

Technology is great when it works, but don't use it to impress customers. It could make them uncomfortable. Never raise the conversation to a level above what your customers have comfortably mastered.

Fortunately, the equipment you need to become a highly successful salesperson has come down in price. In fact, you probably already own many of these items for your own personal use. See Chapter 12 for more information about investing in sales-generating and productivity-boosting technologies.

You may also need some low-tech equipment, such as a car, desk, filing cabinets, bookshelves, and perhaps even a nice office where you can meet clients in person. Although you certainly have to be well aware of the costs, always ask yourself, "What is the cost of not having this?" If not having what you need is going to cost you potentially lucrative sales opportunities in the future, are you really saving money by not buying (or renting) what you need?

Buying the equipment is only the first step. Invest some time and energy finding out how to take full advantage of all the features these devices have to offer. I know dozens of salespeople who have computers and cannot figure out how to type a document and send it as an e-mail attachment. They have fancy all-in-one printers with fax capabilities, and they're still running down to the local print shop to fax documents.

Investing in marketing materials

Regardless of how much money your company invests to market its products and services, you should be spending some company money, or your own money, if necessary, on marketing yourself. As I discuss in Chapter 9, your main goal as an entrepreneurial salesperson is to sell yourself. Your secondary goal is to sell products and services.

At the very least, you should invest in the following marketing materials:

- ✔ Business card
- ✔ Stationery
- ✔ Brochures
- ✔ Blog
- ✔ Web site

For additional strategies and tips on shameless self-promotion, check out Chapter 9.

Investing in support personnel

Whether or not you feel that you're at a point in your career to start hiring people, you are at that point. If you're cleaning your own house, doing your own laundry, balancing your checkbook, preparing your own taxes, or performing any other number of tasks unrelated to selling for no other reason than that you "can't afford to hire someone," you're at a point where you need to hire someone.

To get ahead in sales, realize that first and foremost, you are a salesperson. Your job is to sell, to make deals happen, to make your customers more successful. Don't waste your time performing tasks that other people can do for you better and for less money than what your time and expertise are worth. See Chapter 13 for details about hiring and managing assistants.

Salespeople are often control freaks who have to do everything themselves. If you're not comfortable hiring people, start slowly. Hire someone to clean your house once a week or mow your lawn. If you're having trouble getting organized, hire someone to get everything organized for you. Once you start hiring people and seeing how much more productive it makes you, you soon find yourself hiring more and more people.

Investing in yourself

Don't forget to invest in yourself — your own physical, emotional, and spiritual well-being. Exercise, read a good book, take up a new hobby, travel, spend time with your family, volunteer in the community, have some fun. If you're strapped for time, schedule time for yourself.

If you won't invest in yourself then why would someone want to invest in you and in your products or services?

Financing Your Investments

Coming up with the funding to fuel your investments in your own success can be quite a challenge, especially when you're first starting out. How can you possibly afford a new wardrobe, a powerful computer, a nice car, marketing materials, productivity gadgets and software, and an assistant when you can barely afford yourself?

This question has already been answered by the top salespeople who have blazed the trail before you. The answer is this: Do whatever it takes... short of stealing it. Beg, borrow, barter, look for free tools and assistants, share resources, and think up other clever, creative ways to get what you need. The following sections explain some of the more common procurement strategies in greater detail.

Finding freebies

Acquiring the assets needed for sales success doesn't necessarily mean you have to pay for them. You may be able to obtain some of what you need for free. Here are some ideas to get you started:

- Inquire about internship or coop programs at your local high school or college. Students often need some work experience and on-the-job training and are willing to donate their time and effort to achieve those goals.

- Search the Internet for free Web site or blog hosting and tools you need to create your Web site or blog. WordPress.org is an excellent place to go to find out more about blogging and obtain the tools and resources you need.

- Search the Internet for free productivity software. You can significantly trim your software budget by opting for freeware or shareware (use now, pay later) versions.

- Contact the SBA (Small Business Administration) for additional equipment, tools, and services you may be able to obtain for free or for greatly reduced prices. Visit www.sba.gov for details and to find contact information for the SBA office near you.

You can often trim the costs of marketing materials by teaming up with a company that offers complementary products or services. If you sell cars, for example, you may be able to convince an insurance agent to cover the printing costs in exchange for including her contact information.

Bartering for what you need

Money is just the most common means of exchanging products and services, it's not the only means. You can also barter for what you need. As a salesperson, you probably have several valuable assets you can trade in exchange for products and services you need. I can't tell you exactly what your assets are, but here are some ideas for what you may be able to offer:

- **Consulting:** Ideas for how to increase business.

- **Selling:** You may be able to moonlight for someone who has the goods or services you need.

- **Referrals:** In exchange for goods and services you need, offer to refer your clients to this business. I know of one salesperson who dresses impeccably. She gets all of her outfits at cost because people are constantly asking her, "Where did you get that outfit?" and she tells them.

✔ **Services:** If you have additional services you offer, exchange them for services or products you need. I sell houses, so I can always offer to handle a transaction for free in exchange for something I need.

Consult your accountant or tax expert with any questions you have about how bartering is taxed. Just because money is not changing hands does not give you the right to avoid paying taxes on it.

Consider joining a barter exchange. I belong to several. Check out Tradefirst.com.

Convincing management to invest in you

Although you are ultimately responsible for acquiring everything you need to achieve sales success, you may be able to convince the company you work for to foot the bill or at least a portion of it. Draw up a plan that contains the following details:

✔ **Overview:** Describe your plan and what you hope to accomplish.

✔ **Budget:** Provide a ballpark estimate of how much money you need to put your plan into action.

✔ **Equipment:** Jot down a list of equipment that you need in order to implement your plan. Point out equipment that is already available, and highlight new equipment you need and its cost.

✔ **Human resources:** List any additional human resources required. Your company's staff may already have personnel in place with the expertise required, or it may need to hire someone with unique skills.

✔ **Time required:** If you had all the resources required, how long would it take to implement your plan?

✔ **Measurements of success:** Always specify exactly how you are going to quantifiably measure the success of your plan. Is it going to result in increased sales, increased retention rates of customers, fewer customer complaints, increased sales revenue? How is your plan going to benefit the company's bottom line?

The company you work for is in business to make money. If you can prove that your plan for success can generate a positive return on the company's investment, management is highly likely to buy into your vision. See Chapter 5 for additional details on how to pitch your plan to your supervisor or to the company executives.

Sharing resources

One of the reasons that large companies install computer networks is so employees can share expensive equipment. The company can buy a powerful central computer whose power every employee in the building can tap into. They can also share top-of-the-line printers, high-speed Internet, and backup facilities.

In the same way, you can network with other people to share resources you both need. Here are some suggestions:

✔ Share an office or office building with another businessperson in the area, preferably someone in the same or a related industry.

✔ Rent office space and perhaps even office equipment from another business in the area. Some businesses have office space that they can't use and may offer very affordable rent.

✔ Purchase and share a separate fax line.

✔ Pool resources to acquire the marketing materials you need.

✔ Pitch in with colleagues to hire an assistant to answer phones and shuffle paperwork.

You don't have to be the sole investor in your success. Share the expenses with one or more colleagues to make your investments more affordable.

Securing a small-business loan

When a business needs capital, it either finds investors or it borrows the money. You may be able to find some venture capitalists or perhaps an affluent relative to fund your success, but if that's not an option, consider applying for a small-business loan.

Sketch out a plan similar to the plan discussed in "Convincing management to invest in you," and schedule an appointment with the loan officer at your local bank. Explain what you're trying to accomplish, the amount of money you need, and what you're going to use that money for. Convince the person that you are going to be able to pay back the loan, and you're in.

Don't get discouraged if your loan request is turned down. Find out why, remove all the reasons that the person rejected your request, and try again. You may have to apply for a loan at several banks before you find one that's willing to work with you. Stick to it. The word "no" is just a speed bump. Figure out what put that speed bump in your way and remove it, so you can move forward. "No" may mean "not now" or "I don't *know* enough yet to say yes."

Tabulating Your Time Budget

As all sales gurus can tell you, to be truly successful requires succeeding in all areas of your life — career, finances, relationships, spirituality, recreations, and so on. Occasionally, however, you need to spend more time in one area than another, and you may begin to feel as though you don't have enough time to devote to becoming a highly successful salesperson.

In reality, you probably have more time than you realize. And if you truly don't have enough time to accomplish everything you need to accomplish, you can create more time.

In the following sections, I lead you through the process of drawing up a time budget, and then I suggest various ways to buy yourself more time.

Knowing how you spend your time

When you ask anyone in a financial crisis why they're in a financial crisis, they almost always say, "We just don't know where the money's going." One of the first steps they need to take to get their finances on track is to find out where all that money is going. A good financial advisor would sit the couple down, have them categorize their income in expenses, and then come up with totals for each category. Once they know where all the money is coming from and where it's going, they can then focus on specific expense categories where they need to cut back.

When you never seem to have enough time, the first step is to find out where those 168 hours a week are going. Jot down a list of all activity categories, which may include the following:

- ✔ Working
- ✔ Sleeping
- ✔ Eating
- ✔ Quality family time
- ✔ Watching TV
- ✔ Internet (productive)
- ✔ Internet (unproductive)

- ✔ Reading
- ✔ Commuting
- ✔ Exercising
- ✔ Bathing/getting dressed
- ✔ Searching for stuff, such as misplaced files

When you're jotting down what you do, be brutally honest. If you're at work and not actually working, then don't write down "12 hours working." Write down what you were really doing, like "4 hours working, 2 hours poking around on the Web, 1 hour going through junk e-mail, 45 minutes chatting with fellow salespeople, an hour and a half for lunch." Be honest. How much time are you really working when you're at work?

Over the course of a typical week, jot down all the hours you spend on each activity and total the amount of time you spend on each activity. Now you should know where all that time is going.

Identifying time wasters

After creating your time log, go through and highlight any categories where you may be able to cut back a little. Perhaps 20 hours a week watching TV could be cut to 10. Sleeping more than eight hours a day may be a little excessive. Maybe you can cut back a little on unproductive Internet time by restricting your Internet usage to an hour a day.

Don't strip all of the time-wasting activities from your life. Everybody needs a little downtime to recharge their batteries. Some time-wasting activities, however, are just as draining or even more draining than productive activities. These time and energy wasters should definitely be removed from your schedule. Hopefully this won't keep you from making me your friend on MySpace! While you're wasting time online drop in at myspace.com/ralphroberts.

Finding and making time

Using your time log from the previous week, create a time budget for the following week in which you trim some hours from the time-wasting categories and allocate them to other categories, such as work, quality family time, or exercise.

Whenever you begin to feel as though you don't have enough time, look at your time budget to see where you're slipping. Falling back into old routines is all too easy. The time budget can keep you on track.

Although a time budget can assist you in finding more time, you still have only 24 hours in a day and only seven days in a week, so if you still find that you don't have enough time to be a success, the next step is to make time. Head to Chapter 5 where I show you how to make time by increasing your productivity through technology and assistants.

Chapter 12

Putting the Latest Technologies to Work for You

· ·

In This Chapter

▶ Confronting your tech-phobias

▶ Gathering the tools of the sales trade

▶ Empowering yourself on the Web

▶ Harnessing powerful communication technologies

· ·

*W*ith each passing year, technology changes more and more rapidly. You may feel as though someone's cranking up the speed on your treadmill when you're already having a tough time keeping pace. And here I go telling you that you have to do even more!

Although new technology may seem overwhelming at first, it often opens the doors to new opportunities and improved efficiency. Resist the latest technological advances, and you find yourself working harder and harder just to keep up. Embrace technology, and you soon discover that you're far ahead of the pack, and you don't even have to break a sweat to stay there.

This chapter shows you how to put the latest technologies to work for you in generating a host of new clients and ever-expanding opportunities.

Overcoming Resistance to New Technology

Technology can be pretty scary, especially if you were born prior to Generation X. Most people can handle a cell phone and even fumble their way through the process of typing a document or crunching numbers in a basic spreadsheet. The newer, more challenging technologies, however, can seem somewhat overwhelming at first. Communication is no longer driven primarily by telephones and the mail carriers. To remain competitive, salespeople now have to juggle Blackberries, text messaging, instant messaging, e-mail, blogs, and other communication tools and technologies.

If you get hot flashes every time you think about having to master some new technology, the following sections may be able to calm you down.

Assuming a playful attitude

The absolute worst time you can start learning how to use a new gadget or software package is when you need to use it. You have a presentation to give tomorrow, and you just installed PowerPoint thinking that this is going to make your job a whole lot easier. Now you have two problems — figuring out how to present the material and wrestling with a fairly complicated piece of software. It's like trying to read your new car's owner's manual while you're weaving through city traffic.

Optimizing your technological tools

According to Einstein a genius uses only 10 percent of the brain. I would venture to guess that most people use about 10 percent of the full capacity of their technologies, as well.

When you adopt a new technological tool, I encourage you to get more than 10 percent out of it. By sticking with the features you need most and using what you already know, you may be able to stay on track, but to excel, you have to reach beyond your grasp.

I always embraced the latest technologies, but I've never been able to claim ownership of them. Instead, I purchased the latest gadgets and software and handed them to my more tech savvy assistants who were clearly more comfortable with the tools.

On February 28, 2003, all that changed. I called my IT guy, Pete, and said, "Enough is enough. I need to get up to speed on this thing called the computer." Pete took me shopping. I bought a laptop for myself, my wife, and each of our kids. The kids loved it, of course, and as a family, this became a valuable educational opportunity and bonding experience.

My first real experience using a computer was at the age of 46. I'm 50 now, and I feel very comfortable on my collection of computers. I carry one with me wherever I go.

If you think you're too old for the new technology, that's nonsense. Just start. I suggest you spend 15 minutes to a half hour a day trying something new. Before you know it, you'll discover that you've acquired a whole new skill set.

Try to approach new technologies when you don't need them. Pretend that you just bought yourself a new toy. When you have some free time, play around with it. Try it out on something that doesn't really matter. Show your friends and family some of its coolest features. The more the technology feels like a toy, the more your work is going to seem like play.

Carry around the instruction booklet with you so that when you are waiting in a doctor's office or for some other appointment, you can glean one new piece of information to help you with the technology. Whenever my assistant, Lois and I travel together, she tries to teach me one more feature on my BlackBerry. Don't try to swallow the entire manual — consume the information slowly, one bite at a time.

Overcoming objections to the cost

As a salesperson, you have to buy stuff as a professional courtesy to all of the other salespeople out there who are trying to make a living. If that's not a good enough reason to shell out some cash for the latest technologies, then consider some of the potential benefits in terms of sales and productivity:

- ✔ Increased sales as the new technologies generate leads
- ✔ Enhanced productivity, giving you more time to deal directly with customers or pursue other interests
- ✔ Increased opportunities as you discover innovative uses for new technologies
- ✔ Improved visibility as technologies including Web pages and blogs draw the attention of customers online
- ✔ Increased ability to recommend new technologies to your clients as another way of giving back to your clients and demonstrating your genuine interest in their success

I'm not sure what the culture is like in your industry, but in real estate, top selling agents rarely think about how much a product or service costs. They're more concerned with how much revenue it is going to generate. Even if the return on investment is dubious at best, an agent may try something new and expensive believing it has the potential for a good return.

Consult with someone in your industry who is tech savvy. The last thing you want to do is arrive at a conference thinking you've adopted the latest, greatest technology only to discover that you should have purchased something better — you've blown all your money on cutting-edge technology and have nothing left to invest in bleeding-edge technology.

Getting over the feeling that it's unproven

One school of thought promotes the idea that you should always wait until a technology has proven it has legs before making it a part of your daily business. I didn't graduate from that school. Instead, I analyze the technology on my own and with the assistance of my more technically gifted colleagues to determine whether it can do any of the following:

- ✔ Save me time or money
- ✔ Make me time or money
- ✔ Attract positive attention

If a technology can do any one of those three things, preferably all three, then that's all the proof I need to become an early adopter.

Pumping Up Your Productivity with Computers and Software

When I started selling houses back in the mid 1970s, students were still using slide rules, and all I needed to sell houses was a car, a phone, and a ballpoint pen. I would never have been able to sell over 300 homes in a single year were it not for my assistant. I was one of the very first to see the value in an assistant. Computers and the software deliver similar advantages, enabling you to accomplish more in less time.

Computer technology has enabled me to push home sales into overdrive and eventually attain warp speed. I can instantly pull up a list of thousands of contacts complete with notes about birthdays, anniversaries, and names of spouses and kids; e-mail thousands of contacts with a single click of a button; and broadcast articles, audio, and video across the country and around the world for the cost of a few pennies.

A computer equipped with the right software can significantly increase your productivity, reduce errors, and boost sales. In the following sections, I describe the equipment and types of software that no salesperson should live without.

When you show up with the latest technology in tow and demonstrate that you can use it, you project an image of competence. Clients want to work with a salesperson who's not only old-school personable but also new-school tech savvy.

Becoming a road warrior

Salespeople make up a fair percentage of the road warriors in the business world, and if you're part of this crowd, you carry your office with you. Make sure that your traveling office is properly equipped by purchasing and mastering the following essentials:

✔ **Notebook or Tablet PC:** A high-quality notebook or Tablet PC is a must for delivering presentations on the road, carrying your most important digital documents along with you, and staying connected with the home office and your other clients. For less than $1,000, you should be able to get a fairly high-powered notebook PC with 512MB RAM, a 60GB hard drive, a CD/DVD player, a 15-inch or larger screen, and Wi-Fi capability (so you can get wireless Internet wherever it's available). If you're in a business in which you or your clients may need to sign documents, I highly recommend a computer that enables you to sign on-screen using a stylus.

✔ **Portable printer:** Even if you do everything on the computer and send it back to the office, I recommend that you pack a portable printer, just in case one of your clients is more comfortable looking at marketing materials on paper or requests a paper copy of a contract.

✔ **Wireless Internet access:** Many hotels, coffee shops, and offices have Wi-Fi (wireless Internet access), and most computers have the capability to access it when it's available. But having your own wireless Internet service is a good idea. Sprint, Verizon, T-Mobile, and other communications companies offer wireless Internet. Shop carefully to choose a service with coverage in the areas where you most commonly travel.

✔ **BlackBerry or Pocket PC:** For times when you don't need to lug around your full-featured notebook or Tablet PC, a pocket PC enables you to keep in touch without weighing you down.

✔ **Digital projector:** If you deliver presentations to only one or two clients at a time, you can forego the digital projector. Your clients can easily watch your presentation on the computer screen. If you need to deliver presentations to roomfuls of people, then a digital projector is a must. To choose the right projector, you typically have to make some tradeoffs in terms of image quality, price, and weight.

✔ **Ethernet cable:** Although most hotels are going wireless, some still require a cable to connect to the Internet. Toss an Ethernet cable into your carrying case just in case. Your Ethernet cable can even save you some money; many business hotels charge to use their wireless service, but you can get free high-speed cable connections right in your room.

✔ **Power adapter for a car:** A power adapter that plugs into your car enables you to charge your computer's battery while you travel from one client to another. Make sure you get the right adapter. Visit your local electronics store and explain exactly what you'll be using it for.

- ✔ **Power strip:** Carry a power strip. A power strip not only enables you to plug several devices into a single outlet, but it also functions as an extension cord, so you can reach an outlet a little easier. I often use my power strip at the airport and even share it with others who are waiting for flights — it's an excellent tool for networking with people in need.

- ✔ **Digital audio recorder:** I use a digital audio recorder to take note of any ideas that pop into my head and to record my presentations, so I can review them and improve on them later.

- ✔ **Digital camera:** You never know when you may be presented with a photo op. Some of these cameras are so tiny now, you can practically pack them as easily as a credit card. Better yet, get a cellphone that has a digital camera built right into it; some of these cell phone cameras can even record short video clips.

- ✔ **iPod or MP3 player:** Don't waste a moment acquiring knowledge. If you're not reading a book, you can be listening to a book on tape . . . or get pumped up for your next presentation by listening to your favorite tunes. This is another area where you can lighten your load by buying a cellphone that has digital recording capabilities.

- ✔ **Headset:** If you have Skype or some other VoIP (Voice over Internet Protocol) phone service, carry a headset, so you can plug into your computer to talk on the "phone." Some of these services can even push the signal directly to your cell phone, so you don't have to lug around a headset.

- ✔ **Your copy of *Advanced Selling For Dummies*:** Hey, you're going to need something to read on the plane and in the hotel room. This book can also be a great conversation starter that assists you in meeting new prospects.

If you plan on delivering a sales presentation on the road, make sure you have all the equipment you need and that your equipment is working properly prior to departure and as soon as possible after you reach your destination. You don't want to discover just minutes before giving your presentation that you forgot the cable that connects your notebook PC to your digital projector. If your client has promised to provide the equipment you need, call ahead to remind them and show up early to test everything.

Draw up a checklist of everything you need to pack. I recently went on a trip and was careful to pack all of my electronic gadgets, but I forget to pack my driver's license. That definitely made flying much more difficult. I really had to rely on my sales skills to get on that plane.

Mastering a contact management program

The single piece of software that no salesperson should ever be without is a contact management program. I use Microsoft Outlook. Other salespeople

I know are die-hard ACT users. I'm not about to go on the record saying one is better than the other, but I do recommend that you use a contact management program.

And when I recommend that you use a contact management program, I'm saying that you should use it to its full potential. You can accomplish this by reading up on the program you decide to use. Check out *ACT! 2007 For Dummies* by Karen S. Fredricks or *Outlook 2007 For Dummies* by Bill Dyszel.

If all you're recording are client names and contact information, you're not collecting enough information. Gather and record as much personal information about your clients as possible, including the following:

- ✔ Birthday
- ✔ Spouse's name and birthday
- ✔ Wedding anniversary
- ✔ Children's names and birthdays
- ✔ Hobbies and favorite pastimes

Whenever you contact a customer, you want to make a good impression and an emotional connection. Show your client that you care enough about them personally to remember details about what is most important to them. Although I encourage you to gather details about your customers, don't make your calls sound like interrogations. Gather the information slowly and naturally during the conversation.

Knowing your way around a presentation program

When you're delivering a presentation to prospective clients, you want your presentation to look as professional as possible, and there's no better way to do that than to create it and deliver it with a presentation program, such as PowerPoint.

PowerPoint and other presentation programs almost force you to use your words sparingly and communicate with clients in a more audio-visual format. You can even create notes pages to leave with your clients and post your presentation online, so your more tech-savvy clients have ready access to it. Perhaps best of all, you can simply adjust a presentation you already created for a different client instead of starting from scratch. (For instructions, tips, and tricks for using PowerPoint, check out *PowerPoint 2007 For Dummies* by Doug Lowe.)

Making 100 phone calls in your Hour of Power!

Every weekday, I spend one hour making 100 phone calls. I call it my Hour of Power. My goal is to connect with as many people as possible who may generate leads for me. The Hour of Power is about connecting on a personal level and realizing the rule of 250 — that each person knows at least 250 other people they can tell about you. You have to keep in touch with the people you know in order to meet the people you don't know. And having a contact management program packed with names and information about the people you know is indispensable in making this work.

I picked up the strategy from Philadelphia's "Condo King," Allan Domb. After hearing that he was one of the top real estate agents in America, I shadowed him to witness the secrets of his success. Domb made the calls with the help of an assistant, and he used a collection of sound effects to interrupt calls that started becoming too involved. One sound effect was of a telephone ringing. Another was the sound of someone's voice calling him over an intercom. The Hour of Power isn't a time to get overly involved with one person. It's a time to connect with as many people who may be able to lead you to future prospects as possible.

Prior to my Hour of Power, I select a group of people I want to contact. The group may consist of the people I work with on the Macomb County Voice (a blog we created). It may be the top selling real estate agents I know through Star Power. It may be people I sold houses for or sold houses to. I tell everyone in the office that my Hour of Power is about to commence, and

they know not to disturb me. Then, I shut myself in my office and start placing calls.

If someone answers, I deliver my energetic greeting, ask them how they're doing, and perhaps mention one of the details I've recorded in my contact management program — maybe it's their anniversary or one of their children's birthdays. If nobody answers, I move on to my next call. If I get the answering machine, I leave a message. I may even sing "Happy Birthday," wish the person a happy St. Patrick's Day, or say something goofy right off the top of my head that I think will make them smile. What you say isn't all that important, but it can't be about selling.

When you're doing your Hour of Power, you cannot be interrupted. Make sure anyone who may be tempted to interrupt you knows not to. If you call someone and leave a message and that person calls back, someone in your office should answer the call and take a message, not interrupt you. You can call the person back later, after the hour is up. Your goal is to make it through your list of 100 people, and you have only 60 minutes to do it.

I strongly recommend that you implement the Hour of Power strategy in your business model. Keep a log sheet, and strive to achieve the goal of 100 calls a day. When I coach people, I have them turn in their call logs to me at the end of every week. Making the bare minimum of 25 calls a day delivers some benefit, but the truly successful salespeople are those who do closer to 100 calls a day. The most important part is to start doing it.

If you're still putting together your presentations in a word processing program or relying on printed marketing materials, one of the first software programs you should pick up is a presentation program. Clients are often mesmerized by a presentation on a computer screen that would otherwise put them to sleep, especially if they get to click through at their own pace.

Always have a backup plan in place. Technology is great when it works, but sometimes it doesn't, and when it doesn't, you still need to be able to function. I use PowerPoint for my presentations. I back them up on our server and carry two CDs in different pieces of luggage as well as on a jump drive when I'm traveling. You can usually find someone you can borrow a computer from, but you can't find someone who has your presentation on it. When giving presentations to clients, a backup plan is even more important. The show must go on, even if your computer won't turn on.

Tapping into the Web

The Internet is one of the more powerful and intriguing technologies from which you can benefit as a salesperson, because it's an entirely different world — a digital, virtual, multimedia world where clients and prospective clients not only passively absorb your message but also interact.

In some ways, selling on the Internet in the 21st century is more like selling from a corner store during the 1950s than like selling in the 1990s. The Internet is turning the entire world into a small town in which customers base their purchase decisions more on recommendations from peers than on marketing and advertising. To appeal to these 21st century customers, you had better have a presence on the Internet, particularly on the Web.

In the following sections, I reveal several ways to leverage the power of the Web to boost sales.

Researching customers and competitors

One of the main benefits of the migration of sales from the real world to the virtual world is that you now have easier access to information about your customers and competitors. Your competitors, at least a few of them, probably have Web sites or blogs. Customers who use your products and services may have their own Web sites or blogs and are probably hanging out in communities like MySpace as you're reading this.

Whenever I speak on the topic of marketing online, I almost always focus on the need to establish a presence on the Web, but another way to leverage the power of the Web is to use the information it contains to your advantage, as discussed in the following sections.

Hanging out with your clientele

Go online and hang out where your customers hang out. Get to know them. Become part of the community by contributing to their blogs and message boards. Get involved in their discussions, and offer your expert insights and advice. You don't have to give your sales pitch; in fact, doing so may harm your reputation in the community. By contributing something of value to the discussion, however, you begin to establish a solid reputation online as a knowledgeable and trusted source.

Contributing to the community means giving something of value. As a real estate agent, I often contribute by publishing articles offering tips to home-owners and people looking to buy a home. I also post answers to people's questions and publish articles to assist other real estate professionals. If you sell cars, you may post a newsletter with tips on caring for your car or how to choose the right car for you. If you sell computer software, you may post articles or messages on how to use some little known feature of the program or work around a common problem.

Checking out the competition

When you want to know what your competitors are up to, go online and find out. You can check out their Web sites, see what they're promoting and how they're promoting it, and gather all sorts of ideas on how to promote your products, services, and yourself.

You want to lead, not follow, so check out the competition, but avoid the temptation to mimic others.

Gathering leads

If you've already established a strong presence on the Internet, you may not need to rely on professional lead generation services to steer business your way, but if you don't have a strong Web presence or you need additional leads, check out some of the Internet lead generation services.

In the real estate and mortgage loan industries, lead generation services are a huge industry in and of themselves. I'm the official spokesperson of one of the larger real estate lead generation services — Guthy-Renker Home at HurryHome.com (for consumers) and RealtyTracker.com (for agents). This service offers home buyers and sellers valuable information about buying, selling, and owning a home. When a consumer signs up for the free service and shows interest in speaking with an agent, Guthy-Renker Home gathers their contact information and passes it along to one or more Guthy-Renker Home agents in the person's neighborhood, who can then contact the person.

Assessing the benefits of lead generation services

Lead generation services offer several benefits to you as a salesperson, including the following:

✔ **Advertising:** Lead generation services often do the marketing and advertising for you, so you can focus more resources on following up with motivated customers than trying to find them.

✔ **Screening:** The service commonly weeds out any less-promising prospects, so you deal only with serious candidates who have shown an interest in your product or service.

✔ **Gathering leads 24/7:** While you're performing other tasks, eating, sleeping, or even on vacation, a lead generation service continues to gather leads for you and deliver them on demand.

Before choosing a service, find out how many other salespeople are receiving the same leads, how old the leads are, and how the leads are screened. Bad leads are worse than no leads, taking up precious time and resources you could be spending on more profitable pursuits.

Making the most of your lead generation service

A lead generation service is only as good as you make it. Many salespeople claim that services sell the same leads to more than one salesperson, making it too difficult to actually get that person's business. While you should certainly shop for a service that provides higher quality leads and less competition, you have to do your part as a salesperson to make the most of the leads you receive. Here are some tips on how to optimize the leads you get:

✔ **Qualify those leads.** Your lead generation service may qualify some leads for you to screen out the worst of them, but you should have your own system in place for ranking prospects. Spend the most time on the top prospects.

✔ **Be the first to call and offer the best service.** The Internet is like a fast food restaurant — patrons are looking for instant gratification, immediate contact. Even slight delays can result in lost opportunities.

✔ **Follow up with a welcome e-mail message.** Have some information about you and your company and services prepared well in advance, so you can deliver it without delay.

✔ **Add the customer to a drip e-mail campaign.** A drip campaign may send the prospect a different message once a week or so to remind them of you. If prospects don't hear from you, they can find plenty of other salespeople to deal with.

✔ **Treat your lead like a customer.** Too many salespeople expect leads to be willing buyers. You still have to sell. Treat the prospect well, and you can turn the prospect into a customer. Continue to follow up, so that the person becomes a customer for life.

Every system, even lead generation systems, have drawbacks, but if you put a system in place, make a plan, and then work the plan, you will have more business than you know what to do with.

Marketing and advertising on the Web

The day I started writing this chapter, Google purchased DoubleClick, an online advertising firm, for $3.1 billion. That purchase delivers a very unambiguous message — online advertising works. To be a top salesperson in your industry, you had better be advertising and marketing on the Web, no matter what you sell.

In Chapter 9, I encourage you to set up your own Web site or blog as a form of soft-sell, self-promotion. You should also be looking into other ways of advertising your products and services and driving traffic to your Web site or blog.

Most of the major Internet search tools, including Google (Google AdWords) and Yahoo! offer affordable online advertising in the form of PPC (pay per click) ads. When someone searches for a word or phrase associated with your product or service, up pops a link to where you want the person to go. You pay for the ad only if someone clicks the link. PPC ads aren't foolproof. You really need to study up on them before you dive in, but both Google and Yahoo! have plenty of information to help you get started. (For more about Google AdWords and other tools for improving sales with Google, check out *Building Your Business with Google For Dummies* by Brad Hill.)

In addition to search-engine advertising, identify the sites that people most often visit to find out more about the products or services you sell and see if you can advertise on those sites. This may cost more than PPC advertising, but you have to advertise where your customers hang out.

Networking with colleagues online

With more and more people, especially salespeople, setting up shop on the Internet, you're likely to find colleagues from all over the world online. Every colleague is an opportunity to develop a new relationship, gather strategies and tips, share information, and open yourself to new sales and business opportunities.

To get in touch with the top people in your industry, join one or more professional organizations in your industry and check out what they offer online in terms of message boards, blogs, and other features where you can meet and share information with colleagues. Try to obtain phone numbers and e-mail addresses, and follow up by personally contacting the people you "meet" online.

Most of the top salespeople in any industry have their own Web site or blog, complete with their contact information. Visit their site, and if you like what you see, give them a call or send them an email message introducing yourself.

Tapping the power of pay-per-click advertising

As we were working on this chapter, Lois was reading to me and typing away. I was on another computer setting up Google AdWord campaigns. Currently I have 21 campaigns running at a maximum of $10 per bid.

For the last 90 days I had 2.5 million impressions (number of times the ad appeared on Google or a Google ad network), which led to 2,469 click-throughs to my Web site. I captured 2,469 new sales prospects for a total cost of 23 cents per click through at a three-month cost of $555.

If I converted only 2 of the 2,400 that clicked through, at a average commission of $7,500, that would equal to $15,000. If I can convert 20 then it equals $150,000.

This is definitely a great ROI (return on investment).

Discovering new sales "secrets"

Although some salespeople are very protective of their "secrets of success," top salespeople are so proud of their achievements that they can't help but broadcast them all over the Internet. Take advantage of this immense, free school of sales.

The real reason that top salespeople are so willing to share their "secrets" is usually because everybody already knows the secrets. The real secret of top salespeople is that they actually put into practice what every salesperson knows she *should be* doing.

Tuning in with the Latest Communication Tools

Twenty years ago, relatively few communications media were readily available — typically a phone and hand-delivered mail. Now you have access to fax machines, cellphones, BlackBerries, e-mail, instant messaging, teleconferencing, online seminars, blogs, conference call centers, voice mail, call forwarding, and text messaging. With all of these options, you can remain in contact with your customers 24/7, assuming, of course, that you take advantage of these technologies.

In the following sections, I reveal the communications technologies you should explore and offer some tips on how to maximize their effectiveness.

Optimizing the power of your phone system

If you finally traded in your pager for a cellphone, congratulations. You're one step closer to having the phone capabilities that customers expect in order to contact you at a moment's notice. You can do much more, however, to pump up the power of your phone system and use it to generate more sales. The following sections reveal some options you may want to consider.

Giving customers a toll-free number

Don't discourage customers who live in other states or countries from calling you by having them pay long-distance charges. Set up a toll-free line, so they can call for free. This is particularly important if you're a retailer. Giving customers a quick and easy way to contact you builds trust and makes customers more comfortable placing an order with you.

One of the best features of a toll-free number is that it rings through to your business number, so you don't need a separate phone line. In addition, this allows you to take the toll-free number with you if you move your business.

Implementing automatic call forwarding

Just because you're on the road doesn't mean you're out of touch. With call forwarding you can have any incoming calls routed to whatever phone number you choose — your home phone, cell number, or even the hotel where you're staying in Fiji.

Call your phone company to ask about call forwarding and other services they offer. Phone companies are constantly developing new communications technologies and may have something available that you haven't yet heard about.

Making your voicemail greeting more personal

When customers call or prospective customers return your calls, leave the impression that their call is important to you by playing a special voicemail greeting. Change the greeting daily or at least every week. Instead of using the standard, "Hello, you've reached Plackard Industries, please leave a message after the tone," say something like, "Happy Valentine's Day!" (or whatever day it is), let them know where you are, what you're doing, when you'll be back in the office, and how they can contact you or someone who's covering for you in the meantime.

My attorney, Ralph Margulis, from the Jaffe Raite Law firm is one of the best at leaving detailed and timely greetings. He changes his greeting daily, advises what his schedule is going to be for that day, and ends it with his famous sign-off, "And have a great day!" He tells you whether he'll be out of the office or has a lunch meeting. He tells you the best times to call. He mentions an emergency number. He doesn't use a cellphone, but he always manages to return calls fairly quickly.

In addition to recording an up-beat and memorable voicemail greeting, work on the greeting you use when you answer the phone. "Hello?" Doesn't cut it. If the caller's ID appears, greet the caller by name. Smile when you answer, so you sound happy to hear from the person. Deliver a greeting that the person is unlikely to hear from other salespeople, such as, "Mrs. Dithers! Thanks for returning my call. What can I do for you today?"

Text-messaging customers and clients

Although I wouldn't recommend carrying on a text messaging dialog with one of your customers, text-messaging is a great way to enable your customers to leave you a message . . . especially if your customers are more inclined to type than talk.

With text messaging, your customers or clients can send you a message using their phones, instant messaging software on the their computers, or a wireless handheld device, such as a BlackBerry. They simply type the message and instead of sending it via email, they send it to your phone.

Text messaging is sort of a combination of e-mail and instant messaging for cellphones and portable wireless devices like BlackBerries. On a cellphone, when you receive a text message, the phone typically rings a special tone to indicate that you've received a text message. You can then select a special menu option for checking text messages, read the message, and respond to it using the buttons on your cellphone's keypad.

Always accommodate your customer's preferences, particularly in respect to how they prefer to communicate. Some people love talking on the phone and others hate it. As a salesperson, you should be comfortable with all communications media.

Adding a conference call center

Relatively recently, I installed a conference call center, so my clients, colleagues, and the people I coach can call in and meet one another. I can even record the conference calls and have them transcribed or simply file them in case the calls generate ideas that I may want to follow up on later.

The conference call center has been one of the best investments I have ever made. I can even hold workshops over the phone with real estate agents from across the country. They simply call the central number, enter a secret code on their phone, state their name, and join in the meeting.

Improving e-mail efficiency

You probably know how to send and receive email messages, but you may not be aware of all of the fancy features your e-mail program has that can make your life easier, including the following:

- **Filters:** You can set up e-mail filters to have messages automatically sorted for you into separate folders. You can then prioritize the messages you want to answer first. You can even *filter out* messages that will only waste your time by having them sent to the Deleted Items folder.

- **Groups:** If you find yourself frequently sending the same messages to the same people, consider creating a group that contains everyone's e-mail addresses. Instead of entering each address separately, you can send a message to the group to have it distributed to everyone in that group.

Every week, I send out 9,000 messages to fellow real estate agents and other contacts across the country. In these weekly messages, I usually offer some valuable tip, something inspirational such as the movie *212 Degrees*, or a holiday greeting. This is my way of giving back to the community whose support I value so much. Although you may not want to send out 9,000 -email messages every week, I encourage you to send something to everyone in your address book at least once a month.

Hopping on the BlackBerry bandwagon

BlackBerries and similar portable wireless devices have led the charge of what's called Sales Force Automation (SFA). Equipped with wireless e-mail and phone service, voicemail, GPS, and other features, it enables companies to store information about customers in a central location and provide remote access to that information to everyone in the company, particularly the sales force. It also allows management to track its salespeople in the field.

Salespeople often resist any attempts by management to automate sales. They don't like having to hand over their client portfolios and share the information they spent so much time gathering. They hate the fact that management can trace their movements in the field via GPS. And many salespeople simply don't want to spend time learning how to use a new gadget — time they could be using making sales and earning commissions.

I believe, however, that the benefits far outweigh the potential drawbacks:

- You can carry your contact information with you.

- You can send and receive e-mail on the road.

✔ You can use your BlackBerry to talk on the phone.

✔ You can surf the Web without having to open your notebook computer.

✔ If a customer fails to show up for a meeting, you can connect to your central office and find another prospect in the area to visit.

✔ If your customer does implement some SFA solution, you can compare your performance to other salespeople at your company and discover areas where you need to improve.

✔ You can find the closest Starbucks in the area — you can even get directions to it. Okay, maybe not essential, but I guess that depends on what a cuppa joe can do for you.

BlackBerry devices can become addictive, so be careful. These gadgets are referred to as CrackBerries for a reason.

Keeping in touch with instant messaging

Because I'm on the road a good deal of the time, I rarely use instant messaging to keep in touch with clients, but many salespeople who sell primarily from their computers find that instant messaging (or IMing) is an excellent communications tool.

With an instant messaging program, such as AOL Instant Messenger (AIM), Yahoo! Chat, or iChat, you can communicate via computer and the Internet with someone on the other side of the world instantly . . . assuming you both have computers and compatible instant messaging programs. These programs have become sophisticated enough to handle not only text messages but also voice and video.

You can continue working on your computer with your IM program running in the background, and when a customer sends you an instant message, you're automatically notified of its receipt. You can then type and send the person a message, call the person on the phone, or even teleconference with the customer, as explained in the following section.

Teleconferencing over the Internet

Teleconferencing hasn't quite achieved the promise it had in the Jetsons, but with the Internet, it's getting closer and closer. With your computer, a high-speed Internet connection, and the right software, you can now teleconference with clients and colleagues from all around the world.

One of the most exciting video teleconferencing companies I've seen lately is Extreme Video. It features a product called High Speed Video's Video Meeting, which can connect business locations from around the world. The broadband connections enable on-demand teleconferencing at broadcast quality, so you can call meetings on the spur of the moment and feel as though you're actually sitting in the same room as the people you're talking to. For additional details, visit Extreme Video at `extremevideo.us`.

I mention Extreme Video as a communications technology that's on the horizon. During the writing of this book, it wasn't exactly a mainstream product for your average salesperson, but there was a time, if you can believe it, when not all salespeople carried cellphones and you couldn't get broadband Internet at the airport. Video teleconferencing may seem like Jetson's material, but it's going to be here sooner than you may think.

Chapter 13

Picking the Right People to Fill the Gaps

In This Chapter

▶ Spotting opportunities to outsource your workload

▶ Building a systems-based sales staff

▶ Hiring great people and treating them right

▶ Firing slackers and incompetents

▶ Beefing up your staff with virtual assistants

The "Me" generation fooled us into thinking that we were independent beings — masters of our own destiny able to achieve success without the assistance of others. This sort of thinking limits your upside, which clamps a lid on your goals. With limited people power, you limit your time and availability to pursue other, potentially more lucrative and more intriguing opportunities.

The fact is that you are not just you. You are the sum total of you and all of your relationships. By tapping the power of other people, you expand your potential exponentially. You quickly discover that you can do anything, because what you can't do, you can find someone to do it for you . . . and usually faster, better, and more affordably than you can do it yourself.

In this chapter, I lead you through the process of identifying your limitations, choosing the tasks you find most enjoyable and profitable, and hiring out the rest.

Generally speaking, salespeople are good at building relationships. That's primarily your job, what you should be best at. Hire out all the other tasks, including marketing, Web site or blog design, filing, and so on.

Identifying Outsourcing Opportunities

Throughout this book, I tell you to do about 6,000 more things than you're already doing. You're probably thinking at this point, "Is this Ralph R. Roberts guy for real? Is there one salesperson on the planet who could possibly put all these suggestions into action?" You' may even be wondering whether I practice what I preach. Maybe I'm just all talk. Maybe I'm one of those overpaid sales consultant guru types who's never really sold anything.

Well, I'm here to tell you that I do practice what I preach. I do everything I recommend in this book . . . well, I sort of do it all. Actually, I pay a lot of people to do much of it for me. And you can do the same thing. You just have to figure out what nobody other than you can do, determine what you really love doing, and then hire out the rest.

In the following sections, I show you how to identify responsibilities you can outsource to increase your own productivity and job satisfaction.

Taking inventory of everything that needs to get done

Today, preferably right now, I want you to jot down a list of job responsibilities and tasks you must complete. You can divide your list into work-related and non-work-related items. Why am I including non-work-related items? Because to optimize your schedule, you have to be ready, willing, and able to delegate tasks in both your personal and professional life.

Get 'er done

Salespeople who feel constantly overwhelmed by how much they have to do and how little time they have to do it often make the mistake of thinking in the first person. "*I* have to do this. *I* have to do that. If *I* don't have this report done by Friday, I'll be working all weekend." Blah, blah, blah.

True, all of these things *need to be done*, but that doesn't mean you have to do them. If somebody else does it, it still gets done, but without your having to spend time and energy doing it.

Drop the "I" and start thinking in the passive voice... "this *needs to get done*, that *needs to get done*, this report *needs to be finished*, this customer *needs to be contacted*," and so on. By thinking in the passive voice, you take on less of the burden and focus on the tasks at hand. Identify the tasks, hire people to do them, delegate, and then do what you're best at and what you enjoy.

Remember, "Get 'er done," doesn't mean *you* have to do it.

Your list can include everything from large projects to the tiniest tasks. You may include answering the phone, checking e-mail messages, cleaning house, picking up your kids from school, making lunch, brewing coffee, cooking, visiting with clients, creating presentations, running errands, and so on. Draw up a preliminary list and then add to it as you notice yourself performing different tasks. I want you to know everything you do in a typical day, week, or month.

To make this task a little easier, think of it as though you are in the process of creating a time budget. Instead of finding out where you spend every penny, find out how you spend every minute.

Highlighting tasks that only you can perform

When you have a comprehensive list of things you do in hand (from the previous section), highlight all of the tasks and projects that you and only you can perform. Start with the easy ones like eating, sleeping, and exercising, and then work your way toward more complicated tasks, such as visiting new prospects, coming up with ideas for new advertising and marketing campaigns, and creating reports and presentations.

Before highlighting an item that's in a gray area, ask yourself, "Am I really the only person who could do this?" If you can honestly answer "Yes," then go ahead and highlight it.

You're searching for the maximum number of tasks you can delegate, so go easy with the highlighter.

Highlighting tasks you love doing

Hold on, don't put that highlighter away just yet. Go back over the list and highlight the tasks that you love to do. Maybe you enjoy mowing the lawn or washing the dishes. Perhaps you find folding laundry therapeutic. You love coaching your kid's soccer team and baking cookies for the school. Go ahead and highlight all those activities. If you love doing it, highlight it.

This isn't an exercise in maximizing your time at work or removing all enjoyment from your life. The ultimate goal is to make your life more enjoyable and rewarding by outsourcing all but the most enjoyable, fulfilling, dollar-generating tasks.

Pinpointing what you hate doing

As a child, you probably felt very comfortable expressing your dislike for certain activities. Maybe you hated doing the dishes, cleaning your room, or doing your homework. Chances are, you were probably pretty vocal about it, and if you could get away with not doing those things, you would.

What's funny is that as adults, we become much less vocal about the things we hate to do and much less determined to avoid them, even though we have much more power to delegate them to someone else. If you're like most adults, you just "suck it up" and do what you feel you *have* to do. But sucking it up isn't the best way to accomplish anything. In fact, it usually leads to mediocre results.

Return to that list of tasks you perform and place a star next to all the tasks you hate doing:

- ✓ **Tasks you know you hate doing:** If you find yourself saying "Ugh!" at the mere mention of the task, put a star next to it.

- ✓ **Tasks you avoid:** If you find yourself constantly putting off a certain task and doing something less important instead, you really don't like to do it, no matter what your brain tells you. Another good indication that you don't like doing something is that you're constantly making up excuses for not having it done.

- ✓ **Tasks you dread:** If you break out in a cold sweat or hives or have hot flashes just thinking about having to get started on something, you may need to delegate it or at least find assistance in doing it.

- ✓ **Anything that bores you:** If something bores you, it sucks the energy right out of you, and you shouldn't be doing it.

My first assistant

The first assistant I hired answered the phones. I was working in a real estate office, and we took turns on phone duty. I dreaded the time when my turn would come up, because I hated sitting at a desk waiting for the phone to ring. I wanted to be out there selling houses.

Instead of doing a job I didn't like and that was actually costing me money in missed opportunities, I hired a high school girl to take my place. She was perfectly capable of answering the phone and taking messages, and she had a great phone voice. Clients probably preferred

calling and hearing her voice rather than mine, and she loved it. She could sit at the desk and do her homework or her nails or whatever waiting for the phone to ring.

After hiring this first assistant, I haven't stopped. I know exactly what I need to attend to personally and what others can handle in my place, and I farm out as much of the work as I can. Remember, one of the best services you can provide to another human being who needs a job and income is to hire them.

Taking inventory of missing skills

Whenever you notice that certain tasks are not being completed on a timely basis, are not done as well as they could be, or you and everyone around you feels overwhelmed by the amount of work that's piling up, you should be looking for opportunities to hire someone full or part time to take on some of the work.

Even when you're not in the market for an employee, you should remain on the lookout for any new talent that may assist you in boosting business. Here are some areas you may want to focus on:

- A marketing maven to design and product marketing materials with more pop and sizzle

- Someone to design a newsletter and make sure each issue contains valuable content.

- A computer whiz who can handle Web site and blog design and management along with assisting you when you experience technical difficulties.

- A receptionist to handle phone calls, light filing, and perhaps even screening e-mail messages to call your attention to the most important ones.

Create a list of items you keep putting off or are struggling to get done. If you already have an assistant or two or three, have them add to the list, so you can identify the areas where you need the most help. Hiring someone who is proficient in the areas where you need some assistance will be well worth the money in the end.

Tabulating time-wasting tasks

Another great way to identify outsourcing opportunities is to highlight the biggest time-wasting activities you're involved in over the course of a week. I know, you're probably thinking "sales meetings," but time wasters usually include much more than unproductive meetings.

To analyze where your timewasters are, maintain a calendar for an entire work week, either on paper or on your computer. Make a note of everything you do and how long it takes you. This may seem like a big timewaster itself, but eventually, this investment is going to pay dividends. Log every hour for a week. At the end of the week, review your log and mark any of the following activities:

- Putting out fires

- Spending unproductive time on the Internet

- Wrestling with technology you have no idea how to use

- Pursuing distractions

- Procrastinating

- ✔ Performing tasks not out of necessity but only because you feel responsible

- ✔ Anything someone else could have done better, faster, or for less per hour than you earn

- ✔ Organizing — sorting, filing, deleting, throwing away, cleaning

- ✔ Looking for something — files, folders, supplies, people

- ✔ Waiting for someone to arrive, call, or meet you somewhere

Some of these timewasters, such as pursuing distractions, are things that you have to purge from your day through discipline. I can't help you with those. The rest of the tasks are candidates for delegation.

Designing your own Web site may not be the best use of your time

Kandra Hamric, one of my top virtual assistants who happened to contribute a great deal to the development of this chapter, built her own Web site. She thought it would be a fun, educational experience . . . a nice little weekend project. Well, as she tells the story, it didn't quite end up that way, but it did turn out well in the end:

> "When I first started my business as a virtual assistant for real estate businesses, I thought I could build a Web site. I figured it couldn't be *that* hard. I went out and bought myself a copy of Microsoft's Front Page. It took me a couple of days to figure out how the software worked, but I felt that I had a pretty good understanding of it, and away I went.

> "I started creating what I thought was going to be one of the best Web sites on the net. Boy, was I was wrong! I couldn't for the life of me figure out why my site looked different on different computers. I couldn't get everything to fit on one screen. Visitors were pulling up pages and hitting dead ends. And my site wasn't even showing up in search engines because I had no idea what SEO (Search Engine Optimization) or "keywords" were or how to go about improving my site's ranking.

> "Over the course of several months and with the assistance of some tech-savvy colleagues, I honed my skills. I have a great looking site, mastered Front Page and Dream Weaver, and am now into Open Source.

> "The moral of the story is this: If you don't have the skills to produce something worth showing people, you have two options: get the skills or get somebody with the skills. Because I'm in the business of using technology to support my clients, learning how to build and maintain a Web site was in my long-term best interest, but for you as a salesperson, it may not be. You're likely to lose more on commissions than if you simply hired a skilled web designer."

I have over 200 Web sites and blogs. I love the technology. I enjoy seeing my articles posted online and having visitors comment on them. Did I create them? No. Do I manage them? No. I hire people who are more skilled at building and managing these sites. I enable them to do what they do best by providing them with compensation, and they give me what I need — highly attractive and functional Web sites and blogs that attract a lot of attention.

Designing an Efficient System

Every business I own has a system in place complete with sub-systems for divisions or departments within my business. This is how most corporations are managed, as well, and how you should manage your business as an entrepreneurial salesperson.

A system typically includes the following key components:

- ✔ **Goal:** The stated objective. What you plan to accomplish.
- ✔ **Strategy:** An overall idea of how your business is going to achieve the stated goal.
- ✔ **Tasks:** Everything that needs to be done to launch and manage the business.
- ✔ **Personnel:** Skilled and unskilled personnel to carry out the daily operations.
- ✔ **Resources:** Equipment and supplies required.
- ✔ **Budget:** Money needed to pay for everything.

You're not exactly starting your own business venture, so you don't have to create a formal, detailed business plan, but you should take a systems approach in building and managing your personal sales staff (you and your assistants). Everyone should be aware of the goal and the tasks they are responsible for.

By developing a system for getting things done, you can be much more effective and efficient in hiring the requisite talent and then providing them with the training they need to carry out essential tasks.

You already know what you want your business to accomplish, and you have a pretty good grasp of the tasks that must be performed to accomplish your goals. The next challenge is to break tasks into steps and then assign tasks to the individuals who are best able to perform them, as discussed in the following sections.

Breaking tasks into steps

Document (or hire someone to document) every task you perform. Create a mini, step-by-step instruction manual for each task that's detailed enough so just about anyone can perform it. Leave nothing to question. The more detailed the steps, the fewer questions you have to field later. Include photos, illustrations, and other visuals, to make the information accessible to people with different learning styles.

Store a copy of your step-by-step instruction manuals in an easily accessible binder. You may also want to store a copy electronically on a central computer, assuming your office is networked. Be sure to update your instruction manuals when procedures change.

Consider creating a master binder containing all tasks. You may want to divide tasks by "department" or job title to make them easier to access.

Assigning tasks to assistants

After you have all of your tasks documented, assigning individual tasks to assistants is relatively easy, even if the person is a new hire or a temp. You simply delegate the task and point the person to the instruction manual. From there, the person should be able to figure out the rest . . . assuming, of course, you provided sufficient details in the manual. Of course, I'm assuming here that you have an assistant. If you don't, skip to "Hiring and Firing" or "Scaling Your Work Force with Virtual Assistant," later in this chapter.

As your mini-business becomes larger, you may opt for a more structured approach. You can assemble your instruction manuals into separate binders for specific job titles, perhaps one for your receptionist, another for your marketing coordinator, and your personal assistant.

You can go about planning an efficient system in either of two ways: Do it yourself with the assistance of any people you currently have on staff, or hire someone to come into your office and design a systems manual for you. However you choose to do it, you are likely to be involved in the early stages of identifying tasks that need to be performed.

Targeting specific projects

When you have a specific project to accomplish, such as setting up a new Web site, redesigning your marketing materials, launching a drip e-mail campaign, or installing a new automated phone system, take a systems approach to plan and complete the project:

1. **Set a goal.**

2. **Specify a deadline.**

3. **Identify individual tasks that must be accomplished.** (If you're creating your first blog, for example, you may need someone to design a logo, design the site, provide content, obtain a domain name, find a company to host the blog, figure out how to promote it, and add personnel to handle the increased number of sales calls and contacts.)

4. **Assign specific tasks to the people who are most capable of performing those tasks.**

Designing and implementing systems to perform daily tasks or complete new projects simplifies the process of managing and growing your mini-business by making it more modular. Each individual or group of individuals has one or more very manageable tasks to perform rather than having to do everything. If you implement a systems approach, you soon find that your office runs like clockwork, and you're wasting less time stamping out fires.

Hiring and Firing

You know *what* needs to be done, you know *how* it needs to be done, but you're missing the *who* — *who* is going to do it? You're working with a skeleton crew, and that skeleton crew is you. At this point, you need some staff, at least one person, full or part time, who can pick up the slack.

As a salesperson, you may not feel ready to play the role of personnel director for your personal sales staff, but that's exactly the role you need to play in order to staff up. In the following sections, I offer some guidance on how to hire the right people and fire the wrong ones.

Don't be in too much of a hurry when you're hiring someone to take on some of the workload. Spend some time reviewing resumes, interviewing, and checking references. You want someone who's a good fit, is going to stick around, and is a team player — someone who's willing to play a supportive role and doesn't want your job. You are going to invest time and money training this person, so pick a prospect who promises a handsome return on your investment.

Recruiting top-notch personnel

I'm always in the process of recruiting talented individuals to work with me and for me, and I often find them simply by bumping into them in the course of doing what I do. My secret, if you can call it a secret, for attracting top-notch talent is to be top notch. I provide the opportunities, tools, and direction to execute potentially profitable business ventures that people want to play a role in. I dress the part, play the part, and offer people real value. In exchange, they offer me their talent.

When I need to fill a specific position, however, I often have to go head-hunting, which is a little more difficult. It requires placing and ad, collecting resumes, and interviewing candidates. In the following sections, I lead your through the process.

Creating a job description

Before you can even think about placing an Help Wanted ad in the local newspaper, you'd better have some idea of the position you want the person to fill. Write up a job description, complete with a job title and a list of responsibilities. For details on creating job titles, see "Assigning meaningful job titles," later in this chapter.

If the person is going to be your marketing coordinator, for example, you may need the person to create and manage your Web sites and blogs, coordinate interviews with reporters, design marketing materials, produce copy for newsletters, manage your email campaigns, and so on.

Make the job description as detailed as possible. You want a candidate who's qualified to carry out as many of the tasks as you need done.

Advertising the position

When you're in the market for a talented employee, you want to attract as many qualified candidates as possible, and to accomplish that feat, you have to advertise the position.

Start with the local newspaper. Post a Help Wanted ad that includes the following information:

- ✔ A brief statement of who you are or what you do, such as "Local Salesperson" or "Car Sales" or "Software Sales"
- ✔ The job title
- ✔ A brief description of the type of person you're looking for, such as "organized" and "energetic"
- ✔ A brief description of the main job responsibilities
- ✔ A fax number or P.O. box number where you want applications and resumes sent

Don't include your phone number or address, unless you want to be inundated with phone calls and visits. Have applications and resumes faxed to you or mailed to a specific P.O. box. This gives you time to review the applications and pre-screen for promising candidates.

Consider posting your want ad in several places, including online job sites, such as www.CarreerBuilder.com and www.Monster.com, which advertise both locally and nationally.

Preparing for the interviews

After you receive the majority of job applications, start sorting through the stack. Highlight the top 15 to 20 applicants, and start calling to set up interviews. You can pitch the remaining applications or hold on to any you may be interested in following up on to fill future positions.

Schedule no more than three interviews in a given day. You want to have in-depth interviews, so do fewer interviews better.

When scheduling the interview pay close attention to the person's voice on the phone. You can learn a lot by someone's phone mannerisms. If they are upbeat and motivated when they answer, they're likely to be upbeat and motivated in the office and in the presence of clients. If the person sounds as though she's just going through the motions, make a note, so you can follow up on that during the interview.

Prior to the interview, you may want to do some preparation to determine which candidates hold the most promise for a perfect fit. Here are some options to consider:

- ✔ Develop some way of testing candidates to determine whether they are qualified to perform certain tasks, such as typing, writing ad copy, and so on.

- ✔ Require that candidates take an online skills assessment test on a Web site such as www.BrainBench.com.

- ✔ Assess each candidate's compatibility with the personality type that would be best to fill the position. Several companies offer online personality profiling based on the DISC method — Dominance, Influence, Steadiness, and Conscientiousness.

Salespeople are often extroverts who tend to hire extroverts even when what they really need to fill a certain position is an introvert. Hiring someone of like kind can often be a big mistake that results in major personality conflicts later down the road.

Interviewing promising candidates

When you're unaccustomed to interviewing candidates for employment, you may not even know which questions to ask. Here are some key questions to get the conversation going:

Are you currently employed? Why are you looking to leave your current employer?

What do you feel is your biggest accomplishment in life?

What are your future goals?

What was your worst customer service experience and how would you have handled it differently?

Describe your best boss.

Describe your worst boss.

During the interview take note of some important qualities you should be looking for:

✔ Did the person smile while talking?

✔ Is the candidate a problem solver or a problem creator?

✔ Is the person's ultimate goal to take your position?

✔ How well did the person perform on any tests or tasks you had them do?

Never hire on the first interview. Take your time and interview all the candidates to see what they all offer, then narrow your list down again for a second interview. This process does take time, but is going to result in the hiring of a superior employee.

Assigning meaningful job titles

Everyone you hire is essentially your assistant, but they probably don't want to think of themselves as an "assistant." After work, they're going go out with their friends or home to their families, and somebody is going to ask, "What do you do?" They don't want to say, "I'm so-and-so's assistant." Your employees need titles that give them a sense of purpose and self-respect, something that conveys a sense that they play key roles in your organization. Here are some job titles you may want to consider:

✔ Public Relations Liaison

✔ Director of Sales

✔ Director of Marketing

✔ Director of Operations

✔ Senior Sales Manager

✔ Client Care Manager

✔ Executive Assistant

✔ Business Manager

✔ Senior Business Developer

✔ Customer Service Supervisor

When you start looking for someone to fill a position, dangling an elite title often draws more and better candidates. Advertising a position for Executive Office Manager sounds a lot better than advertising for a Receptionist. In addition, when a client calls and wants to talk to someone in charge, they would probably rather talk to the Customer Service Supervisor rather than to a Customer Service Representative.

Empowering your personnel and letting go

Salespeople tend to be overachieving control freaks. I know, because I'm one of them, but micromanaging won't further your business or sales goals. In order to be a top salesperson, do what you do best and enable your staff to do what they do best:

- ✔ Trust your judgment in hiring qualified personnel.

- ✔ Let go of any thoughts that "nobody can do it better than me," "my way is best," and "my way or the highway."

- ✔ Give your employees the tools and resources they need to do the job right.

- ✔ Empower your employees to make decisions, and then don't question every decision they make. You don't want to have a staff that's always waiting around for approval and afraid to pull the trigger and make a decision.

- ✔ Involve your employees in setting the direction and goals for the company and for themselves. Employees who have a sense of ownership in the company are more likely to be highly motivated and offer suggestions for positive change.

If you micromanage your business, you essentially have a stranglehold on it that can choke the very creativity and energy out of your staff that you need to succeed. Anyone who begins to feel as though they are wasting their time and creative energy is going to be spending more energy developing an exit strategy. You don't want your employees to have one foot out of the boat, you want then to be rowing the boat with you.

Rewarding productive personnel

People don't generally work for the sheer pleasure of it. They usually need or want something — money, status, power, benefits, a pat on the back, and often a combination of all of the above. To retain your best people and motivate them to give you 100 percent, you have to reward them in some way. Here are some suggestions to add to your incentive program:

- ✔ Pay raises based on performance

- ✔ Bonuses, to show them that the more successful you are, the more successful they are

- ✔ Praise, both verbal and in writing

- ✔ A thank-you card showing that you recognize their efforts

- ✔ Employee of the month plaques and special recognition

- Dinner on the boss
- Special parking privileges
- An extra hour for lunch
- A gift card to a favorite restaurant or store
- A spotlight in the company newsletter
- More freedom and responsibility
- Free or subsidized classes to improve their job skills and stimulate their minds
- A fun office environment where it doesn't even feel like work

Some people work for the sheer pleasure of working, others for money, some for titles, and others for praise. Find out what motivates each of your employees and give them what they value most.

Knowing when to fire an employee

When an employee just isn't working out, you first have to determine whether it's his fault or your fault. You may have hired an incompetent slacker by mistake, the person may have undisclosed problems outside of work, or perhaps you failed to provide essential training and resources.

Before you send your employee packing, ask yourself the following questions:

Has the person been trained adequately by me or by another knowledgeable staff member?

Am I expecting too much? Reducing the person's workload or allowing more time to complete tasks may result in better performance.

Do other staff members view this person as an asset to the company? Maybe your estimate of the person's value is off.

Are communication lines open? Maybe the person feels as though she can't talk with you.

Can the office function without this person?

Does this person have all the tools and resources she needs to do her job?

Is something going on that I don't know about? Before pointing blame, ask questions. Don't make a snap judgment or decision based on false or missing information. Describe your dissatisfaction and ask questions. The person may be struggling with serious personal issues.

Don't set up an employee to fail by not providing the proper training and resources to do the job well and then blame the employee. If you haven't empowered the person, that's your fault, not theirs.

Although employees often have valid reasons for performing poorly on the job, they often have no good reason. These are the employees you need to fire, and the sooner, the better. To stay on the safe side, legally speaking, consult your attorney before firing anyone on your staff. The following list describes some common grounds for firing an employee:

- Steals from the company
- Draws negative attention to the company through words or deeds
- Doesn't pay attention to problems that keep recurring
- Procrastinates to the point of missing deadlines — shows no sense of urgency in respect to deadlines
- Takes no initiative — never volunteers for anything
- Becomes annoyed and confrontational when someone disagrees
- Requires constant supervision and reminders
- Rarely or never takes work home to meet fast approaching deadlines
- Doesn't take advantage of additional training or educational opportunities
- Blames others when things don't quite go right
- Consistently late or tardy for work
- Fails to attend or participate in office meetings
- Resists necessary changes to office procedures
- Socializes or gossips too much in the office
- Drags down office morale with a persistent negative attitude
- Criticizes or allows criticism of the company
- Refuses to adhere to the policies you've communicated to the staff
- Constantly pushes work off onto other staff members

Few people enjoy firing others, but you have to fire people who fail to fulfill the job requirements. If you won't do it for yourself, do it for the rest of your staff members who are hard working and conscientious.

Scaling Your Work Force with Virtual Assistants

You don't always have to hire full- or part-time staff to work in-house. You can staff up with virtual assistants, instead. *Virtual assistants* are freelancers who generally market their services on the Internet — that's where the "virtual" part comes from. They can do everything from processing forms to designing and managing Web sites to processing payroll and doing your taxes. And because they're freelancers, you simply buy as much work as you need and pay a flat hourly fee or by-project fee. You don't have to worry about paying taxes, offering additional benefits, or paying for vacations.

Most virtual assistants specialize in a certain field — writing, editing, Web design, transcription, database management, accounting, you name it. Each assistant typically has specialized training and all the resources required to perform a task better and more efficiently and affordably than you can do it yourself. They can be retained for one-time jobs or become an integral part of your team, devoting a certain number of hours to your business every month.

Following are some of the many benefits that virtual assistants offer:

- You pay only for the time the assistant works for you.
- You don't have to constantly find tasks to keep the person busy.
- You don't withhold payroll taxes or pay into unemployment.
- You don't pay for insurance or other benefits.
- They don't take paid sick days, holidays, or vacation days.
- They come fully equipped, so you have no overhead on office space or additional equipment.
- You don't have to fire them if they fail to perform — you just find someone else.

Perhaps the biggest benefit of using virtual assistants is that they enable you to scale your business immediately when business conditions change. You can scale up when you have more work to do and scale back when business tapers off. When you have in-house employees, you can't simply fire and rehire at a moment's notice, and you end up with constant overhead.

According to the 2nd annual survey by America Online and Salary.com in 2006, the average worker admitted to squandering 1.86 hours per 8-hour workday, not including lunch and scheduled break-time, which is down from 2.09 hours in 2005.

For more about virtual assistants, visit the International Virtual Assistants Association at www.ivaa.org and the Virtual Real Estate Assistant blog at www.vrea.com.

Part IV

Prospecting for Sales Opportunities

The 5th Wave   By Rich Tennant

In this part . . .

*B*usiness just isn't what it used to be. In the old days, you could hang out your shingle, post an ad in the local newspaper, take out a listing in the Yellow Pages, and attract enough customers to keep yourself and your employees pretty busy.

Now, more and more people are consulting the Internet to research products and services and buy them online. Relationship selling is becoming much more important. And if you want to remain competitive, you need to establish a strong presence on the Internet and in online communities.

How can you possibly keep up? The chapters in this part show you not only how to survive in this age of digital sales, but also how to beat out the competition.

Chapter 14

Harnessing People Power with R-Commerce

In This Chapter

▶ Building long-term success with an R-Commerce strategy

▶ Connecting the four C's of R-Commerce

▶ Establishing connections *before* you need them

▶ Leveraging the power of your R-Commerce network

▶ Strengthening relationships with your clientele

---

*I*n sales, the word "commerce" refers to exchanging goods and services typically with some sort of currency involved. Market conditions define the value of a product or service, and the value of everything that changes hands can be measured and quantified. You can measure the success of a business by examining its profit and loss statement. You can estimate an employee's worth by looking at productivity. You can even rank the value of your customers by the amount of revenue they bring in.

Underlying this quantifiable commerce is another commerce — *R-Commerce* (Relationship-Commerce). R-Commerce is the power that fuels the exchange of goods and services. Although it's not something you can easily measure, it's the force that generates new ideas, draws people together to execute those ideas, and functions as the infrastructure for advertising, marketing, and distributing the products and services spawned from those ideas. Yet, salespeople and other business professionals often limit their opportunities by focusing too much on commerce and not enough on R-Commerce.

In this chapter, I reveal the secret of R-Commerce — a powerful networking concept developed by business consultant and visionary Terry Brock — to refocus your attention and energy on the qualitative components of success. Here you discover how to establish synergistic relationships that ultimately deliver measurable results in the form of increased sales and profits.

Embracing the R-Commerce Philosophy

Those who build sales on the R-Commerce model are less like hunters and more like farmers. They invest time in learning the land, cultivating the soil, and nurturing prospects. They may not see the fruits of their labor for several months or several years, and some of the relationships they cultivate may not bear fruit, but over time, they reap a bountiful harvest and spend very little time chasing down leads.

In the following sections, I reveal why R-Commerce is so critical to your success and show you how to shift your thinking to focus less on your bottom line and more on building productive and profitable relationships.

Exploring R-Commerce applications

Entertaining the concept of an economy built on the foundation of relationships may seem like a time-wasting intellectual exercise devised by some professor of business who took many sociology classes, but it actually has several practical applications, including the following:

- **Generating ideas:** People from complementary and sometimes even contradictory fields or disciplines can often collaborate to inspire one another to invent the next big thing.

- **Boosting productivity:** Strengthening relationships among coworkers and between management and employees motivates everyone to work together to build a more positive and productive workplace.

- **Increasing sales:** Making your customers more successful typically results in increased sales, as your customers grow their businesses and expose you to new opportunities. Chapter 18 shows you how to focus on your customer's success.

- **Streamlining operations:** R-Commerce is often the driving force behind mergers. Competitors may realize that by combining their companies, they can slash costs. When I was considering moving my office, I contacted a colleague who owns a business that offers complementary real estate services. In addition to saving on the cost of the building and other resources, we hope to generate business for one another.

- **Combining strengths:** Individuals or companies with specialties that complement one another can often capitalize on relationships that benefit both partners.

✔ **Improving scalability:** Relationships can develop and dissolve as needed to provide expertise and resources on-demand, enabling small businesses to act like big businesses and vice versa.

✔ **Adapting to change:** In the fast-paced global economy, change ripples through the system like a lightning bolt. You can't stay on top of these changes by yourself. Having relationships with people in numerous, diverse fields enables you to spot impending change earlier, adapt more quickly, and seize new opportunities.

R-Commerce is often driven by mutually beneficial partnerships. When looking for productive partnership candidates, consider anyone you would like to sell your product or services to and anyone you would like to receive referrals from.

Noting the importance of R-Commerce

My friend and colleague, international speaker and business consultant Terry Brock witnessed the negative effects that result when companies overlook the importance of R-Commerce. Terry shares his story:

"In college, I worked for Goodyear Tire and Rubber Company as a member of United Rubber Workers Local 185 in Jackson, Michigan. I had a union job . . . great benefits, super salary, and a relatively secure position, just like many of my coworkers.

Yet, throughout my time at the company, I never once heard any of the union members express a desire to help the company achieve greater profitability, greater respect in the community, or anything positive. The prevailing attitude was 'company bad, union good,' and most of the workers invested most of their time trying to think up ways of getting more out of the big, bad corporation. Those who were with the company the longest and had the highest salaries and best benefit packages were the worst, having little else to say about the company than, 'Well, they've got us by the beanies.'

Job security worked against the health of the company. Employees had no incentive to improve intellectually or acquire new skills. They thought they were doing the company a favor simply by showing up on time and putting in their eight hours a day. The only time they took some initiative was to file a grievance with their union rep if anything went wrong.

The attitude was not one to foster an atmosphere of innovation and productivity. It simply generated animosity, which ultimately hurt the business and everyone who benefited from that business. This same sort of thing is what's destroying the U.S. auto industry."

As Terry points out, R-Commerce is what drives success. Without a strong foundation of R-Commerce, a business is almost destined to fail. It may survive for a short time, but eventually it won't be able to compete against companies who build stronger, more productive relationships.

Retooling your mind

Refocusing your sales strategy on something as vague as relationships requires a fairly large shift in how you think about business. Toss out any concerns you may have about profit margins, sales quotas, and revenue. Think about building relationships. Think customer service. Treat everyone you meet as a partner — someone you can potentially team up with in a way that raises you both to a new level.

To build your sales career on the R-Commerce model requires patience and persistence. Don't expect an immediate payoff for your efforts. In fact, you may invest in several relationships that provide you with no observable benefit. Over time, however, you begin to see real progress. Focus on building productive relationships. Increased commissions and job satisfaction naturally follow. Be prepared to give R-Commerce time to work.

Discovering the Four C's of R-Commerce

When you think of R-Commerce in terms of sales, most people naturally think "customer." That's only one of the four "C" words that apply to R-Commerce. The other three are "company," "colleagues," and "community." As a salesperson, tending to relationships in all four C categories builds the strongest R-Commerce foundation for future success:

- ✔ **Company:** What's good for your company is good for your customers, colleagues, and community, and for you, as well. Look for opportunities to improve your company's success.

- ✔ **Colleagues:** Your colleagues include everyone you work for and with and anyone who works for you. Do whatever you can to surround yourself with the best people, and then make them better.

- ✔ **Customers (or clients):** Every customer who fails is a customer lost. Team up with your customers to make them as successful as they can be. As I show you in Chapter 18, this doesn't mean simply placating them. A customer or client often needs to be challenged to make a positive change.

- ✔ **Community:** Dynamic, vibrant communities are places where people want to invest and spend money. People want to do business with people they trust, people who are known in the community and working to effect positive changes. By investing time and resources in building and bettering communities, you build a dynamic, ever-growing consumer base, while making the world a better place.

When I talk about building communities, I'm not only talking about building communities in the real world. I'm also talking about online communities. I host a blog called Macomb County Voice (macombcountyvoice.com) where I invite others from my community to participate in a positive way.

With an R-Commerce mindset, you realize that money doesn't define an economy. The flow of money is simply a measure of how healthy the real economy, R-Commerce, really is.

Getting Well Connected

To be successful in the new R-Commerce economy, networking is key. It enables you to establish connections and discover a never-ending supply of leads simply by talking to people, letting them know what you do, and then kicking back and letting your network work for you.

Where do you start? A better question would be "Where don't you start." I network constantly, everywhere I go. Whether I'm rubbing elbows with colleagues at a convention, eating out with my family, buying a car, or attending a ball game, I'm meeting people and building relationships. As a salesperson, you should be doing the same.

Join or start a Meetup

A Meetup is a group of people who live in the same geographical area and gather regularly in an informal setting to share a common interest. You can go online at Meetup.com, search for a topic of interest, find a group of people in your area that share your interests, and find out the location and time of the next meeting. If no Meetup group exists, you can create your own.

Meetup groups cover every interest imaginable, from learning a foreign language to acquiring technical expertise or business skills. If you're living in Central Florida, for example, and are interested in learning Russian, you can join a group started by Jef Gray, a guy who works at the local utility company. The group meets regularly, usually monthly, at a restaurant or other location in a local community. Jef's wife, Lena, a Russian immigrant, has teamed up with Jef to organize the group and plan meetings and other activities. Students of the Russian language can meet with Russian immigrants and others interested in Russian language and culture to speak Russian, talk about the vagaries of being a Russian immigrant, and discover more about America from a Russian point of view.

Jef and Lena demonstrate the value of gathering various people together to acquire new skills and build lasting relationships in a fun-filled atmosphere. The meetings may or may not generate direct sales leads, but they open opportunities and build communities in which both personal and professional opportunities can flourish.

By *networking*, you never find yourself *not working*. Networking delivers more leads and opportunities for productive relationships than you're likely to have the time and resources to pursue.

Don't get sucked into believing that everyone you meet is committed to establishing mutually beneficial relationships. Opportunists may see you as a way to further their cause without having any desire or ability to further your cause. Watch out for these one-sided relationships. They can often drain your resources and energy.

Identifying networking opportunities

I didn't coin the 250 rule, but according to my field studies (at weddings and anniversaries), I have confirmed it — every person on the planet knows at least 250 other people. So I view every encounter I have with someone as a networking opportunity — a chance to connect with 250 people. If you're not quite ready to network with everyone you meet, consider the focusing on more formal networking opportunities:

- ✔ **Meet people on the job.** Get to know everyone you work with a little better.

- ✔ **Get involved in professional organizations.** Connect with people in your industry and with other salespeople. Join your trade association and start making a difference. See "Joining and Leading Your Trade Association," as discussed later in this chapter.

- ✔ **Join a community service organization.** Rotary, Kiwanis, Toastmasters, and other national organizations may have chapters in your area. These are excellent places to meet the most ambitious and successful businesspeople while giving something back to your community.

  Don't join an organization just for the sake of joining. Check out several organizations until you find an organization whose mission you can passionately support and whose people you feel comfortable around.

- ✔ **Join the local Chamber of Commerce.** I've never found the local Chamber of Commerce to be very effective in nurturing a business-friendly environment. The real benefit of the Chamber of Commerce is that it provides another meeting place for local business owners and community leaders.

When you join a club or organization, resist the temptation to sit with the same friends. Mingle. Also, unless the organization prohibits the handing out of business cards, don't forget to hand your card to everyone you meet, as discussed later in the section "Giving memorable tokens."

Soft-networking

In sales, you hear about the hard-sell and the soft-sell approach. You can network the same way. Hard-networking is a more aggressive strategy, in which you're generally driven to connect with people who may be able to do something for you in the future — generate leads, find you a better job, and so on. Soft-networking is more like socializing — you build relationships. Soft-networking is less business and more pleasure.

Think of networking as socializing, and you're likely to network more effectively.

Soft-networking builds relationships in which people are more comfortable approaching you because they know you're not just out to get something. To establish relationships that make you more approachable, be aware of the following do's and don'ts of networking:

- **Do belong.** Become a part of the community and donate your time and resources, so you're not the guy who shows up at meetings just to pass out his business card.

- **Do show interest in others.** Ask questions, contribute ideas, and offer assistance. People are more inclined to approach you if they feel as though you know something about them and their business and are concerned about their welfare.

- **Don't ask favors.** Build trust and a positive rapport first. You can ask for favors and barter talents and resources more naturally as friends than you can as acquaintances. Friends stay in touch even when they don't need anything, but when a need arises, the friend is there to help. Follow the age-old advice of "Make friends *before* you need them."

Take a break. Write down the names of five new people you want to reach out to and five old friends you'd like to get back in touch with. Contact one person from each list and see what happens.

Scouting for force multipliers

Who are *you* really? When you think about it, you're more than just you. You are the sum total of all of your relationships, past and present. The more relationships you have and the more productive each of those relationships is, the more you accomplish and achieve. Continuing your personal and professional growth process demands a constant pursuit of new talent and resources.

Woodrow Wilson said, "I not only use all the brains that I have, but all that I can borrow." When you embrace R-Commerce principles, you tap the brainpower and resources of others. You get more done by being with others than you ever could accomplish by yourself.

When you're networking, remain on the lookout for *force multipliers* — a term the military uses to describe any factor that dramatically increases the effectiveness of a military unit. This could be something high-tech, like satellite imagery revealing the positions of enemy troops to something environmental, such as having the sun at your back. In sales, a force multiplier can be a software program, a lead generating service (such as Guthy-Renker Home, for real estate agents), a drip e-mail campaign or any number of other tools that enable you to sell more efficiently. A force multiplier can also be a person with the attitude, intelligence, or other talents you need to take your career to the next level.

R-Commerce is about looking at a vast network of people whom you know and filtering problems and opportunities through that group. Who is particularly good at accounting? Who is particularly good at designing and building Web sites? Who's outstanding at motivating and communicating with team members? Identify these key people, these force multipliers, and add them to resource pool. When you have a great idea for making money, you can quickly assemble your all-star team and get to work.

Don't forget the role you play in assembling R-Commerce communities to work on projects. As the rainmaker — the person making this all happen — you're responsible for giving what you have to offer to these talented force multipliers:

- ✔ **Trade value for value.** Identify what the others on the team need most, and deliver it. Compensation may be in the form of money and benefits, new opportunities, increased status or credibility, assistance in a professional or personal matter, or something else you can offer. Remember that all people must benefit in some way from this association. No one will keep contributing to a task or project if they are not being compensated.

- ✔ **Find the right fit.** Align people with work that they're qualified to do and are going to find rewarding. Don't try to force a square peg into a round hole just to get something done. If someone isn't perfect for this particular project, they may be perfect for the next project.

- ✔ **Accommodate different personalities.** You may find one or two areas where you disagree, but don't throw the baby out with the bathwater. Embrace areas where you agree, and let the rest go.

Just as some people can be force multipliers, others can be force dividers. They can ruin the morale of an entire staff, ruin projects with their incompetence, and destroy dreams, visions, and creativity. R-Commerce does not work with negative people. I have had negative people in my life and tried to change them. It didn't work.

Gathering vital information

Whenever you meet someone new, whether you bump into them in person, over the phone, or online, use your sales skills to ask questions and gather the following information about the person:

- ✔ Career, work, or major in school
- ✔ Interests and hobbies
- ✔ Goals or dreams
- ✔ Special talents
- ✔ Contact information

Ask the person for a business card, and if she doesn't have one available, jot down the information in a notebook. You can enter the information into your database, as described in the following section, later. If the person does provide you with a business card, jot down some additional notes to remind yourself later of any details that aren't included on the card.

When I return to the office at the end of the day, I scan the card and then pass along any additional details to my assistant who types the information into my contact management program. I don't want to loose any shred of valuable information, so I try to tell the entire story of the person, including where and how we met and everything that person told me.

Building a database

Unless you have a photographic memory with total recall, I suggest that you start building a database of everyone you come in contact with . . . and I do mean *everyone*. Over my 30 years in real estate, I've built a database of more than 7,000 contacts, including real estate agents, mortgage brokers, loan officers, attorneys, Web site designers, corporate bloggers, marketing people, writers, editors, and people in every field imaginable. When I have an idea for a new project or need something done, I can immediately pull up my database and gather together a team of talented individuals to tackle the project. Moreover, if a customer mentions needing assistance in an area that's outside my circle of expertise, I can usually provide at least one, if not dozens, of referrals.

I'd like to meet you. Take a moment and email me with your information at ralphroberts@ralphroberts.com.

Categorizing your contacts

When you're gathering contacts and building your database, consider categorizing those contacts in terms of how urgently you need their services or how likely a customer is going to purchase your products or services. I generally place contacts in one of the following three categories:

- **Hot prospects:** Those whose services I need most or who need my products or services most urgently. You can feel the excitement or electricity as you discuss a future relationship. These are the prospects you should pursue most ambitiously. Give them laser-beam attention.

- **Warm welcomes:** Those with whom you would feel comfortable working or who are likely to need your products or services almost immediately but aren't exactly drooling over the prospect of working with you. These are the people you pursue as time allows.

- **Sooner or later:** Those who haven't quite showed up on the radar. You can't really see their talents or expertise serving you, and they really don't need what you have to offer, but you never know, so you add them to your contact list just in case.

Don't ever throw someone away. You never know when people can move from the "Sooner or later" category to the "Hot prospects" category. Keep them in the loop, using some automated technology, such as a newsletter or e-mail messages, but don't invest a great deal of time or energy trying to force a relationship.

Managing your list of contacts

I use Microsoft Outlook as my contact-management program. Some people love ACT! Others use a spreadsheet or database program or simply type the information into standard document, but these general-purpose programs don't offer the same power and flexibility as you get in a dedicated contact-management program. Using Outlook, I can store names, addresses, phone numbers, e-mail addresses, birthdays, anniversaries, and additional information about each of my contacts. I can print mailing labels, set up Outlook to notify me of meetings and important dates, and even transfer data to my PDA (personal digital assistant) to take it on the road. For additional guidance on how to get the most mileage out of Outlook, check out *Outlook 2007 For Dummies* by Bill Dyszel.

Consider purchasing a business card scanner, such as CardScan or Worldcard to simplify the process of entering information from business cards into your contact management program. CardScan can read a business card; transfer entries to the appropriate fields in your contact management program, PDA, or smart phone; and save the data online, so you can pull it up on any computer anywhere in the world that's connected to the Internet.

Giving memorable tokens

You have a relationship when someone returns home or heads back to the office thinking of you and when you return home or head back to the office thinking of that other person. Making a great first impression is certainly the most important step, as discussed in Chapter 4, but leaving the person with some tangible memorabilia is a great way to seal that first impression in their memories.

Carry some "gifts" with you wherever you go, so you always have something new to give to someone you already handed your card to. Here's a list items you may consider passing out:

- ✔ **Your business card:** A classy business card printed on high-quality card stock with raised lettering is the gold standard for memorable business tokens.

- ✔ **Your brochure:** Print up a professional brochure explaining who you are, what you do, and what you sell. Remember, you're not simply selling a product. You're selling yourself. Check out Chapter 9 for additional details on how to sell yourself.

- ✔ **An inspirational book:** For less than ten bucks, you can purchase inspirational books that can touch a person deeply and cause them to remember you for the rest of their lives. I used to carry around several copies of *The Platinum Rule* by Art Fettig (see the following sidebar, "Living by the Platinum Rule"). If someone already had my business card and brochure, I'd give them a copy of the book.

- ✔ **A thank-you card:** Nothing says "thank-you" better than a big, fat bonus or tip, but a thank-you card runs a close second. Have thank-you cards printed that include your contact information, and whenever someone does something deserving of a thank-you, write a personal message on the inside of the card and leave the card behind.

- ✔ **Flowers or candy:** For those deserving of a special thank-you, consider leaving behind a box of chocolates or sending a bouquet of flowers.

Joining and leading your trade association

If you don't already belong to your trade association, shame on you. You're missing one of the best R-Commerce opportunities on the planet. Your trade association is your community, and if you're not actively involved in that community, you're not tending to one of the four C's of R-Commerce — Community.

Living by the Platinum Rule

When giving, don't make the mistake of giving to get. Give for the sheer privilege of giving. Pay it forward. Art Fettig clearly points out the distinction between giving to get and giving to give in his book *The Platinum Rule*, but the best way to illustrate the rule is to look back at giving experiences you've had.

Think back to the last time you gave or loaned someone money or something else with the understanding that someday that person would return what you gave or repay you in some way and never did. Chances are pretty good that over time, your relationship with that person became strained. You may have avoided the person, because you didn't know what to say and felt uncomfortable bringing up the issue and clearing the air. Unbeknownst to you, the other person probably felt even worse than you did. Instead of resolving the issue, the relationship simply dissolved. What a tragedy! Giving actually ruined the relationship.

To avoid the ugliness that often results from giving and lending, Art recommends the Platinum Rule — give without expectations. The next time you give somebody something and that person says he'll pay you back, say, "Here's how you can repay me — never try to repay me. Instead, help someone else someday." The next thing you tell him is, "Please don't ever bring this up again. Consider the matter closed. I'm not going to say anything about it, and I don't want you telling anyone about it."

Shortly after I read *The Platinum Rule*, I called Art Fettig, and we struck up a conversation that led to a friendship that has lasted all these years. I started practicing the Platinum Rule, and the more I did, the more confused I became. I called Art and said, "I'm following your advice. I'm telling people not to tell people what I did for them, and they're telling people all sorts of good stuff about me anyway." Art replied, "Of course, that's what happens with the Platinum Rule. There's nothing you can do about it. You can tell people not to say anything to anyone, but they're going to do it anyway. They're going to say great things about you for the rest of your life. And now they're going to do something nice for another person in need."

Pay it forward. Start living by the Platinum Rule, and make the world a better place.

If you're already a member of your trade association, you deserve a pat on the back for taking the initiative, but now I want you to work your way to a leadership position. In every organization, the leaders have more stage presence, a higher profile. You don't even have to introduce yourself to others in the organization, because their goal is to introduce themselves to you.

Getting noticed in the community

Every businessperson, regardless of position, should be actively involved in the community. Communities not only buy products, but they support businesses, supply talented personnel, and spread the word outside of the community. You should be even more involved in the community if you're selling products and services directly to people in the community — for example, if you're a real estate agent, car dealer, insurance salesperson, restaurant owner, or retailer.

In the following sections, I guide you in identifying the communities in which you're a member and then offers some suggestions on how to become more involved.

Identifying your communities

Instead of advising you to get involved in your community, I should really be advising you to get involved in your *communities*, plural. Depending on how you define "community," you can be involved in several communities, including your family, neighborhood, city, state, nation, professional organizations, online communities (such as MySpace), and a host of others.

Jot down a list of all of the communities in which you live and sell. When you're done with that list, continue adding communities into which you believe you can expand your R-Commerce activities. This may include churches, service organizations, online communities (as discussed in Chapter 17), user groups, political organizations, schools . . . the list goes on and on.

Volunteering your services

Showing up for meetings is only the first step to becoming involved in your community. Take the next step — volunteer. Most organizations are in dire need of your skills as a salesperson to promote the organization and raise funds. When you volunteer, you join an elite group of community leaders, who usually happen to be the business leaders in the community, as well. Followers don't volunteer for anything.

Don't restrict yourself to volunteering for jobs you're good at. Volunteer organizations are one of the best places to acquire a free education and plenty of on-the-job training. Identify skills you want to acquire or improve, and see if the organization has any positions that require those skills. Better yet, team up with someone who has those skills and work as their assistant.

Don't just be a check writer. Giving money is great, but your time and expertise are even more valuable. Participate.

Giving free speeches and presentations

Service organizations often focus their meetings on specific topics and invite accomplished professionals to speak at these meetings. They may even offer you a token payment, but whether or not they pay, seize the opportunity to speak at meetings or special events. Again, this raises your profile in the community and opens you to new opportunities.

Speaking engagements also enable you to practice your public speaking skills, and if those are a little rusty (or non-existent), consider joining Toastmasters. Check out Chapter 9 for more about public speaking or buy (and read) *Public Speaking For Dummies,* 2nd Edition, by Malcolm Kushner.

Taking on a leadership role

Like businesses, organizations have hierarchies that start with "members" and go all the way up to "president." Don't settle for being a member. As I discussed earlier in this chapter in the section "Joining and leading your trade association," the higher your position in an organization, the more visible you are and the more opportunity you have to improve the organization.

When elections for officers roll around or the organization is appointing people to sit on the board of directors, get your name on the ballot. If you don't feel comfortable gunning for the presidency, start slow with a position as treasurer or secretary. The more comfortable you become in that position, the more likely you are to feel qualified to take on a more responsible role.

Becoming the Go-To Guy or Gal

After you've built a solid R-Commerce network, it begins to take on a life of its own and requires much less time and energy to maintain and grow. With your overstuffed Rolodex and your generosity, you now become the "go to" guy or gal, the communications hub that people come to whether they have a problem to solve or a brilliant idea to make tons of money.

Sometimes, you can charge a finder's fee or referral fee to put people in touch with one another, but in most cases, paying forward is the best approach.

As the person who knows everyone, you suddenly become the person everyone wants to know. People will seek you out when they need a good dentist, doctor, attorney, building contractor, web designer, graphic artist, you name it. And every time someone new comes to you with a question, you have the answer or the next best thing — someone else who can answer the question.

This provides you with the golden opportunity to give to two people; you assist the person who needs assistance and business to one of your contacts. You may not receive any monetary reward or compensation, nor should you expect it, but you've just made a huge deposit into your R-Commerce bank. Assuming the relationship you created is a positive one, both recipients of your gift are likely think fondly of you well into the future.

Healthcare professionals recommend that you exercise 30 minutes a day. Don't forget to exercise your give muscle. Live in a world of abundance and assist others in achieving their goals. By doing this, you create magnetism around you and people just naturally want to be near that positive energy. I know this can sound like a bunch of "woo woo stuff" and really "out there," but when you follow this approach, you really do generate a magnetic field around yourself.

Building R-Commerce with Your Clientele

Visit any comparison shopping site on the Internet, such as Froogle (`froogle.google.com`) or Dealio (`www.dealio.com`), and you're likely to find the absolute lowest prices for products you can find anywhere, online or off. Yet, most people continue to buy from major retailers. Why is that? And why is someone willing to pay over $3 for a cup of coffee at a posh coffee shop when they can grab a perfectly good cup of coffee at a fast-food restaurant for less than a buck?

The reason is that people don't just buy products or services. They're buying relationships. They're paying extra to feel special and to do business with someone they trust.

R-commerce is all about enhancing the total experience your clients have when they do business with you. When you're selling to a customer and doing it right, your customer feels a sense of partnership and security. Your customer knows that you're looking out for her best interest. In Chapter 18, I offer specific suggestions on how to use R-Commerce strategies to focus on your customer's success and improve your own success as a result.

Chapter 15

Prospecting for Untapped and Under-Tapped Markets

In This Chapter

▶ Identifying new markets for products and services

▶ Focusing on demographics

▶ Going global

▶ Bundling your goods and services

▶ Inventing other uses for your products

*W*hen you run out of leads, it's often tempting to think that you've run out of market. You may discover additional opportunities, however, in untapped and under-tapped markets — opportunities you may not yet have considered.

In their early days, for example, cellphones were primarily used for business. They quickly made their way into the home markets, and now even kids are packing cellphones. Why? Because clever marketing people were able to convince families that a cellphone is an essential communications tool for every single family member. When they discovered they were running out of road, they made more road.

Whatever you happen to sell, you can usually find untapped or under-tapped markets that could use your product but simply don't know about it or haven't thought of using it in a particular way. In this chapter, I encourage you to explore other markets and provide several clues on where to begin looking for ideas.

Seeing Business Where It Isn't

Sales opportunities don't exactly slap you in the face. They're extremely difficult to notice, because opportunities, by their very nature, are vacuums — they're invisible. You have to train your mind to look for the signs of a vacuum and, even better, envision something filling that open space. You have to train yourself to see business where it isn't.

The birth of FlippingFrenzy.com

For several years, I had been researching real estate and mortgage fraud and could see that they were big problems in the real estate industry. Con artists, many of whom were industry insiders, were fleecing the system and homeowners out of billions of dollars. Illegal house flipping and other forms real estate crime were increasing foreclosure rates and destroying neighborhoods.

Thousands of files crossed my desk and I was fielding phone calls from victims on a daily basis, but the media was clueless. I spend millions of dollars of my own but was still unable to get anyone from the media or government agencies to pay attention. I was ringing the

alarm bell, but nobody heard or took notice. I could see the trend, but I really didn't know what to do about it.

One evening, one of my real estate assistants, Sarah Hodges, came into my office, and we discovered blogs. The people who created these intriguing new online community centers seemed pretty excited about them, and visitors apparently loved the interaction and lively banter that these blogs seemed to generate.

Sarah and I were excited at the prospect of engaging the public in this innovative forum. Then, it hit me . . . a real estate and mortgage fraud blog . . . FlippingFrenzy.com! We were off to the races!

When I tell you to "See business where it isn't," what I mean is that you should look for markets that you and your competitors are not serving. Say you're selling satellite phones, for example. Ask yourself, who could really use a satellite phone that I'm not selling to? If you're only selling to business people who travel to areas where cellphone service is unavailable, you're missing out on other potentially lucrative markets, including the following:

- ✔ Foreign exchange students
- ✔ College students who may travel abroad
- ✔ Mountain climbers
- ✔ People who go on cruises
- ✔ Oceanographers
- ✔ Pilots

Some people can naturally think of a thousand and one ways to market a product, but you don't have to be born with a gift for it. You can train your mind to look for business where it's not and spot new opportunities. Here are some suggestions that can open you to new sales and marketing opportunities:

- ✔ **Look for trouble.** As a salesperson, you're selling solutions. Find a group of people with a problem that your product or service can solve, and you've discovered a new market. In my industry, the real estate business, I've been able to build entire new divisions on problem areas, including foreclosure, probate, and divorce.

✔ **Network extensively.** People often want to talk about their problems in the hopes that someone can solve them or simply to vent some frustration. In either case, networking enables you to hear more problems and discover more opportunities for solving those problems. Networking can also open you up to partnerships that may lead to other markets.

✔ **Read extensively.** Reading articles, especially articles that seem to have nothing to do with what you're selling, can often make your mind more receptive to opportunities.

✔ **Juxtapose two or more ideas.** Sometimes, neither of two separate ideas or technologies can open any doors for you, but when you combine the two, something magical happens — sort of like combining chocolate and peanut butter. The creation of one of my most popular Web sites happened that way, as I relate in the following sidebar — the birth of FlippingFrenzy.com.

You've probably seen clever new startup businesses and said to yourself, "Now why didn't I think of that?" The people who start these businesses see business where it isn't. Recently, I received a letter from a company informing me that they were aware that my name was on title for a piece of real estate I purchased about a year ago. It went on to say that many property owners don't have a certified copy of their deed and offered to get that for me. All I had to do was mail the completed, signed form back to them with a check for $69, and I would receive my paperwork with in four weeks. What a great idea! You can go down to the county and get a copy of your deed for about $1 through the Freedom of Information Act, but someone realized that property owners don't even know that's an option and would really like to have a piece of paper showing that they officially own their property.

 Become a lifetime learner to continuously open yourself to new ideas, markets, and opportunities. Just because the phone isn't ringing off the hook doesn't mean you should go into lockdown mode. You should be doing just the opposite — get out there and find out what's happening. Seek out the most recent trends and discover ways to tap into their momentum. Only by becoming a lifelong learner is this possible. Fill your mind, keep it active, and it will do the rest for you, intuitively making the connections that open the doors to new opportunities.

Considering a Different Demographic

Are you serving all markets, regardless of race, ethnicity, beliefs, or lifestyle choices? If you're not, then you're not tapping the full potential of your consumer base. You may be completely unaware that your marketing materials target a particular group of people at the expense of missing opportunities with different groups. By catering to these under-served customers, you can often win over a huge segment of the market that your competitors have neglected.

On Wheels

What Randi Payton, future CEO of On Wheels, Inc. had noticed about the automobile magazines stuffing the shelves at the local newsstands and grocery stores, would eventually lead him to build a multi-million dollar business of his own. Or perhaps it was what he had noticed was missing.

All of the magazines for automobile aficionados at the time catered to Caucasians. Randi knew full well that other ethnic groups loved their cars, too. He decided to create a company to provide multimedia information to Asian, Hispanic and African-American automotive enthusiasts, and

he started rolling out three national magazines — *Latinos on Wheels*, *Asians on Wheels* and *African Americans on Wheels*.

His magazines have a readership of over 1.3 million people monthly, and the publications generate $2.5 million in advertising sales.

Through his vision and insight, Payton stands as a glowing example of how you, as an entrepreneurial salesperson, can begin to see business where business isn't and capitalize on it. For more about On Wheels, Inc., visit www.OnWheels.com.

To appeal to different demographics, you have two options — revise your marketing to be all-inclusive or develop new marketing materials to target specific groups that your other marketing materials seem to miss.

In the following sections, I provide additional insights and tips on who to serve certain market segments that traditionally have been neglected — specific generations, people who are disabled, racial or ethnic groups that may be under-serviced, and global markets.

Targeting a generation

Salespeople often focus on people who are part of the same generation they are. Plastered all over their brochures, Web sites, and other marketing materials are people who look and dress just like them. After all, selling anything is easier when you're selling it to someone who have more in common with.

When you're looking to boost sales, however, you may need to be a little more accommodating in both your marketing and sales. The following sections offer some tips on how to bridge the generation gap.

Every generation has a set of common experiences, values, and way of doing things that distinguish it from past and future generations. By remaining sensitive to these differences, as discussed in the following sections, you can market and sell more effectively to people from different generations:

- **G.I. ("Greatest") Generation:** 1901–1924
- **Silent ("Post War") Generation:** 1925–1945

- **Baby Boomers:** 1946–1964
- **Generation X (a.k.a. Baby Busters):** 1965–1976
- **Generation Y (a.k.a. Millenials or Echo Boomers):** 1977–1994

G.I. Generation

The G.I. Generation experienced the two Great Wars — World War I and World War II and managed to survive the Great Depression. People in this generation tend to be frugal, have a great respect for traditional values, and generally own their homes, which they don't plan on selling any time soon.

When selling to the G.I. Generation, be prepared to focus on quality and value. Most of your customers are likely to be living on fixed incomes and are very focused on making their money last.

Silent Generation

The so-called Silent Generation was born and raised between two great periods of global upheaval — the two World Wars and the Vietnam Era, complete with its Cold War. They may not have fought in the Great Wars, but they certainly suffered through them and, perhaps as a result, came to value family and security above all else. Because of this, the Silent Generation has been officially labeled the generation of the "withdrawn, cautious, unimaginative, indifferent, unadventurous, and silent."

When marketing and selling to people in the Silent Generation, keep the following information in mind:

- Risk assessment is likely to play a major role in the purchase decision.
- Work ethic is highly valued. Don't be late, and be prepared to work hard to gain your client's respect.
- Treat your clients with respect, addressing them as Mr., Mrs., or Miss, followed by their last names. These folks are likely to prefer being treated more formally.
- Be prepared to talk about costs. This generation grew up during tough times when food and other goods were rationed. They are generally very conscious of price and value.
- Speak and act conservatively.
- Focus on convenience, simplicity, ease of use, service, and support.
- Present your products and services with a "you earned it" message. Give them permission to spend their money.
- Don't waste their time.
- Face-to-face meetings are generally most productive.

✔ Although people of this generation may be fairly affluent "retirees," they are living in a time when medical advances have greatly increased life expectancies, and many worry about outliving their savings. Depending on what you're selling, this could be good or bad, but you should be aware of it.

Don't assume that the Silent Generation is technologically illiterate. Many members of this generation are quite skilled on the computer and spend hours on the Internet, even in some of the "hip" social areas, such as MySpace. And whatever you do, don't refer to them as "seniors."

Baby Boomers

Baby boomers grew up during a time of unprecedented wealth and freedom that happened to collide with the perceived hypocrisy of the world around them. As a result, they collectively formed what's often referred to as the Me Generation, relying on the guidance of their own inner visions and resources rather than what society was telling them. Baby boomers generally feel a sense of entitlement — they deserve the "good life" and believe that they have what it takes to ensure it.

When marketing and selling to baby boomers, take an approach that's more in line with their thinking and the way they perceive the world. Here are some suggestions:

✔ Appeal to the boomers' sense of independence and rebelliousness.

✔ Play up the convenience of products. Boomers are money rich and time hungry. They crave anything that will save them time and effort.

✔ To boomers, the Internet is a tool, not an end in itself. Although some boomers are geeks, most simply see technology as a necessity.

✔ Keep it simple. Provide boomers with enough information to make a well-informed purchase decision without burying them in details. Remember, they don't have time for that.

✔ Don't quote "company policy" as a reason you *can't* do something your customer requests. Boomers don't trust organizations and think of rules and policies as a way of controlling them. Flexibility is key.

✔ External image is important to boomers. Even if they try to play it down, possessions, status, and appearances count.

✔ Boomers tend to be less trusting than other generations, so communicate honestly and openly and be prepared to answer questions. If the boomer senses that you're not genuine, you haven't got a chance.

✔ Word-of-mouth referrals carry a great deal of weight with this group, both in real and virtual communities, so network effectively. See Chapter 14 for additional guidance on developing productive relationships.

Generation X

Generation X has been saddled with all of the problems caused by the G.I. and Silent Generations that the baby boomers have failed to fix. In addition, they're facing a future of increased insecurity and decreased financial opportunities while having to deal with the media labeling them as slackers. In defense of this generation, I have to say that they're a very capable group, particularly in regards to technology.

Xers have grown accustomed to a chronically unstable job market, protected neither by the government nor the unions. As a result of this and increased opportunities via the Internet, they've become much more entrepreneurial. Some estimates claim that Xers start 70 percent of the new businesses in the United States.

When marketing and selling to Generation Xers, keep the following information in mind:

- ✔ Most Xers shop online or at least do some portion of their product research online when making a purchase decision. Make sure you have a strong presence online.

- ✔ Reassure Xers that they are making a savvy purchase or investment decision. Xers tend to feel insecure about their decisions.

- ✔ Give Xers more control. They tend not to be team players and may cringe from long-term commitments. Forcing them to sign a multi-year commitment for service may scare them off.

- ✔ Offer time-saving solutions. Xers aren't slackers, but they will seize any opportunity to perform a task in less time with less effort, so they can go back to having fun.

- ✔ Present information in snippets, avoiding any kind of lengthy discourse.

- ✔ Brutal honesty trumps any slick marketing and advertising. Xers demand an honest, straightforward presentation that's fun and unique without being pretentious.

Generation Y

Although the members of Generation Y were born later, they're a step ahead of their Gen X parents and siblings in terms of technology and communications. When you're marketing and selling to members of Generation Y, the Internet and newer communications technologies are even more important:

- ✔ Never underestimate a Yer's reliance on technology for massive amounts of information.

- ✔ Yers are truly democratic. They don't rely on traditional establishments to tell them what's safe to buy. They rely more on community, especially online, virtual communities for referrals.

> ✔ Yers are open to all forms of communication, including face-to-face, cell-phones, text messaging, and instant messaging. The more communications media you can handle, the better you are going to be able to accommodate their needs.
>
> ✔ Maximize the use of multimedia marketing. Yers require a lot of sensory stimulation to stay interested in whatever it is you're selling. Whatever you do, don't bore them with a stodgy presentation.

Yers grew up downloading music, video, podcasts, and a host of other media and information from the Internet for free. Be prepared to deliver quality, dynamic content to win their business.

Selling to the disabled

A friend of mine was born without arms. Whenever I see him, I shake his shoulder. He likes that. He tells me that most people turn away. They get uncomfortable. They don't know how to act, so they choose avoidance. That hurts. After all, this guy is a human being. He wants the same thing everybody else wants — respect, dignity, human interaction, some emotional attachment.

When your competitors are busy avoiding the disabled, do yourself a favor and embrace them. This under-served market demands some attention and service, and you could be the one salesperson in your area that provides it for them. In addition to increasing sales, you receive a much more valuable benefit — the friendship of entire groups of people who have a very unique perspective and something to offer that you can't get anywhere else.

If you have a disability, you already know this, but for those who don't have the advantage of the insight that comes with the experience, I can tell you that most people who have a disability don't want to be treated any differently. You may need to adapt in some way, however, so you can provide them with the same level of enthusiasm and service you offer your other clients. At one time, I had a teletype machine in my office to communicate with my clients who couldn't hear. I found that the hearing impaired were much easier to work with than the *listening impaired*. You can't change the situation they're in, so don't try, and don't pity them. Just adapt to their needs. Every time you do, you open yourself to a new valuable relationships and a host of new opportunities. When I meet a client who's wheel-chair bound and can drive a modified vehicle, I ride with them. It makes us both feel more comfortable.

Overcoming racial and ethnic barriers

Some salespeople actually let their prejudices get in the way of making money. Personally, I think that's borderline insanity, but it does leave more opportunities out there for the rest of us.

If you're not prejudiced or you can at least overcome any prejudice feelings you have, consider tapping into the multicultural marketplace. In Chapter 19, my colleague, diversity expert Michael Soon Lee, and I size up your multicultural expertise with a simple ten-question quiz and then lead you through the basics of becoming more sensitive and accommodating to clients from other cultures.

Whenever I work with homeowners who hire me to list their home or coach or consult with other real estate agents, sales people, or businesses around the country, I always advise that the only color you should see when you're doing business is the color green. I've encountered homeowners who have placed themselves in serious legal predicaments and have jeopardized the sale of their home simply because they didn't want to sell to "those kind of people" as if they were any better.

Seeing only green

About ten years ago, I was working with a minority couple to help them find a home — a pair of young professionals, both of whom had solid incomes. They were excellent, highly qualified buyers, whom any seller should have felt fortunate to find.

When one of my buyer's agents took them for the first showing of one particular house, the garage door was locked, and the owner wouldn't allow them access to one of the bedrooms or the basement.

They looked at other houses, but just couldn't find anything that fit their needs as well has that house they were blocked from touring completely. They wanted to see the rest of the house. We scheduled a second showing. My buyer's agent, the couple, and the wife's father went to look at the house again. This time, the seller wouldn't even let them inside. The seller told them, "You kind of people don't want to be in this neighborhood."

Somewhat shaken, the couple sought legal advice and soon learned that the seller had broken several equal opportunity statutes. Under the law, they were clearly entitled to relief or damages for the way they had been treated.

As soon as he learned what had happened, the listing broker immediately released the seller from the listing agreement. A real estate agent can lose his license for assisting people whom he knows have broken equal opportunity laws.

The couple was getting ready to take the seller to court and there was a good chance that the seller would lose his house in the dispute. At this point I intervened. I convinced the seller that he had been wrong in the way he treated the couple and he eventually settled the matter with the couple out of court, paying them about $10,000. Thanks to that money, which the couple used as a down payment, they were now able to afford their dream house instead of settling for something in a lower price range.

The take-home message here is that green should be the only color you see when you're selling. If your goal is to maximize your profit, what difference does it make who buys it? If someone wants your product, offers you the right price for it, and is intent on closing the transaction, why on earth would you not grab that deal?

Shifting your gender focus

Now that the 21st century has arrived, I find it difficult to believe that sexist salesmen still exist, but they do. I meet them on a daily basis. They meet a woman and instantly ask to deal with her husband, as if she were some second-class citizen.

The fact is that in 60 percent of relationships, the woman is the decision maker. Women literally hold the purse strings. In addition, women are naturally gifted at networking, so if you upset a female client, she's much more likely to pass the word along to her 250+ network of other men and women who make decisions and have purchasing power. Over the course of my 30 years in real estate, I have witnessed significant changes — more women are heads of households, primary wage earners, and decision makers. More men are stay-at-home dads.

Saga of the sexist salesman

I've met some sexist salesmen in my days, but the guy who used to deliver firewood to my house was perhaps one of the worst. As you read this story, you soon discover why he "used to" deliver firewood to my house.

Every year, I spend about $350 on firewood. The guy who delivered it guaranteed that the wood would be properly seasoned. (If it's green, it doesn't burn right, coats the inside of the chimney with creosote, which is highly combustible, and fouls the air.)

One season, we received some green wood. My wife, Kathleen, called the company and talked with the sales rep who came over to inspect the wood. He told Kathleen that the wood was perfectly fine and that perhaps he should speak with her husband. She replied that there was no need to call her husband, because she's the one who deals with the wood, but he insisted.

To keep the peace with the firewood company and Kathleen, I got involved and suggested that I keep the green wood and they deliver some seasoned wood, which I would also pay for. I figured that the green wood could season while

I burned the wood that was already seasoned. Well, they never delivered the seasoned wood. I called the company about a dozen times, and they never returned my calls.

The company lost me as a client, but even worse, they lost all of the referral business I stood to send their way. Had they dealt with the "little lady" in the first place, they could have resolved the issue, kept me as a client, and had hundreds of additional clients from my referrals. Instead, they chose to fire me as a client.

In contrast, we had a non-sexist plumber by the name of Bruce Hassick. We were having a few plumbing issues in the house, so I called Bruce. He said he would stop by and take a look. When he did, he discovered that my two hot water tanks had gone out. He said he would make sure we had at least one of them up and running, and then he could replace the other one. I asked whether he needed me, and he quickly replied that he would go over everything with Kathy — I was busy enough, and she was just as capable. I was happy, Bruce was happy, and most importantly, Kathleen was happy. That's how you sell.

Treat all of your clients equally, with the same respect, regardless of race, ethnicity, beliefs, or sex. Not only is this the right way to act, but it's also the best way to sell.

Going Global: Exploring International Markets

Today's global marketplace hasn't quite flattened the world, but it has made it much easier to sell in foreign lands. With the Internet and global shipping at your fingertips, you can create a Web store from the convenience of your living room and sell and ship products to customers in Canada, Mexico, South America, Europe, Asia, and anywhere else.

You may not even have to ship the products yourself. By hooking up with a drop ship supplier such as Doba (www.doba.com), you can sell the products, collect the money, and then have the supplier ship the products directly to your customers. With the world population at over six billion people, many of whom have Internet connections, just think of the potential boost in sales you would see if you could connect with even one percent of that market!

Before reaching out to the global market, I suggest you do some research and expand slowly:

- ✔ Research any laws that may govern the sale of your products in foreign lands.

- ✔ Consider establishing a partnership with foreign companies who sell the same or similar products or services.

- ✔ Address the language barrier. Although many people in other countries speak English, you may need to hire someone who speaks the language to be most effective. Fortunately, in the United States, you can usually find someone who can fill the position.

If you're interested in marketing and selling products online, Wiley offers a small library that covers just about every aspect of Internet marketing and sales, including *Selling Online For Dummies* by Leslie Heeter Lundquist, *eBay For Dummies* by Marsha Collier, *Blogging For Dummies* by Brad Hill, and *Buzz Marketing with Blogs For Dummies* by Susannah Gardner. I could go on.

Exploring Other Sales Channels

Customers want what they want, when they want it, and how they want to buy it — in a store, from a catalog, over the phone, online, at a shopping kiosk or even from a handheld device. The way customers prefer to pay for their orders also varies. Some prefer to pay with cash or check, some buy everything with a credit or debit card, and online shoppers may enjoy the convenience of PayPal.

To appeal to the broadest selection of customers, accommodate a wider selection of preferences. If you sell goods primarily through a traditional brick-and-mortar storefront, consider expanding to online sales. If you're selling online, you may be able to increase sales by opening a local store. Or, if you're already selling online and through a local store, think about advertising in a magazine and having readers phone in their orders.

This is an age in which customers want to customize and personalize everything. Just look how popular ring tones have become. Just about everyone who owns a cell phone has it set up to play a different ring tone. This says a lot about customers — people like options. It's like that Burger King commercial that encourages you to "Have it your way." By expanding your sales channels, you deliver goods however your customers want to order and pay for them.

Looking for Bundling Opportunities

Clever bundling of products and services can often make your products and services more appealing seem more valuable. In the real estate business, I often encourage the home sellers I represent to "bundle" a home warranty with the house. These warranties cost only a few hundred dollars, but to buyers who are worried about having to replace a $5,000 furnace right after they purchase the home, the warranty appears to be worth much more. It makes the buyer feel much more comfortable about spending a hundred thousands dollars or more for the house.

I don't know what you sell, so I can't point out bundling opportunities that may be available to you, but I can provide some general guidance on how to select among different bundling options. The first step is to decide on the purpose of the bundle:

- ✔ **To attract new customers:** Bundling can often be used to attract new customers by offering increased value or convenience, or (as in the case of extended warranties) reducing the worry a customer has when making a major purchase.

- ✔ **To retain existing customers:** If your customer-retention rate is slipping, offering additional products and services at a reduced rate may boost revenue while at the same time increasing retention rates.

> ✔ **To bring ex-customers back to the fold:** Bundled products may be used to encourage ex-customers to try the service again, particularly if you have improved your products and services and prices have dropped since the time they left.
>
> ✔ **To introduce an unproven product to the market:** Bundling new, unproven products and services with highly successful ones is a common strategy for gaining market share.

The purpose of the bundle should drive your choice of which products and services to bundle and how to most effectively market the bundle. A bundle designed to introduce new products to the market is obviously going to differ from one that's designed to attract or retain customers.

The next step in introducing an appealing bundle is to select the products and services you want to bundle and then research the market to determine which bundling opportunity is likely to be most successful. Your market research should be designed to turn up information about the following:

> ✔ Identify the market segments you want to target.
>
> ✔ Analyze the needs of those market segments.
>
> ✔ Investigate product and service combinations that can best meet the needs of the targeted market segments. This may include checking out bundles that your competition is offering and determining how you can improve the bundle.
>
> ✔ Investigate the buying habits of the targeted market segments, so you have a clear idea of how to market and sell the bundle.

Bundling doesn't mean giving away the store. You can bundle products and services and charge even more than if the customer purchased everything separately. The key is to put together a bundle that separates you from the competition and convince your customer that your bundle has value that justifies or more than justifies the sticker price.

Partnering with Other Product or Service Providers

Bundling products doesn't always require that you have all the products and services available to piece together an attractive package. You may be able to partner with other businesses and salespeople who sell complementary offerings.

A real estate broker, for example, could partner with a mortgage broker to offer home buyers a one-stop solution to buying a home and securing the financing to pay for it. They could even bring a title company on board to handle the closing or partner with builders to sell newly built homes.

Think of what you're selling and what you can add without having to do any more work. Make sure you're not getting yourself into a conflict-of-interest situation and that the partnership offers your clients a real value-add.

Think creatively and remain on the lookout for partnership opportunities. Whenever you notice that your customers tend to use certain goods and services that you don't offer, you have an opportunity to either add those products to your product line or team up with another business that offers those products and services.

Discovering Another Use for Your Product or Service

Products and services often have more than one use. You just have to become somewhat of a visionary to identify new uses. If this notion seems a little vague to you at first, just think of how satellite technology applications have expanded over the course of about 50 years:

- Telecommunications
- Satellite television
- Satellite imaging systems
- Broadband Internet
- GPS (Global Positioning System)
- Satellite radio
- Satellite telephones

Even in real estate, the product I'm selling can have different uses. Some buyers use a house to live in, while investors may want a house to lease, and someone else may want the same house as a vacation property. Sometimes by shifting your focus and marketing a specific use for a product or service, you can make it more appealing to the different markets.

When you're in sales, keep in mind that you're not only selling products and services. To make sure you're earning a profit that justifies the time and effort you put into your work, think of yourself as selling time — your time. The more efficiently you can sell, the more money you make per minute. As long as you're constantly improving your $/minute rate, you're making progress.

Chapter 16

Tapping the Power of the Multimedia Marketplace

In This Chapter

▶ Making headlines in the print media

▶ Establishing a presence on television and radio

▶ Erecting your own billboard on the Internet

▶ Marketing via mail and e-mail

*A*dvertising is everywhere. You see it on TV and the Internet, hear it on the radio, and read it in newspapers and magazines. It pops up in your mailbox and your e-mail box. It lines the streets and drives past you painted on trucks and cars. Sometimes it even talks to you when you walk past a special display in your hardware or grocery store!

Why do these ads permeate our world? Because they work. And when they work, the company producing the ads is successful in taking up mind-space — etching the image of a person, product, service, or brand on your mind and the minds of any others who've encountered the ad.

As a salesperson, you want to consume as much mind-space as possible, and the most effective way to do that is to create a media blitz that uses every form of media available — television, radio, print, Internet, and anything else you have at your disposal. Wherever people go, in the real world or the virtual world, you want to be there, reinforcing your message.

In this chapter, I introduce the various types of media that offer the most bang for your buck and suggest ways for creating the media buzz that drives customers right to your door.

Marketing Yourself and Your Product in Print

Although more and more people rely on TV and the Internet to stay informed and entertained, a good number of people still turn to newspapers and magazines for their information. Establishing a presence in the print media enables you to reach the offline readers of the world.

By "establishing a presence" in print media, I'm not just talking about purchasing advertising space, although that's certainly one option. I'm also talking about making yourself available to reporters and perhaps even submitting your own articles. The following sections discuss all three of these options.

You've probably seen advertisements cleverly disguised as newspaper or magazine articles, the headline announcing a "New Medical Breakthrough for Weight Loss!" Look a little closer, and you see "Advertisement" printed across the top of the article in small print. The theory that drives these ads and print-based marketing is that people tend to believe what they read, unless they have good reason not to.

Advertising in print publications

The most obvious way to establish a presence in newspapers and magazines is to take out an ad. That's certainly easy enough. You contact the newspaper or magazine, tell them what you want the ad to say, and submit your payment. Most publications have layout people who can design the ad for you, so you don't have to mess with fonts, graphics, and other stuff you may find challenging.

To get the biggest bang for your advertising dollar, consider your clientele:

- ✔ **Target the publications that your customers read.** Placing an advertisement in the local newspaper may be a good idea if you're selling cars, but an ad for productivity software may be better placed in a business journal or trade publication.

- ✔ **Sell the benefits.** Don't simply list the features of whatever you're selling. Analyze the needs of prospective customers, and then pitch the ad to those needs.

- ✔ **Focus on the headline.** People generally skim print publications for interesting headlines and then invest time reading more only if the headline engages them. Make that headline snap, crackle, and pop off the page.

- ✔ **Choose an effective color scheme and design.** Flip through the publication you're thinking of advertising in and select the ads that catch your eye. Ask some colleagues to pick the ads they like best. Then, select some samples and cut them out to show the designer. If you have a good eye for what works, feel free to provide input, perhaps even a rough sketch of what you're looking for; otherwise, trust someone else who has a proven track record.

To write an eye-popping headline, get in character. Pretend you're a prospective customer. What would grab your attention and speak to your needs? Check out the following sidebar, "In Transition?" for an example.

Moonlighting as a journalist

Your sales career makes you an expert. You become somewhat of an expert on the products and services you sell, and from talking with your customers, you become an expert on the applications and benefits of those products and services. To anyone who's in the market or may someday be in the market for your products and services, this knowledge and expertise are pure gold.

The best way to invest this gold is to spend it freely. Write articles for newspapers, magazines, trade publications, journals, Web sites, blogs, and any other "print" media where you can get those articles published and where prospective customers are most likely to read them.

In Transition?

Ed Primeau, proprietor of Primeau Productions, Inc., a video production company I use to produce my videos, tells the story of how he maximized the use of headlines in print media to find tenants for a couple of his rental homes.

"Awhile back I had two rental homes without tenants. My fiancé and I decided to advertise in our community newspaper, and when we sat down to write the ad copy, we did what people normally do — we started describing all the great features of the homes. We listed the lot size, square footage, number of bedrooms and baths, and so on. We jotted down the benefits, as well — great school district, nearby shopping, convenient access to the expressway, and low taxes.

When we were done, we had a great list, but nothing that really spoke to potential tenants.

That's when my fiancé suggested the title, 'In Transition?' It was brilliant! Instead of focusing on the home, it focused on the situation that people who may be inclined to rent a home were likely to be in.

We spent a total of $95 advertising in all of our county community newspapers (12 in all, if I remember correctly), and we received 12 calls between 3pm and 9pm on the first day alone. The homes rented immediately!"

The headline is like a big fishing net that catches readers as they're swimming through life not really paying attention. When advertising in print, make sure your headline speaks to prospective customers. If you're sending out e-mail ads, take the same approach when composing the subject line.

This is the information age. Companies online and off are starving for original content that draws traffic. Original, insightful articles that engage and entertain people are a valuable commodity, and companies are more than willing to publish great articles for free, so don't pass up the opportunity. Following are some suggestions to get the most distance out of the articles you publish:

- ✓ **Offer valuable information and guidance.** Offer information and guidance that empowers your audience to do something faster, better, or for less money. Articles should be able to pass the "Who cares?" test.

- ✓ **Focus on the title.** People skim the headlines, so make sure your headline grabs their attention and pulls them into the article.

- ✓ **Get to the point.** You have even less time to capture a prospective customer's attention in print than you have over the phone or in person. State your point in the first or second sentence.

- ✓ **Target articles for specific publications.** Read the publication to get a feel for the audience, tone, and style, and write your articles accordingly. Talk with the publisher to determine word-count limitations, and strictly adhere to those limitations.

- ✓ **Edit carefully.** Write, rewrite, revise, edit, and have someone else read through the article before submitting it. You want to make it as easy for the publisher as possible to simply drop the article into the publication without having to do anything to it. (Ask if the publication has any writing guidelines you can look at before your get started.)

- ✓ **Make sure you can re-use the articles.** Give the publisher of the article first publishing rights, but make sure you retain the rights to the article, so you can re-use it on your Web site or blog.

- ✓ **Add your contact information.** Insert a credit line at the end of every article that contains your name, area of expertise, the company you work for, your phone number and e-mail address, and your Web site address.

You don't have to be a professional writer in order to get published, but you may need to hire a writer. As a sales person you have valuable experiences that you should be sharing. Don't let an inability to write get in the way.

Avoid the temptation to turn an article into a full-blown advertisement. Take the soft-sell approach. Address the topic, offer your readers knowledge and wisdom, and follow up with your name and contact information.

Writing and distributing your own press releases

Another way to generate some marketing buzz, particular amongst industry insiders, is to write and distribute a press release announcing a major product release, a new service, a change in management, or any other newsworthy item. If you can't think of anything newsworthy right now, spend your time searching for press release services that can get the word out the next time some newsworthy event occurs.

In the following sections, I offer some tips on penning your press release and then actually releasing it.

Penning your press release

When a newsworthy event occurs (or is about to occur), start writing. Announcing something that happened a week ago doesn't exactly qualify as news . . . it's more like a historical account. As you write, follow these guidelines for composing your press release:

- **Read some sample press releases first.** Model your press release after others that you find compelling. After attending a conference for real estate professionals, I penned the release shown in Figure 16-1.

- **Include contact information.** You want the press calling or e-mailing you or your assistant to set up interviews and perhaps appearances.

- **Add an intriguing headline.** Nobody is going to read your press release if the heading sounds boring.

- **Start the first paragraph with the city, state, and date.** Location and time set the stage for the rest of what you have to say.

- **Limit your release to a single page.** You have very little time to make your point. Remember, your goal is to convince people who read the release to call you. 300 to 750 words is best.

- **Don't advertise.** A press release is an announcement worthy of the news, not an advertisement for products or services.

- **Edit carefully.** Your press release is a reflection of you, so make sure it is well-written and free of typos and grammatical errors.

- **Avoid using exclamation points or all uppercase characters.** To make your press release appear objective, keep the emotion out of it.

- **Obtain permissions for quoted material.** If you want to quote someone in a press release, obtain permission from the person or company you're quoting.

Press Release
For Immediate Release

'Divide & Conquer: Creating Virtual Offices & Expanding Market Area"

Ralph Roberts Realty, llc creating virtual offices and opening branches in several Metro Detroit Areas

Warren, MI April 26, 2007- Ralph Roberts Realty, llc, which has been serving the Metro Detroit area for almost 2 decades, from their 13 Mile and Schoenherr office, will be moving their main office and establishing several virtual offices in 4 suburban cities (for a total of 4 offices).

"The time of specialization and virtual offices is here now." Says Ralph R. Roberts, broker of Ralph Roberts Realty, llc. "With technology today, like internet faxing, cell phones, wireless internet, and PDAs, we can "divide and conquer," and more efficiently service our market areas in Oakland County, Northern Macomb, and Wayne Counties.

Additional branch locations will include Southfield, Warren, and Washington Township with the main headquarters moving to Clinton Township. Plans to open other branches in Detroit and other cities are in the works. "As the need arises, we will open branches in other cites as the market area expands," says Roberts.

"So many buyers and sellers nowadays, use the internet and phone to sell and purchase homes. We can email them purchase agreements, send them virtual tours, and communicate with them in other ways via the Internet. Marketing virtually through websites, blogging, and emails is becoming more the norm than the exception. The need for having a 28,000 square foot office is obsolete," says Roberts, "Most agents work from home and from their cars, and the need for a permanent desk in an office has diminished. I have agents who work from Starbucks sometimes, because it's close and Starbucks has broadband wi-fi," says Jocelyn Santiago, Sales Manager for Ralph Roberts Realty. All agents for the company will be able to use any of the 4 locations to meet clients, make copies, etc.

Ralph Roberts Realty, llc is the home of "The Big Nail," the giant nail from the I-94 Uniroyal Tire that Roberts acquired in 2003. Ralph R. Roberts is the author of Flipping Houses for Dummies published by Wiley in 2007 and numerous other books on real estate, sales, and marketing.

Figure 16-1:
Compose
your own
press
release.

Contact
Lois Maljak
loismaljak@ralphroberts.com
Ralph Roberts Realty, llc
810-533-3448
586-751-0000
586-752-8959
www.RalphRoberts.com

Releasing your press release

After you've written and carefully edited your press release, you have to find some way to get it into the media channels. Several companies offer such services, including PRWeb at www.prwebdirect.com, 24-7 Press release at www.24-7pressrelease.com, and RISMedia at www.rismedia.com. You can search the web for "press release distribution" or other related words and phrases to find a hundred other such companies, or e-mail me at RalphRoberts@RalphRoberts.com and I can recommend a few options.

Another option is to add a publicist to your team. Your publicist can handle the writing and distribution of the press release, so you won't have to do it yourself. Most publicists offer different levels of service, so you can usually find a package that meets your budget needs.

Getting Some Free Publicity

The only thing better than writing your own articles is to have someone writing them for you or have TV and radio stations calling you for interviews. Assuming you're pretty good at handling the interview process, a few minutes of your time can lead to some valuable free publicity and really get the marketing buzz in full swing.

Call your local TV and radio stations and send them a marketing packet that includes your business card, a brief letter of introduction, brochures, and other marketing materials. Explain who you are, what you do, and your areas of expertise. Whenever a story crops up in the media about your industry, reporters start combing the area for local experts, and that local expert they interview should be you. While others are paying top dollar for advertising, you could be getting advertising for free — the type of advertising that TiVo users are less likely to fast-forward through.

Build relationships with news desks, reporters, and producers. Often, I read a great story, see it on TV, or hear it on the radio and blog about it. I then send a copy of my post and a link to it to the reporter who broke the story. After I make the initial contact, I try to set up a meeting, typically over lunch. Nothing works better than a face-to-face meeting to build a long-term relationship.

Don't wait for the local news to dig up a story that requires an expert like you. If you have an idea for a story, contact the stations and let them know. They wrack their brains every day to come up with intriguing stories. By delivering them a story, complete with a topic expert, you've just enabled them to go home early while creating a golden media opportunity for yourself. You may even want to consider creating your own newsworthy events — perhaps spearheading a community-improvement project.

Riding the wave of major media events

You don't always need to be at the center of a major media event in order to capitalize on it. My good friend Ed Primeau of Primeau Productions, Inc. tells the story of how he capitalized on the closing of Detroit's Tiger Stadium:

"In 1998 when Detroit's Tiger Stadium closed down, Tiger Stadium, my local production company produced an audio CD entitled 'Echoes of Tiger Stadium.' We partnered with a local AM radio station WJR who put their logo on the CD packaging. At the same time, we put out press releases to all the newspapers and radio and television stations in the state of Michigan. We scored 43 interviews in ten days!

We didn't exactly stage the event that drew media attention. Instead, we took full advantage of a city- and state-wide event that we knew would appeal to a wide variety of people, many of whom would be prospective customers."

Read the papers, listen to the radio, and watch the local news with an eye to discovering major events that you can transform into major marketing opportunities for yourself and your company.

When giving interviews, train yourself to talk in sound bytes. I often jot down a list of bullet points I want to make and then I repeat those bullet points during the interview. When I first purchased the Big Nail, which I talk about in Chapter 9, one of the quotes I repeated over and over again to every reporter was, "The nail is to Detroit what the Stanley Cup is to hockey." The more you repeat your quote, the more likely it is to get picked up and coined.

Advertising on Television

According to a study released by Nielsen Media Research in September of 2006, the average home now has more TV sets than people, and the average person in the U.S. watches four hours and 35 minutes of TV per day. A single commercial during a popular TV broadcast can give you the opportunity to reach millions of potential customers. Even a relatively inexpensive commercial on a local channel can expose you to thousands of people you may otherwise fail to reach through other media.

In the following section, Ed Primeau and I cover the basics of producing a 30-second television commercial and then choosing an advertising slot that gives you the most exposure to the demographic you're trying to reach.

Producing your commercial

Unless you have a film studio in your basement, you're probably not equipped to produce your own commercial, so crack open the Yellow Pages to and look under Video Production Services for the names of some candidates. Call around, ask about commercials the company produced, and set up an appointment with the company that seems the best able to meet your needs. The company should be able to provide you with excellent ideas and guidance on how to proceed.

Avoid using an advertising agency to produce your commercial. The ad agency simply hires a crew, just as you can do yourself, but adds a markup for the service and simply subcontracts with a video production company. Look in the Yellow Pages or online or ask another business owner in your community who already has a successful TV campaign who they used.

Your goal is to produce an engaging, informative, 30-second commercial. Although some commercials run 60 seconds, a vast majority are 30 seconds, because 30-second clips provide the station with more flexibility in fitting the commercials in specific slots, and they cost less to produce and air.

Although the process for actually creating the 30-second ad varies depending on the type of commercial and the production service, the process for producing a commercial, typically requires the following steps:

1. **Conceptualize the commercial, perhaps drawing it out on a storyboard showing how you envision it playing out.** Obtain additional input from the video production specialists.

2. **Write a 30-second script.** Consider using a voice-over — instead of having a person in the video talking, the speaker talks in the background as the video plays. This costs less and simplifies the revision process.

3. **Record a *scratch track* before calling in the voice over talent to do the real read.** A scratch track is a practice recording that enables you to fine-tune the script before calling in the real voice-over talent.

4. **Get timings from your script so you know how much footage needs to be shot of each scene.**

5. **Schedule a day to shoot.** Shoot the video footage required for the commercial and then some. Always shoot more footage than you need. Editing the video later is much easier and less expensive than calling the film crew back for re-shoots.

6. **Review all footage and take notes before you get into the edit session.** The crew that did the shoot can make you a DVD *window dub* of all the footage. A window dub is a work copy of the video that includes time code numbers, so you can jot down sections of the video you want to cut or keep as you watch the video.

7. **Add the voice-over narration and any background music or sound effects to evoke the emotion you want the viewer to feel while viewing the video.** Omni Music at www.omnimusic.com offers one of the best production music libraries around.

8. **With the assistance of the video production service or a separate edit house, edit the footage and mix in the narration and music to obtain the best 30-minute spot you can imagine.** Better editing houses may charge a higher hourly rate, but the total production cost may actually be lower if the editor works more efficiently.

At the end of the process, the production company or edit house supplies you with a *broadcast dub* — a final version of the commercial which you can send to the TV station, and a *master edit,* that contains all the footage, just in case you want to change something later.

Contact your local college or high school to see if they have any students who are skilled in video production and looking for some real world experience. I've discovered a great deal of talent through the coop program at the local high schools. Most recently, we discovered Jessica Ruddle, who is very talented and has teamed up with me and Ed Primeau to produce my videos. We plan to continue working with Jessica through her college years. When partnering with students, look for ways to promote their interests and careers, as well.

Picking the right station and time slot

TV stations charge you every time they play your commercial, and they charge you more for prime-time slots, but cost alone shouldn't drive your decision of which station to choose, when to air your commercial, or how often it plays. What you're looking for is the most bang for your advertising buck:

- ✔ Choose a station that your target customer is more likely to be watching.

- ✔ Choose a timeframe when you want your commercials to air. Is your target customer more likely to be watching Monday through Friday mornings, weekend afternoons, or evenings?

- ✔ Call the television station's sales department and ask which times are available and at what price. You may be able to look up advertising rates online.

Don't buy a time slot just because it's affordable. Consider the demographic you're targeting — stay-at-home moms, seniors, working parents, or whoever they may be. Pick time slots during which your targeted demographic is likely to tune in. The television station should be able to offer some guidance.

Prepare in advance for the increased business that your television commercial is likely to generate. Do you have enough phone lines to handle the increase volume of phone calls? Do you have enough staff to follow up when more customers start contacting you?

Strategically airing your TV commercial

Here's another entertaining educational story from my good friend Ed Primeau:

"A few years ago, my production company produced a campaign for a local window replacement company. We used 3D computer-generated animation to create fun commercials — something that would capture the interest of kids. Sure, we knew that kids weren't exactly the decision-makers when it came down to purchasing replacement windows, but we figured the kids could get us to the decision-makers.

By talking with the window company, we learned that the decision-makers for buying replacement windows were usually women. We told the salesperson at the TV station that we wanted the ads to target women, primarily homeowners with young children. The salesperson told us that between the hours of 6 am and 9 am were probably best, because their viewing audience was made up of stay-at-home and working moms who were getting ready for their day.

We picked time slots between 6 am and 9 am. When our commercials came on, the cartoon-like window characters and custom music grabbed the children's attention and thus the mom's attention. The campaign did very well and the window company's business tripled that first year."

Getting on the Radio

Radio advertising used to be an affordable way to get the word out about your products and services, but that's changed over recent years with the introduction of satellite radio. Satellite (pay) radio has drawn listeners away from standard (free) radio stations, and radio stations have been slow to adjust the pricing of radio commercials to account for the loss of listeners. In short, paying for a radio ad may not be the best use of your advertising dollars.

This doesn't mean that you should avoid local radio stations altogether. You can still garner a great deal of exposure by establishing relationships with local radio stations and offering your expertise as a consultant on stories relating to your industry and anything else you're involved with.

Programming is key to a radio station's success, which is evident in the growing popularity of talk radio. If you have a lot to say and plenty of connections, consider pitching an idea for your own talk show and describing your plans for retaining and growing their listening audience. Don't give up. If one station turns you down, pitch your idea to the next station on the list.

Radio stations need your expertise as much or more than you need their ability to reach listeners, so don't be shy about approaching radio stations. A perceptive station manager sees you as an opportunity to deliver three items of value:

> ✔ **Programming content:** The station needs valuable content to fill its daily programming schedule.
>
> ✔ **Listeners:** Assuming you make a pretty good radio personality and have valuable information and insight for listeners, your contribution can assist in retaining existing listeners and attracting new ones.
>
> ✔ **Sponsors:** If you establish a following, and the station can prove that people are actually listening, the station's salespeople can sell more commercials for more money to other businesses in the community.

Convince enough listeners and sponsors to tune into your show, and you may be able work out a deal with the station for some free or discounted advertising. You may also be able to get some free advertising through your community service efforts.

Marketing on the Internet

Even if you don't take orders on the Internet, you should be selling on the Internet. This always-on, on-demand global community and resource center is packed with people looking for information, answers, and camaraderie, not to mention great products and services. To have a shot at these potential customers, you need to establish a presence on the Internet.

In the following sections, I describe a host of marketing opportunities that the Internet offers, including Web sites and blogs, email, audio and video podcasting, and instant messaging. I encourage you to explore and then integrate at least a few, if not all, of these technologies into your marketing program.

Cross-market your real and virtual worlds. Your stationery, business card, brochures, and every other paper communication you provide your client should have your Web site address, blog address, and e-mail address. Likewise, your Web site, blog, and e-mail messages should contain your business address, phone number, fax number, and other pertinent information.

Setting up your own Web site

The most obvious way to establish a presence on the Internet is to build your own Web site, where people can visit 24/7 to find out more about you and your products, have their questions answered, and perhaps even purchase products and services.

Other experts are more qualified to lead you through the step-by-step process of setting up your own Web site, including David A. Crowder, author of *Building a Web site For Dummies*. I can, however, provide some tips that can assist you in making your Web site a better vehicle for marketing yourself and your products:

✔ **Obtain your own unique domain name.** If you work for a company that has its own Web site, creating your own area on that Web site is fine, but it's no replacement for having your own Web site with your own, unique domain name (address, like `www.ralphroberts.com`). By having your own domain name, you can build a following that travels with you if you choose to change companies. To check if a domain name has already been spoken for, visit `www.internic.net/whois.html`. Several companies offer domain name registration services. Simply use your favorite search tool to search for "domain name registration" or visit `www.internic.net/regist.html` for a list of accredited domain name registrars. Compare prices and services carefully before placing your order.

If the domain name that matches your name is available, purchase that domain. Also, secure the domain names that match the names of your children. As the Internet grows, more and more domain names will be taken, so secure them now.

✔ **Invest in an attractive design.** If you have a good eye for designs and colors and can handle the technical side of creating Web pages, feel free to do it yourself. Otherwise, hire a qualified designer.

You can find a good collection of Web site design and hosting companies on the Internet that provide you with powerful tools and templates that can simplify the process. You may even be able to purchase your domain name through these sites. Look for Web site design and hosting companies that specialize in creating Web sites for salespeople in your industry.

✔ **Offer valuable content.** Prospective customers may visit your Web site for the first time out of curiosity, but unless you offer something of value, such as information, advice, entertainment, discounts, quality customer service, they won't come back.

✔ **Make it interactive.** Offer more than an online catalog of products. Feature articles, brochures, a Q&A area, and other features that visitors can explore. On a real estate site, for example, you may provide links that enable visitors to find out more about local schools, property taxes, area parks, and more.

✔ **Keep it up-to-date.** Visitors want a dynamic site with up-to-date content. If you're having trouble coming up with enough fresh content, consider asking for contributions from other experts in the field. You may be able to cross-promote one another's Web sites.

If possible and beneficial for your customer, consider implementing a tool that enables visitors to obtain personalized content. Guthy-Renker Home has a tool for home buyers that enables them to enter the zip code for the area in which they want to live. The Web site then displays a custom page with details about area schools, shopping centers, parks, and other amenities.

Launching and maintaining a blog

A web log or blog, for short, is a shared online journal, often a collaborative effort in which visitors can comment on articles and other entries. Why should you care? For several reasons:

- ✔ **Blogs are hot.** People who avoid commercialized Web sites gravitate to blogs because they tend to be more personal and offer timely information.

- ✔ **Blogs are communities that drive R-Commerce.** Becoming established as a knowledgeable and trusted expert in the blogging community enables you to build strong relationships that sell product. For more about R-Commerce, check out Chapter 14.

- ✔ **Blogs are easier than standard Web sites to maintain.** Keeping your blog up to date requires no knowledge of HTML (hypertext markup language) — the tags used to format content on Web pages. You simply type a message in a form, click a button, and your message appears on your blog.

- ✔ **Blogs are a great way to drive traffic to your Web site.** A blog offers a more approachable, less commercial venue that draws visitors. You can then steer those visitors toward a more commercial Web site where they can find additional information about products and services and perhaps even place an order.

The investment required to launch and maintain a blog is minimal. You can set up your blog and have it up and running in about 15 minutes. Several sites, including www.BlogSpot.com, enable you to create your own blog for free, although I highly recommend that your blog have a unique domain name (address), as mentioned in the previous section on Web sites. If you're looking for a full-featured blogging and blog hosting service, e-mail me at RalphRoberts@RalphRoberts.com, and I will recommend one. Some of these services change so often and so drastically that I would hate to place my recommendation in the book and have it change three weeks from the time the book goes to press.

Be sure to offer your visitors something of value. To promote *Flipping Houses For Dummies*, I hired a company called Grip Media (www.gripmedia.net) to build a combination Web site and blog called GetFlipping.com at www.getflipping.com. From this site, visitors can view a flipping tip of the day, view a sample chapter from the book, sign up for a 31-day e-mail course on flipping houses, and much more. Of course, the site also provides a convenient link users can click to order the book. I currently have over 200 Web sites and blogs, creating what I like to refer to as my own *spider web.*

For more about using your blog to market your products and services, check out *Buzz Marketing with Blogs For Dummies* by Susannah Gardner.

Driving traffic to your Web site and blog

Erecting a Web site or blog on the Internet is no guarantee that people are going to start flocking to it. You have to drive traffic to your site using any and all means possible, including the following:

- **Increasing hits with SEO (search engine optimization):** Pack your Web page with key words and phrases that people commonly search for on the Internet when they're looking for content that your Web site or blog offers. Using HTML tags, such as <em> for emphasis, to call attention to key words and phrases. For additional tips and strategies for giving your Web pages and blogs a higher profile, check out *Search Engine Optimization For Dummies* by Peter Kent.

- **Trading links with partners:** If you know other people and companies who write on the same topics as you do, consider trading links. You can post a link on your site pointing to theirs and they can return the favor.

- **Contributing content to other sites:** Check out the Web sites and blogs of others who write on the same topics that you cover and contribute content to their site, if that's permissible. You may also be able to include a link to your site or your contact information if the person allows it.

- **Buying ads on search engines:** Google has a feature called AdWords. For a price, you can have a link for your Web site or blog pop up whenever someone searches for one of your AdWords. Visit `adwords.google.com` for more information. Other search sites may have similar features.

Adding audio and video content

The Internet, particularly the Web, is the perfect venue for multimedia presentations that include text, graphics, animation, audio, and video. When designing your site and lining up content to offer visitors, don't overlook the audio-visuals. Stimulate the senses . . . as many as possible, to reinforce your message through all available media.

You can even offer downloadable audio or video podcasts that prospective customers can play on their computers or transfer to their iPods or other portable players to carry with them:

- ✔ **Podcast:** A podcast is an audio file that Internet users can download and play on their computers or transfer to a portable music player such as an iPod. You no longer need to hire a production company to create books on tape. With a computer, microphone, and recording software, you can record your own audio files and post them to your Web site or blog. For details on creating podcasts, check out *Podcasting For Dummies* by Tee Morris, Evo Terra, Dawn Miceli, and Drew Domkus.

- ✔ **Video podcast:** A video podcast (vidcast or vodcast for short) is a video recording that Internet users can download and play on their computers or transfer to a portable video player such as a video iPod. With a digital camera, a tripod, and video editing software, you can create your own video Podcasts to feature products, distribute how-to videos, or simply deliver your message in a more personal format. For more about using video on your web site and blog, check out *Videoblogging For Dummies* by Stephanie Cottrell Bryant.

When recording for a video podcast, think about the screen size for a minute. Unlike a television set, which has a lot of viewing real estate, portable video devices have small screens and limited storage capabilities. Limit the size and resolution of your video clip to accommodate these portable devices.

Connecting with customers via e-mail

Nobody likes receiving useless, unsolicited email messages, especially from salespeople, but if you offer your customers and prospective customers something they value, they're going to be happy to opt in to whatever e-mail marketing campaign your running.

Don't send unsolicited commercial e-mail messages (spam). Even if it's legal in your state, most people find it annoying, and it makes you look bad. Use an opt-in system in which customers request to be added to your mailing list. In addition to being the courteous way to handle mass mailings, this challenges you to offer something of value in your messages.

To make your e-mail messages most effective as a marketing tool, follow these guidelines:

- ✔ **Use a catchy, descriptive Subject line.** An email Subject line is like a newspaper headline. It should catch the recipient's attention and convince her to read the message.

✔ **Keep your message short.** Write your message, cut it in half, and cut it in half again, and you should have the right number of words. When reading e-mail, customers aren't exactly patient.

✔ **Edit carefully.** If your e-mail program doesn't check grammar and spelling, compose the message in your word processing program first and then copy it to your email program. Check every message yourself for typos and grammatical errors; if editing isn't your forte, have some who's more qualified review the message.

✔ **Don't sell.** Your goal is to encourage your customer to contact you or visit your Web site for more information. Announce new products, services, or promotions; offer business tips; relate case studies of customers (with their permission, of course); but don't sell.

✔ **Include your contact information.** Every e-mail message should contain a host of ways the recipient can contact your or obtain more information. Everyone is different. Some people prefer calling, some prefer e-mailing, and others would rather grab the information off your Web site. Accommodate all preferences.

✔ **Automate distribution.** E-mail programs have features that enable you to send thousands of messages with a single click of the mouse button. Explore your email program to discover its advanced features for composing and sending messages.

✔ **Add a signature file.** All e-mail programs include a feature that enables you to create a signature file that the program adds to all outgoing messages. Create a signature file that contains your name, contact information and Web site and blog addresses. This enables people to contact you for more information, and it gives you a way to drive more traffic to your Web site and blog.

Drip, drip, drip e-mail marketing

When you're selling to customers who often take several months before deciding to purchase a product or service, a drip campaign can be the most effective tool for wooing a customer. A drip campaign is a system in which you send a prospective customer some form of communication on a regular basis, so the customer doesn't forget about you and defect to some other salesperson.

Whenever a prospective customer contacts you for information, request the customer's e-mail address and ask the customer for permission to send them email notifications of products, services, and additional information. If the customer gives you permission, add the person's e-mail address to your mailing list, so they receive regular correspondence from you. When they're ready to buy, you want to be the first person they call.

Make it easy for customers to opt out. At the end of every e-mail message, provide instructions that enable your customers to remove themselves from your e-mailing list. You always want to make your customers feel in control of the situation.

Keeping customers posted with a newsletter

Losing contact with a customer for more than a month is one of the best ways to lose a customer, but you don't want to sound like a nag. One way to walk the fine line of keeping in touch with your customers without annoying them is to publish a monthly newsletter via email.

In the following sections, I provide guidance and tips on designing your newsletter, finessing the content, encouraging customers to subscribe (without sounding too pushy), and automating distribution to save time.

Designing an attractive newsletter

You want your first newsletter to be the best, because you may not have a second chance to make a good first impression. In any publication, your first impression hinges on the design:

- **Keep it simple.** Include your company name and logo at the top, stick with a single-column format (two columns at the most), and use graphics sparingly and tastefully.

- **Optimize your brand presence.** Make the design consistent with the look of your business cards, stationery, brochures, and other marketing materials. See Chapter 9 for more about branding.

- **Keep it short.** Shoot for one page max; cover one to three topics per newsletter, 200 to 500 words per article; give each article a descriptive heading; opt for lists over text-heavy paragraphs.

Editing your newsletter

The professionalism demonstrated by your newsletter reinforces your own professionalism, so make sure your newsletter is well written and error-free:

- **Make it interesting.** Every article should be able to pass the "So what?" test. If you read the article and find yourself saying, "So what?" cut it. Avoid bragging about your own or your company's accomplishments — save that for your family Christmas letter. Following are some ideas of what to include:

  - Tips and tricks for doing something better or faster or for enjoying a particular product even more than they already do

- S.olutions to common problems

- Answers to frequently asked questions

- Announcements of new products or services

- Special promotions or deals

- A dash of humor

✔ **Punch up the style.** Grab the customer's attention in the first line of each article and keep them moving along with short, simple sentences.

✔ **Pick the most precise and powerful words.** Start each sentence with a strong noun and follow with a strong verb. Avoid starting a sentence with "There are . . ." or "It is . . .".

✔ **Remove the errors.** Check your spelling, grammar, and punctuation, and then have someone else do a read-through. If your newsletter is riddled with errors, your customers may wonder whether you can get their accounts right.

Advertising your newsletter

After overcoming the challenge of producing a killer newsletter, you should be highly motivated to get it into the hands of your customers and future prospects. Advertise your newsletter everywhere your customer is likely to come in contact with you, including:

✔ The opening page on your Web site or blog

✔ E-mail correspondence

✔ Brochures

✔ Letters

Distributing your newsletter

Although you can certainly distribute your newsletter as an e-mail attachment, perhaps as a PDF file, I recommend you publish it in a separate section on your Web site, instead. You can then e-mail your customers a link to the newsletter. Better yet, send an e-mail with a summary of each article linking back to the newsletter.

Why publish your newsletter to your Web site instead of sending the full version to customers? I can think of several reasons, including:

✔ Some customers may choose to view text-only messages, in which case all graphics are going to be stripped out.

✔ The e-mail reader may have a limited amount of space for displaying your newsletter.

✔ If the newsletter is a fairly large file, and your customer has a slow Internet connection, your customer may find the download time annoying.

Plan on publishing your newsletter once a month. Customers are likely to forget about you if they don't hear from you in a month. Some salespeople publish a short weekly newsletter and then follow up with something more lengthy each month, but don't overdo it. Quality trumps quantity.

Re-use information. You can use the same information to create a press release, post an article on your Web site or blog, and submit the article to your local newspaper.

Staying in touch via instant messaging

Instant messaging programs, including America Online Instant Messenger (AIM), Yahoo! Messenger, and ICQ are the communication tools of choice for those who spend a good part of their day on the Internet. With an instant messaging program, you can type and send messages back and forth between two computers in real time and, with the addition of a camera and microphone, videoconference with clients.

I'm away from my computer too much to implement this very effective tool in marketing and customer service, but if you spend most of your day in front of your computer and on the Internet and your customers use instant messaging programs as their preferred method of communication, I highly recommend that you do the same.

Launching a Direct-Mail Campaign

Although many proponents of email marketing want to proclaim the death of direct mail campaigns (through the postal service), direct mail campaigns can still be highly successful.

This isn't something I would recommend that you do on your own. Hire a company that specializes in managing direct mail campaigns. These specialists offer the following benefits:

- ✔ Highly targeted mailing lists based on market research.
- ✔ Editorial services to enable you to compose a timely and relevant message.
- ✔ Design services to make your direct mail package look professional.
- ✔ Integration with other components of your marketing program.

Avoid the temptation of offering discounts or reduced rates to prospective customers. You don't always have to give away something to get the phone to ring, and discounts often make customers think that your products and services are overpriced to begin with. Instead, consider offering package deals that create the impression of offering value without a discount.

Chapter 17

Exploring Opportunities in the Virtual World: Social Media

In This Chapter

▶ Understanding the marketing power of social media and networking

▶ Building a high profile online with blogs

▶ Using your blog as a lead-generation tools to boost sales

▶ Mixing it up in social networking communities

*T*raditional media isn't what it used to be, pretty much because there's so darned much media nowadays. Not so long ago, consumers had a very limited selection — they could get relatively good reception on maybe ten TV channels if they were lucky, tune into the radio, read the local newspaper and national magazines, and take in a movie at the local theater.

Now, people have an infinite selection of channel-surfing opportunities — hundreds of TV and cable channels, radio stations, satellite radio stations, newspapers, magazines, movies (at theaters, on DVDs, and through pay per view), Web sites, blogs, instant messaging, social networking sites like MySpace, virtual worlds like Second Life. In addition, everything it offers is free (or at least affordable), available 24/7, interactive, and on-demand.

This is good news and bad news for people in marketing and sales. The good news is that you have a host of new opportunities to market products. The bad news is that you have a host of new opportunities to market products — you can't just advertise on prime time TV anymore and think that you're reaching a majority of your target consumers.

Various factors, the biggest of which is perhaps the Internet, are fragmenting the delivery of media, marketing, and communication. Traditional media channels are not engaging consumers and prospects as they once did. Increasingly, consumers are tuning out traditional messages and turning in to new communication channels to fill the void.

As a salesperson, you need to connect with clients and prospects in a whole new way to get your message across to them. Social media (or the so-called *new media*) and online networking tools are the newest and most effective communication media, and in this chapter, my blogging colleague, Richard Nacht, founder and CEO of Blogging Systems Group, and I show you how to harness their power and start rubbing elbows in the vast online network of social media and networking.

Grasping the Concept of Social Media

Every day, millions of Internet users commune on sites like YouTube (to share video), Second Life (to work and play in virtual reality, and now to market), MySpace (to network with friends, family, and colleagues), Digg (to share news), and Flickr (to swap photos) to name only a few of the more popular online destinations.

With more and more prospective customers spending more and more time online, the most successful salespeople are setting up shop online to reach prospects where their prospects and clients hang out. They are replacing their traditional marketing toolkits with 21st century marketing tools, as shown in Table 17-1.

Table 17-1	Out with the Old Marketing Toolkit, and in with the New
Old Media Marketing Toolkit	*New (Social) Media Marketing Toolkit*
TV/Cable	Online video
Radio	Podcasting
Magazine	Blogs
Newspaper	RSS (Really Simple Syndication)
Consumer groups	Social networks
Direct Mail	E-mail drip campaigns
	Wikis
	Virtual life
	Online games
	Tagging, Local, Niche Search

In a way, like most Internet features, social media just happened. Early in the development of the Internet, Web sites were fairly static. People visited them, but they didn't quite interact with the sites. The Web was pretty much an information kiosk. If you wanted to interact with people, you did it through discussion forums or online chat.

I'm not sure who invented blogging. I'm pretty sure it wasn't Al Gore. Whoever invented it or started doing it first, however, must have though it would be pretty cool to combine the simplicity of the Web with the social networking aspect of discussion forums. That's basically what a blog is — a more attractive, robust discussion forum. Other social networking sites, like Second Life and YouTube are merely variations on the theme.

Applying social media to marketing and advertising

How do you define the word, "advertising?" In the old days, advertising could be characterized as "repeated messages which emphasized a product's or service's desirable qualities in such a way that captured the consumer's attention and aroused within them the desire to buy." The goal was *mass appeal* — targeting the biggest potential markets.

Those days are over. Mass is out. Niche is in. The consumer has become the real advertiser. In social media, you build a partnership with your consumer. You build a relationship in which your client is so excited about you and your product that she spreads the word for you, calling attention to your products and services. Your online content strategy can achieve what's known as a *franchise in the mind* — a collective, community consciousness that ripples around the world through the underlying currents of the Internet.

One of the most powerful aspects of social media marketing is that it's so affordable. Initially, you may have a substantial investment of time and money creating a low-level buzz, but once the buzz starts, it catches on like a wildfire with very little effort on your part. You start the buzz, and your clients convert that buzz into brand presence or a franchise in their minds.

Putting the "social" in marketing media

While traditional marketing and advertising centers around product and service, social media marketing gathers its energy from personality, values, and community — R-Commerce, as discussed in Chapter 14.

What *they* are saying about social media

Many old-school salespeople and marketing mavens I talk to about social media are initially reticent to jump on the social media and networking bandwagon. They think social media is just for teenagers who have nothing better to do with their time than hang out on the Internet.

Industry insiders across the board, however, envision the true potential marketing power. People of all ages are flocking to the Internet for their entertainment, educational, and social needs. It has become clearly evident that industries who successfully make the transition are going to thrive, while those who don't are likely to fizzle.

According to Peter Daboll, president and CEO of comScore Media Metrix, "The popularity of social networking is not expected to wane in the near future. This is a phenomenon we're seeing not only in the U.S., but also around the world."

Contrary to what many business people think, social networking is not just for personal use. Here's a quote from a *Business Week* cover story from as far back as June 5, 2005 addressing Web 2.0 tools such as blogs and wikis: "These services haven't had much to offer the vast world of business — until now . . . Web 2.0 portends a real sea change on the Internet . . . . For all its appeal to the young and the wired, Web 2.0 may end up making its greatest impact in business."

Edelman Research reports that consumers are now less brand-loyal, less trusting of traditional media messaging and more independent. Social media and networking provide a solution to these challenges in a spontaneous, real time and participatory manner. Consumer-generated content created via an online community in which you are participating is going to provide buzz and insight to companies.

Fortunately, it's not too late for any company to take advantage of social networking. According to a recent iProspect study:

> "Though sites such as YouTube and MySpace were designed to appeal to a high percentage of the online user population, many social search engines have been built to serve and attract, a community that is defined by their affinity to a vertical industry, a business model, or an interactive activity type."

It's still early in the history of social networking, yet one out of three Internet users is already taking advantage of a site containing user-generated content to help make a decision to buy, or not buy something. This bodes well for the future of these sites that take advantage of our human nature to trust the recommendations (and warnings) of fellow consumers more than we do the claims and 'marketing-speak' of professional marketers."

Most salespeople try to build a brand on a single feature or benefit, such as experience, knowledge, education, or service. But creating a strong emotional appeal by focusing on features and benefits is nearly impossible. The best branding campaigns are built on a personality, philosophy, or set of values. These qualities are inherently emotional and, when used consistently, give you a huge competitive advantage in the marketplace over time.

Social media puts the social and emotional back into marketing. It enables you to establish a strong positive rapport with your community of clients and prospects, and, over time, build the trust that makes clients comfortable buying whatever you have to sell.

For 21st century salespeople looking to engage hundreds or thousands of prospects and customers, social media provides a powerful solution for creating, organizing, managing, and distributing your content online.

Assessing the pros and cons of social media and networking

Putting yourself and your company out there on the Internet can be a little scary at first. After all, the Internet is the consummate democracy . . . total freedom, almost to the point of anarchy. Say the wrong thing at the wrong time, and somebody is likely to pick it up and use it against you. Hordes of prospects and clients may inundate your site with questions, complaints, and outright attacks. This thing can potentially do more harm than good.

This is all true, but I believe that the potential benefits far outweigh the potential drawbacks. In the following sections, I reveal the potential benefits and drawbacks, so you can decide for yourself, and then point out some options that may set your mind at ease.

I feel a little silly including a discussion of the benefits of blogging, as though I have to convince you of its value. The overriding reason that every salesperson should be blogging is that prospects and clients want it. If you don't do it and your competition does, you've already conceded a good slice of the pie to your competitors. Unfortunately, the IRS won't let you write it off as a loss on your taxes.

Considering the benefits of social media and networking

If you need some convincing about the value of blogging and other social media and networking tools for marketing purposes, I could probably deliver an hour-long presentation, complete with graphics, and still have plenty more to say. I'll spare you that experience and simply list ten key areas where social media and networking can benefit your marketing efforts:

- **Search engine marketing:** Blogs give you an increased presence on major search engines like Google and Yahoo. Some search engines pick up new blog content in as little as five minutes! One veteran blogger put it this way, "BLOG stands for *Better Listings On Google.*"

- ✔ **Direct communications:** Social media and networking provide a way for you to speak directly and candidly with customers and prospects and provide your customers and prospects with a forum for establishing their own voice on the Internet.

- ✔ **Brand building:** Social media and networking serve as other channels to put your brand in front of the customer and keep shaping its identity in real-time.

- ✔ **Competitive differentiation:** You gain the opportunity to tell your story over and over and set yourself apart from the competition. Over time, you build brand awareness and increase customer loyalty.

- ✔ **Relationship marketing:** Blogs and other social media and networking tools enable you to build personal, long-lasting relationships with your customers that foster trust. Your prospects and customers come to know you in a personal way never before achieved. Over time, you develop lifelong relationships with your customers.

- ✔ **Niche marketing:** Blogs are very niche-specific. You can use them to penetrate niche markets that are underserved.

- ✔ **Media and public relations:** The media relies on social media and networking, particularly in the form of blogs, for source material. As a result, journalists call you, not your competition.

- ✔ **Lead generation:** Social networking tools offer a more personal form of lead generation in that they enable you to establish rapport with readers which fosters trust. Because of the personal interactions that social media facilitates, prospects and clients respond to you with comments, e-mails and other interactive opportunities. Over time that can mean additional contacts from prospects and customers.

- ✔ **Expert positioning:** Social media and networking enable you to articulate your viewpoints, knowledge, and expertise on matters pertaining to your industry, your local community, and other areas of interest to you, your clients, and your prospects.

- ✔ **Customer referrals:** Not only does social media and networking foster customer loyalty, but they also create a mini-lead-generation service for you. These "brand evangelists" promote you to family, friends, and associates, demanding little, if any, additional effort on your part. For additional details, check out the following section on word-of-mouth marketing.

Blogs require very little technical expertise, although you may need some training or assistance to customize your blog — to give it the desired look and feel. Once it's set up, posting messages is as easy as sending email messages.

Creating buzz with word-of-mouth (WOM) marketing

Word-of-mouth (WOM) marketing, often referred to as *viral marketing,* is the best marketing that ever was, is, and likely will be, and on the Internet, social media and networking are like WOM on steroids. You can't assign a dollar figure to the value of having others talk positively about you, your company, and your products and services, but you can certainly see the results.

Not only do clients and prospects interact with you via your social media platform, they also talk to one another . . . for good or bad. The people in your social network can become your best brand-building evangelists, spreading your message and your presence throughout their networks. Instead of artificial, biased commercial messages, people can now get genuine advice and answers from their peers on anything they're looking for.

WOM marketing derives its power from the ability of consumers to influence one another when making purchasing decisions. Blogging and other social media and networking activities enable consumers to create an informal consumer's digest for recommending products and services. Consumers who are placing lest trust in the marketing messages that corporate America has been spewing out for years and who are more empowered to taking ownership of the buying process, are now relying more on the word on the street to decide where to spend their hard-earned money.

Sizing up the potential drawbacks

Social media and networking is not all positive. It adds transparency, which is always a little dangerous. If you're phony, somebody is going to spot it and cry foul. If you upset a customer, that customer is likely to post a note of criticism on your blog and perhaps other blogs where community members are likely to see it. If you write in the wrong tone or voice, a sensitive individual can take issue with what you said. In other words, people are going to talk about you.

Some other potential drawbacks, especially relating to blogging are these:

- Social networking requires a time commitment to create posts, monitor comments, answer questions, and respond to the messages that others post.

- People can vandalize your blog by posting obscenities, vulgarities, or racial epithets or by hacking into or crashing your site.

- Someone may try to use your blog to advertise their own products and services.

- Competitors can pose as clients and post nasty messages.

The business blogging tsunami

Beginning with Business Week's cover feature in May of 2005, mainstream business media has trumpeted the effectiveness of blogs as a marketing medium. The following are a few examples:

> "The blog as business tool has arrived. Some eight million Americans now publish blogs and 32 million people read them, according to the Pew Internet & American Life Project. What began as a form of public diary-keeping has become an important supplement to a business's online strategy: Blogs can connect with consumers on a personal level -- and keep them visiting a company's Web site regularly." — *Wall Street Journal*

Harvard Business School recently said that businesses "need to embrace the benefits of blogging." In a recent Harvard Management Communication letter the revered business school gave full support to corporate blogging, saying blogs enable companies "to connect with customers online and advance corporate communications and marketing goals." — *Harvard Management Communication*

David Sifry, creator of blog search engine Technorati reports, "New blog creation continues to grow. We currently track over 100,000 new weblogs created every day, which means that on average, two new weblogs are created every second of every day." Technorati is tracking nearly 57 million blogs in its database.

Certainly, something this phenomenal cannot be overlooked. As *Business Week* strongly asserts, blogs are not a business elective, but indeed a prerequisite.

You can minimize the effects of potential drawbacks by knowing what you're doing or hiring a professional to create and manage your blog. You can draw up an editorial schedule and compose a post once every week to ease the burden of creating content, or take on guest bloggers to write content for you. Vandalism can be controlled by putting the proper security checks in place, monitoring posts, and automatically censoring obscenities. You can even require that visitors provide their email address when posting a comment to cut down on anonymous posts, which are more likely to contain objectionable material.

Don't throw the baby out with the bathwater. Just because you have a concern about a particular aspect of social media or networking, don't let that spook you. You can usually find a solution or compromise to address your concern. You may even be able to disable certain features of your blog that you don't want to deal with.

Drawing Attention to Yourself with Blogs

Blogs are consumer magnets, primarily because search engines, such as Google and Yahoo! love blogs. Keep in mind that when people start searching for information on the Internet, they use a search engine. The higher your Web site or blog ranking, the higher profile it has. Blogs do a much better job than standard Web sites at feeding search engines what they're hungry for — fresh content and relevant links. While you may create a small Web site and attract a small amount of traffic, a comparably sized blog can attract huge crowds.

In the following sections, I show you how to keep your blog on center stage by updating its content regularly and populating it with relevant links that attract attention.

Add a Google Site Map to your blog to improve its ranking with Google and other search engines. To create a sitemap, you create a sitemap file and copy it to the directory on your domain server where your site is stored. You then sign into Google and tell Google the location of the sitemap file. For additional details about Google Site Map, visit www.google.com/webmasters/sitemaps. If you're not technically inclined, check our *Blogging For Dummies* by Brad Hill or hire a Web designer.

Updating your blog with fresh content

More than anything else, search engines value unique content. When a search engine visits a Web site or blog, it looks for content that it hasn't "seen" since the last time it visited your site. Sites that are constantly updated with new information tend to get higher rankings, so freshen up that content regularly. When a search engine discovers a site that hasn't been changed in weeks or months, it "assumes" that the information is older or that nobody cares about the site.

When posting entries in your blog, carefully select the words you use in post titles and the bodies of the posts. Search engines look for repeated *key words* and *phrases* to index. Think of very descriptive words or phrases that apply to the content on your site and that the people you want to visit your site are most likely to search for, and use them repeatedly. Over time, this "teaches" the search engine what your site is about.

Another way to include fresh content on your blog is to get other people to freshen the content for you — encourage visitors to post comments.

Populating your blog with relevant links

Search engines also love Web sites and blogs that are "well connected" — that is, the site contains plenty of links pointing to other sites and is pointed *to* by plenty of other sites. This sends a message to the search engine that the site is a credible member of a community of Web sites and blogs, and not just some fly-by-night operation.

The following items suggest a few ways you can use a search engine's preference for well-connected sites to your advantage:

- ✔ **Cross-market your Web site and blog:** Insert links in your blog entries to your company Web site and link to your blog from your company Web site. The more links into and out of your blog, the more "Google Juice" your produce and the higher your search engine listings.

- ✔ **Populate our Blogroll with relevant listings:** Woven into the fabric of blogging are lists of blogs called *blogrolls* — links to other relevant blogs and Web sites. Think of them as mini-directories to other sites in the niche-neighborhood. Blogrolls enable search engines to better understand the proposition of the site. In addition, as a blog gains credibility, other bloggers link to the site, creating a wealth of inbound links from other relevant sites that raise the blog's credibility.

- ✔ **Add relevant links to posts:** In addition to packing your blog posts with relevant key words and phrases, add links to your posts that point to other high-profile Web sites and blogs with content that's related to yours. In addition to drawing attention to your blog, this raises the profile and credibility of other Web sites and blogs in your community.

Google offers a free tool called Google Analytics that can automatically track and report on traffic streaming into your blog or Web site. It tracks the number of visitors, the number of pages they view, which site directed them to your site, and much more. All you do is copy a small script that Google creates for you and paste it on every page of your blog or Web site. If you don't know how, check out *Blogging For Dummies* by Brad Hill or call a tech savvy colleague. In a blog, all you have to do is paste it in one location, and every page you create contains the tracking code. For details, check out Google Analytics at www.google.com/analytics.

Getting your blog discovered on Technorati

Technorati (www.technorati.com) is a search engine that focuses exclusively on blogs. Until recently, it was considered the most comprehensive blog search engine on the Internet, but recent statistics suggest that Google's blog search engine has surpassed it. Nevertheless, if you have a blog, you should register it (*claim it*) on Technorati.

The process for claiming your blog on Technorati is fairly straightforward. Visit www.technorati.com, register to become a member, click the link for claiming your blog, and follow the instructions. You can enter keyword tabs to raise your blog's rank when Technorati visitors search for particular key words or phrases.

Blogging software typically includes a *ping* feature that "pings" a search engine automatically to notify it when information on your blog is updated, such as when you post a new message. After you claim your blog on Technorati, look for instructions on how to have your blog automatically ping Technorati. In WordPress, select Options, Writing, and then scroll down to the Update Services box and insert http://rpc.technorati.com/rpc/ping. Then, click Update Options. Google's Site Map feature, discussed earlier, automatically pings Google whenever you update content on your blog.

Distributing your content with Really Simple Syndication (RSS)

Are you wondering what that orange button is that you have seen on blogs and other websites? It represents something called RSS, which stands for *Really Simple Syndication*, among other things. RSS provides Internet users a way of gathering and organizing content from websites and blogs through a syndicated feed. It essentially allows you to create your own custom online newspaper that pulls news and other information from a wide selection of Web sites and blogs.

What makes RSS so valuable is that it prevents users from having to spend hours surfing the Internet for fresh content because it's all sent to the user via an RSS newsreader, also called a *feedreader* or *aggregator*. A newsreader is a type of software whose purpose is to retrieve RSS "feeds." If some subscribes to your feed, whenever you update your blog, the person automatically receives the new content.

This is called *permission marketing* and it creates connections with consumers and clients that are much stronger than spam e-mail and other unsolicited forms of marketing.

Just how important is RSS for selling? Renowned Microsoft blogger Robert Scoble summed it up best, "[I]f you have a marketing site and don't have an RSS feed today you should be fired."

For additional details about creating RSS feeds, go to the source. Visit Feedburner at www.feedburner.com or Newsgator at www.newsgator.com. I also recommend *Syndicating Web Sites with RSS Feeds For Dummies* by Ellen Finkelstein.

Converting blog traffic into sales

Attracting Internet traffic is nice, but it's not an end in itself. At the end of the day, a blog is a Web site, and any Web site can attract visitors. It's what becomes of the visitors when they arrive at the site that matters most. A marketing Web site, whether static or dynamic (like a blog), has two goals:

- ✔ Establish credibility in the marketplace or industry. You establish credibility by offering valuable information and resources. Credibility leads to trust, and clients and prospects who trust you lead to sales.

- ✔ Capture leads to promising prospects. Web surfers are not looking for blogs for blogs' sake; they are looking for pertinent, useful content. Sites that provide valuable content generate interest, comments, and leads. By positioning your blog as a site with valuable content, you automatically get more opportunities to capture leads owing to your increased visibility in search engines.

The ultimate goal of your blog is to turn traffic into business. In the world of sales and marketing, this is called *lead generation.* In Internet parlance, it's called *conversions.* It does little good to have traffic if that traffic does not translate into something more tangible, such as an e-mail contact, phone call, or other type of actionable item with the potential for generating additional business transactions.

Traditional lead-generation systems are designed to highlight comparisons and give readers the opportunity to compare features and benefits of different products, services, and companies. This approach is a *competitive perspective.* An effective blog, however, *establishes meaningful relationships* with its readers. The sole purpose is to create a substantive bond based on qualities of trust, goodwill, respect, mutual appreciation, and open communication.

Establishing a Presence in Virtual Communities

Building relationships on the Internet freelance style by setting up your own blog is like having your own booth at a sales convention. Clients and prospects can choose to visit if they want to, and if they can find you using Internet search engines or perhaps links from other Web sites and blogs.

Another way to rub elbows online is to register at any of several existing virtual communities, such as MySpace, Facebook, YouTube, and Digg. Each community has its own culture that attracts a unique crowd, so you may find one community a better fit for you than another.

In the following sections, I lead you on a guided tour of some of the more popular virtual communities, to assist you in choosing a hangout that's best suited to you and what you sell and optimize its marketing potential.

Marketing on MySpace

MySpace is the King and Queen of social networking communities, reporting over 150 million users, although how many of those user are actively blogging on MySpace is up for debate. MySpace currently drives more traffic to online retailers than MSN Search, and that traffic isn't all from kids who are too young to drive. More than half of MySpace visitors are at least 35 years old, and two-thirds are 25 or older.

If you think MySpace has no commercial use, think again. Companies that actively market on MySpace include Apple, Nokia, Honda, and Microsoft.

Prior to the Internet, word-of-mouth marketing was limited to the relatively small social circles most people were part of. For the most part, church groups, neighbors, golfing buddies, work associates, fellow classmates, and client referrals comprised the entirety of a salesperson's network. Social media networks like MySpace can reach far beyond that and grow organically and exponentially. The Internet has made the "six degrees of separation" idea a reality.

I'm not about to provide you with complete instructions on how to create your own MySpace page and navigate the community. You can visit MySpace yourself at www.myspace.com and poke around to discover the basics or check out *MySpace For Dummies* by Ryan Hupfer, Mitch Maxson, and Ryan Williams. In the following sections, I highlight the key points of using MySpace as a marketing tool.

Making "friends" on MySpace

Marketing successfully on MySpace is all about creating friends, not pushing product. In fact, if you try to push product, you're either going to drive away all of your friends or get booted off of MySpace. Either way, it's a lose-lose scenario.

After you create a MySpace page and enter information to define your profile, MySpace presents you with a list of prospective friends. I suggest that you add all the people from your prospect list to your "friends" list, and then add all of their friends, and so on. Don't expect everyone to accept your invitation to become friend. Establishing a circle of friends takes time, so have patience. Reports suggest that one-third of those who receive your invitation eventually accept it.

You have to be a friend to have a friend. Contribute to other MySpace member pages to populate those pages with valuable content, insights, and other items of interest. When people see that you take an interest in them and in their pages, they're more likely to take an interest in yours.

Taking the soft-sell approach

Post content that isn't sell, sell, sell. If you do so, it is unlikely your Friends will stay Friendly. Write as if you're speaking to a real friend, not as a company. If you're an expert on a particular topic, offer advice, answer questions, suggest ways to do something faster, cheaper, or better.

By offering content that engages, entertains, and educates, you build a loyal following of MySpace members who are more likely to trust you, and when the time is right, more likely to buy from you.

Targeting a demographic

MySpace enables you to target a specific demographic or a group with similar interests. Upon arriving at MySpace, click on browse then on advanced. You can then browse user profiles by age, sex, religion, education, location, hobbies, disposable income, and other information provided by the MySpace Members.

Targeting the correct demographic enables you to maximize the power of your marketing efforts rather than coming across as a spammer who's simply taking up Internet bandwidth through mass mailings.

Linking into and out of your MySpace page

Even if you do nothing else on MySpace, I recommend that you create a page that links to your other Web sites or blogs. If someone happens upon your page on MySpace, you can then use your MySpace page to drive traffic to your Web site or blog.

Weaving your own spider web

Successful social networking hinges on your ability to weave your own spider web to snare clients. It's all about making contacts. Build strategic contact points on the Internet wherever your clients and promising prospects tend to gather and then cross-promote these contact points (your Web sites, blogs, and social networking pages). This creates a mini spider web that can begin to expand both organically and exponentially.

The most effective online salespeople create multiple *participation points* — places where clients and prospects want to interact and engage. By testing these new social media tools you can determine which ones have participants who appreciate innovative new approaches and the opportunity to connect with salespeople who are people first and salespeople second.

Your prospects and clients need to feel empowered to search and find the information they are looking for without being pressured. Then need interaction, participation, and the approval of the online community to buy your products from you. Social networking provides them with all this and more.

Create a link from your Web site or blog to your MySpace page, as well. By cross-linking your MySpace page with your other sites, you create your own mini spider Web, an online community of pages that may eventually attract more attention from search engines like Google and Yahoo!

Buying banner ads

Marketing by building friendships isn't the only way to sell on MySpace. You can also buy banner impressions for somewhere in the neighborhood of $5 per 1,000 impressions (appearances). The minimum buy for a banner campaign is reportedly $5,000 to $10,000.

To find out more about advertising on MySpace, click the Advertise link at the very bottom of the page.

Getting some air time on YouTube

YouTube became a cultural phenomenon seemingly overnight, allowing anyone with a creative imagination and a digital camcorder to produce and distribute their own short video clips online. Commercial applications of YouTube in marketing, advertising, and sales, however, are still in their early stages. While corporations have dipped their toes into online video as a new advertising vehicle, success stories from salespeople are still anecdotal.

Having said that, however, I'm sure that some salespeople are going to harness the power of YouTube and put it to work for them in boosting sales. As I currently see it, the biggest opportunities for driving sales with YouTube come in the form of soft-sell videos, such as the following:

- ✔ Educational videos that show how to use a new product or one of its more complicated features.

- ✔ Entertaining videos that contain some mention or appearance of the product, perhaps even a video that makes fun of the product.

- ✔ Third-party testimonials, in which a YouTube member posts a video clip of herself singing the praises of a particular product or company.

Stay away from posting any obviously commercial ads on YouTube. They're likely to drive away more customers than they can possibly attract. If you find a video on YouTube, however, that promotes a product or service you sell, consider linking to it, adding it to your marketing materials, and tagging it (adding a search term to it, so clients and prospects can easily find it by performing a search).

Dig it, man, Digg it!

Looking for a way to generate links to your business website or blog, drive traffic and increase search engine rankings? The social news site Digg (www. digg.com) may be the answer you've been looking for. Digg is a site where regular folks like you and me can submit stories for consideration. Other users read the stories and "digg" them. That's Web 2.0 nomenclature for rating a story. If your story receives enough diggs, it gets promoted to the front page.

The site, which averages 1.5 million visits per day, utilizes the "wisdom of crowds." In other words, no editorial staff is at work screening stories and deciding on what makes the headlines and what get's buried. It's all up to you and your peers to make the news.

What are the marketing benefits? Let's say you write an informational article and post it to your Web site or blog. By submitting it to Digg, which you can do with a single click if you install Digg on your blog, you leverage the chance of that article getting linked to by a large number of readers, including other bloggers.

Digg facilitates viral marketing. The end result is that many more people may read the article than would otherwise read it, more are likely visit your blog, and search engines see this activity and reward you for it. All in all, Digg provides an excellent means by which your quality content can get read, linked to, and ranked in the search engines. As always, remember not to be overtly selling in your blog posts. You may send those posts to Digg, but no one else is going to dig 'em.

Living a "Second Life"

I was recently asked when blogs would become the "neighborhoods we choose to live in." What the inquirer meant was how long will it be before we communicate and collaborate with people more via our blogs than in real life? I'm not sure that will happen, but many people are now spending at least a portion of their lives as virtual creatures in the online world of Second Life (www.secondlife.com). As a salesperson, if you want to hook up with these folks, you'd better get a second life of your own.

Second Life is a fast-expanding online world, "imagined, created and owned by its residents." It has been attracting tech savvy marketers, including Toyota, Starwood Hotels, IBM, GM, and music and book companies. These firms are using the Second Life world for branding purposes.

As a salesperson, as an entrepreneur, you have a chance to move faster than large corporations and establish yourself as an early adopter. If you wait too long to establish your presence in your target market with any social media tools, you may find yourself competing in a marketplace that is already dominated by earlier adopters. Gen X and Gen Y consumers are using these online social communities to communicate, collaborate, and find information. Don't you want to be where they are?

Second Life branding, a case study

Second Life marketers aren't just large companies. A Second Life resident who has created an "in world" brand and products is Gareth Lancaster — who sells "in world" roller skates. Yes, you read that right, he *sells* virtual roller skates — 50,000 pairs to date. According to Second Life, residents of this virtual world sold goods and services in the amount of $328,517 — that's *real* dollars for *virtual* goods. This kind of money wouldn't be spent if there weren't lots of like minded people taking this online social networking thing very seriously.

In discussing how real world brands might think about how to access this lucrative market, Lancaster was quoted in the *New York Times* article as comparing "the situation with a company doing business in China for the first time and belatedly realizing that the place is already teeming with companies that know the market inside out." While these "RL" (real life) firms might have years of experience and knowledge about branding and marketing, what they do not realize, says Lancaster, is "that they're going to have to compete against a completely different marketplace, which is basically the residents of Second Life." In other words, while they may only be kids or RL employed people creating "in world" lives and businesses, they got there first, and the old school "experts" have some catching up to do.

Second Life can be a bit intimidating for nontechnical users. It isn't quite as intuitive as creating a blog, but if you stick with it, you can create your own avatar (a representative of you online), buy and sell property, and set up a store where you can sell real goods or offer RL services. You can also set up a press conference, build a community of fans of your product, or set up mock demos of your product or service for Second Life residents to try out.

Second Life may be online, but it can have real-world results.

Part V

Teaming Up with Your Customers . . . and Competitors

The 5th Wave   By Rich Tennant

In this part . . .

Your success may be limited by the lackluster success of the people around you — particularly your customers, but curiously enough, your competitors, too. Surround yourself with success, and you soon find that the crowds you've assisted are the ones who are lifting you upward toward and perhaps even beyond your goals.

While the rest of this book is all about you, the chapters in this part turn your focus to those around you. Here, you discover various ways to reach out and achieve much more than you could possibly achieve on your own by investing in the success of others.

Chapter 18

Focusing on Your Client's Success

In This Chapter

▶ Familiarizing yourself with your clients' business

▶ Documenting your clients' needs

▶ Tailoring products and services to specific clients

▶ Letting your client know how much you care

▶ Shedding any sexist sales techniques

*F*or your business to thrive, your clients must thrive, so part of your job as a top salesperson is to provide your clients with the products, services, and information they need to achieve success. This may include providing your clients with training and support to effectively implement a new software system, offering articles and tips on how to use your product or service more efficiently and effectively, developing financing solutions to make purchases more affordable, and even referring business to your clients.

When clients see that you're committed to their success, they're much more committed to your success and more capable of doing something about it — by purchasing more products and services, referring business to you, and perhaps even presenting opportunities that can make your business more profitable.

This chapter takes the focus off of your own success and refocuses your efforts on the success of your clients. By putting the techniques and tips I reveal in this chapter to work for you, you soon realized that this client-focused approach delivers immeasurable benefits to you and your company.

Throughout this book, I use the words "customer" and "client" interchangeably, but these two words do have different meanings. A customer is someone who buys a product or service from you without having much of a relationship with you, either implied or in writing. A client, on the other hand, is someone with whom you develop a lasting relationship.

Getting to Know Your Client's Business

Prospective clients don't care about the products you're peddling. They don't care about *your* business. They care about *their own* business. If they're smart, they also care about the success of their clients. What they need from you are products and services that enable them to achieve their goals faster, cheaper, or with fewer hassles.

To make your products more attractive, you have to know a little something about your client's business — the challenges they must overcome, the daily annoyances, the clients they serve, and the most pressing problem they are currently trying to solve. By understanding how your clients run their business, you can tailor your products and presentation to better meet the needs of each individual client.

People don't care how much you know until they know how much you care. Ask questions to identify the problem they are trying to solve. Asking questions shows you care. Once they realize that you understand their circumstance, they are more likely to listen to the solution you have to offer.

Hiring an assistant who knows how to sell

As I discuss in Chapter 13, I often hire and use virtual assistants (freelancers who market their services on the Internet) to take on much of the workload. Like employees, virtual assistants can be good or bad, and you may have to go through a few of them before you find one that's right for you.

One evening I was working on finding another virtual assistant to take on some responsibilities in my real estate business, and I came across an assistant who looked promising. I called over to my close advisor, Lois, who was working nearby and told her that I thought I had found the perfect fit. She said she wasn't so sure. She came over to my desk and asked me keep searching as she supervised my search.

We came across the Web site of Hamric Enterprises. Lois liked the site and what Hamric Enterprises apparently had to offer, so I called

and left a voicemail message. About an hour later, we received a call from Kandra Hamric, owner and operator.

Wow! Were we impressed! Kandra was energetic, knowledgeable, and understood my needs immediately. But what knocked it out of the park for me was that she had taken the time to Google me, visit my Web sites, and understand who I was before she called, so that she could address me and my company's needs better. I have always appreciated that about Kandra. She has since become my number-one virtual assistant, oversees many of our other assistants, and has become an integral part of our one-on-one coaching team.

If you're hiring an assistant to work directly with clients, I recommend you find someone who knows how to sell — how to show your clients she cares and build relationships.

One of the best ways to establish a mutually beneficial relationship with business clients is to refer your clients to their business. Be sure to tell the clients you refer to mention that they were referred by you. This sends a message loud and clear that you are dedicated to the success of your client.

Researching your client's business

You can hire a marketing research firm to gather information about your clients, but doing your own research may provide you with more valuable information as well as giving you the opportunity to connect with your clients without the pressure of having to make a sale.

How do you go about doing this market research on your own? Following are some suggestions:

- **Visit the company's Web site.** If the company has a press area, check out the latest press releases and other publicly available information about the company.

- **Do a thorough Web search:** Google the company, Google your contact person, Google the company's phone number, and Google the industry. This gives you details you may not find on the company's Web site, including advertisements and what that company's customers are saying about the company.

  Google allows you to perform several types of searches. In addition to searching the Web, search Google News. Also, click the **more>>** link to search blogs, products, and discussion groups. You can even use Google Earth to view an aerial photo of the company. The more you *know* about the company, the less likely they will say *No* when you call.

- **Distribute a questionnaire.** Post a questionnaire on the Web or send it via email, and let your clients know that any information they offer is confidential. Don't burden your clients with a lot of questions. Simply request the person's name, e-mail address, phone number, mailing address, job title, purchasing power, how they use your product, and the biggest issue or problem they are currently facing.

- **Attend industry conferences.** Find out the which conferences your best clients attend, and try to get into those conferences, so you can discover more about your client's business and perhaps even network with more clients like these.

- **Host a client forum.** You can do this online or in person. Invite your clients to gather and talk shop, and state clearly up front, that during this time, you're not going to be selling anything. Let your clients know that you simply want to connect with them personally and hear what they really need from you.

✔ **Talk to your client service reps.** If your company has separate departments for sales and client service, open the lines of communication. As a salesperson, you should know what the client service reps know about your clients.

Professionals who are passionate about their business love to describe what they do and are often more willing than you may think to provide information about their company. Ask to speak with the president, CEO, or CFO. Express an interest in taking a tour of the company. This enables you to connect with company personnel in a low-pressure setting and gather information without immediately delivering some heavy-handed sales pitch.

Finding out about your client's client

Although your primary focus should always be on your client, knowing about the needs of your client's client can often give you a competitive advantage.

Identify the people that your client needs to please in order to be successful, and then do what you can in terms of product development and your sales presentation to prove that you can assist your client in pleasing her client.

When I'm working on selling a house for a client, I have to constantly remain aware of the needs of my client's client — the person looking to buy a house. To better serve my clients, I find out from their clients what they thought of the house after looking at it. I then pass that feedback along to my clients who can then, perhaps, make a few adjustments to make their property more marketable. If the prospective buyers commented that the yard looks cluttered or the house seems dark, my clients can attend to those areas before another set of prospective buyers tour the premises. I have to know what buyers are looking for in order give my seller a competitive edge in the market.

I also have to be aware of my client's clients needs during the negotiating process. I can think of countless numbers of times when a prospective buyer said something like, "I would buy the house if it only had . . ." I have to be able to end that sentence, so I can relay the information to my client and determine whether we can supply that missing piece.

Of course, knowing the needs of your client's client isn't always enough. You still have to convince your client to make the necessary adjustments. You have to be able to prove that the change or sacrifice is in your client's best interest. This is where your hand-to-hand sales skills really come into play.

Golden Tee Golf

My co-author, Joe, co-authored another book with Incredible Technologies, the creators of the popular coin-op video game, Golden Tee Golf. *Deconstructing Golden Tee LIVE* describes how developers designed the game to appeal to several clients, including the players, the operators (who purchased, delivered, and maintained the games), and the location owners (the owners of the establishments where the games were placed).

The players obviously wanted a game that was loads of fun to play, and the developers certainly focused on making the best video golf game on the planet, but the operators and location owners had other needs. The operators needed an accounting system, for example, that could automatically calculate the splits — how much the operator received, how much he had to pay the location owner, how much of the money went to Incredible Technologies, and how much he would owe in taxes. The game developers

designed an accounting system right into the game and made it accessible online, so operators could check their machines from a remote location using a personal computer and the Internet.

The location owners had a different need. They needed patrons to stick around and order more food and drinks, so developers added a display to the top of the game that showed tournament standings — patrons would stick around after playing a round of golf to see how they did, and when they stuck around, they usually ate and drank more.

By focusing on the needs of its clients and its clients' clients, Incredible Technologies was able to carve out a niche in the declining market of coin-op video games and take the lead in a highly competitive industry. Follow their lead by focusing on the needs of all the people in the food chain who stand to benefit from your products and services.

Discovering What Your Client Needs to Succeed

Your client may not always need what you have to offer, but you should be aware of those needs all the same and assist in any way possible to meet them. When I sell homes, for example, most of my paying clients haven't the cash to buy a home — they have to finance the purchase. I'm not a bank, but I can put the buyer in touch with a loan officer who can assist them.

Someone who's selling a house has other needs. They may need to find a new home, have the roof repaired, or have the house painted before we can list it. I can refer the seller to people who can handle that. A client facing foreclosure is likely to have entirely different needs — primarily the need to know her options and the deadline to make a decision. I offer the person education and guidance. I become a conduit for putting people in touch with one another, and by helping them, I strengthen my relationship with the people I put in touch.

The point here is that each client may be in a unique situation with needs that differ from those of your other clients. Place yourself in a position in which you can meet all those needs, and you immediately expand your client base.

In the following sections, I touch on the various types of needs your clients are likely to have and offer suggestions on how to more effectively cater to those needs.

Identifying specific needs

You profit by selling a product or service, but products and services are not always what your clients need most. They may need money, education, qualified personnel, and so on. By being able to offer your clients more of what they need, even if doing so does not directly improve your bottom line, you gain client loyalty.

Following are some suggestions of what your clients may need that you can offer indirectly:

- **Products:** If you're in a service industry and you know of products that your client may need, refer your client to a supplier who carries those products. In addition to assisting your client, you steer some business to the supplier, who may return the favor later.

- **Services:** If you sell products and know of a service that could benefit your client, refer the client to the service provider.

- **Information:** Information is power, or, as my co-author Joe tells me they say in the publishing business, "Content is King!" Offer your clients the information they need to become more successful in their businesses. You can do this in person, by creating a newsletter or posting the information on your Web site or blog, e-mailing your clients, or even mailing the information via the postal service.

- **Training:** Businesses often suffer by selling products or services and then failing to properly train clients on how to use them or optimize their use. Consider offering free or premium training to get clients up to speed. You may be able to automate the training by posting training materials online — text-based training, online seminars, training videos, podcasts, and so on. See Chapter 16 for more about selling in the multi-media marketplace.

- **Financing:** Are your products and services affordable for most of your clients and prospective clients? If not, consider offering some form of financing or recommending a lender who can work with the client to design a personalized financing package. You may be able to open another sales channel by selling your products and services to startup companies. When selling to startups, you have an added incentive to team up with the client for success, because if that startup business doesn't make it, you may not get paid!

✔ **Community:** Clients, especially those who are just starting out in business, often crave a community from which they can obtain support and resources. By becoming a community center for related businesses in your area, you boost your own credibility and feed your clients' need for community.

✔ **Personnel:** In Chapter 14, I encourage you to tap the power of R-Commerce (Relationship-Commerce) by gathering the names and contact information of everyone you meet. When a client's success is limited by a lack of qualified personnel, you may be able to recommend qualified candidates for specific positions. Assuming you recommend high-quality candidates, they will sell for you every day they show up for work and do an outstanding job.

You may be able to save a considerable amount of money by combining training with community. On your Web site, create a discussion forum area where clients can gather to share information, post questions, and answer one another's questions. One or more employees at your company who are in charge of client support and training can monitor the forums or blog.

Rack your brain and go back through your files to find questions that clients have asked in the past and you have answered. Post these questions first. Most questions are common, and the answers benefit even those who don't raise their hands.

Getting down to business

Although you want to show genuine concern for a client's current situation, you don't always have to be overly nice about it. Sometimes, being curt and getting down to brass tacks is the best approach.

When I'm dealing with clients who are facing foreclosure, for example, I often hit them with a rat-at-tat-tat series of very targeted personal questions to find out exactly what's going on and how the homeowners arrived at this point. My questions can make any of my associates who accompany me very uncomfortable. Some of them feel as though I'm being too blunt and not compassionate enough.

I've found, however, that my approach is most effective and expedient. By asking personal questions (the "ugly" questions) early on, I can quickly assess the situation, find out who I'm really dealing with, take the "personal" out of it, and get on with the business of assisting the homeowners either save their home or at least make their loss less painful.

Ask questions in the right tone of voice, but don't avoid asking ugly questions if you have to. The more information you have, the better the assistance you can provide.

Adapting to client needs in the real estate market

In the Detroit metropolitan area that I service, drastic changes in our local market and economy have forced us to make sweeping changes in the way we service our customers, particularly home buyers. Currently, the average person is carrying more debt and has less cash than in previous years. Clients are no longer receiving yearly bonuses and many have taken pay cuts to maintain jobs. Many people simply do not have a great deal of cash anymore, but they still want to own a home.

We are finding that we need to do much more matchmaking with buyers and sellers than in the past. We have to find sellers who are willing and able to assist with the financing — to contribute toward down payments and closing costs for a potential buyer. Not every seller is in the position, so every transaction requires a different approach and some creative thinking.

We've also had to build a larger referral network of lenders, mortgage brokers, and loan officers to service our clients. Not all lenders offer the same financing options, and many clients today have specific needs for financing. We need to be able to hook up buyers with people who can help them. We've developed relationships with multiple lenders and have to keep an open flow of communication to provide clients with accurate, timely financing information.

With the increase in the foreclosures and REO (Real Estate Owned or bank-owned) business, potential buyers are in greater need of contractors and repair services than ever before. In today's market, a buyer is more apt to buy a bank-owned home in as-is condition. We must have a large base of professionals to refer to our clients — professionals who will represent us in the best possible fashion and not damage our relationship with the client. We have to find people who do outstanding, affordable work, because their performance reflects on us.

When changes in the economy, your industry, and other areas affect your clients, you have to be ready, willing, and able to embrace the change, adapt, and serve your clients in a way that brings them closer to success. You can't spend time and waste energy complaining about it.

When I am with a client and they ask a question, I often respond with "Wow, that's a great question." Instead of making the client feel stupid for asking a question, it makes them feel like a genius and encourages them to ask more questions, which makes my job even easier.

Adjusting your business model to meet client needs

When I'm out coaching and mentoring salespeople, I notice two kinds of businesses — those that adapt to the changing needs of clients and those that fail. As a salesperson, you may think that your company's CEO should be in charge of guiding the business to success, but you're the person battling on the front line. You're the one who has direct contact with clients on a daily basis. And you're the one who feels the pain most directly when your company is failing to meet the needs of your clients.

Whenever you become aware that your company is dropping the ball, communicate your perceptions to company management. Describe exactly what you think needs to be done to better serve the clients. You have a vested interest in your company's success, so act like it.

Whenever anyone has an unmet need, the person takes action to fill that need. This is usually what happens when married couples get divorced, but it happens in business, too. If you're not offering your clients what they need, they are going to find it elsewhere. Be constantly vigilant of their changing needs. What your clients need today may not be what they needed yesterday.

You are only as good as your last transaction, your last sale. If you fail someone you have lost the referral of 200 to 250 people. That is why you must align yourself with people that have the same integrity and the same commitment.

Integrating Sales with Product Development and Client Service

When clients choose a supplier, they're usually looking for more than a product or service. They're buying your reputation for quality and reliability, the promise of excellent client service, perhaps additional education and training, and a host of other things you may consider intangible. What you're selling is a whole package, including yourself.

Tossing your clients a bonus

Remain on the lookout for anything you can do to make your client's life a little easier. I do this myself, and I observe other top-producing salespeople do the same thing in their own, unique ways.

Sharon, a top-notch car salesperson who happened to sell a car to my wife, Kathleen, is a natural at looking out for her clients. She accommodates the client. Instead of calling to have her client drive to the dealership to pick up their new car, she delivers it and picks up the trade-in.

When Sharon found a great deal on garage door openers, she bought about a dozen of them at 50 percent off. She sold them to her clients at

cost. None of her clients complained, but an envious colleague mentioned it to management, and Sharon was fired. Now perhaps Sharon should have gone to management to ask permission first, but if I were her manager, I'd be giving her a bonus rather than a pink slip. Sharon is a perfect example of a salesperson who provided her clients with something extra.

Sharon became a salesperson for another dealership for a while. After time, the dealership that fired her realized that they had made a huge mistake and recruited her again. So she is back selling and servicing her clients.

Take the extra step. Look for opportunities to pay your clients a bonus.

As you present your products and services to prospective clients, don't leave out these "intangibles," especially when you're selling to a client who just fired her previous supplier on the grounds of being unable to meet these other needs.

Some companies keep their departments overly isolated. Product development, customer service, sales, and other departments pretty much keep to themselves. To serve your clients more effectively, open up the lines of communication. Knowledge is power. The more you distribute the knowledge, the more you empower everyone in your company to make a difference.

If you don't know, say so. In an effort to appear as though you know everything, you can bruise your credibility. Salespeople often answer a questions before fully understanding them. Worse yet, they fake it, pretending to know the answer. When a client asks a question, take a moment to digest it before offering an answer. If you don't know, say you don't know and that you are going to have to look into it and get back with them.

Your client needs to have the confidence that you "know your stuff' better than anyone else out there — that you give them an advantage over the next person. This isn't easy, because first you really do have to "know your stuff," and that takes time, research, and experience. You have to be the total package before you can deliver it. If your client believes that you are a smart, honest, hard-working professional who is an expert in your field, and you care about their needs, they will use you and refer you to their friends and family.

Communicating Your Commitment to Your Client

Your clients need to feel the love, and the only way they can feel it is if you show it, both by words, non-verbal cues, and decisive action that shows you care:

1. **Listen to what your client has to say.** You have two ears and one mouth, so use them in that proportion. Don't go on the defensive, no matter how confrontational your client becomes. Absorb the hit.

2. **Respond, first by restating the client's concern or complaint to show that you fully understand and then go one step further to express your empathy — you not only understand the situation, but you also feel the client's pain.** Most clients simply want someone to validate their feelings. Make a note of what they have to say so you can review their questions and concerns later and address them in a way that fills your client with confidence.

3. **Present one or more solutions.** After giving the client's situation or problem due consideration, try to formulate one or more solutions, and present those as some possibilities.

4. **Ask your client for any additional solutions she can think of.**

5. **Team up with your client to arrive at a solution you can both live with and that serves both of your interests.**

6. **Take action immediately, if not sooner.** Once you've arrived at a solution, implement it as soon as possible. A sure way to lose a client is to make a promise and then fail to follow up on it.

7. **Keep the client informed of the progress.** Your client may not notice that you're making an effort unless you keep that client posted throughout the process, from the time you agree on a solution until the time you've resolved the issue. You can keep the client in the loop in any number of ways — email, phone calls, or a Web site that gives them access to the service, product, or progress on a particular project.

You don't have to wait until your client has a problem or an issue that needs tending to. Become proactive in serving your clients' needs, especially their need to know that you care about them. In Chapter 12, I talk about my daily *Hour of Power*, in which I get on the phone for an hour and place 100 calls to people I know to express in various ways just how much I care about them. The key to the *Hour of Power* is to not sell. Simply show your clients that you're thinking about them.

All of your clients don't speak the same language. Some of them want to hear that you're looking out for their best interests. Others would rather see it in your performance and what you do on a daily basis to make them more successful. Some clients prefer receiving gifts, special deals, referrals, or additional training. Identify the language that each client speaks, and then speak to your client in that language.

Reinforcing a positive relationship

Clients, especially your best clients, need and deserve praise and other forms of positive reinforcement throughout your relationship. Here are a few tips on how to provide these positive strokes:

- ✔ **Let them talk.** People love to talk about themselves, so let them. Spend less time talking about how great you are and how great your company and products are and more time listening to how great your client is.

- ✔ **Pat them on the back.** When a customer asks a good question or makes a suggestion, give them a "Wow," as in "Wow, that's an excellent question," or "Wow, that's a great idea."

✔ **KISS up to the client.** No, I'm not saying that you need to cater to the client's every whim. I'm saying KISS: Keep It Simple, Stupid. Don't over-complicate issues with clients. They have better things to think about.

✔ **Let your client set the pace, but you drive.** From the beginning, let the client take the lead and set the pace. You want to be driving the car but making your client feel as though she's steering.

✔ **Know your stuff.** You need to know the product, service or process so well that you have the ability to educate and overcome any pre-conceived ideas.

Ask for endorsements and testimonials. My executive assistant, Lois, led our foreclosure department and collected a host of testimonials and endorsements from clients. I told her to create a book and lay it out in the front lobby, so other clients could look at them while they were waiting. If you do this, make sure you have a backup copy, just in case the book "disappears." Remember that complaints come naturally, but unless you ask for an endorsement, testimo-nial, or reference, you are likely to receive only a few.

Fielding complaints

A certain portion of the population consists of natural complainers. If you handed them five bags of gold nuggets, they would whine about the bags being too heavy. Over time, you pick up various techniques for spotting these people and can avoid taking them on as clients, but you're still going to have to handle some complaints, particularly valid complaints. Here are some tips for dealing with complaints most expeditiously:

✔ **Address complaints immediately.** Small problems can escalate in a hurry if they are not addressed immediately. You don't want to give your client time to stew about it and post a bunch of negative PR on the Web.

✔ **Clear up misunderstandings.** Most complaints result from miscommuni-cation, so you can address the problem simply by clarifying something you said or wrote. In many cases, a client simply wants someone to listen and show genuine concern.

✔ **Keep clients posted.** If the problem is due to something other than a communication issue, fix the problem and then let your client know that the problem has been taken care of. If you receive a complaint in writing, respond in writing and follow up with a phone call.

✔ **Keep management posted.** If you feel that you have done all that you can do and you know that management will be contacted next you need to go to management first, explaining the whole situation, and if you have been wrong disclose that as well. This will help. A good manager ultimately gets you involved again to resolve the issue and use it as an educational experience.

The customer is not always right. If a client becomes completely unmanageable, fire them. Let them down softly by saying something like, "I don't think that we are compatible, and I believe that you would be better served by someone else." This isn't easy when you are first starting out or when you are in a sales slump, but this is the best option for both you and your client. Cumbersome clients sap your energy and detract from more productive pursuits.

Chapter 19

Selling to Multicultural Customers

· ·

In This Chapter

▶ Understanding the multicultural buyer mindset

▶ Meeting and greeting customers from other cultures

▶ Adjusting your approach to accommodate cultural differences

▶ Haggling to win respect

▶ Adapting customer service to diverse needs

· ·

*U*nknowingly and unintentionally, you could be limiting the scope of future sales by ignoring or even offending a huge potential market — minorities.

Now, "minority" may sound like a tiny market, but the combined annual buying power of this group in America exceeds the gross domestic product of all but nine countries in the entire world. The Hispanic population alone in the U.S. is larger than the entire population of Canada. Yet sadly, this is an opportunity that many salespeople overlook. Most American sales professionals actually turn off minority buyers without ever knowing how or why they offend them.

To grab your fair share of the multicultural market, you have to adjust your practices to meet the unique needs of people who have come here from all over the globe: Hispanics, African Americans, Asians, Middle Easterners, and other groups. Collectively, these minorities in America buy nearly $2 trillion in goods and services every year. Are you getting your share of that market?

In this chapter, I team up with diversity and sales expert Michael Soon Lee of EthnoConnect (www.EthnoConnect.com) to show you how to adjust your strategies to the needs of buyers from other cultures, so you can instantly grow your market by at least a third!

You may have had interactions with people from diverse cultures already, but they seemed uninterested in what you had to offer or you just never got to the point of doing business with them. This probably means that they put you to the test and somehow you failed. It doesn't mean they didn't *want* to buy. When minorities return over and over without buying, it means they don't trust the environment enough to make a commitment. Only you can turn that around and create an environment in which they feel more comfortable buying something.

Testing Your Multicultural Aptitude

The first step in becoming more aware of other cultures as a salesperson is to determine just how tuned in or tuned out you already are. On EthnoConnect. com, Michael has an online quiz that you can take to determine how much you know about dealing with customers and clients from other countries and cultures. If you register (by entering your name and email address) and take the quiz online, you can have your quiz automatically graded. Figure 19-1 features a subset of questions from that quiz, so you can test your knowledge about selling to multicultural customers.

To grade yourself, check your answers against the following answer key:

1. **What is the most appropriate greeting when first meeting a male multicultural customer?**

   C. Wait for him to do what's comfortable for him

   Do not automatically stick your hand out. Wait for him to do what is comfortable for his culture. See details below.

2. **When a major purchase will be financed, what should you never ask?**

   A. How much of a down payment do you have?

   Many groups, particularly Hispanics and Asians, tend not to trust banks so may keep cash hidden in and around their homes. Asking about the down payment could subject them to home invasion robberies.

3. **When exchanging business cards with a multicultural customer you should be sure to:**

   C. Present your card with both hands

   Always present your card with both hands with the lettering facing the customer. Accept their card with your right hand because the left hand is considered to be "unclean". Asking for two cards implies you will likely lose one of them which is an insult.

1. What is the most appropriate greeting when first meeting a male multicultural customer?
A. Shake his hand since this is the universal greeting.
B. Pat him on the back
C. Wait for him to do what's comfortable for him
D. Present your business card
E. Bow since this is the most common greeting in the world

2. When a major purchase will be financed, what should you never ask?
A. How much of a down payment do you have?
B. How many years do you want to pay back the loan?
C. Have you been pre-approved for a loan?
D. What amount of loan would you like?
E. Do you have a favorite bank?

3. When exchanging business cards with a multicultural customer you should be sure to:
A. Bow as you present it
B. Accept their card with your left hand
C. Present your card with both hands
D. Hand them your card with the wording facing you
E. Always ask them for two so you can staple one into their file

4. It is acceptable to make notes about multicultural customers:
A. On the back of their business card
B. On the front of their business card
C. On a separate note pad
D. On the back of one of your own business cards
E. On the front of one of your cards

5. A product demonstration with Hispanic buyers is likely to be most effective by:
A. Giving them a manual to read
B. Letting them try it for themselves
C. Showing them a diagram
D. Verbally explaining its operations to them
E. Playing them a video

6. When talking with new immigrant buyers who show no body language which would be a definite buying sign?
A. Smiling
B. Nodding
C. Talking in their own language
D. Laughing
E. Asking questions

7. Which gesture is most universally offensive?
A. Pointing with the finger
B. The "OK" sign
C. Thumbs up
D. Talking with hands in pants pockets
E. Whistling at the opposite sex

8. Which group is mostly likely to openly display emotions during negotiations?
A. Whites
B. Hispanics
C. African Americans
D. Asians
E. Middle Easterners

Figure 19-1:
Test your
knowledge
of how
to treat
customers
from other
cultures.

9. Which group is least likely to try to negotiate the price of your product?
A. Whites
B. Hispanics
C. African Americans
D. Asians
E. Middle Easterners

10. Which "Thank you" gift would be least appropriate for Asians?
A. Watch
B. Box of candy
C. Pen & pencil set
D. Key chain
E. Kitchen utensils

4. It is acceptable to make notes about a multicultural customer:

C. On a separate note pad

Writing on the customer's card is equivalent to writing on their face! Writing on your own card disrespects it as well.

5. A product demonstration with a Hispanic buyer is likely to be most effective by:

B. Letting them try it for themselves

Studies show that Hispanics tend to be more kinesthetic than other cultures preferring to actually examine and operate products as opposed to just hearing about its features.

6. When talking with new immigrant buyers who show no body language which would be a definite buying sign?

C. Talking in their own language

Smiling and laughing often indicated uneasiness or lack of understanding and nodding often simply means they are listening, but not agreeing with you.

7. Which gesture is most universally offensive?

A. Pointing with the finger

Pointing with the finger is generally the most universally offensive gesture. In most cultures outside the United States it is preferred that the entire closed hand or a head nod be used to indicate a specific direction. In many cultures the pointed finger is considered rude or even obscene.

8. Which group is mostly likely to openly display emotions during negotiations?

E. Middle Easterners

Middle Easterners tend to be very emotional and emphatic as part of their negotiating technique.

9. Which group is least likely to try to negotiate the price of your product?

A. Whites

European Americans come from non-negotiating cultures where only large purchases are regularly bargained on.

10. Which "thank you" gift would be least appropriate for Asians?

A. Watch

Watches and clocks tend to remind Asians of the "winding down of life" so giving a watch would be taken to mean "I wish you were dead". Probably not the sentiment you had in mind!

To score your test, total your number of correct answers. You can then determine just how knowledgeable you are about selling to customers of diverse cultures:

Your score:

9–10: Outstanding! You're culturally competent and probably have many diverse customers. Heck, you ought to be writing this chapter.

7–8: Very good. With a few minor adjustments, you are well prepared to take full advantage of the global economy.

5–6: Pretty good. You can handle most situations, but could use some fine-tuning.

3–4: Not bad. You're not about to get kicked out of a foreign country for a major faux pas, but you're not ready for the U.N., either.

0–2: Yikes! You'd better stick with your own people until you get the proper training. Keep reading.

To take the full Multicultural Sales Quiz or other cultural-readiness quizzes, visit Michael's site at www.EthnoConnect.com and click Take a Quiz. Michael offers several free quizzes including Company Cultural Competency, Multicultural Marketing, and Multicultural Negotiating.

Busting Common Myths

As an adult learner, you often have to unlearn before you're ready to learn. This is especially true when you're building skills required to deal with customers from other cultures. Your own culture is so ingrained that it has become second nature, and assuming that everyone else thinks and acts the same way is far too easy.

So, before you begin your re-education, take some time de-educating yourself by questioning some commonly held beliefs you may have picked up:

Myth: Minorities want to buy only from salespeople of their own culture.

Fact: This may be true for a few individuals, but not for most. People who speak very little English often prefer communicating with someone who speaks their language, but other than that, people generally don't care what your background is as long as you're respectful, competent, and sensitive to their traditions. In fact, many people prefer to work with a salesperson from outside their own culture. Asians, for example, can be very private about their financial affairs, and many are afraid that if they work with a fellow Asian, she may disclose their income, debts, and purchases to others in the community. Newly immigrated Hispanics often want to improve their English skills by interacting with people who won't speak Spanish to them.

Myth: We should treat everyone the same, regardless of culture.

Fact: Yes, it's true that we should treat every customer fairly but this does not necessarily mean treating them exactly the same way. For example, if a buyer who is blind comes into your store or office, you wouldn't think of handing them a printed brochure to read. You may read the brochure to the person or present the information in some other format. In the same way, you have to adapt your sales presentation to meet the needs of those from other countries and cultures.

Applying multicultural sales techniques

Lee's clients often write to him to express their appreciation for something they learned at one of his seminars. One client in particular, a real estate broker, had put Lee's advice into practice and was quite impressed with the results.

A prospective client of Chinese descent invited the broker and his wife over to his house for dinner. The broker reviewed the notes from Lee's seminar prior to the dinner date and prepared himself and his wife to expect to meet more people than just the client. He knew that other family members were likely to be in attendance, so when he arrived to find 25 people from three generations, he was not surprised.

He had also informed his wife that they wouldn't be talking business. They would simply treat this as a social gathering and an opportunity to meet some new friends. When they drove up, Cheng (the prospective client and patriarch of the family) came out to greet them personally and lead them into the house. Before entering Cheng's home, the broker took off his shoes and signaled his wife to do the same. He noticed that everyone had left their shoes out by the porch.

The broker informed Cheng, as Lee had suggested, that he was afraid he would say or do something wrong that the family would find offensive to his culture, and he asked Cheng to assist him. Cheng sat the broker next to him at the head of the table while the children sat on little wooden stools.

Well into dinner, Cheng mentioned to the broker that family is most important. He turned to the broker and said, "One family for life," and then he smiled and said, "And one real estate broker for life." The broker replied, "And good friends for life." Cheng smiled broadly.

Cheng hired the broker to manage his family's properties, and it seemed as though everyone in the family owned a rental property. He also asked the broker to represent him in commercial and residential real estate investment purchases.

The broker managed to develop what he believes is going to be a lifetime relationship with Cheng and his family primarily because he followed Lee's advice and didn't rush into a business discussion. He showed respect for Cheng's culture and focused on the relationship rather than what he could get out of it.

Myth: People should do as Americans do when they're in this country.

Fact: People in other countries often refer to visitors from the United States as "Ugly Americans." Why? Because many tourists from the states fly to Germany, France, China, or other foreign lands and expect the people there to accommodate them. These less worldly tourists expect to receive the same food and other amenities they are familiar with. They expect to be served pizza in Asia and to speak English in France. Just as it's difficult for us Americans to leave our 200-year-old culture at the gate when we travel abroad it's even harder for those coming here from cultures that are thousands of years old to do as we do here. While they do try to assimilate, it is hard for them. If you want a piece of business from the fastest-growing segment of the retail market it is you who need to adjust . . . at least a little. Take the time to learn about other cultures, languages, and foods. As a bonus you will become a much more interesting person.

Myth: We don't have that many minority customers so why should we bother changing the way we do business?

Fact: You may be missing out on a huge opportunity. If you have few or no minority customers the reason may be that you haven't changed the way you do business. Studies show that minorities go out of their way to shop at establishments that are sensitive to their culture and meet their unique needs. Go to the U.S. Census Web site at www.census.gov and look at the percent of the population you serve who are non-white, and ask yourself if you are getting your fair share of this business. It's hard to imagine any area of this country where you couldn't boost your sales with a substantial percentage of minorities.

Mastering the Multicultural Meet and Greet

Even at family gatherings, people greet one another differently. Demonstrative family members may offer a full-body hug, while the more self-conscious are careful not to let any body parts below the ribcage come in contact. Others may prefer shaking hands, offering a peck on the cheek, or simply fleeing to another room until the customary pressing of flesh has ended.

Of course, in business situations with customers, you can usually get by with a handshake, as I explain in Chapter 4. When dealing with customers from other cultures, however, even the tried-and-true handshake comes into question. What may seem like a friendly handshake to you, could make a customer instantly uncomfortable, and in sales, that's not exactly the emotion you're looking for.

In the following sections, I offer a strategy for handling the first meeting that should work for every situation you're in. I then reveal a few tips for dealing with special circumstances, including meeting couples for the first time.

Following your customer's lead

In the Unites States, we often assume that a firm handshake is universal, but that's simply a Western custom. The most common greeting in the world is the bow, not the handshake. Joining hands can actually be offensive to people who don't believe in touching people they don't know.

To build rapport with any customer, regardless of culture, never assume you know how they want to be greeted. To be safe, let them make the first move. Hesitate a moment to see what they do, and then follow their lead. Most multicultural men in the United States have become used to our customs and are not particularly bothered by shaking hands. They may even offer their hand, knowing that this is the customary greeting. Asians may nod as they shake hands. Simply do likewise.

Following a customer's lead is fairly easy when the customer bows instead of offering to shake your hand, but the first time a customer goes to hug you or kiss you on the cheek, you're likely to go into culture shock. This is especially true if you're a man meeting a male customer. In the United States, guys just don't do that. For many Hispanic and Middle Eastern men, however, a kiss on the cheek is the preferred greeting.

If a customer attempts to hug you, hug back. If he kisses you on the cheek, return the gesture. Avoid acting offended; take it as a sign that the person is comfortable with you. Most importantly, if a customer kisses you once on the cheek, don't try to turn away to avoid that second kiss, because it's likely to land squarely on your lips, which could be most uncomfortable for you and your customer.

The rule of greeting people from outside the American culture is this: Never assume anything. Greet your customer verbally, let your customer make the first move, and then follow his lead.

Gauging your customer's personal space

You can't see it, but surrounding your body and extending out for anywhere from a few inches to several feet is an extension of your body commonly referred to as your *personal space*. Your body immediately identifies anyone crossing the border into that space as an intruder. Instinctively, your body moves to constantly re-establish its comfort zone.

In the United States we shake hands and then stand about two-and-a-half feet away from the other person. People from more formal countries, including Japan, may bow or shake hands and then step back about four feet. At four feet apart, you may feel as though you're yelling across the Grand Canyon. To close the gap, you step forward. Your Japanese customer steps back. If the situation continues, you could end up chasing him around the store.

People from the Middle East and Spanish-speaking countries tend to stand much closer than Americans are accustomed to. They may hug you and then stand about six inches away, making you feel as though, at any minute, you're in for another hug. If you're not ready for it, your natural impulse is to move away, to establish your two-and-a-half-foot comfort zone. As soon as you do, however, your customer feels as though you're wandering off and inches closer. If this keeps up, your customer may feel as though you don't like him.

Let customers determine the personal space that's comfortable for them. If they step back after the greeting, get used to the distance and just speak a bit more loudly to bridge the gap. If they step toward you after your greeting, resist the temptation to back up, and be sure to have a breath mint handy.

Establishing eye contact . . . or not

When a customer in the United States looks away, you're likely to think that the person isn't interested in what you have to say. The culture teaches that establishing eye contact demonstrates interest and respect.

Many groups, however, including the Vietnamese, Japanese, and Koreans, avoid direct eye contact as a way of showing respect. To them, looking someone in the eye is intrusive and rude. To honor the other party, they look down. Naturally, the uninformed salesperson does everything in her power to draw the person's attention back to the conversation and may become visibly frustrated or even offended.

When a customer looks down, don't automatically assume the person is not interested, considers you unattractive, or doesn't trust you. Just look down and try to find something else your customer can look down at — the product itself, product brochures, rate charts, flyers, or other material.

Of course, not all cultures interpret eye contact or the lack of it the same way. Middle Easterners and Hispanics, for example, may crave even more direct eye contact than most Americans are used to. This can make the average salesperson in the United States feel as though the customer is being confrontational. Feeling challenged, you may become a little too aggressive or simply look away, and either move could jeopardize the sale. Simply adjust your eye contact accordingly. Mirror your customer.

Keep reminding yourself that what your instincts are telling you is based on cultural habit. It doesn't mean what you think it means. Don't trust the voice inside your head that's the product of decades of cultural training. Trust the facts you know about other cultures to point you in the right direction.

Greeting the female companion

People of all cultures usually try to fit in, so don't be surprised if a male customer from another culture greets you with a handshake. If he's accompanied by a female companion, however, avoid the natural urge to shake her hand, as well. After shaking the man's hand, drop yours to your side, turn to the female companion, and nod respectfully . . . unless, of course, she extends her hand to greet you.

What's acceptable for a man is not always acceptable for a woman in other cultures. Many traditional Middle Eastern, Indian, and Japanese women, for instance, are distressed by touching any male who is not their husband, often because in their own country it is forbidden. If you turn to her with your hand now at your side, and she does not extend hers, you know this to be the case. Just politely nod in her direction to acknowledge her presence. This simple act alone speaks volumes about your cultural sensitivity and your willingness to accommodate her needs.

Asking customers to explain their culture

When you meet up with someone from a culture you haven't encountered before, don't feel as though you should already know everything about that culture. Ask questions. If you don't voice your thoughts, they start to produce *cultural static* — an energy field that interferes with communications. If you're secretly wondering about the way your customer is dressed or how she acts or speaks or you have unspoken questions about their cultural or religious practices, your customer is going to sense that.

Ask questions in a non-threatening way. Chances are good that your customer wants to talk about her culture to assist you in gaining understanding and acceptance, and perhaps even talk about something that's more interesting than the weather. You're likely to be very surprised at just how much you can discover about other cultures as well as how people from other cultures perceive your culture.

If you're going to ask one customer about her culture, ask all of them, including those who may not appear to be culturally different. You don't want to create the appearance of singling out anyone.

Adjusting Your Sales Presentation for Cultural Differences

Salespeople often ask whether they need to adapt their sales presentation for multicultural customers. Michael's answer is always the same, "Only if you want them to buy from you." When you're working on commissions, selling is all about establishing relationships with your customers, and you can't establish solid relationships if you're not communicating in a way that your customers can clearly understand.

Tweaking presentations for different cultures

Salespeople from a wide variety of industries attend Lee's seminars to discover techniques for tapping the multicultural market for sales opportunities. One attendee, an insurance salesperson, discovered that she could sell better to different ethnic groups simply by adjusting her presentation.

One important lesson she took away from the seminar was that multicultural customers didn't necessarily want to buy from an agent from their own culture. This simple truth gave her the motivation to reach out to customers of different races and cultures.

First, she began reaching out to African American clients, because Lee had mentioned that only 32 percent of them had life insurance while 92 percent believed that life insurance was essential. She started taking more time with these prospects because of their historic mistrust of insurance companies. She got to know them as people, helped educate them about the various life insurance options, and let them get to know her as a person, which helped build trust. It took longer than usual but it was worth it.

With Asians, she remembered that Lee had advised to avoid talking about death, because Asians generally believe that discussions of death could bring bad luck. Instead, she emphasized the protection that insurance provides for families now and in the future. There was much less resistance to discussing this aspect of insurance than when she focused on the death benefit.

With Hispanics, she highlighted the savings feature of whole-life policies, which people from this background seemed to value most. They seemed to consider the death benefit almost as an added bonus.

I encourage you to take Lee's advice and make the modifications necessary to your sales techniques and presentations make yourself more appealing to these un-served and under-served groups. In addition to boosting sales, you can open your mind and your life to a host of new insights and experiences.

In the following sections, I offer some suggestions for redecorating your office, choosing effective media, and guiding multicultural customers through a purchase process that may be even more complicated for them than it is for your other customers.

Changing your office décor

Many salespeople try to impress prospective customers by hanging sales awards on the walls of their office. Although your sales achievements may impress customers who come from highly competitive cultures, people from other cultures may find them much less remarkable. Diplomas, certifications, and family photos often carry much more weight. They show that you're a well-informed individual who values relationships.

Choosing effective presentation media

Educators often discuss different learning styles. One student may be more of a visual learner, who needs to see things in order to comprehend the lesson. Another student may learn more effectively in lecture or by having a tutor explain it. Other students may be experiential, hands-on learners.

You can observe these same tendencies in different cultures. In general, Asians are more visual learners. After all, their written language essentially consists of pictures. Hispanics are generally more tactile learners — they want to see a product and perhaps even try it out. African Americans are typically more comfortable processing spoken language.

By knowing that people of other cultures may be able to process information more effectively when it's presented in a certain medium, you can prepare a presentation that makes effective use of all media. If you sense that a customer requires more visuals, you can present photos or illustrations or even videos. If another customer needs to see the product in action, demonstrating the product or letting the customer try it out may be more effective.

Speaking the language

Unless you're bilingual or multilingual, you're likely to find yourself struggling to communicate with some potential customers. In some cases, the language barrier may be a hurdle you can't clear. If the customer can speak a little

English, however, you may be able to work around the obstacles together. The following tips offer some additional assistance:

- Speak a little more slowly, but not so slowly that your tone seems condescending.

- Streamline your presentation to explain only the most important features and benefits of your product. Don't overwhelm your customer with details.

- Enunciate your words clearly.

- Don't shout. Your customer's understanding doesn't increase in proportion to the volume level.

- Choose the most basic words possible and avoid technical jargon.

- Avoid using idiomatic expressions, such as "We'll cross that bridge when we come to it."

- If your customer doesn't seem to understand you, try explaining what you just said another way. A different choice of words might work better or try a different teaching style.

- If you don't understand the person, accept the blame for your inability to understand. Rather than saying, "Could you repeat that? I can't understand you," consider saying something like, "I'm sorry, I'm having trouble understanding you. Could you please repeat that for me?"

Leading customers through the purchase process

When selling to people from other cultures, expect to spend more time and effort educating the customer. Although most of your customers, those who grew up in the country, probably understand the basics of buying a car, a house, or whatever it is you're selling and have a general idea of what contracts are all about, a customer from another country may need a brief primer. The more complex the transaction, the more you can expect to invest in education.

Cultivate patience, not condescension. You don't want to sound as if you're talking to a first grader. As you speak, you can illustrate your point with pictures or diagrams. Many immigrants are unfamiliar with products and services that Americans take for granted. Slowly step them through the purchase process, unless they have some level familiarity with it.

Haggling with Multicultural Buyers

The world can be divided into two types of countries — hagglers and non-hagglers, negotiators and non-negotiators. In non-negotiating countries, including the United States, Germany, and Great Britain, money is relatively plentiful and time is scarce. To save time, most people in these countries are willing to pay sticker price, rather than haggle to save a few bucks. The exception to the rule is when people are buying big-ticket items, such as homes or cars. Then, they force themselves to haggle, but most people don't enjoy it.

In negotiating countries, people barter for everything, because time has traditionally been plentiful and money scarce. Saving a few dollars on meat or vegetables could place more food on the table. As a result of the constant practice, people from these countries are really good at haggling, so I recommend that you hone your own haggling skills. Check out *Negotiating For Dummies* by Michael C. Donaldson and David Frohnmayer.

In the following sections, I point out a couple key areas of negotiating that apply specifically to situations in which you need to negotiate with people from other cultures.

Surviving your first group negotiation

In some countries, sometimes referred to as "collectivist countries," shopping is a team sport. An entire family or village is likely to show up to check out what the local merchant is selling and decide as a group, whether to buy the product. When these folks move to the United States, they may bring this style of shopping with them.

 Highly collectivist countries include Pakistan, Venezuela, Colombia, Peru, Taiwan, Thailand, Japan, and China. The United States, Australia, Great Britain, Canada, the Netherlands, and New Zealand are highly individualistic countries.

When you're confronted with a group of collectivist shoppers, the real trick is to figure out who is really making the purchase decision. Sometimes, it's not so easy. It may not even be the person who is actually going to take out his wallet and pay for your product. I've seen cases in which the grandparent or even a teenager is the ultimate decision-maker. Your best option in such cases is to deliver your sales presentation to the entire group, treating them all as equals.

You can spot the decision-maker at the very end when you ask your closing question, "Would you like to take this home today?" Everyone in the group looks to the decision-maker, and now you finally know the person to whom you were selling.

Negotiating before, during, and after the signing of the contract

In the United States, once the ink dries on the contract, the deal is done . . . you can stick a fork in it. People from other countries often don't see it that way. They may continue to negotiate after signing a contract. Michael constantly hears complaints from salespeople about how "unethical" certain groups of buyers appear to be, because they don't seem to grasp the concept of a contract. The truth is that they view contracts a little differently.

In the United States, bargaining stops when everyone signs on the dotted lines. In countries like China, however, signing a purchase agreement is simply proof that the parties have decided to negotiate — price, terms, and conditions, are all open to negotiation. These people are not being unethical; they just have a different approach to contractual relationships.

Whenever you're dealing with strong negotiators, regardless of culture, always save something for the end. If you sign a contract that's truly based on your "best offer," you leave yourself with little to negotiate later, which is likely to cause some bad feelings. Hold off on offering that extended warranty or free installation until the product has been delivered.

Adjusting Customer Service for Different Cultures

Customer service is a universal language. No matter where your customer is from and which language she speaks, she wants to be treated fairly and with respect. The differences in how people from different cultures deal with poor customer service are expressed in how the people react to receiving poor customer service.

In the United States, people are trained to complain. They contact customer service, and if customer service resolves the problem, the customer typically forgives and forgets. Only after several unsuccessful attempts at obtaining satisfaction is the customer likely to become bitter and start complaining about the company to family and friends, and perhaps even complete strangers.

When dealing with customers from other cultures, you're likely to hear less complaining. Disappointed with your product or customer service, the person is likely to go elsewhere in the future. Even worse, the customer is more likely than someone from the United States to speak badly of your company and products to their friends and family members.

Because you're not likely to hear complaints from your multicultural customers, being proactive is the best option:

- ✔ Pay more attention to your customer's body language than what she says. A facial expression showing dissatisfaction or confusion may say more than you're likely to hear.

- ✔ Address any issues earlier rather than later. If possible, address any concerns before the customer steps out that door. You may not have another chance.

- ✔ Ask a few trusted minority customers what you could do to better serve customers from their community or describe an interaction you had and ask them for a critique.

Working with customers from other cultures may take more time and effort, but most salespeople find it very rewarding. When you satisfy customers from other cultures, they're much more likely to remain loyal and refer others in their community to you. Because they're coming to you from a referral, they're much more ready to buy. Take the effort to learn about every customer's background and you'll be rewarded not only with increased sales, but also with fascinating facts about the world. And you won't lose one piece of luggage on an airplane!

Chapter 20

Playing Nice with the Competition

. . . .

In This Chapter

▶ Understanding the benefits of being nice to your competitors

▶ Picking up a few tricks from the competition

▶ Leading the pack

▶ Sending your worst customers to your competitors

▶ Building synergies with the competition

. . . .

Tempting as it is to criticize and drive a wedge between yourself and your competitor, this is often counterproductive. Follow the adage, "Keep your friends close and your enemies closer." Spend less time criticizing your competitor and more time studying the competition and exploring ways to take advantage of what they have to offer.

What are your competitors doing that you should be doing? What could they do better? Are there any opportunities for you to work together? Do you have any customers who would work better with one of your competitors? By playing fair and working with your competition in addition to working against them, you can often reap unparalleled rewards.

In this chapter, I point out some of the benefits of playing nice with the competition and offer suggestions on how to leverage cooperation to give yourself a competitive edge.

Seeing the Upside of Letting Down Your Guard

I'm fiercely competitive and usually want to squash anyone who goes head-to-head with me. That's one reason why I send someone else in the office to do my bidding at foreclosure auctions. I get so caught up in the bidding war, so obsessed with preventing someone else from buying a property I want, that I bid myself out of what would otherwise have been a profitable investment. I end up paying way too much, so when I try to sell it, I can't turn a profit.

Most top salespeople I know are the same way, but this type of over-competitive nature is counterproductive. It slams shut and locks the doors to information and relationships the can be very valuable in protecting your interests, generating new business, and opening future opportunities and even potential partnerships.

By being overly competitive, you may be missing out on the following benefits:

- ✔ **Getting free advice:** Talking shop, telling stories of success and failure, and trading information (to some degree) enables everyone in the industry to climb one rung up on the ladder of success. This is part of what trade associations are all about. You don't have to give up closely guarded company secrets, but by sharing a little information, you and your competitor can both achieve more.

- ✔ **Offering complementary products and services:** You and your competitor may not be offering exactly the same products and services. If that's the case, you can often share customers, recommending your competitor for products and services you don't offer and having your competitor recommend you for products and services she doesn't offer.

- ✔ **Picking up the slack for one another:** When you can't possibly fill an order, rather than disappointing your customers, you can purchase merchandise from your competitor to cover the shortfall. Your competitor may need to return the favor someday by purchasing products from you. You may even be able to share leads if you or your competitor can't handle a huge new influx of customers.

- ✔ **Referring clients to one another:** A client who gives you trouble may be perfect for one of your competitors and vice versa. In my business, for example, some home sellers find me too aggressive, so I may refer them to someone who's less aggressive. By referring customers who aren't right for you to your competitors, you create a win-win-win scenario — you, your ex-client, and your competitor all win out. In some industries, you may even be able to charge a referral fee. See "Referring Customers to Your Competitors and Affiliates," later in this chapter, for details.

- ✔ **Warning one another about challenging customers:** Customers, especially the most challenging ones, often play hopscotch, skipping from one salesperson to the next to find the perfect fit. By communicating openly with your competitors, you may be able to create an informal dossier on these folks and warn one another of specific problems to watch out for. You may find out that the customer has a history of not paying, for example, which could enable you to be more proactive about receiving payment.

✔ **Watching one another's backs:** If you have a customer or former employee posting negative comments about you on the Internet or an employee who's acting unethically, you want to know about it. By having a close, cordial relationship with your competitors, you're much more likely to hear about something than if you remain isolated.

✔ **Attracting customers . . . together:** When attending industry events, stick close to the competition. This gives your customers the convenience of one-stop-shopping for the products and services they need. This is the whole idea behind consumer shows. The key is to have the best people running your booth — high-energy people with integrity, who make your business stand head and shoulders above the competition.

✔ **Cutting in on one another's profits:** By remaining close with your competition, you may lose some clients, but you also gain an opportunity to win more clients. Free and open competition works best when clients have a choice. You just need to prove that you're better.

✔ **Making your company a more attractive investment opportunity:** Competing companies often merge to generate increased revenue and cut costs. By remaining friendly with the competition, you make your company a more attractive target and you discover more about your competitor, so your company can make a well-informed decision of whether to move ahead with a merger.

Successful businesses don't isolate themselves by walling out competitors. They expand by walling them in — embracing and encompassing the competition. Never let your highly competitive nature get in the way of making money. Without competition, you become complacent and stagnant. Competition produces healthy accelerants to fire us ahead of the pack and improve everyone's performance and bottom line.

Studying Your Competitors

I always say "Hind side is 20/20." If you're getting your hind side kicked by the competition, you have 20/20 vision on what you need to do to remedy the problem — just study the competition.

As I explain later, you never simply want to mimic the competition. Doing so simply makes you equal at best. You want to be superior. Keeping your competition in sight is important, but make sure you're looking at them through your rearview mirror. Your competition can open your mind to new ideas, but don't get overly obsessed with them. Set your sights on what you know you have to do to be number one.

In the following sections, I lead you through the process of identifying the competition, and then I offer some suggestions on how to do a little corporate espionage.

Never badmouth your competition, no matter how tempting that may be. It only reflects poorly on you. If a customer points out something good about one of your competitors, acknowledge it. Once you know what the customer needs, you have an opportunity to point out what your company offers that your competitors don't. Remain positive.

Identifying your competitors

I was talking to a fellow who ran a chain of movie theaters. I asked him about the competition. According to him, his competition was everything that pulled a dollar out of the pockets of prospective patrons. He wasn't in competition simply with other movie theaters. He saw himself in competition with local bars, video arcades, bowling alleys, miniature golf courses, movie rental businesses, casinos online and off, online movie rental businesses, television, televised sports, and on and on.

He was right.

The moral of the story is that your competitor may not always be obvious. It may not be someone in the same industry. Your competitor is anyone or anything that your customer is paying for with money that you should be getting. In fact, some of your stiffest competition is likely to come from businesses you're completely unaware of. It's like being on a highway driving 80 miles an hour thinking nobody is going to pass you when someone zips around you going 90. You wonder, "Where the heck did she come from?" Don't let this happen to you. Think of all the unforeseen competitors lurking in all the corners.

To identify your competition, ask yourself the following questions:

- ✔ Who are my direct competitors in the industry?
- ✔ Who's behind me? Who has their sights on me?
- ✔ What else do my customers spend their money on?

✔ Are any new technologies on the horizon that could threaten my business?

✔ Are there any changes to the market or the industry that are likely to affect my bottom line — either positively or negatively?

The competition is anyone or anything that draws your customers' cash outlays away from you.

Scoping out the competition

Before I became the spokesperson for Guthy-Renker Home, an Internet lead-generation service for the real estate industry, one of the first things I did was visit the Web site of every company that competes with Guthy-Renker Home. I signed up for their services, downloaded all of their promotional materials, poked around on their Web sites, and gathered all the information I possibly could. I wanted to know why Guthy-Renker Home was superior, so I could tell prospective customers of Guthy-Renker Home when they asked me.

As a salesperson, you need to know first that your company, products, services, and you are superior. Then, you need to know what it is that makes you superior. And the only way to do that is by researching the competition:

✔ **Visit your competitors' Web sites and blogs.** If they feature newsletters, discussion forums, a mailing list, brochures, or anything else, register to receive it.

✔ **Talk to your customers.** Ask your customers if they've done business with a particular competitor and what the experience was like. If the customer only considered doing business with the competitor, ask why she ultimately chose you, instead.

✔ **Talk to your competitors' customers, if possible.** If a customer chooses your competitor over you, find out why. What did your competitor offer that you didn't?

✔ **Attend the awards banquet for your industry and seek out the top players in your field.** Their exemplary careers serve as inspiration in your own growing business. After all, they started in this business in the same manner you did. After the awards, drop by the winner's circle and strike up a conversation. On their special night, your competitor will be happy to receive congratulatory accolades. Ask questions, and you will receive golden nuggets of information. Use what you gather to fuel your own personal drive to success.

✔ **Study your competition's advertising campaigns.** Approach their marketing as though you were a prospective customer rather than a competitor. What catches your attention? Do they offer something different from what you offer or simply offer the same thing in a different way? Is their area of expertise different yet related to your field? Perhaps you can change your marketing to draw on your strengths and their weaknesses without openly criticizing the competitor. If the competition is missing a particular aspect to their campaign, is there a reason for it? Perhaps that missing aspect is not profitable. If it is feasible, yet they have overlooked its potential, change your own marketing strategies to include what they're missing.

When you're scoping out the competition, search for lessons to be learned. Ask yourself the following questions:

✔ Why did past competitors who failed go extinct? What did they do wrong that I should never, ever repeat?

✔ What does the competition do right and what does my competition do wrong that affects their income?

✔ Are there any "add-ons" I can create to liven up my revenue strategies?

When comparing what you offer to what your competitors offer, be brutally honest. If your competition is better than you, admit it, and then get down to the business of fixing what's wrong. I've talked with many salespeople and business owners who merely criticize the competition so they can feel good about themselves. This only blinds you to what you really need to do.

Avoiding the Copy Cat Syndrome

When I tell you to check out the competition and find out what it's up to, I'm not suggesting that you become a "me too" salesperson. Researching the competition merely enables you to see what the competition is doing and hopefully give you insight into why your competitors may or may not be achieving greater levels of success.

Trying to confuse the market or merely mimic the competition usually results in becoming a cheap copy of the original. You may win over a few confused customers, but you won't gain any respect in the industry, and you certainly can never hope to take on a leadership role with such an approach.

In the following sections, I show you how to keep an eye on what's important, develop a creative vision, and become an early adopter, so you can gain an edge over your competition.

As fast as the world changes, you can no longer succeed by playing follow the leader. You need to develop your own vision and either work harder to eventually catch up and take the lead or work smarter to find a shortcut that puts you in the lead.

Focusing on your business

Copy cat corporations often fail to realize that they don't have the same structure and personnel as their competitors. They're ill-equipped to do what the competition does, because they don't have identical people and resources. Focus on your business, on the unique talent and resources you have at your disposal. Don't try to be something you're not.

When deciding on a direction to take, first ask yourself what you have that the competition doesn't. Then, explore various ways to leverage the unique skills and talents of your staff and other resources you have at your disposal to maximize results.

In your quest to become the leader, never lose site of your customer. Your customer's needs should influence every decision you make.

Sparking creativity

Incremental progress is okay in some cases, but when you're shooting to gain a few steps in the market, you often have to take a creative leap. Staring longingly at the competition usually doesn't do it. You have to immerse yourself in a creative atmosphere and give your brain license to play. Here are some suggestions for building an atmosphere that's more conducive to creativity:

- **Surround yourself with creative people.** Gather a roomful of creative people, grab a whiteboard, and get to work. Toss around ideas on where to find new customers, how to more effectively market your products and services, and how to serve your clients better. Two or three or four heads are often better than one.

- **Surround yourself with stuff.** Ideas don't pop out of a vacuum. They usually arise when two or more things come together. Think of an innovation, and you often find the juxtaposition of two great things — "satellite" and "TV," "video" and "game," "Internet" and "marketing," "online" and "lead-generation," "chocolate" and "peanut butter." The more you have floating around in your head, the more connections you can make.

✔ **Stop thinking.** Your mind needs time and space to freely make connections on its own. Give yourself some quiet time. Spend time with your family or alone. Relax. Let your mind sort things out on its own.

✔ **Identify your creative time.** Are you most creative first thing in the morning, later in the afternoon, or late at night? Note when you're most creative and block that off as your creative time. Some people, like my assistant, Lois, go to bed with a problem and wake up with the perfect solution. Lois used to wake up her husband in the middle of the night and ask him to remember her ideas, but then he bought her a leather-bound notebook and pen to keep on the nightstand, so he could get some sleep.

✔ **Play a game of free association.** Some of my best creativity comes when I first wake up in the morning. The phones aren't ringing, the world is still asleep, and I can concentrate with a rested and cleared mind. Sit quietly and think of your particular obstacle and freely associate ideas. Do not allow interruptions. Often, the answer will come. After all, nobody knows all the details involved in a particular situation than you.

Keep an idea book with you at all times. I can almost guarantee that unless you jot down your ideas, you are going to forget more than 90 percent of them. Write down every idea you have, no matter how crazy or unrealistic it may seem, and then read through your ideas every few weeks. You may be surprised at just how many of them really do have legs.

Launching ideas into action

The difference between success and failure is often in the execution. Second-rate sales people often have big ideas, great ideas that ultimately turn not into great plans and brilliant accomplishments but into deep regrets — shoulda, coulda, woulda . . . didn't. Once you think of some fabulous new idea, move it from the boardroom to the drawing room and then on to the launch pad:

✔ **Put together a plan of action.** Once you have these exciting new ideas for increasing business, write them down with specific goals in mind and what to expect from each stage of implementation. Put time limits, goals, and expectations into place. Then, stick with it. See Chapter 3 for details about setting goals and planning.

✔ **Admit the weak points in yourself and your plan.** This is a healthy exercise and has great advantages for your career. If you shy away from acknowledging the weaknesses in your business, you can't solve the issue. Recognize your weaknesses and then work (or delegate) your way around them.

✔ **Accountability is a must:** Without written accountability to measure your new plans, you will fail. Hold to your original plan of action and make the necessary adjustments along the way.

Playing nice with competition is fine, but keep your new plans to yourself.

Gaining a gadget edge

As soon as any new technology hits the streets, I gotta have it. Everyone around me thinks I'm just fascinated by gadgets and toys, and they may be right, but I like to think of my obsession with having the latest, greatest gear a savvy way of staying one step ahead of the competition.

Sure, when something first comes out, you pay more for it, and it may be slower, less reliable, and buggier than future versions, but by being the first one on the block with the latest technology, you rake in a host of benefits:

- ✔ Potential to gain an edge on the competition — because technology has a shelf life of about three minutes your competition may just be getting up to speed on the new technology while you're upgrading to the latest version

- ✔ More time to experiment with and master the new technology before it becomes mainstream

- ✔ More time to implement the new technology in your business model

- ✔ Pioneer plugs — the distinct advantages you have to market yourself as the very first in your field to offer the benefits of the new technology

- ✔ The time to think up creative new ideas and applications for the new technology, so you can start the bandwagon before anyone else has a chance to jump on it

- ✔ The opportunity to establish yourself as the voice of authority on a new technology or system

If you don't pioneer new gadgets as tools for your business, be assured, your competition or someone else will.

For additional tips on the types of technology that can be most useful to you as a salesperson, check out Chapter 12.

Referring Customers to Your Competitors and Affiliates

Although you can certainly generate gobs of business with the right marketing and advertising, that's usually fairly costly in terms of time, money, and effort. An easier and often free alternative is to focus on referrals, but you have to handle these referrals strategically. Your goal? Get rid of your worst customers and replace them with better customers.

In the following sections, I show you how to deliver this one-two punch by sending your worst customers to your competitors and teaming up with affiliates to generate business for yourself and your affiliates.

Redirecting your worst customers to the competition

Whenever I tell the salespeople I coach to send their worst customers to the competition, I always get a chuckle. They think I'm telling them to make their competitors suffer by sending bad customers their way. Although that's certainly part of it, a bigger reason to do it is to create a win-win-win situation for everyone involved:

- ✔ You get rid of a customer who was demanding too much time and energy. In certain industries, you may have the additional benefit of charging your competitor a finder's fee for the new client.

- ✔ Your ex-customer has the opportunity to start fresh, hopefully with a salesperson who's a better fit.

- ✔ Your competitor obtains a new customer and may be more open to referring customers to you.

When a customer isn't working out for you, fire them, but let them down easy. Tell them that you'd love to continue working with them, but so-and-so would probably be a better match. Take the blame for the relationship not working out. The old "It's not you, it's me . . ." line works wonders.

Sending business to your affiliates

Most salespeople are well aware that they need to give referrals to get referrals, but many salespeople handle the referral process all wrong. They end up losing control and losing out on opportunities to maximize the actual number of referrals they receive. When giving referrals, be aware of the wrong way and the right way to do it:

- ✔ **Wrong way:** Say you're selling cars. A customer comes in to buy a car and mentions that she gets her auto insurance from XYZ Insurance, Inc. You ask how much she's paying and then mention that she may want to get a second opinion from ABC Insurance, Inc., a company you know of in town. This referral is not going to expand your business.

✔ **Right way:** Same scenario — you're selling a car, and the customer mentions her insurance company. You realize that this is certainly a reputable company. You ask your customer if she has the name and contact information of the person she deals with at the insurance company. You call the insurance agent, introduce yourself, tell the person you have met one of his clients, say that you would like to offer your services to him in the future, and tell him that you would appreciate it if he would send his clients your way, as well. You now have a new source for referrals.

Partnering with Your Competitors to Create Win-Win Opportunities

Going head-to-head with the competition isn't always the best move, especially if your competitor has a harder head. I've seen companies nearly destroy each other in all-out war, when it wasn't really necessary. The companies perceived each other as competitors, but they were actually offering something quite different. Some competing companies continue to battle it out even though both of them could become more profitable by cooperating.

In the following sections, I offer some guidance on how to team up with your competition to create win-win opportunities.

Harnessing the power of affiliates and competitors

Throughout the book, particularly in Chapters 7 and 14, I show you how to network with colleagues and other "friendly" business associates, but you can network productively with foes, as well. When you need to expand sales, you usually need to expand your human resources, so start recruiting the top talent, wherever it may be:

✔ **Find talented affiliates and competitors:** The first key is to get out there and talk with anyone related to your type of business. Don't worry if they are your competition. Get the word out that you are looking for talented individuals. Think of the advantages of spreading the workload with more talent on your team — more ideas and more energy. A team can accomplish far more than one player can ever hope to accomplish on her own.

✔ **Fill your voids with the talents of others:** When you're missing the inner resources to accomplish a particular goal, find someone in possession of the skills or talents you're missing. Your weaknesses could be their strengths. Find the talent. Then let them fly. Let them get fired up and bring plans that can intertwine with yours. For more about finding the right people to fill the gaps, check out Chapter 13.

Whenever you spot a business that, at first glance, seems to be competing against you, ask yourself whether that business is a true competitor. Are they selling exactly what you're selling or something slightly different? If another business can offer your customers a product or service that your customers may need, consider promoting the other business as an affiliate. You may even be able to charge them a fee for referrals or obtain referrals in exchange.

Collective marketing

Fierce competitors don't always play rough. Lending institutions, for example, often compete for clientele, but they've been known to join forces at times to the mutual benefit of all involved. I've witnessed these collaborative marketing efforts unfold particularly when lending institutions are trying to get referrals from new home builders.

Lenders know that if they can make one builder happy, they stand to reap the benefits of many mortgage loans as builders refer prospective buyers to lenders for financing. They also know that if the builder's representative can rely on them for steady service, the representative is going to recommend that lender to every potential customer that walks in the builder's model home. On the lender's behalf, the builder's representative delivers a mini-commercial to each and every customer. It is a perfect marriage because the builder and sales representative want smooth transactions and no hassles, while the lending institutions gather lots of loans and new clientele.

How does a lending institution get to all these builders? Marching around to each and every builder could be brutal. However, if they could find a place where builder's congregate, imagine what they could accomplish in that single room full of builders. And that's exactly what they do. They host wine and cheese parties and informative gatherings for builders at the building association levels and ingratiate themselves with that world. It's big business and it works. The building association is thrilled to offer interesting opportunities to their builders, and the lending institutions can pitch their products and services to the entire group at once. Everybody wins. Everybody prospers.

Teaming up with the competition

For many years, I realized that I was competing against new home builders — what we real estate agents refer to as *new construction*. When I'm trying to sell "used" homes to first-time buyers, these builders were offering homes in pristine condition. I managed to out-compete them in many cases by pointing out the value of an established home — affordability, no waiting for the home to be built, the mature landscape, and so on.

Later, I realized that I could sell new homes, too! I contacted the builders in the area and worked out a deal in which if I delivered buyers, I would receive a commission. This increased business for me in two ways — I had more homes to sell, and I could offer buyers more options.

 Consider selling for the competition. If your competitor is selling something that many of your customers want, why not offer it as an option? I realize that this is not always an option, it depends on what you and your competitors sell, but it is an option in some cases, as I point out in the following sidebar, "Teaming up with the competition."

 Your focus should be on pleasing your customer. If that means referring your customer to the competition, that may be the best decision for your long-term success. News of your commitment to your customer's success and happiness travels fast and is sure to draw customers in your direction.

Bridge burning creates tiny towns

I learned a long time ago never to create enemies along the way, especially with the competition. Inevitably, you will run into the same people time and time again. Just when you need the support to make a deal fly, you run into the old toad you told off in 1963!

Secretary saves the day! Fifteen years ago, I had a competitor friend who happened to have a fabulous assistant. She offered to help me with one of my deals and botched it up terribly. For the sake of the relationship with my competitor, I worked with her to correct the issues and consummate the deal. I always treated her with great respect, despite the mistakes.

Cutthroat competition: Is it worth it?

I recently ran into the son of a man I once knew. Chip Jenkins was the son of Mr. Pete Jenkins, whom I always knew simply as "Mr. Jenkins." Mr. Jenkins was a great salesperson and a successful businessman, but he had no personal life or close friends. Chip told me that his father was still alive, but he hadn't seen his father in over five years. His father had never met his grandchildren.

Mr. Jenkins' family had owned strawberry fields in California. He eventually sold the fields and purchased a shopping center in Michigan. The department of transportation needed the land for road improvements, so they were forced to pay him millions of dollars for the shopping center because of all the improvements to the land.

He used part of his small fortune to invest in building condominiums, and he hired me to sell them. One of the buyers I found had recently lost her husband. She said she just wanted to sell her home and buy a condo, and she gave me a $30,000 deposit. A few days later, she came back to me and explained that she had made a rash decision and wanted to stay in her house for a year to sort things out. This was a wise choice. Whenever you lose a spouse, you really should wait a year before making any major decisions.

I went to Mr. Jenkins and told him that we needed to refund the widow's deposit. He refused, we argued, and he fired me, refusing to pay me the commissions I had earned. I ended up paying thousands of dollars in legal fees to force him to pay me the commissions I had earned.

When I heard from Chip that he had not seen his father for five years and that his father had never seen his own grandchildren, I was not surprised. The way Mr. Jenkins handled business was the way he navigated life in general — it was his way or the highway.

The point of all this is that life is short. Compete to the point of winning, but never to the point of isolating yourself from the rest of humanity. Play fair, do the right thing, and you are going to have more business and more profit than you ever expected.

Years later, I needed a fundraiser chairman and didn't know where to find one. During this dilemma, one of my affiliates arrived for a meeting we had previously arranged. Who do you think he had with him? A new assistant! Yes, it was the same girl from years ago. As it turns out, she loved raising money for causes and remembered my kindness. She raised over $36,000 for the cause I was supporting.

Part VI
The Part of Tens

The 5th Wave

By Rich Tennant

"For a more aggressive sales approach, we have our 'Or Else' series of motivational posters."

In this part . . .

Each and every *For Dummies* book you pick up includes a Part of Tens, with at least a couple chapters packed with tips, tricks, and other bit-sized tidbits that you can munch on whenever you have a few minutes to spare and need a little brain food.

In this Part of Tens, I reveal my top ten power selling tactics and techniques, recommend ten ways to break a sales slump (or avoid a slump from ever occurring), and tell you ten stories of awesome salespeople who can inspire you to overcome whatever obstacles you may think are keeping you from achieving your dreams.

Chapter 21

Ten Power-Selling Tactics and Techniques

In This Chapter
- ▶ Building relationships for long-term sales success
- ▶ Producing positive buzz on the streets
- ▶ Keeping focused on the end result
- ▶ Avoiding the temptation to job hop
- ▶ Putting your ideas in action

I'm not a big fan of canned sales pitches, but I do rely on a toolbox packed with strategies, techniques, and tips to place prospective clients at ease and make them more receptive to my presentation.

In the following sections, I share my ten most effective methods, but remember to personalize these methods for your own use. You don't want to look and sound like some other sales rep who just met with these same clients.

Focusing on Relationships, Not Sales

Do you know anyone who calls you only when they need something from you? Chances are good that you know more than one person like this, and they probably make you a little uncomfortable or even bitter. You probably avoid them. You may even screen their calls.

Customers and clients are the same way with salespeople, because salespeople usually call when they want something, when they want the customer to buy something. This is why building relationships is so important.

Chapters 14 and 18 offer plenty of ideas for how to build mutually beneficial relationships with customers, but here are a couple more:

✔ Develop and implement a customer relationship program, in which you are in regular contact with customers *without* selling them anything. This should include regular phone calls, e-mail messages, newsletters, and a blog that they can visit at their leisure.

✔ Arrange business development meetings with existing, past, and prospective clients on a regular basis.

✔ Conduct focused seminars and workshops of interest for your target markets.

✔ Arrange speaking engagements with your target market's industry and professional organizations.

✔ Network, network, network!

Generating Positive Publicity for You and Your Company

In addition to targeting prospective customers, become a high-profile target by generating positive publicity for yourself and your company:

✔ Create at least one blog for your business.

✔ Create at least one community-based blog to support your community.

✔ Write articles for professional and trade publications on current topics of interest to your target markets.

✔ Publish and distribute a press release on a regular basis announcing something important and of current interest.

✔ Get involved in the communities in which you work and live. Give, give, give.

Implementing an Hour of Power

In Chapter 12, I talk about my Hour of Power — an hour I set aside every day of the week to place 100 phone calls to people in my address book just to keep in touch. Here's how you do it:

1. **Pick a group of 100 people in your address book you want to contact.** The group may consist of people in a volunteer organization in which you participate, customers you service, or colleagues.

2. **Think of something clever to say that is unrelated to selling.** Do not sell on these calls. Simply establish contact and let the person know you are thinking about her.

3. **Let everyone in the office know that your Hour of Power is about to commence, and that they should not disturb you during this time.** If you leave a message and someone returns your call, your staff can take a message, and you can return the call later.

4. **Lock yourself in your office and start placing the calls.**

Keep a log sheet of how many calls you make per day. You can start out slow, with maybe 10 or 25 calls a day, but I strongly urge you to set a goal of 100 calls per day. This seems to be the optimum number for success.

Working Your Way to the Decision Maker

Salespeople often get screened out by receptionists or other employees who are a little lower on the totem pole than the company executives — the decision makers. I have a trick to work my way past these sales screeners.

When I call someone, even if they have know idea who I am, I say, in the most authoritative voice I can muster up, like I'm some kind of rock star, "Hi! This is Ralph Roberts!" The person I called is too embarrassed to admit that she has no idea who I am. I keep the conversation going, and then after some time, I say something like, ". . . Okay, you really don't know who I am, do you?" The person I was talking to usually admits the fact and typically puts me through to the person in charge.

Being Yourself

Before customers are going to buy from you, they have to buy into you, and that you had better look, act, and sound genuine. Even though I step it up when I'm selling and try to infuse a little more energy in the relationship than I normally do when I'm not selling, I'm always Ralph R. Roberts. People know what they're getting — a somewhat, nay, overzealous madman.

Some people won't like what you have to offer, but if you're going to have any staying power in sales, you'd better be real and true to yourself. Trying to act the way you think others want you to act is only going to exhaust you.

Focusing on Ends . . . and Letting the Means Fall into Place

Far too many salespeople get so wrapped up in planning their success and worrying about how they're going to achieve it that they never take the first step to attaining their goals. Those who ultimately succeed set their eyes on the prize and then deal with all the details.

Remember back to when you were first learning how to ride a two-wheeler (without the training wheels). You knew that balance was the key, but you probably were so focused on balance that you forgot to pedal and you'd keep falling down or teetering at best. Your dad or mom or whoever was training you, probably held the bike and ran alongside you to give you the confidence you needed and to keep you mind off the balancing act. Then, the person would let go, tricking you into thinking that he still "had" you. Pedaling is the secret to keeping your balance — you have to keep moving forward with your eyes on the goal and not worry so much about how you're going to get there.

Categorizing Your Customers

Being a salesperson often seems like being a migrant farm worker. You're busy during the planting season and when the crop is ready to harvest, and business is dead in between. To keep this from happening, you may be tempted to over-commit, taking on too many clients and being unable to provide them with quality customer service.

In the best of all possible worlds, you would have a steady stream of business, but that's a pipe dream — it's probably not going to happen. The next best thing you can do is to categorize your customers:

- ✔ **A customers — the most dollar-productive customers:** Paying customers receive your full attention when they demand it. These are the people who are going to continue to drive business, leads, and opportunities in your direction. Keep them happy.

- ✔ **B customers — top prospects:** These may be existing customers who aren't exactly in the top bracket or prospects who you strongly believe could reach that upper bracket. These are the people you want to spend the most time nurturing.

- ✓ *C customers — good prospects:* These prospective customers are very promising candidates with whom you want to spend sufficient time and resources to nurture.

- ✓ *D customers — for "deleted":* These are existing customers or prospective customers who are going to drain you of time and resources offering little if any return on your investment. You want to let these people go or refer them to some other salesperson down the road.

List your top 5 customers, your top 25 customers, and your top 100 customers and then assign them to your slots — A, B, and C. These are the customers you want to focus on, in that order.

Asking for Referrals

When you've earned a customer's satisfaction, don't hesitate to ask the customer to refer you to others who may need your products or services. Supply your customer with a stack of business cards and ask him to hand them out freely and call you if he needs more.

Better yet, ask for the names and contact information for two or three people your customer knows who may be in need of what you're selling. If your customer can't think of anyone right off the top of her head, ask whether you can call back in a couple days. You may even offer the person some incentive to provide you with referrals, perhaps a discount or rebate of some sort.

The best time to ask a customer for a referral is when the person thanks you for going above and beyond the call of duty. The person says "thank you" probably because she has no better way of showing her appreciation. Give her that better way by asking for a referral.

Staying Put . . . Rather Than Job Hopping

The temptation to change jobs whenever the commissions splits are unsatisfactory or your company seems unsupportive can be overwhelming. From what I've seen in the field, however, job hopping is generally counterproductive. You waste a great deal of time and energy getting re-established.

Sometimes the grass looks greener on the other side of the valley, so you change jobs. During the change, you happen to get back to the basics, and you achieve success, so you tend to think that the job change is what did it. But if you would have focused on the basics before you left rather then letting your resentment fester, you could have gained success without interrupting it and probably achieved an even higher level of success.

The most important resources you have at your disposal are not the external resources that your company offers you, but your own internal resources — your skills and your determination to succeed. Sell more, earn more, and your boss is likely to be very eager to negotiate better splits with you. You have to take the first step, and it doesn't have to be a step out the door.

I'm not saying that you should always stick with a job no matter what. Sometimes, you have to walk, but try renegotiating with your supervisor before making a final decision.

Just Do It!

The single one huge mistake that all mediocre or lousy salespeople make is that they don't follow through. They pay for books, seminars, tapes, classes, coaching, and everything else they need to know to succeed, and then they fail to follow through on one single thing they've learned. When choosing people to coach, I try to screen out people like this, but I still meet far too many of them.

Whenever you pick up a new tip, discover a new technique, or hear about a great technology that can make you more productive, try it out — put the idea into action. Even if it doesn't work for you, you've made some progress. You now know more than before you tried it. And if it works, all the better. You now have one more tool in your sales arsenal.

I owe my success to what I like to refer to as sticktoitism, a word I made up in place of stick-to-itiveness. Sticktoitism is a dogged determination in the face of challenge or perceived failure. Very often, you are closest to success just before giving up. Even if you don't see positive results immediately, keep at it. As long as you stick to it, you will eventually succeed.

Chapter 22

Ten Ways to Break Your Sales Slump . . . or Avoid It Entirely

In This Chapter

▶ Dodging a sales slump before it happens

▶ Giving yourself even more reasons to sell

▶ Flexing your marketing muscle

▶ Seeking inspiration from your mentor or partner

▶ Putting your family to work for you

*E*ven power sellers have slow days . . . or weeks or months. The trick is to keep working and more importantly keep *networking,* marketing, and pounding the pavement to pull yourself out of that slump.

In this chapter, I offer ten proven methods for cranking up sales after a slowdown . . . or even a meltdown and a few tips for keeping that momentum flowing.

Steering Clear of Sales Slumps

I consider a slump any time I wander off task. I find that I work better when someone else is around — a staff person who can keep me focused. Sometimes, I leave the building and take a short walk, and then I tell myself to get back at it.

The key factor in avoiding a slump is knowing what usually triggers it. Here are some common triggers and other causes to look out for:

✔ **Making the sale:** When you make a sale, especially a big sale you worked hard on, the tendency is to breathe a big sigh of relief and celebrate. That's great, but don't party too long.

✔ **Focusing too much on the present:** When you focus too much on the present and not enough on building your future, you may lull yourself into thinking that just because you don't have a client or prospect to deal with, you have nothing to do. Turn down time into productive time.

✔ **Getting distracted:** Even a minor distraction can push your wheels off the tracks. Either ignore the distraction or deal with it and then get back to what you were doing.

✔ **Being able to pay your bills:** If you're highly motivated by commissions, you may tend to ease up whenever all your bills are paid up. To keep this from happing, work ahead. Have a goal to save up a certain amount of money, so you're not selling in "feast or famine mode" — working too hard when bills stack up and not hard enough when times are good.

✔ **Dealing with negative people:** Naysayers and other people with bad attitudes can drag you down and take the wind right out of your sails . . . and your sales. See "Steering Clear of Negative People and Situations," later in this chapter.

You may also experience slumps on a regular basis due to the nature of your business. In real estate, for example, people buy and sell fewer homes over the winter and more in the spring. Recognize the timing of these slumps and plan for them. Don't worry or fret about these slumps, because worry is a sure way to kill future sales. Keep a confident and positive attitude.

Motivating Yourself with Added Incentives

Ideally, everyone should be motivated by the inner desire to compete and win, but the world is not an ideal place, and selling may not be what you really want to be doing right now. Or perhaps you recently achieved a goal and no longer have anything to shoot for.

Whatever the case, you get up and go, got up and went, and now you need something to kick you into gear. Try dangling a carrot in front of yourself. Plan a vacation. Go car shopping. Look at new houses. Find something that you really want to work for, and dangle that reward in front of yourself. Sometimes a little added incentive is all it takes. Eventually you find that you don't work for things anymore — you work for the thrill of the deal. Putting a deal together and knowing that you ultimately helped is a real hoot and a great motivator.

A reward doesn't always have to be a possession. You may want to set the goal of spending more quality time with your family, setting aside more time to volunteer in the community, or even earning some extra money for your favorite charity. Anything that gives you a purpose to sell is fair game. I call this moving from success to significance. Once you've met the needs of yourself and your family, you can focus on more meaningful endeavors.

Steering Clear of Negative People and Situations

When your entire office or the entire industry is experiencing a sales slump, all the Negative Nancy's start crawling out of the woodwork to whine about how bad it is, berate management, and complain. Don't get caught up in this downward spiral of negativity. It will suck the positive energy right out of you.

Avoid the break room, coffee room, lunch room, water cooler, and wherever else the negative people congregate. Seek out the positive people and spend time with them planning on how to pull yourselves and your company out of the current slump. You may be able to turn a negative person positive, but don't expend too much energy on such pursuits, and never let someone drag you in the same hole they're in (hey, isn't that a Dylan song?).

Its not about being surrounded by "Yes" people. It's about balance — surrounding yourself with positive people who challenge you to be your best and who bring out the best in you.

Starting Right Now

One method to quit smoking is to pick a date on which you are going to be smoke-free. Theoretically, this gives you a few final days to indulge yourself prior to making an all-out commitment to stop.

What some people do, however, is set to start on Monday, indulge themselves over the weekend, manage to make it through Monday, and then start back on Tuesday with the goal of quitting again on Monday. It reminds me of a restaurant I frequent that has a sign posted saying "Free Beer Tomorrow." Every time someone enters the place, they're promised free beer tomorrow.

Instead of setting a date on which to begin doing something positive or stop doing something negative, start now. Even if you take the tiniest step toward your goal, you're making progress. Don't put it off until tomorrow. Tomorrow never comes.

Don't delay the launch! You will miss the boat. Speaking of boats, I recently read some words of wisdom that apply to this topic at `www.suddenlysenior.com/noahsark.html`.

Re-Committing Yourself to Success

A sales slump is often a sign that you're operating off plan. You made a commitment to success, carefully drew up an effective plan, worked your plan for a few days or weeks or months, and then became so busy that you completely forgot about your plan. You're now back to where you started. Even worse, you may begin to think the *plan* failed.

Get rid of any thoughts you may have of ditching your plan. If your plan for success really didn't work, tweak the plan and try again. If you simply drifted off plan, then regroup and re-commit to getting back on plan. Refer to Chapter 3 for a brief refresher course on drawing up and implementing your plan.

A failed plan can also indicate that you're spending too little time on real business and too much time on monkey business. Get rid of the time wasters and back to dollar productive activities. Stop the feel good stuff and get on to the business of business.

Ramping Up Your Marketing Efforts

When you're selling little or nothing, that usually means people have forgotten about you. Unfortunately, far too many salespeople mistakenly think it means that they need to sit by the phone and wait for it to ring.

People get caught up in making a living and living their lives. Don't take this personally, but many of your customers and people who would be your customers if they knew about you don't really give you much thought on a daily basis. . . unless, of course, you give them reason to think about you.

When sales slip, you have much more time on your hands to shake the bushes for business. Ramp up your marketing efforts by exploring a marketing medium you haven't yet tried. Chapter 16 is packed with ideas. Also, check out Chapter 15 for tips on how to explore opportunities in other markets. You could be in the sales slump because you are doing all the wrong stuff. Go back and see what worked before, re-visit the basics, and then get creative.

After your increased marketing efforts pull you out of your current slump, keep at it. Salespeople who ignore marketing when sales are brisk and attend to it only when sales taper off discover that their sales slumps are deeper, longer, and more frequent. Market in good times and bad, especially in bad times. When you find yourself thinking, "I can't afford to advertise," you're probably at a point where you can't afford not to advertise.

Revisiting Your Relationships

One of the best sales prospecting tools you have are the relationships you've nurtured with customers, colleagues, and other people you've bumped into as a part of your networking activities. When business tapers off, use the extra time to rekindle old relationships and begin new ones.

As I explain in Chapter 14, don't contact people only when you need them. Make a habit of keeping in touch with your contacts and strengthening your relationships over the course of the year. When you're in a sales slump, contacting these people for assistance or leads won't feel as though you just call when you need something. When you make a habit of keeping in touch with contacts over the course of your career, you soon discover that your sales slumps become more shallow and less frequent.

Reviewing Your Records

Sometimes, you may not be able to easily identify why you're experiencing a slow time. Maybe it's the market. Perhaps it's something you're doing or not doing.

Keep impeccable records and then review those records when you've had a string of what appears to be bad luck or good luck. You can often spot patterns in what you're doing or not doing that correspond to the hills and valleys you're experiencing. The only catch is that you need good records.

If you don't already keep a journal, day planner, or some other log of what you're doing to improve sales, start today. You can't identify what's working and not working unless you have clear records showing what you tried and when.

Consulting Your Supervisor, Mentor, Personal Partner, or Coach

When a baseball player has a batting slump, the batting coach steps up to the plate and assists in analyzing the batter's swing. Even though you're a professional salesperson (and probably not an athlete), you may not have a clear, unbiased view of your sales technique.

Consult an expert. Ask another salesperson whose opinion you respect or ask your mentor, coach, supervisor, or personal partner for some advice. Describe your current situation in detail, including what you were doing when sales were good, what you were doing when the slump started, and what you're doing now. Ask your sales doctors for their diagnoses and treatment plans, and then sit down and then consult with them to decide on a cure.

Outside experts may not be able to offer any real solution, but even so, they can often make you feel less isolated and offer a compassionate ear that may be sufficient in assisting you with working through the problem yourself. When you're in a rut, falling off the face of the earth is too easy. Keep in touch with people. Call a positive friend and go out to lunch. Get jazzed up. You know what gets you motivated, so do it.

Getting Your Friends and Family Involved

Your family holds a significant stake in your sales success, so get them involved in motivating you and generating ideas. Make a contest out of it. Tell your family that if you become the top salesperson for the month, you can all go on some mini-vacation. Set a sales goal for the week, and when you achieve that goal, you can all go out to dinner and a movie.

Get your family excited about your success. The more excited they become, the more they can motivate you with their support and suggestions. Excitement is contagious!

Index

• Numerics •

10/10/20 technique, 147–148
360-degree feedback, 107

• A •

accountability, 52
ACT! 2007 For Dummies (Fredricks), 185
ADD and ADHD For Dummies (Strong,
    Flanagan, and Tejada-Flores), 66
adversity, capitalizing on, 160–161
advertising
  branding yourself, 20
  as buyer motivation, 92
  Internet, 190
  job positions, 206
  by lead generation services, 189
  newsletters, 263
  in print publications, 246–247
  problem or need, calling attention to, 93
advisory board, assembling your own, 158
affirmations
  anywhere technique used to reinforce, 34
  basic affirmations, 31
  believing, 33
  burning bowl technique used to
      reinforce, 34
  candle technique used to reinforce, 34
  composing your own advanced
      affirmations, 31–32
  consistency in, 33
  emotional expression of, 33
  examples of advanced affirmations, 32
  exercise technique used to reinforce, 34
  feeling, affirmations spoken with strong, 32
  integration technique used to reinforce, 35
  meditation technique used to reinforce, 34
  mirror technique used to reinforce, 34
  overview, 30–31
  persistence with, 33
  personalizing, 33
  positive statement, affirmations
      expressing, 32
  present tense, stating affirmations in
      the, 31
  recorder technique used to reinforce,
      33–34
  reinforcing, techniques for, 33–35
  repeating, 33
  short affirmations, 32
  specific affirmations, 32
  subconscious, imprinting your
      affirmations into your, 32–33
  subconscious mind, power of the, 30
  trash can technique used to reinforce, 34
  writing technique used to reinforce, 33
aggregator, 275
airports, negotiating upgrades at, 71–72
answering a question with a question, 100
Antion, Tom (public speaker), 27
anywhere technique used to reinforce
    affirmations, 34
articles, writing, 247–248
assistants
  assigning tasks to, 204
  hiring, 16
  overview, 18
attentive listening, 115
attitude, improving your, 61–62
automatic call forwarding, 192

• B •

Baby Boomers, marketing to, 236
BACKUP, providing, 114
banner ads, buying, 279
Bannister, Roger (athlete), 15
bartering for what you need, 173–174
basic affirmations, 31
believing affirmations, 33
Beson, Dave (expert), 158
best customers,, discovering more, 82–83
best thing that can happen, 153
Big Nail (marketing tool), 134–135

billboards, using, 140

BlackBerry, 183, 194–195

Blogging For Dummies (Hill), 141, 241, 273, 274

Blogging Systems (blog hosting service), 258

blogrolls, 274

blogs
building and maintaining, 141
communicating with millions of people by, 158
content, 273–274
cross-marketing, 274
effectiveness of, 272
key words and phrases, 273
lead generation, 276
links on, 274
marketing, 258–259
overview, 273
RSS used to distribute content, 275–276
sales, converting blog traffic into, 276
Technorati, getting your blog discovered on, 275
updating, 273–274

bonus for clients, 293

books, communicating with millions of people by writing, 158

The Booth Company Web site, 107

Bott, Kathy (expert), 158

Boufford, Dave (Mr. Positive), 13, 30

branding
advertising everywhere, 20
Big Nail, 134–135
billboards, using, 140
business cards, handing out, 140
consistent look and feel, designing, 139–140
expert in your industry, becoming, 142–148
on the Internet, 20, 140–142
local groups, speaking to, 143–145
media, marketing yourself in the, 20
meeting and greeting the general public, 147–148
name, changing your, 136
newspaper, marketing yourself in the, 20
overview, 20
with social media, 270
10/10/20 technique, 147–148
unique selling proposition (USP), 136–139
unique trait, focusing on, 132–134
volunteering your time and expertise, 145–146

Branding For Dummies (Chiaravalle and Schnenck), 139

breakout sessions, 66

Brinton, Howard (Star Power), 111, 158

broadcast dub, 254

Brock, Terry (business consultant), 158, 215, 217

Brophy, Dan (expert), 158

Brown, Les (salesperson), 27

Building a Web Site For Dummies (Crowder), 256–257

Building Your Business with Google For Dummies (Hill), 190

bundling opportunities, 242–243

burning bowl technique used to reinforce affirmations, 34

business cards
handing out, 140
scanner, 224

business model adjustment to meet client needs, 292–293

business settings, decision makers in, 97–98

buyer motivations
in advertising, 92
fatigue, 91
fear, 91
greed, 90
identifying, 90–91
impulse, 91
need/problem, 90
overview, 90
pleasure, 91
vanity, 91

buyer's remorse, 95–96

buying to learn, 67

Buzz Marketing with Blogs For Dummies (Gardner), 141, 241, 259

● *C* ●

calculated risks, 150

candle technique used to reinforce affirmations, 34

capitalizing on major media events, 252

CardScan (business card scanner), 224

categorization
  of database of contacts, 224
  of your customers, 334–335
CDs, listening to, 65
celebrating your success
  overview, 53
  personal partnering, 116
  rewarding yourself for a job about to be
    well done, 54
  rewarding yourself for a job well done, 53
  sales plan, 53–54
change as growth strategy
  cross-selling opportunities, 121–122
  current marketing and sales strategy,
    improving your, 125–128
  how customers buy, monitoring, 118–121
  industry changes, capitalizing on, 128–130
  new selling methods, identifying, 123
  "no" from customer, finding the reason
    for, 127–128
  overview, 117, 118
  preparing your customers for change, 124
  proven products, leaving alone, 128
  purchase-decision process, 118–119
  questions about decision-making process,
    119–120
  references, using, 121
  revenue-generating opportunities,
    identifying, 123–124
  serving the consumer, 124–125
  testimonials, using, 121
  tracking progress of changes you've
    made, 126–127
channels, exploring other sales, 241–242
checklists for tracking your progress, 52
Chiaravalle, Bill (*Branding
  For Dummies*), 139
Chicken Soup for the Soul (Hansen), 27
clients/customers. *See also* commitment to
    client; success of client
  best customers, discovering more, 82–83
  client's client, finding out about your, 288
  feedback, collecting, 108
  good customers, identifying qualities of, 81
  knowing your customers, 82
  as personal partner, avoiding, 111
  pursuing high-quality customers, 81–83
  R-Commerce, 218, 229

referrals with social media, 270
research, 169
success, 22
coaches, advice from, 18
cold feet, 95–96
collaborating on purchase decision, 93–96
collaborative competition, 114
collaborative partnering, 112
colleagues
  personal partnering, 107
  R-Commerce, 218
collective marketing, 326
Collier, Marsha (*eBay For Dummies*), 241
Comcast, 129
comfort zone
  boundaries of your, 149–152
  envisioning life outside of your, 152–156
commitment to client
  communicating your, 294–297
  complaints, fielding, 296–297
  overview, 294–295
  positive relationship, reinforcing, 295–296
communicating with millions of people
  by blogging, 158
  by e-mail, 159
  by online videos, 159
  by podcasts, 159
  by radio broadcasts, 159
  by writing articles for magazines and
    journals, 159
  by writing books, 158
  by writing press releases, 159
communicating your commitment to client,
    294–297
communication tools. *See also* e-mail
  BlackBerry, 183, 194–195
  instant messaging, 195
  overview, 191
  phone system, 192–193
  teleconferencing, 195–196
  video teleconferencing, 195–196
community
  getting noticed in the, 226–228
  as need of client, 291
  R-Commerce, 218–219
community involvement
  identifying your communities, 227
  leadership role, taking on, 228

community involvement *(continued)*
 overview, 226–227
 speeches and presentations, giving free, 227–228
 volunteering your services, 227
companies
 lack of support from your, 77
 lack of training from your, 77
 overbearing sales managers, 77
 R-Commerce, 218
 staying with your company, 335–336
competition research, education on, 169
competitive differentiation with social media, 270
competitive perspective, 276
competitors
 advantages of working with your, 316–317
 copying, avoiding, 320–323
 creativity used to get ahead of your, 321–322
 cutthroat competition, 328
 execution of ideas used to get ahead of your, 322
 focusing on your business to get ahead of your, 321
 identifying your, 318–319
 overly competitive, disadvantages of being, 315–317
 partnering with, 325–328
 referring customers to, 323–325
 researching, 319–320
 selling for your, 327
 studying your, 317–320
 technological edge used to get ahead of your, 323
 worst customers redirected to your, 324
complaints, fielding, 296–297
comScore Media Metrix, 268
conference call center, 193
conferences, attending, 130
confidence, sales quotas negative effect on, 45
connections, establishing, 68
consistency
 in affirmations, 33
 in brand presence, 139–140
 in grooming and attire, 168
consumer base, reliable, 79

contact management program, 184–185
content of blogs, 273–274
continuing education, 28
control issues limiting your upside, 78
conversation, 99, 276
cooperative partnering, 112
copying competitors, avoiding, 320–323
cost
 objections to, overcoming, 181
 productivity focused on instead of, 166
coworkers as personal partner, avoiding, 111
creativity used to get ahead of your competitors, 321–322
cross-marketing blogs, 274
cross-selling opportunities, 121–122
Crowder, David A. (*Building a Web Site For Dummies*), 256–257
cultural static, 308
Cummings, Chip (expert), 158
customer. See clients/customers
customer service for multicultural customers, 313–314
customers' customer's success, 23
cutthroat competition, 328

• *D* •

Daboll, Peter (comScore Media Metrix), 268
database of contacts
 building, 223–224
 categorizing, 224
 managing, 224
 overview, 223
day job, not quitting your, 166
deadlines
 for sales plan, 46
 unrealistic deadlines, 55
decision makers
 in business settings, 97–98
 dealing with, 96–98
 overview, 96–97
 spotting, 97
 working your way to, 333
Deconstructing Golden Tee LIVE (Kraynak), 289
delegating time-consuming tasks, 14, 84–85

demographics
  in MySpace, 278
  in untapped/under-tapped markets, 233–241
Desmond, Tom (real estate agent), 27
destiny, 12
Dice, Karen (expert), 158
Digg (virtual community), 280
digital audio recorder, 184
digital camera, 184
digital projector, 183
direct mail campaigns, 264
disabled customers, 238
Disney, Walt (Walt Disney Company), 129
dollar investment per dollar of sales, 44–45
Dollar, Rachel (expert), 158
dollar-productive activities, 51
domain name, registering your own, 141
Domb, Allan (real estate agent), 186
Donaldson, Michael C. (*Negotiating For Dummies*), 312
Dress For Success (Malloy), 168
dressing for success, 167–168
drip campaigns, 261
driving traffic to your Web site and blog, 259
Dyszel, Bill (*Outlook 2007 For Dummies*), 185, 224

• E •

easiest thing first option for task prioritization, 51
eBay For Dummies (Collier), 241
Ebner, Dave (expert), 158
education
  on competition research, 169
  on customer research, 169
  overview, 169–170
  on product research, 169
  pursuing, 169–170
  on sales craft, 169
Eisenhower, Dwight D. (President), 152
Eisner, Michael (Walt Disney Company), 162
elevator speech, 144
e-mail
  communicating with millions of people by, 159
  filters, 194
  groups, 194
  improving e-mail efficiency, 194
  Internet marketing through, 260–262
  overview, 194
  signature, adding, 142
emotional appeal of social media, 267–269
emotional expression of affirmations, 33
empowering your personnel, 209
end result, focusing on, 334
eNewsletter, publishing, 142
engaging people throughout the day
  first impression, making a great, 63–64
  overview, 62
  professional image, projecting, 63
entrepreneur, thinking like, 59–61
envisioning your future success
  acting as if you've achieved your destiny, 40
  acting successful, 39
  ideal, envisioning your, 39
  overview, 15
  sales, applying visualization to, 40–41
equipment, investing in your success with, 170–171
Ethernet cable, 183
EthnoConnect Web site, 299, 300, 303
execution of ideas used to get ahead of your competitors, 322
exercise technique used to reinforce affirmations, 34
expert in your industry
  becoming, 142–148
  local groups, speaking to, 143–145
  meeting and greeting the general public, 147–148
  overview, 142–143
  10/10/20 technique, 147–148
  volunteering your time and expertise, 145–146
expert positioning with social media, 270
Extreme Home Makeover (Pennington, Ty), 120
Extreme Video Web site for video teleconferencing, 196
eye contact
  multicultural customers, 307–308
  overview, 63

• F •

fad items, 75
failure, recovering from, 161–162
family members
  family limitations as reason for not doing something, 150, 151
  sales slump, involving family members in, 342
fatigue as buyer motivation, 91
fear as buyer motivation, 91
fear of failure
  advisory board, assembling your own, 158
  milestones, setting achievable, 158–159
  overview, 156–157
  present, focusing on the, 159–160
  as reason for not doing something, 150, 151
  reducing, 156–160
  research and planning on the viability of an idea, 157
  tactical use of your fears, making, 156
  trailblazers, following, 157–158
fear of success as reason for not doing something, 150, 151
Feedburner Web site, 276
feedreader, 275
female companion of multicultural customers, greeting the, 308
Ferris, Tony (expert), 158
Fettig, Art
  expert, 158
  salesperson, 27
  motivational speaker, 12
  The Platinum Rule, 145, 225, 226
filters for e-mail, 194
financing as need of client, 290–291
financing your investments
  bartering for what you need, 173–174
  freebies, 173
  management, through your company's, 174
  overview, 172
  sharing resources, 175
  small-business loan, securing, 175
Finkelstein, Ellen (*Syndicating Web Sites with RSS Feeds For Dummies*), 276
firing an employee, 210–211
first impressions
  eye, looking people in the, 63
  how you say it, 64
  moving with conviction and confidence, 64
  shaking hands, 64
  smiling, 63
  standing up straight, 64
  what you say, 64
Flag Day, sponsoring your own, 148
Flanagan, Michael O. (*ADD and ADHD For Dummies*), 66
flawed sales plans, 55
Flipping Houses For Dummies (Roberts), 258–259
FlippingFrenzy real estate fraud blog, 232
focusing on your business to get ahead of your competitors, 321
follow through, 336
force multipliers, 221–222
foreclosures, opportunities in, 161
Fox, Tony and Noel (Fox Brothers Real Estate), 26
franchise in the mind, 267
franchise opportunities, spotting, 80
Fraser, Marge (expert), 158
Fredricks, Karen S. (*ACT! 2007 For Dummies*), 185
freebies, 173
friends in MySpace, making, 278
Frohnmayer, David (*Negotiating For Dummies*), 312
future success, envisioning your, 38–41

• G •

Gardner, Susannah (*Buzz Marketing with Blogs For Dummies*), 141, 241, 259
gender focus, shifting your, 240–241
generating ideas with R-Commerce, 216
generation, targeting, 234–238
Generation X, 237
Generation Y, 237–238
G.I. Generation, 235
gifts, items to give as, 225
Girard, Joe (salesperson), 27, 29
giving without expectations, 16
global marketplace, 241
go to person, becoming, 228–229
goals
  rewards, connecting goals with, 54
  setting, 13, 45–46

Golden Tee Golf (Incredible Technologies), 14–15, 289
good customers, identifying qualities of, 81
Google AdWords, 190, 191
Google Analytics, 274
Google News Alerts, 69
Gray, Jef and Lena (Meetup example), 219
greed as buyer motivation, 90
Grip Media Web site, 258
groups, e-mail, 194
Guthy-Renker Home, 129, 188

• *H* •

Hamric, Kandra (virtual assistant), 202, 286
Hansen, Mark Victor
  Chicken Soup for the Soul, 27
  expert, 158
hardest thing first option for task prioritization, 50
Hassick, Bruce (plumber), 240
hate to do, determining which tasks you, 199–200
Hayes, Ira (salesperson), 24, 26
headset, 184
high-quality customers, 81–83
Hill, Brad
  Blogging For Dummies, 141, 241, 273, 274
  Building Your Business with Google For Dummies, 190
hiring
  advertising the job position, 206
  empowering your personnel, 209
  grounds for firing an employee, 211
  interviews, preparing for, 206–207
  job description, creating, 206
  overview, 14, 205
  qualities to look for in applicants, 208
  questions to ask in interviews, 207
  recruiting personnel, 205–208
  rewarding personnel, 209–210
  titles, assigning meaningful job, 208
  when to fire an employee, 210–211
hobby, making selling your, 58–59
Hodges, Sarah (assistant), 232
home, practicing your sales skills at, 70
Hopkins, Tom
  expert, 158
  Selling for Dummies, 3, 26, 28, 103

Hour of Power
  implementing, 332–333
  overview, 186
how you say it, 64
Hupfer, Ryan (*MySpace For Dummies*), 277
Hurry Home Web site, lead generation, 188

• *I* •

Iacocca, Lee (former Chrysler CEO), 27
idea of the week book for tracking your progress, 52
ideal, envisioning your, 39
implementing your plan, 14
improvement, determining areas for, 106–108
impulse as buyer motivation, 91
incentives, motivating yourself with, 338–339
increased opportunities, 22
Incredible Technologies (Golden Tee Golf) video game creator, 14–15, 289
independent contractor, salesperson functioning as, 60
industry changes
  capitalizing on, 128–130
  conferences, attending, 130
  Internet research on, 130
  keeping up with, 68–69
  reading about current events, 129
  reading industry publications, 129
  talking with others to learn about, 130
information
  gathering, 223
  as need of client, 290
instant messaging
  Internet marketing, 264
  overview, 195
insufficient funds as reason for not doing something, 150, 151
insufficient time as reason for not doing something, 150, 151
integration technique used to reinforce affirmations, 35
international markets, 241
International Virtual Assistants Association Web site, 212

Internet
  advertising, 190
  blog, building and maintaining, 141
  brand presence on the, 140–142
  domain name, registering your own, 141
  e-mail messages, adding a signature to
      your, 142
  eNewsletter, publishing, 142
  leads, gathering, 188–189
  marketing, 190
  networking with colleagues online, 190
  online communities, contributing to, 141
  overview, 187
  pay-per-click advertising, 191
  research on industry changes, 130
  researching competitors, 187–188
  researching customers, 187–188
  search-engine advertising, 191
  secrets, discovering new sales, 191
Internet marketing
  audio content, 259–260
  blogs, launching and maintaining,
      258–259
  branding yourself, 20
  drip campaigns, 261
  driving traffic to your Web site and
      blog, 259
  instant messaging, 264
  media, 256–264
  newsletters, 262–264
  overview, 256
  podcasts, 260
  through e-mail, 260–262
  video content, 259–260
  video podcasts, 260
  Web site, setting up your own, 141,
      256–258
interns, 18
interviews
  preparing for, 206–207
  problem or need, calling attention to, 93
inventorying everything that needs to get
      done, 198–199
investing in your success. *See also*
      financing your investments
  cost, focusing on productivity
      instead of, 166
  day job, not quitting your, 166
  dressing for success, 167–168
  education and training, pursuing, 169–170
  with equipment, 170–171
  with marketing materials, 171
  off-the-job training, 169–170
  overview, 16, 165
  prioritizing your investment needs,
      167–172
  productivity, focusing on, 166
  with support personnel, 171–172
  time budgets, 176–178
  yourself, investing in, 172
iPod, 184

• *J* •

Jaffe Raite Law firm, 192
job description, creating, 206
Jones, Charlie (salesperson), 26, 27
journaling the journey, 35

• *K* •

Karpovich, Michael Scott (National
      Speaker's Association member), 132
Keim, Earl (real estate agent), 27
Kennedy, Danielle (real estate agent),
      27, 158
Kennedy, Joseph Senior
      (businessman), 118
Kent, Peter (*Search Engine Optimization
      For Dummies*), 259
keynote speakers, 66
Kiyosaki, Robert (expert), 158
"know," changing "no" to, 102
knowing your customers, 82
Knox, David (expert), 158
Kraynak, Joe, (*Deconstructing Golden Tee
      LIVE*), 289
Kushner, Malcolm (*Public Speaking
      For Dummies*, 2 Ed.), 145

• *L* •

Lancaster, Gareth (Second Life
      resident), 281
language barriers, 310–311
lead, following your customer's, 306

lead generation
  on blogs, 276
  on the Internet, 188–189
  with social media, 270
lead generation services
  advantages of, 188–189
  advertising by, 189
  marketing by, 189
  optimizing your use of, 189
  overview, 188
leadership role in community,
    taking on, 228
leading customers through the purchase
    process, 311
leads, recommendations for, 21
learning about your client's business,
    286–288
Lee, Michael Soon
  EthnoConnect, 299, 300, 303
  sales expert, 64, 158, 239
lesser strengths, 106
lifestyle, achieving balanced, 16
lifetime achievement book for tracking
    your progress, 52
Liniger, Dave (ReMax), 129
links
  on blogs, 274
  on MySpace, 278–279
listening skills
  attentive listening, 115
  first, letting other person talk, 115
  nonverbal communication, 115
  note taking, 115
  positive environment, creating, 115
  probing questions, 115
  sharpening your, 115
local groups
  delivering speech to, 145
  public relations value of, 144
  public speaking skills, improving
    your, 144
  speaking to, 143–145
love to do, determining which
    tasks you, 199
Lowe, Doug (*PowerPoint 2007
    For Dummies*), 185
Lundquist, Leslie Heeter (*Selling Online
    For Dummies*), 241
Lyons, Darlene (expert), 158

• M •

magazines and journals, communicating
    with millions of people by writing
    articles for, 159
Maljak, Lois (assistant), 35, 133, 152
Malloy, John (*Dress For Success*), 168
manager or supervisor, feedback from, 108
managing database of contacts, 224
Mandino, Og (salesperson), 27
Margulis, Ralph (attorney), 192
marketing. *See also* Internet marketing
  efforts, increasing your, 340–341
  lead generation services, 189
  materials, investing in your success with
    marketing, 171
  on MySpace, 277–279
  social media, 267
mass appeal, 267
master edit, 254
maximum potential. *See* upside
Maxson, Mitch (*MySpace
    For Dummies*), 277
Mazur, Dick (real estate investment), 154
Me generation (Baby Boomers),
    marketing to, 236
media
  branding yourself, 20
  capitalizing on major media events, 252
  Internet marketing, 256–264
  multicultural customers, 310
  print media, 246–251
  publicity, 251–252
  radio advertising, 255–256
  television advertising, 252–255
meditation technique used to reinforce
    affirmations, 34
meet and greet
  the general public, 147–148
  mastering, 98
  for multicultural customers, 305–309
Meetup groups, attending and creating 219
mentor
  advice from, 18
  becoming, 18
  consulting your, 342
milestones, setting achievable, 158–159
Mills, Stanley (expert), 158

mirror technique used to reinforce affirmations, 34

mirroring your customer, 101

missed goals, correcting for, 55

most obvious first option for task prioritization, 51

most profitable first option for task prioritization, 50

moving with conviction and confidence, 64

MP3 player, 184

Mr. Positive Web site, 13, 30

multicultural customers
adjusting your sales presentation for, 309–311
applying multicultural sales techniques, 304
customer service for, 313–314
eye contact, 307–308
female companion, greeting the, 308
following your customer's lead, 306
language barriers, 310–311
leading customers through the purchase process, 311
media, choosing effective presentation, 310
meet and greet for, 305–309
myths about, 303–305
negotiations with, 312–313
office decor, changing your, 310
overview, 299–300
personal space, gauging your customer's, 306–307
questions about their culture, asking, 308–309
testing your multicultural aptitude, 300–303

multicultural marketplace, 238–239

multimedia marketing opportunities, assessing, 80

mutual success
customers' customer's success, 23
customer's success, 22
increased opportunities, 22
overview, 21–22
peace with your competitors, declaring, 23–24
positive referrals, 22
positive testimonials, 22
professional associations, using, 24

return business, 22

sales volume, increased, 22

underserved clientele, focusing your efforts on, 23

MySpace
banner ads, buying, 279
demographic, targeting, 278
friends, making, 278
links, 278–279
marketing on, 277–279
overview, 277
soft-sell approach, 278

MySpace For Dummies (Hupfer, Maxson, and Williams), 277

myths about multicultural customers, 303–305

• *N* •

Nacht, Richard (expert), 158

name, changing your, 136

need/problem as buyer motivation, 90

needs of client, discovering, 289–293

negative people and situations, avoiding, 339

Negotiating For Dummies (Donaldson and Frohnmayer), 312

negotiations with multicultural customers, 312–313

network marketing, 80

networking
database, building, 223–224
force multipliers, 221–222
identifying opportunities for, 220
information, gathering, 223
Meetup groups, 219
online, with colleagues, 190
overview, 219–220
soft-networking, 221
time for, 66

Neumann, Chip (expert), 158

new construction, 327

new media, 266

new selling methods, identifying, 123

Newsgator Web site, 276

newsletters
advertising, 263
designing, 262

distributing, 263–264
editing, 262–263
Internet marketing, 262–264
overview, 262
newspaper, marketing yourself in the, 20
niche marketing, 270
Nickel, Sandra (real estate agent), 132
"no" from customer, finding the reason for, 127–128
nonverbal communication, 115
note taking, 115
notebook, 183
Nutrition For Dummies (Wiley Publishing), 62

• O •

objectives, identifying your, 46–47
office decor, changing your, 310
office, negotiating in the, 70
off-the-job training, 169–170
On Wheels, 234
one-time purchases, 75
online communities, contributing to, 141
online videos, communicating with millions of people by, 159
optimizing your technological tools, 180
order of importance option for task prioritization, 50
order takers, 59–60
Outlook 2007 For Dummies (Dyszel), 185, 224
outsourcing opportunities
  assistants, assigning tasks to, 204
  hate to do, determining which tasks you, 199–200
  hiring and firing, 205–211
  inventorying everything that needs to get done, 198–199
  love to do, determining which tasks you, 199
  missing skills, taking inventory of your, 201
  only you can perform, determining which tasks, 199
  overview, 198
  system for accomplishing tasks, designing an efficient, 203–205
  time-wasting tasks, 201–202
  virtual assistants, 211–212
  Web site creation as, 202

overbearing sales managers, 77
overly competitive, disadvantages of being, 315–317

• P •

panels of top producers, 66
participation points, 279
Partnering To Success, LLC, 106
partnering with competitors, 325–328
partnering with other product or service providers, 243–244
pay-per-click advertising, 191
Payton, Randi (On Wheels), 234
peace with your competitors, declaring, 23–24
Peale, Norman Vincent (*The Power of Positive Thinking*), 27
Pennington, Ty (*Extreme Home Makeover*), 120
Perks, Bob (motivational speaker), 52
permission marketing, 276
persistence with affirmations, 33
personal partnering
  avoid clients as personal partner, 111
  avoid competing coworkers as personal partner, 111
  avoid customers as personal partner, 111
  BACKUP, providing, 114
  building on past success, 116
  celebrating your success, 116
  collaborative partnering, 112
  colleagues, gathering insight from, 107
  cooperative partnering, 112
  customer feedback, collecting, 108
  finding a personal partner, 111–112
  ground rules for, 113
  improvement, determining areas for, 106–108
  listening skills, sharpening your, 115
  manager or supervisor, feedback from, 108
  overview, 105–106, 110
  plans, sharing your, 112
  priorities, sharing your, 112
  progress, tracking, 113–114
  recruiting people, 18

personal partnering *(continued)*
  reviewing your overall performance, 115–116
  sales skills assessment test, 107
  sales slump, consulting your personal partner during, 342
  self assessments, 106–107
  skills, targeting key, 108–110
  360-degree feedback, 107
  track, keeping each other on, 113–115
personal space, gauging your customer's, 306–307
personalizing affirmations, 33
personnel as need of client, 291
phone system
  automatic call forwarding, 192
  communication tools, 192–193
  conference call center, 193
  overview, 192
  text-messaging, 193
  toll-free numbers, 192
  voicemail greeting, personalizing, 192–193
The Platinum Rule (Fettig), 145, 225, 226
playful attitude about technologies, 180–181
pleasure as buyer motivation, 91
pocket PC, 183
podcasts
  communicating with millions of people by, 159
  Internet marketing, 260
poor quality items, 75
positive attitude, suggestions for achieving, 12–13
positive environment, creating, 115
positive mindset, establishing, 12
positive people, 36
positive referrals, 22
positive relationship, reinforcing, 295–296
positive statement, affirmations expressing, 32
positive testimonials, 22
potential, listing products and services with, 79
power adapter for car, 183
The Power of Positive Thinking (Peale), 27

power selling
  affirmations, 30–35
  categorizing your customers, 334–335
  company, staying with your, 335–336
  conversation, energizing the, 99
  decision maker, dealing with the, 96–98
  decision maker, working your way to, 333
  defining success in your own terms, 37–38
  end result, focusing on, 334
  follow through, 336
  future success, envisioning your, 38–41
  hour of power, implementing, 332–333
  "know," changing "no" to, 102
  meet and greet, mastering the, 98
  mirroring your customer, 101
  overview, 25
  positive people, surrounding yourself with, 36
  publicity for you and your company, generating positive, 332
  questions, asking pertinent, 99–101
  referrals, asking for, 335
  relationships, focusing on, 331–332
  reminiscing on past successes, 35
  role models, 25–35
  sales, applying visualization to, 40–41
  stop, knowing when to, 102
  to-do lists, 37
  top sellers, shadowing, 29–30
  win-win opportunities, 101
  yourself, being, 333–334
power strip, 184
PowerPoint, 185
PowerPoint 2007 For Dummies (Lowe), 185
practicing sales. *See* real-world scenarios for practicing sales skills
preparing your customers for change, 124
present, focusing on the, 159–160
present tense, stating affirmations in the, 31
presentation programs, 185–187
press releases
  communicating with millions of people by writing, 159
  example of a press release, 250
  guidelines for, 249
  overview, 249

releasing to the media, 251
writing, 249–250
Primeau, Ed
  expert, 158
  Primeau Productions, Inc., 247, 252
print media
  advertising in print publications, 246–247
  articles, writing, 247–248
  media, 246–251
  overview, 246
  press releases, writing and distributing your own, 249–251
  soft-sell approach, 248
printer, portable, 183
priorities, sharing your, 112
probing questions, 115
problem or need
  advertising, 93
  calling attention to, 93–94
  interviewing, 93
producing your commercial, 252–254
product development and client service, integrating sales with, 293–294
product research, education on, 169
product selection
  consumer base, reliable, 79
  finding the right product or service, 78–81
  franchise opportunities, spotting, 80
  multimedia marketing opportunities, assessing, 80
  network marketing, 80
  overview, 78
  potential, listing products and services with, 79
  repeat sales, opportunities for, 79
  universal appeal, 79
productivity
  boosting, 216
  focusing on, 166
  technology used to increase, 182–187
products as need of client, 290
professional associations, using, 24
professional image, projecting, 63
profit-per-sale reduced by sales quotas, 45
progress assessment
  overview, 55
  personal partnering, 113–114
  sales plan, 52

proven products, leaving alone, 128
Pruitt, Eric (expert), 158
public relations value of local groups, 144
Public Speaking For Dummies, 2nd Edition (Kushner), 145
public speaking skills, improving your, 144
publicity
  media, 251–252
  for you and your company, generating positive, 332
purchase decision
  buyer's remorse, 95–96
  cold feet, 95–96
  collaborating on, 93–96
  costs and benefits, weighing, 95
  overview, 93
  problem or need, calling attention to, 93–94
  process, 118–119
  second guessing, 95–96
  solutions, identifying possible, 94–95

• *Q* •

qualities to look for in applicants, 208
questions
  answering a question with a question, 100
  culture, asking multicultural customers about their, 308–309
  about decision-making process, 119–120
  interviews, to ask in, 207
  overview, 99
  pertinent questions, asking, 99–101
  thought-provoking questions, asking, 99–100
  uncomfortable, asking questions that make people, 291
  yes/no questions used tactically, 101
quotas. *See* sales quotas

• *R* •

radio advertising, 255–256
radio broadcasts, communicating with millions of people by, 159
R-Commerce (Relationship-Commerce)
  applications for, 216–217
  change, adapting to, 217

R-Commerce *(continued)*
  clientele, building R-commerce
    with your, 229
  colleagues, 218
  community, 218–219, 226–228
  company, 218
  customers, 218
  for generating ideas, 216
  gifts, items to give as, 225
  "go to" person, becoming, 228–229
  networking, 219–228
  productivity, boosting, 216
  recruiting people, 18
  refocusing your sales strategy on, 218
  sales, increasing, 216
  scalability, improving, 217
  streamlining operations, 216
  strengths, combining, 216
  trade associations, 225–226
real estate market, adapting to client needs
    in the, 292
Really Simple Syndication (RSS), 275–276
RealtyTracker Web site for lead
    generation, 188
real-world scenarios for practicing sales
    skills
  airports, negotiating upgrades at, 71–72
  home, practicing your sales skills at, 70
  office, negotiating in the, 70
  overview, 69
  restaurants, practicing your sales
    skills at, 70–71
  situational fluency, 69
  taxi drivers, engaging in conversations
    with, 72
re-committing yourself to success, 340
recorder technique used to reinforce
    affirmations, 33–34
records, reviewing your, 341
recruiting personnel, 17–18, 205–208
references, using, 121
referrals
  asking for, 335
  overview, 324–325
refocusing your sales strategy on
    R-Commerce, 218
relationship marketing with social
    media, 270

Relationship-Commerce. *See* R-Commerce
relationships
  focusing on, 331–332
  revisiting your, 341
ReMax, 129
reminiscing on past successes, 35
repeat sales, opportunities for, 79
repeating affirmations, 33
research and planning on the viability of an
    idea, 157
researching competitors, 187–188, 319–320
researching customers, 187–188
researching your client's business, 287–288
resistance to new technology, overcoming,
    179–182
resources
  acquiring, 83–84
  identifying, 49–50
restaurants, practicing your sales skills at,
    70–71
return business, 22
return on risk (ROR), 155–156
revenue-generating opportunities,
    identifying, 123–124
reviewing your overall performance,
    115–116
revising your sales plan
  missed goals, correcting for, 55
  overview, 54–55
  progress, assessing your, 55
  success, building on, 56
rewarding personnel, 209–210
rewarding yourself for a job about to be
    well done, 54
rewarding yourself for a job well done, 53
risk taking
  adversity, capitalizing on, 160–161
  best thing that can happen, 153
  calculated risks, 150
  comfort zone, boundaries of your,
    149–152
  comfort zone, envisioning life outside of
    your, 152–156
  failure, recovering from, 161–162
  family limitations as reason for not doing
    something, 150, 151
  fear factor, reducing the, 156–160

fear of failure as reason for not doing
     something, 150, 151
fear of success as reason for not doing
     something, 150, 151
insufficient funds as reason for not doing
     something, 150, 151
insufficient time as reason for not doing
     something, 150, 151
lack of knowledge or skills as reason for
     not doing something, 150, 151
not trying, 153–155
ROR (return on risk), estimating your,
     155–156
stretching your limits, 16
systems approach, 160
worst thing that can happen, 152–153
Roberts, David W. (expert), 110, 158
Roberts, Ralph J. (Comcast), 129
Roberts, Ralph R.
     Flipping Houses For Dummies, 258–259
     Walk Like a Giant, Sell Like a Madman, 59
Roebuck, Alva (Sears, Roebuck &
     Company), 120
role models
     continuing education, resource for, 28
     finding, 28–29
     identifying your sales heroes, 26–29
     overview, 25–26
     shortcuts to success, 28
     success, inspiration to strive for higher
          levels of, 28
     top sellers, shadowing, 29–30
role playing, 103
ROR (return on risk), 155–156
Rowland, Julia (business owner), 26
RSS (Really Simple Syndication), 275–276
Ruddle, Jessica (video production), 254
Runstatler, Dick (sales manager), 27
Russell, Cathy (expert), 158

• *S* •

sales craft, education on, 169
sales efficiency ratings, 45
sales heroes
     Antion, Tom (public speaker), 27
     Brown, Les (salesperson), 27
     Desmond, Tom (real estate agent), 27
     Fettig, Art (salesperson), 27

Fox, Noel (business owner), 26
Fox, Tony (business owner), 26
Girard, Joe (salesperson), 27
Hansen, Mark Victor (*Chicken Soup for the
     Soul*), 27
Hayes, Ira (salesperson), 26
Hopkins, Tom (*Selling for Dummies*), 3, 26,
     28, 103
Iacocca, Lee (former Chrysler CEO), 27
Jones, Charlie (salesperson), 27
Keim, Earl (real estate agent), 27
Mandino, Og (salesperson), 27
Peale, Norman Vincent (*The Power of
     Positive Thinking*), 27
Rowland, Julia (business owner), 26
Runstatler, Dick (sales manager), 27
Wickman, Floyd (real estate agent), 27
Ziglar, Zig (salesperson), 27
sales manager
     sales goals, letting salespeople help set
          their, 49
     turning down position of, 15
sales plan
     accountability, 52
     celebrating your success, 53–54
     deadlines for, 46, 55
     dollar investment per dollar of sales,
          44–45
     failure to execute, 55
     flawed sales plans, 55
     goal, setting, 45–46
     objectives, identifying your, 46–47
     overview, 43–44
     progress, tracking your, 52
     resources, identifying, 49–50
     revising, 54–56
     sales-per-hour earnings, 44–45
     steps for, 44
     strategy, figuring out, 47–48
     Strebor System, 51
     task prioritization for, 50–51
     tasks, identifying, 48–49
     timeframe, setting, 46
     where you are, determining, 44–45
sales presentation
     multicultural customers, adjusting sales
          presentation for, 309–311
     overview, 102
     role playing, 103

sales presentation *(continued)*
  trainer, working with, 104
  watching and listening to yourself
    work, 103
sales quotas
  confidence, negative effect on, 45
  derailing the sales process with, 45
  disadvantages of, 13, 45
  profit-per-sale reduced by, 45
sales skills assessment test, 107
sales slumps
  family, involving, 342
  incentives, motivating yourself with,
    338–339
  marketing efforts, increasing your,
    340–341
  mentor, consulting your, 342
  negative people and situations,
    avoiding, 339
  now, starting, 339–340
  personal partner, consulting your, 342
  re-committing yourself to success, 340
  records, reviewing your, 341
  relationships, revisiting your, 341
  supervisor, consulting your, 342
  triggers for, avoiding, 337–338
sales techniques
  buying to learn, 67
  CDs, listening to, 65
  discovering new, 64–68
  reading up on new selling strategies, 65
  secrets, sharing with colleagues, 67
  seminars, attending, 66
  tapes, listening to, 65
  testing new, 67–68
  workshops, attending, 66
sales visionaries, list of, 129
sales volume, increased, 22
sales-per-hour earnings, 44–45
Santiago, Jocelyn (sales manager), 250
saturated markets, 75
SBA (Small Business Administration), 173
scalability, improving, 217
Schnenck, Barbara Findlay (*Branding
    For Dummies*), 139
Schwarzkopf, Norman (expert), 158
Scoble, Robert (Microsoft blogger), 276
scratch track, 253
search engine marketing, 191, 269

Search Engine Optimization For Dummies
    (Kent), 259
Sears, Richard (Sears, Roebuck &
    Company), 120
Sears, Roebuck & Company marketing
    strategies, 120
second guessing, 95–96
Second Life (virtual community), 281–282
secrets
  discovering new sales, 191
  share secrets, why you should, 24
  sharing with colleagues, 67
self assessments, 106–107
self-promotion
  branding yourself, 20
  overview, 19
  unique selling point, identifying your,
    19–20
Selling For Dummies (Hopkins),
    3, 26, 28, 103
Selling Online For Dummies
    (Lundquist), 241
seminars, attending, 66
services as need of client, 290
serving the consumer, 124–125
sexist salesmen, 240
shaking hands, 64
sharing resources, 175
short affirmations, 32
shortcuts to success, 28
Sifry, David (Technorati), 272
Silent Generation, 235–236
Sirianni, Joe (expert), 158
situational fluency, 69
skills
  missing skills, taking inventory
    of your, 201
  personal partnering used for targeting
    key, 108–110
slumps. *See* sales slumps
Small Business Administration (SBA), 173
small-business loan, securing, 175
SMART plan, 109
smiling, 63
social media. *See also* blogs
  advantages of, 269–270
  brand building with, 270
  competitive differentiation with, 270
  customer referrals with, 270

Digg, 280
direct communication with, 270
disadvantages of, 271–272
emotional appeal, 267–269
expert positioning with, 270
lead generation with, 270
marketing and advertising,
applied to, 267
MySpace, marketing on, 277–279
niche marketing with, 270
overview, 266–267
participation points, 279
relationship marketing with, 270
search engine marketing, 269
Second Life, 281–282
viral marketing, 271
virtual communities, establishing
presence in, 277–282
word-of-mouth (WOM) marketing, 271
YouTube, 279–280
soft-networking, 221
soft-sell approach
MySpace, 278
print media, 248
solutions, identifying possible, 94–95
Spanish For Dummies (Wiley Publishing), 48
speeches
giving free, 227–228
to local groups, 143–145
spider web, 259
spotting the decision maker, 97
spouse, 36
standing up straight, 64
Star Power, 111, 158
station, picking the right television, 254
stay the course, 17
steps, breaking tasks into individual,
203–204
Stewart, Steve (expert), 158
sticktoitism, 3, 51
stop, knowing when to, 102
strategically airing your commercial, 255
strategy, figuring out, 47–48
streamlining operations, 216
Strebor System, 51
Strong, Jeff (*ADD and ADHD
For Dummies*), 66
studying your competitors, 317–320

subconscious
affirmations imprinted into your, 32–33
power of the subconscious mind, 30
success
building on, 56, 116
creating a plan for, 13–14
defining, 12, 37–38
envisioning your, 15, 39–41
goals, setting, 13
implementing your plan, 14
inspiration to strive for higher
levels of, 28
mutual success, 21–24
positive mindset, establishing, 12
recruiting people to fuel your, 17–18
stay the course, 17
walking the walk, 15–16
success journal for tracking your
progress, 52
success of client
bonus for clients, 293
business model adjustment to meet client
needs, 292–293
client's client, finding out about your, 288
commitment to client, communicating
your, 294–297
community as need of client, 291
financing as need of client, 290–291
information as need of client, 290
integrating sales with product
development and client service,
293–294
learning about your client's business,
286–288
needs of client, discovering, 289–293
personnel as need of client, 291
products as need of client, 290
questions that make people
uncomfortable, asking, 291
researching your client's business,
287–288
services as need of client, 290
training as need of client, 290
supervisor, consulting your, 342
support
acquiring, 83–84
lack of support from your company, 77
support personnel, 171–172

Swanepoel, Stefan (expert), 158
*Syndicating Web Sites with RSS Feeds
For Dummies* (Finkelstein), 276
system for accomplishing tasks, designing
an efficient, 203–205
systems approach
assistants, assigning tasks to, 204
overview, 160
specific projects, targeting, 204–205
steps, breaking tasks into individual,
203–204

• T •

Tablet PC, 183
tactical use of your fears, making, 156
talking with others to learn about industry
changes, 130
tapes, listening to, 65
Tarzy, Steve (expert), 158
task prioritization
easiest thing first option for, 51
hardest thing first option for, 50
most obvious first option for, 51
most profitable first option for, 50
order of importance option for, 50
overview, 50
for sales plan, 50–51
step-by-step option for, 50
tasks, identifying, 48–49
taxi drivers, engaging in conversations
with, 72
technological edge used to get ahead of
your competitors, 323
technologies
BlackBerry, 183, 194–195
communication tools, 191–196
contact management program, 184–185
cost, overcoming objections to, 181
digital audio recorder, 184
digital camera, 184
digital projector, 183
essentials, list of, 183–184
Ethernet cable, 183
headset, 184
Internet, 187–191
iPod, 184
knowledge about, 16
MP3 player, 184

notebook, 183
optimizing your technological tools, 180
playful attitude about, 180–181
pocket PC, 183
power adapter for car, 183
power strip, 184
PowerPoint, 185
presentation programs, 185–187
printer, portable, 183
productivity, increasing your, 182–187
resistance to new technology,
overcoming, 179–182
Tablet PC, 183
unproven technologies, 182
wireless Internet access (Wi-Fi), 183
Technorati
getting your blog discovered on, 275
Sifry, David (creator), 272
Tejada-Flores, Lito (*ADD and ADHD
For Dummies*), 66
teleconferencing, 195–196
television advertising
overview, 252
producing your commercial, 252–254
station, picking the right television, 254
strategically airing your commercial, 255
time slot, choosing, 254
10/10/20 technique, 147–148
testimonials, using, 121
testing new sales techniques, 67–68
testing your multicultural aptitude,
300–303
text-messaging, 193
Thomas, Pete
expert, 158
reality star, 74
thought-provoking questions, asking,
99–100
360-degree feedback, 107
time budget
expanding, 85–86
finding time, 177–178
knowing how you spend your time,
176–177
overview, 176
time wasters, identifying, 177
time-consuming tasks, 18, 84–85, 201–202
titles, assigning meaningful job, 208
Toastmasters Web site, 144

to-do lists, 37
Toler, Jerry (expert), 158
toll-free numbers, 192
top sellers, shadowing, 29–30
tracking your progress
  of changes you've implemented, 126–127
  checklists for, 52
  idea of the week book for, 52
  lifetime achievement book for, 52
  overview, 52
  success journal for, 52
trade associations, 225–226
trailblazers, following, 157–158
trainer, working with, 104
training
  lack of training from your company, 77
  as need of client, 290
  pursuing, 169–170
trash can technique used to reinforce
  affirmations, 34
triggers for sales slumps, avoiding, 337–338
turnkey solutions, 257

• U •

underserved clientele, focusing your
  efforts on, 23
unique selling proposition (USP)
  elements included in, 138
  implementation of, 139
  overview, 136–137
  steps for creating, 137–138
unique trait, focusing on, 132–134
universal appeal, 79
unproven technologies, 182
untapped/under-tapped markets
  Baby Boomers, 236
  bundling opportunities, 242–243
  channels, exploring other sales, 241–242
  demographic, considering a different,
    233–241
  disabled customers, 238
  gender focus, shifting your, 240–241
  generation, targeting, 234–238
  Generation X, 237
  Generation Y, 237–238
  G.I. Generation, 235
  global marketplace, 241
  international markets, 241

multicultural marketplace, 238–239
  overview, 231–233
  partnering with other product or service
    providers, 243–244
  Silent Generation, 235–236
  uses for your product or service,
    discovering other, 244
updating blogs, 273–274
upside
  control issues limiting your, 78
  limitations to, 74–78
  overview, 74
  time constraints limiting your, 78
  wrong company or manager limiting
    your, 77
  wrong customer or client limiting your,
    75–77
  wrong product or service limiting your, 75
uses for your product or service,
  discovering other, 244
USP. *See* unique selling proposition

• V •

VanGoethem, Bob (expert), 158
vanity as buyer motivation, 91
video podcasts, 260
video teleconferencing, 195–196
viral marketing
  with Digg, 280
  social media, 271
virtual assistants, 211–212
virtual communities
  Digg, 280
  establishing a presence in, 277–282
  MySpace, marketing on, 277–279
  Second Life, 281–282
  YouTube, 279–280
Virtual Real Estate Assistant blog, 212
voicemail greeting, personalizing, 192–193
volunteering
  your services to community, 227
  your time and expertise, 145–146

• W •

Waitley, Dennis (expert), 158
Walk Like a Giant, Sell Like a Madman
  (Roberts), 59

walking the walk, 15–16
Walt Disney Company
  Disney, Walt, 129
  Eisner, Michael, 162
watching and listening to yourself
    work, 103
Web site
  building your own, 141
  creation, 202
  overview, 256–258
Westmark, Steve (expert), 158
Wickman, Floyd (expert), 27, 158
Williams, Ryan (*MySpace
    For Dummies*), 277
window dub, 253
win-win opportunities, 101
wireless Internet access (Wi-Fi), 183
Wisner, Terry
  expert, 158
  Partnering To Success, LLC, 106

word-of-mouth (WOM) marketing, 271
workshops, attending, 66
Worldcard (business card scanner), 224
worst customers
  criteria to identify your, 76
  redirected to your competitors, 324
worst thing that can happen, 152–153
writing
  press releases, 249–250
  technique used to reinforce
    affirmations, 33

• *Y* •

yes/no questions used tactically, 101
YouTube, 279–280

• *Z* •

Ziglar, Zig (expert), 27, 158

BUSINESS, CAREERS & PERSONAL FINANCE

0-7645-9847-3

0-7645-2431-3

Also available:

- Business Plans Kit For Dummies
  0-7645-9794-9
- Economics For Dummies
  0-7645-5726-2
- Grant Writing For Dummies
  0-7645-8416-2
- Home Buying For Dummies
  0-7645-5331-3
- Managing For Dummies
  0-7645-1771-6
- Marketing For Dummies
  0-7645-5600-2

- Personal Finance For Dummies
  0-7645-2590-5*
- Resumes For Dummies
  0-7645-5471-9
- Selling For Dummies
  0-7645-5363-1
- Six Sigma For Dummies
  0-7645-6798-5
- Small Business Kit For Dummies
  0-7645-5984-2
- Starting an eBay Business For Dummies
  0-7645-6924-4
- Your Dream Career For Dummies
  0-7645-9795-7

HOME & BUSINESS COMPUTER BASICS

0-470-05432-8

0-471-75421-8

Also available:

- Cleaning Windows Vista For Dummies
  0-471-78293-9
- Excel 2007 For Dummies
  0-470-03737-7
- Mac OS X Tiger For Dummies
  0-7645-7675-5
- MacBook For Dummies
  0-470-04859-X
- Macs For Dummies
  0-470-04849-2
- Office 2007 For Dummies
  0-470-00923-3

- Outlook 2007 For Dummies
  0-470-03830-6
- PCs For Dummies
  0-7645-8958-X
- Salesforce.com For Dummies
  0-470-04893-X
- Upgrading & Fixing Laptops For Dummies
  0-7645-8959-8
- Word 2007 For Dummies
  0-470-03658-3
- Quicken 2007 For Dummies
  0-470-04600-7

FOOD, HOME, GARDEN, HOBBIES, MUSIC & PETS

0-7645-8404-9

0-7645-9904-6

Also available:

- Candy Making For Dummies
  0-7645-9734-5
- Card Games For Dummies
  0-7645-9910-0
- Crocheting For Dummies
  0-7645-4151-X
- Dog Training For Dummies
  0-7645-8418-9
- Healthy Carb Cookbook For Dummies
  0-7645-8476-6
- Home Maintenance For Dummies
  0-7645-5215-5

- Horses For Dummies
  0-7645-9797-3
- Jewelry Making & Beading For Dummies
  0-7645-2571-9
- Orchids For Dummies
  0-7645-6759-4
- Puppies For Dummies
  0-7645-5255-4
- Rock Guitar For Dummies
  0-7645-5356-9
- Sewing For Dummies
  0-7645-6847-7
- Singing For Dummies
  0-7645-2475-5

INTERNET & DIGITAL MEDIA

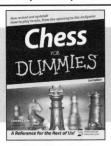

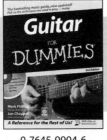

0-470-04529-9

0-470-04894-8

Also available:

- Blogging For Dummies
  0-471-77084-1
- Digital Photography For Dummies
  0-7645-9802-3
- Digital Photography All-in-One Desk Reference For Dummies
  0-470-03743-1
- Digital SLR Cameras and Photography For Dummies
  0-7645-9803-1
- eBay Business All-in-One Desk Reference For Dummies
  0-7645-8438-3
- HDTV For Dummies
  0-470-09673-X

- Home Entertainment PCs For Dummies
  0-470-05523-5
- MySpace For Dummies
  0-470-09529-6
- Search Engine Optimization For Dummies
  0-471-97998-8
- Skype For Dummies
  0-470-04891-3
- The Internet For Dummies
  0-7645-8996-2
- Wiring Your Digital Home For Dummies
  0-471-91830-X

* Separate Canadian edition also available
† Separate U.K. edition also available

Available wherever books are sold. For more information or to order direct: U.S. customers visit www.dummies.com or call 1-877-762-2974.
U.K. customers visit www.wileyeurope.com or call 0800 243407. Canadian customers visit www.wiley.ca or call 1-800-567-4797.

SPORTS, FITNESS, PARENTING, RELIGION & SPIRITUALITY

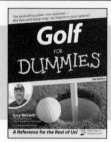

0-471-76871-5

0-7645-7841-3

Also available:
- Catholicism For Dummies
  0-7645-5391-7
- Exercise Balls For Dummies
  0-7645-5623-1
- Fitness For Dummies
  0-7645-7851-0
- Football For Dummies
  0-7645-3936-1
- Judaism For Dummies
  0-7645-5299-6
- Potty Training For Dummies
  0-7645-5417-4
- Buddhism For Dummies
  0-7645-5359-3

- Pregnancy For Dummies
  0-7645-4483-7 †
- Ten Minute Tone-Ups For Dummies
  0-7645-7207-5
- NASCAR For Dummies
  0-7645-7681-X
- Religion For Dummies
  0-7645-5264-3
- Soccer For Dummies
  0-7645-5229-5
- Women in the Bible For Dummies
  0-7645-8475-8

TRAVEL

0-7645-7749-2

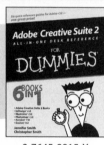

0-7645-6945-7

Also available:
- Alaska For Dummies
  0-7645-7746-8
- Cruise Vacations For Dummies
  0-7645-6941-4
- England For Dummies
  0-7645-4276-1
- Europe For Dummies
  0-7645-7529-5
- Germany For Dummies
  0-7645-7823-5
- Hawaii For Dummies
  0-7645-7402-7

- Italy For Dummies
  0-7645-7386-1
- Las Vegas For Dummies
  0-7645-7382-9
- London For Dummies
  0-7645-4277-X
- Paris For Dummies
  0-7645-7630-5
- RV Vacations For Dummies
  0-7645-4442-X
- Walt Disney World & Orlando
  For Dummies
  0-7645-9660-8

GRAPHICS, DESIGN & WEB DEVELOPMENT

0-7645-8815-X

0-7645-9571-7

Also available:
- 3D Game Animation For Dummies
  0-7645-8789-7
- AutoCAD 2006 For Dummies
  0-7645-8925-3
- Building a Web Site For Dummies
  0-7645-7144-3
- Creating Web Pages For Dummies
  0-470-08030-2
- Creating Web Pages All-in-One Desk
  Reference For Dummies
  0-7645-4345-8
- Dreamweaver 8 For Dummies
  0-7645-9649-7

- InDesign CS2 For Dummies
  0-7645-9572-5
- Macromedia Flash 8 For Dummies
  0-7645-9691-8
- Photoshop CS2 and Digital
  Photography For Dummies
  0-7645-9580-6
- Photoshop Elements 4 For Dummies
  0-471-77483-9
- Syndicating Web Sites with RSS Feeds
  For Dummies
  0-7645-8848-6
- Yahoo! SiteBuilder For Dummies
  0-7645-9800-7

NETWORKING, SECURITY, PROGRAMMING & DATABASES

0-7645-7728-X

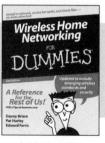

0-471-74940-0

Also available:
- Access 2007 For Dummies
  0-470-04612-0
- ASP.NET 2 For Dummies
  0-7645-7907-X
- C# 2005 For Dummies
  0-7645-9704-3
- Hacking For Dummies
  0-470-05235-X
- Hacking Wireless Networks
  For Dummies
  0-7645-9730-2
- Java For Dummies
  0-470-08716-1

- Microsoft SQL Server 2005 For Dummies
  0-7645-7755-7
- Networking All-in-One Desk Reference
  For Dummies
  0-7645-9939-9
- Preventing Identity Theft For Dummies
  0-7645-7336-5
- Telecom For Dummies
  0-471-77085-X
- Visual Studio 2005 All-in-One Desk
  Reference For Dummies
  0-7645-9775-2
- XML For Dummies
  0-7645-8845-1